DICK TRACY

THE COLLINS CASEFILES, VOLUME 3

MAX ALLAN COLLINS

CHECKER GROUP

"...the approach of the strip has always been, and continues to be, one of pitting our urban Sherlock Holmes against topical crimes."

Max Allan Collins, in his pitch to the Tribune syndicate regarding Dick Tracy

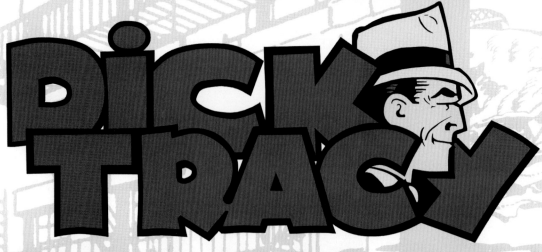

DICK TRACY

THE COLLINS CASEFILES, VOLUME 3

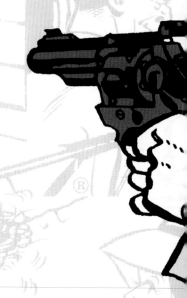

Contributors:

Max Allan Collins ....*Writer*
Chester Gould ....*Creator*
Rick Fletcher ....*Artist*

Compilation:

Mark Thompson ....*Publisher*
Constance Taylor ....*Marketing Director*
Angie Dayton ....*Graphic Design*
Trevor Goodman ....*Graphic Design*
Mike Gregg ....*Graphic Design*

Checker Book Publishing Group would also like to recognize the invaluable assistance of the University of Iowa Library.

Originally published by Tribune Media

Checker Book Publishing Group
228 Byers Road, Suite 201
Miamisburg, OH 45342
Visit us online at www.checkerbpg.com

No solicitations accepted

ISBN# 0-9753808-8-5
Printed in China

Table of Contents

Dick Tracy: The Collins Casefiles Volume 3

"I decided that if the police couldn't catch the gangsters, I'd create a fellow who could."
- Chester Gould

Inspired by a need to somehow combat the social and political corruption in the post-Depression era, Gould took it upon himself to create an incorruptible yet street-savvy detective that could bring to justice the mobsters and crooks that he believed were being glorified by the media. Within these pages lies more than just mere comic strips – it is the continuation of one man's endeavor to create a refuge of hope for a nation that had been stricken by the worst economic disaster in its history.

Gould had Tracy solving crimes that paralleled what was actually going on in the violent, gangster-saturated world of the 1930's; even the names of the Tracy's nemeses rang similar to the monikers given to the high-profile criminals of the day. In 1932, when the infant son of Anne and Charles Lindbergh was kidnapped and the entire nation was transfixed by the unfolding story, Gould gave the public what it wanted and had Tracy find a kidnapped toddler safe and unharmed, despite the eventual real-life tragic outcome of the crime. Tracy was well-loved by newspaper readers around the world, mostly because of this optimistically realistic slant that Gould insisted the strip have – he even went so far as to hire a retired police detective to make sure all of the details of Tracy's crime-fighting tactics were as accurate and believable as possible. Gould's inspired vision of police integrity made Tracy the first, and by far the most popular, detective hero in the comic strips.

When Gould decided to retire from the creation of the strip, Max Allan Collins was the natural choice for the next writer. With an ambition that matched Gould's, this budding crime novelist decided to take Tracy back to his roots, and back to the street. The overall plot for Dick Tracy had been floundering in the final years of Gould's writing, but under Collins' masterful scripting, Tracy was once again solving crimes inspired by headlines of the day, but with grittier undertones and more social satire.

Collins, like Gould, used Dick Tracy to address societal problems that were (and still are) hot-potato political issues, and also to call attention to the more subtle undertones of society and the negative ways they can influence us if we're not aware of them. Take, for example, the misguided attempts of Art Dekko to carve out a place for himself in a fast-paced, high society world that he desperately wants to be a part of. Or in "The Computer Killer" (you'll have to look in Checker's Dick Tracy: Volume 2 for this story), in which our tragic antagonist "Z.Z. Rowe" takes out his frustration borne of an impersonal society by blowing computers to bits. Collins has Tracy solving crimes committed by everyone from criminal masterminds to desperate sons with sick mothers. The motivations and the delinquents vary dramatically throughout the run of the strip, but Tracy handles it all with his impartial fairness and Everyman compassion.

Gould created Dick Tracy because he believed that the public needed him. Perhaps we still do.

-- Constance Taylor

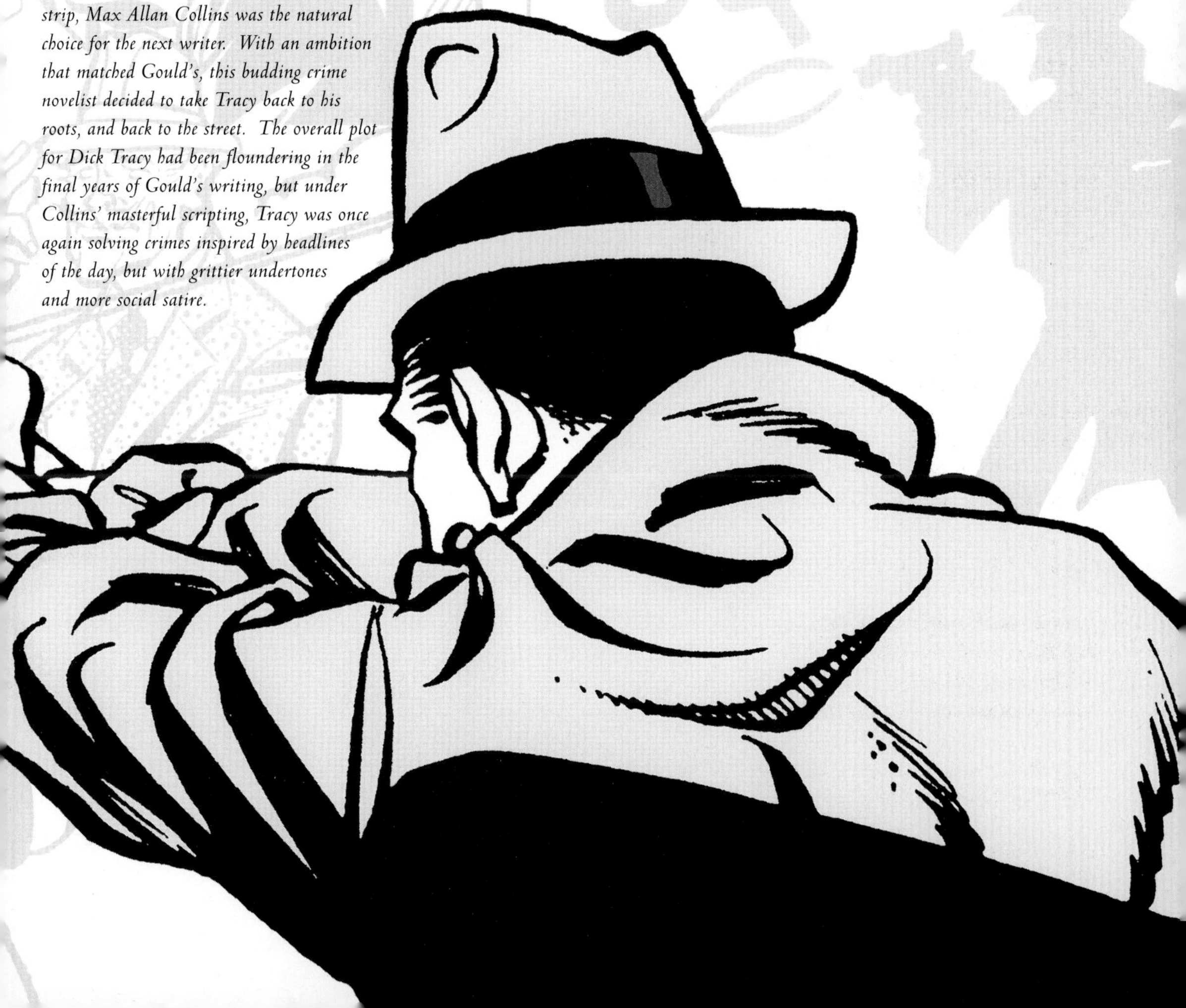

DICK TRACY

THE COLLINS CASEFILES, VOLUME 3

CHAPTER 1
DICK TRACY MEETS ART DEKKO

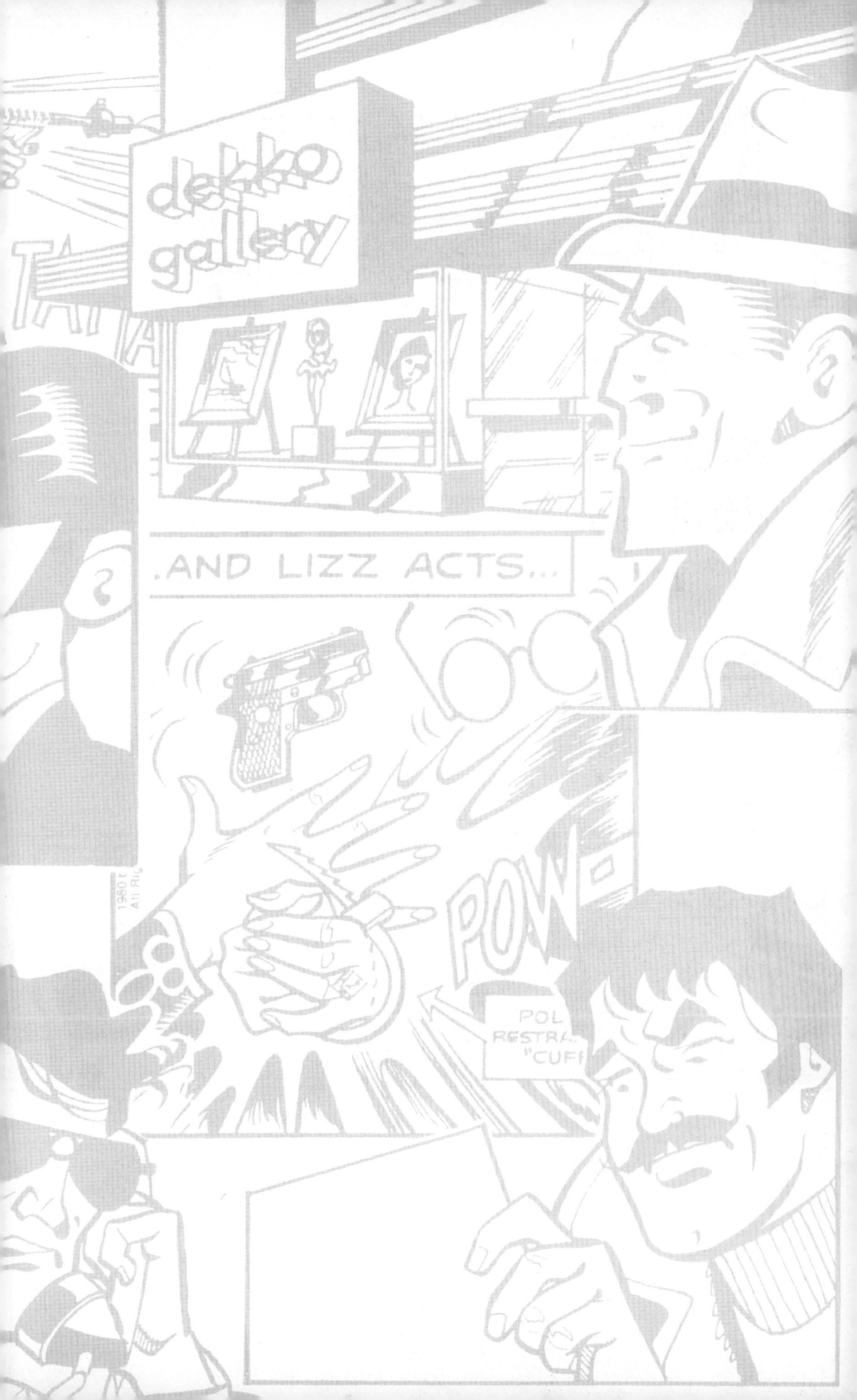

dekko gallery
.AND LIZZ ACTS...
POW

COLT 25 ACP
WELL, WELL— LOOK WHO DROPPED IN.
DON'T I KNOW YOU? DIDN'T YOU USED TO WORK HERE?
HE STILL DOES— TRACY, STEP INTO MY OFFICE.
SOMETHING UP, PAT?
IT'S THESE ART HEISTS —SAY, IS THE FBI THROUGH WITH YOU?
PATRICK L. PATTON CHIEF OF POLICE

ON THE QUIVER TREMBLY THING? YEAH, FOR NOW.
WHAT WAS SHE AFTER, ANYWAY?
ALL I KNOW IS SHE SAID SHE WAS WILLING TO DIE FOR HER CAUSE.
"WHAT WAS HER CAUSE?" ASKS PATTON. "SHE DIDN'T SAY," SAYS TRACY.
1-6-80
While AT CITY ART MUSEUM—
THE CÉZANNE? GONE?
© 1980 by Chicago Tribune-N.Y. News Synd. Inc. All Rights Reserved

TRACY, THESE ART HEISTS HAVE REACHED EPIDEMIC PROPORTIONS.
Pat
1-7-80
LAST YEAR IN THIS COUNTRY, THIEVES MADE OFF WITH $50 MILLION IN STOLEN ART—
"AND A GOOD SHARE OF IT HAPPENED RIGHT HERE—IN OUR CITY!"
NOT THE CÉZANNE— STOLEN?

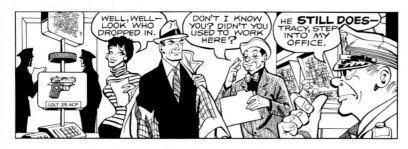

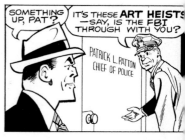

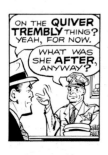

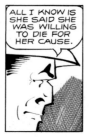

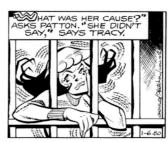

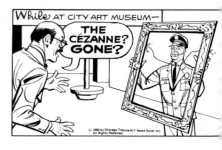

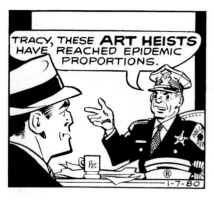

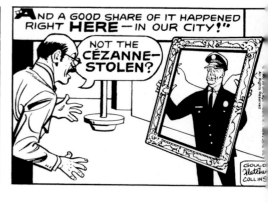

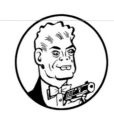

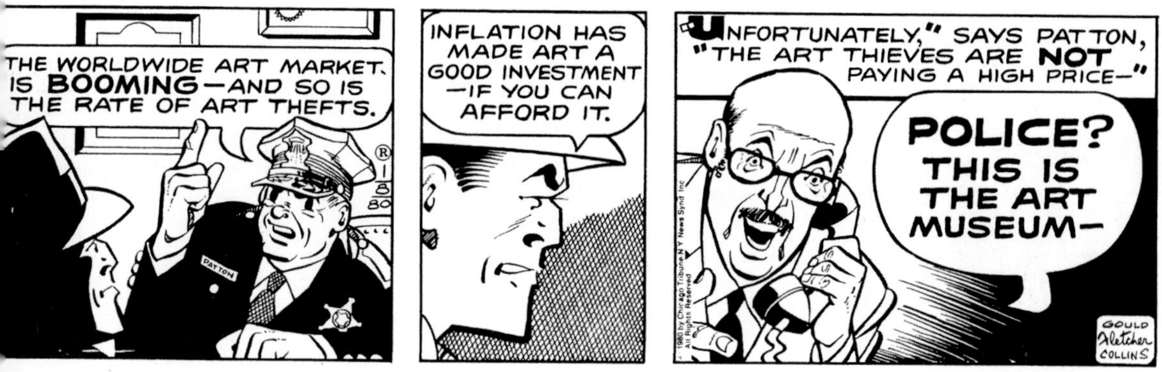
THE WORLDWIDE ART MARKET IS **BOOMING**—AND SO IS THE RATE OF ART THEFTS.
PATTON
® 1 8 80
INFLATION HAS MADE ART A GOOD INVESTMENT —IF YOU CAN AFFORD IT.
"UNFORTUNATELY," SAYS PATTON, "THE ART THIEVES ARE **NOT** PAYING A HIGH PRICE—"
POLICE? THIS IS THE ART MUSEUM—
© 1980 by Chicago Tribune N.Y. News Synd Inc All Rights Reserved
GOULD Fletcher COLLINS

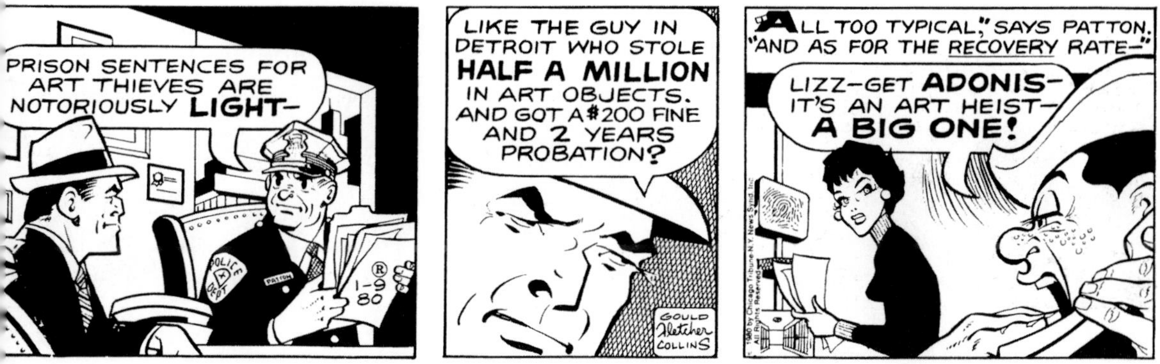
PRISON SENTENCES FOR ART THIEVES ARE NOTORIOUSLY **LIGHT**—
POLICE DEPT
PATTON
® 1-9 80
LIKE THE GUY IN DETROIT WHO STOLE **HALF A MILLION** IN ART OBJECTS. AND GOT A $200 FINE AND 2 YEARS PROBATION?
GOULD Fletcher COLLINS
"ALL TOO TYPICAL," SAYS PATTON. "AND AS FOR THE RECOVERY RATE—"
LIZZ—GET **ADONIS**— IT'S AN ART HEIST— **A BIG ONE!**
© 1980 by Chicago Tribune N.Y. News Synd Inc All Rights Reserved

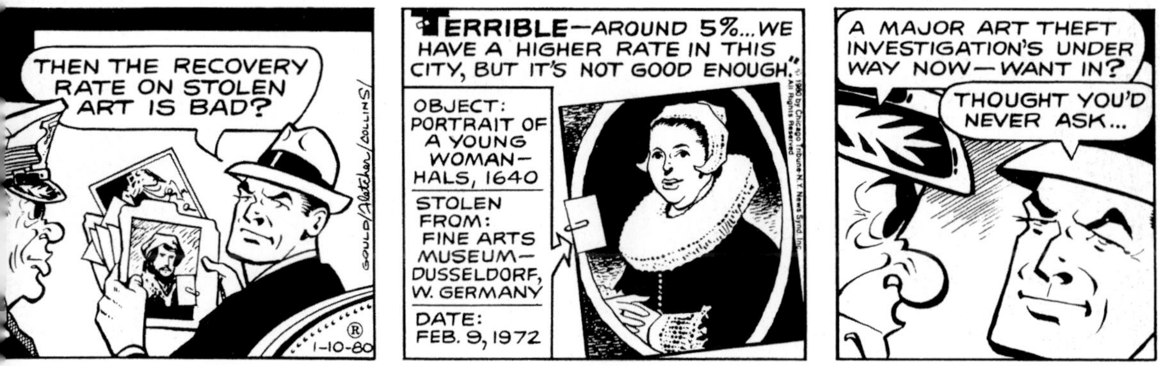
THEN THE RECOVERY RATE ON STOLEN ART IS BAD?
GOULD/Fletcher/COLLINS
® 1-10-80
"TERRIBLE—AROUND 5%... WE HAVE A HIGHER RATE IN THIS CITY, BUT IT'S NOT GOOD ENOUGH."
OBJECT: PORTRAIT OF A YOUNG WOMAN—HALS, 1640
STOLEN FROM: FINE ARTS MUSEUM—DUSSELDORF, W. GERMANY
DATE: FEB. 9, 1972
© 1980 by Chicago Tribune N.Y. News Synd Inc All Rights Reserved
A MAJOR ART THEFT INVESTIGATION'S UNDER WAY NOW—WANT IN?
THOUGHT YOU'D NEVER ASK...

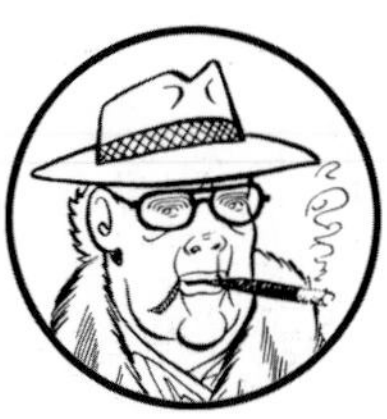

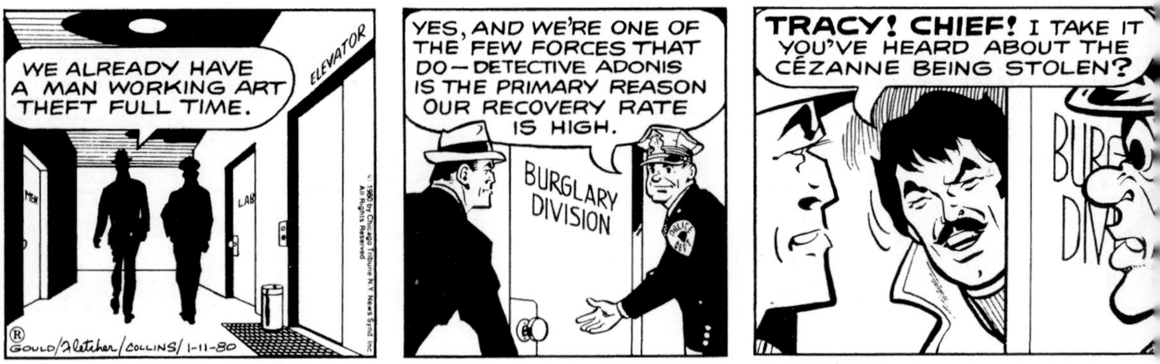
WE ALREADY HAVE A MAN WORKING ART THEFT FULL TIME.
ELEVATOR
MEN
LAB
© 1980 by Chicago Tribune N.Y. News Synd. Inc. All Rights Reserved
GOULD/Fletcher/COLLINS/ 1-11-80
YES, AND WE'RE ONE OF THE FEW FORCES THAT DO—DETECTIVE ADONIS IS THE PRIMARY REASON OUR RECOVERY RATE IS HIGH.
BURGLARY DIVISION
POLICE DEPT
TRACY! CHIEF! I TAKE IT YOU'VE HEARD ABOUT THE CÉZANNE BEING STOLEN?

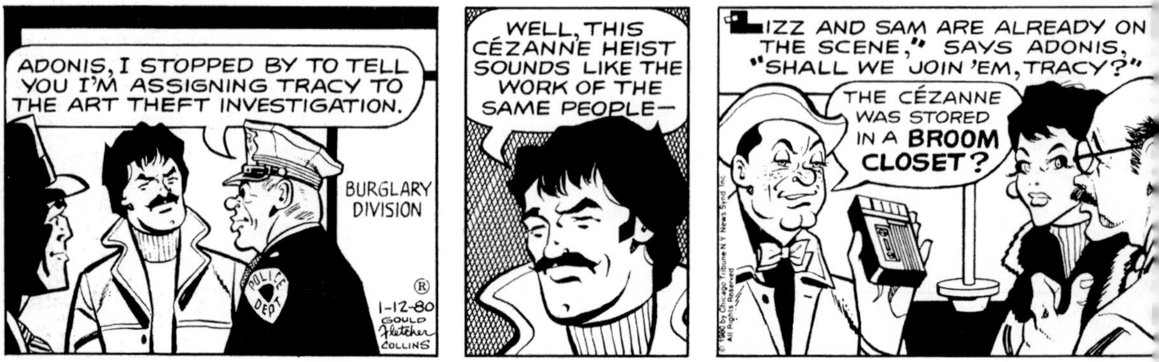
ADONIS, I STOPPED BY TO TELL YOU I'M ASSIGNING TRACY TO THE ART THEFT INVESTIGATION.
BURGLARY DIVISION
POLICE DEPT
1-12-80 GOULD Fletcher COLLINS
WELL, THIS CÉZANNE HEIST SOUNDS LIKE THE WORK OF THE SAME PEOPLE—
LIZZ AND SAM ARE ALREADY ON THE SCENE," SAYS ADONIS, "SHALL WE JOIN 'EM, TRACY?"
THE CÉZANNE WAS STORED IN A BROOM CLOSET?
© 1980 by Chicago Tribune N.Y. News Synd. Inc. All Rights Reserved

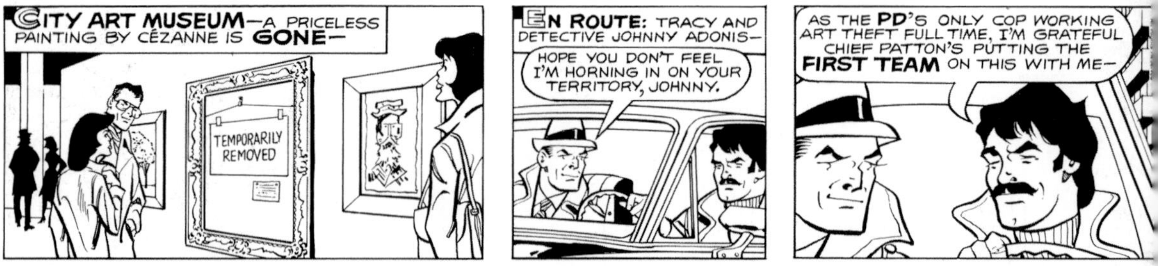
CITY ART MUSEUM—A PRICELESS PAINTING BY CÉZANNE IS GONE—
TEMPORARILY REMOVED
EN ROUTE: TRACY AND DETECTIVE JOHNNY ADONIS—
HOPE YOU DON'T FEEL I'M HORNING IN ON YOUR TERRITORY, JOHNNY.
AS THE PD'S ONLY COP WORKING ART THEFT FULL TIME, I'M GRATEFUL CHIEF PATTON'S PUTTING THE FIRST TEAM ON THIS WITH ME—

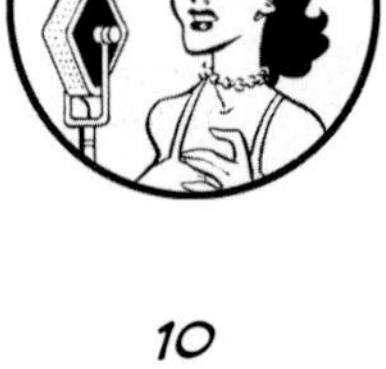
LOVE, YOU'VE.....

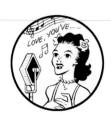

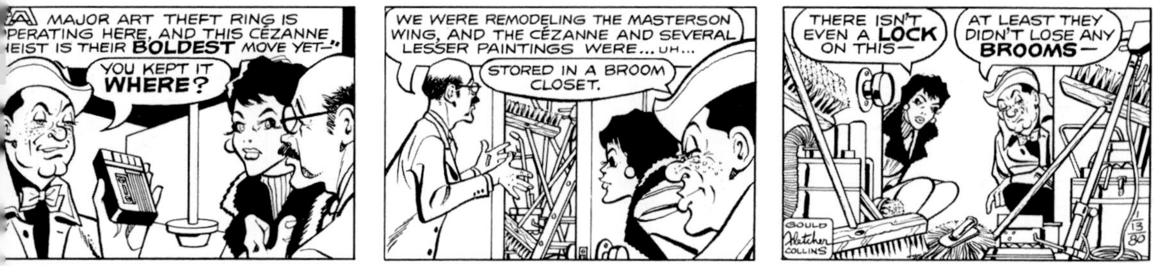

A MAJOR ART THEFT RING IS 'PERATING HERE, AND THIS CÉZANNE IEIST IS THEIR **BOLDEST** MOVE YET—"
YOU KEPT IT **WHERE?**
WE WERE REMODELING THE MASTERSON WING, AND THE CÉZANNE AND SEVERAL LESSER PAINTINGS WERE... UH...
STORED IN A BROOM CLOSET.
THERE ISN'T EVEN A **LOCK** ON THIS—
AT LEAST THEY DIDN'T LOSE ANY **BROOMS**—
GOULD Fletcher COLLINS
1/13/80

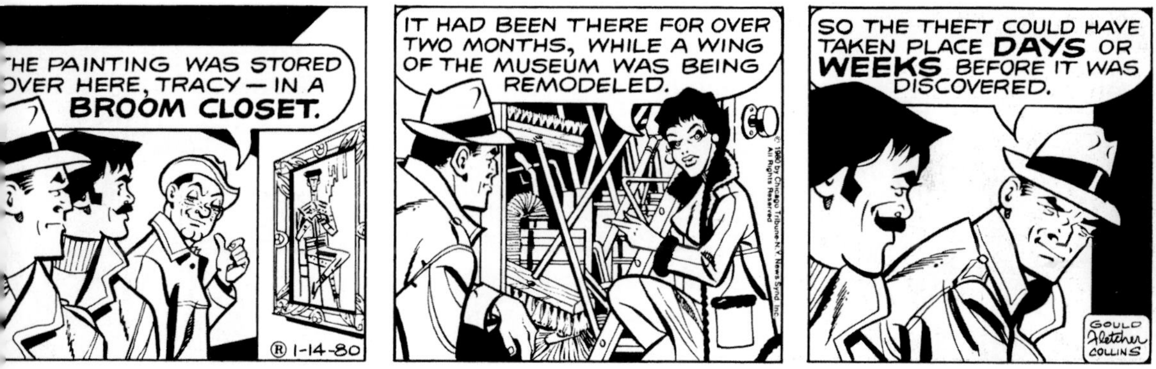

HE PAINTING WAS STORED VER HERE, TRACY— IN A **BROOM CLOSET.**
® 1-14-80
IT HAD BEEN THERE FOR OVER TWO MONTHS, WHILE A WING OF THE MUSEUM WAS BEING REMODELED.
© 1980 by Chicago Tribune-N.Y. News Synd. Inc. All Rights Reserved
SO THE THEFT COULD HAVE TAKEN PLACE **DAYS** OR **WEEKS** BEFORE IT WAS DISCOVERED.
GOULD Fletcher COLLINS

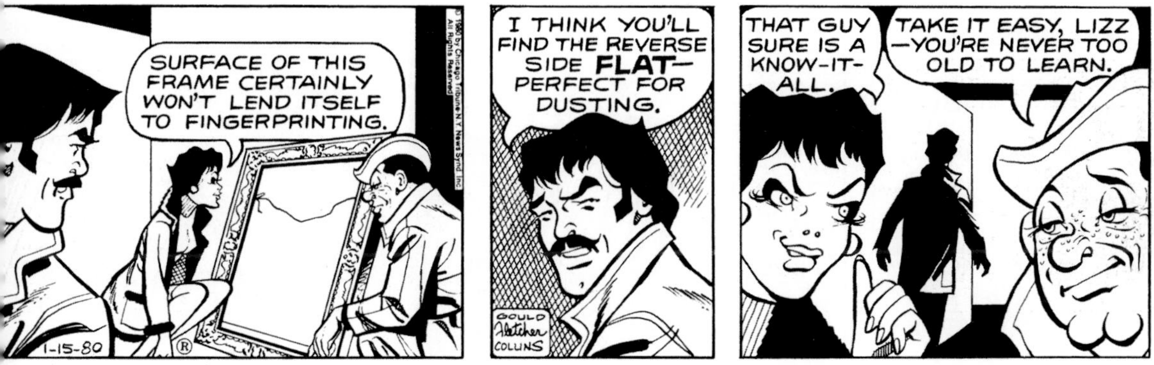

SURFACE OF THIS FRAME CERTAINLY WON'T LEND ITSELF TO FINGERPRINTING.
© 1980 by Chicago Tribune-N.Y. News Synd. Inc. All Rights Reserved
1-15-80 ®
I THINK YOU'LL FIND THE REVERSE SIDE **FLAT**— PERFECT FOR DUSTING.
GOULD Fletcher COLLINS
THAT GUY SURE IS A KNOW-IT-ALL.
TAKE IT EASY, LIZZ —YOU'RE NEVER TOO OLD TO LEARN.

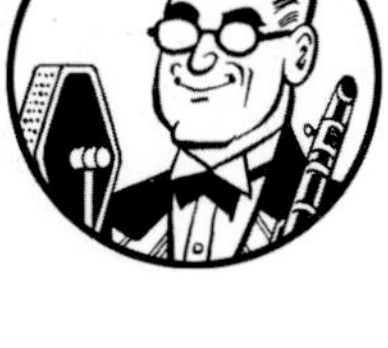

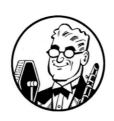

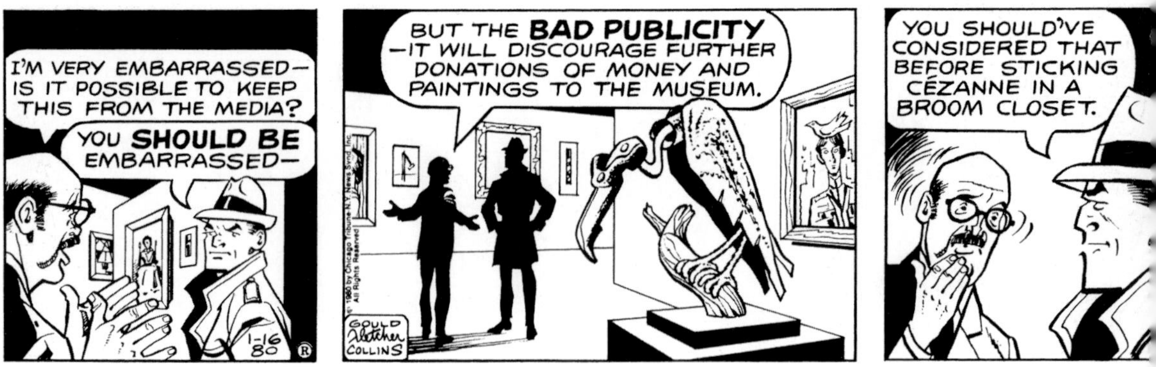
I'M VERY EMBARRASSED—IS IT POSSIBLE TO KEEP THIS FROM THE MEDIA?
YOU SHOULD BE EMBARRASSED—
1-16 80
BUT THE BAD PUBLICITY—IT WILL DISCOURAGE FURTHER DONATIONS OF MONEY AND PAINTINGS TO THE MUSEUM.
© 1980 by Chicago Tribune-N.Y. News Synd. Inc. All Rights Reserved
GOULD Fletcher COLLINS
YOU SHOULD'VE CONSIDERED THAT BEFORE STICKING CÉZANNE IN A BROOM CLOSET.

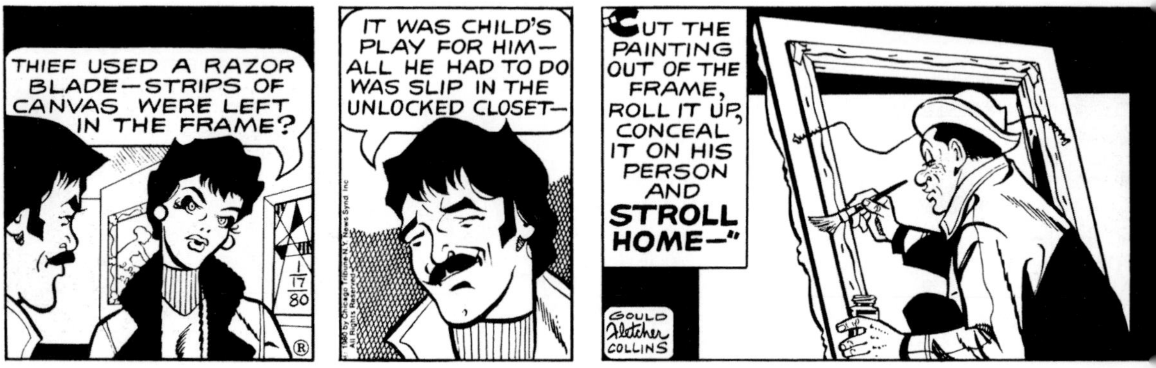
THIEF USED A RAZOR BLADE—STRIPS OF CANVAS WERE LEFT IN THE FRAME?
1/17/80
IT WAS CHILD'S PLAY FOR HIM—ALL HE HAD TO DO WAS SLIP IN THE UNLOCKED CLOSET—
© 1980 by Chicago Tribune-N.Y. News Synd. Inc. All Rights Reserved
"CUT THE PAINTING OUT OF THE FRAME, ROLL IT UP, CONCEAL IT ON HIS PERSON AND STROLL HOME—"
GOULD Fletcher COLLINS

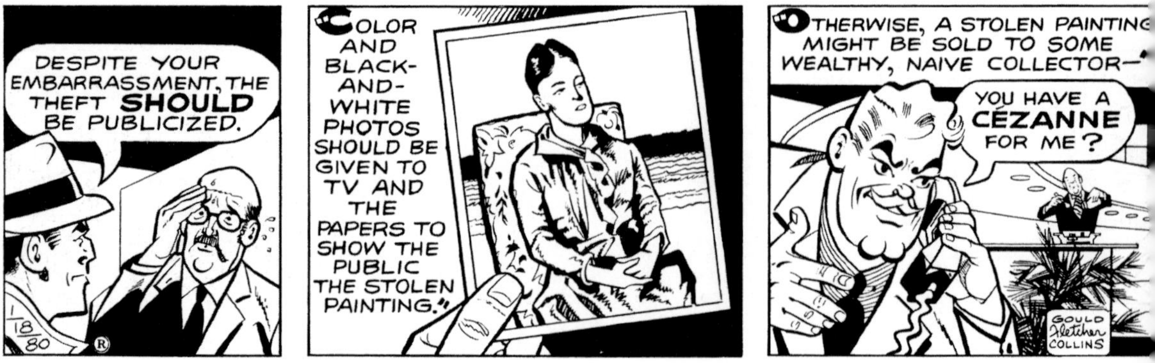
DESPITE YOUR EMBARRASSMENT, THE THEFT SHOULD BE PUBLICIZED.
1/18/80
"COLOR AND BLACK-AND-WHITE PHOTOS SHOULD BE GIVEN TO TV AND THE PAPERS TO SHOW THE PUBLIC THE STOLEN PAINTING."
"OTHERWISE, A STOLEN PAINTING MIGHT BE SOLD TO SOME WEALTHY, NAIVE COLLECTOR—"
YOU HAVE A CÉZANNE FOR ME?
GOULD Fletcher COLLINS

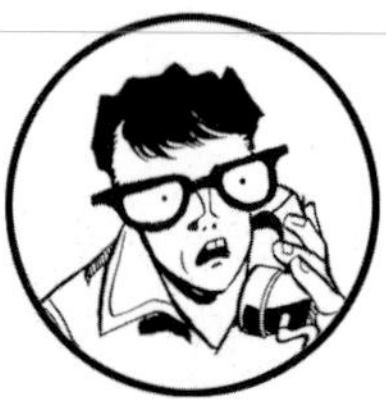

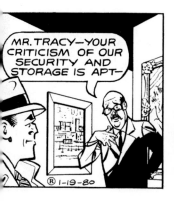

MR. TRACY—YOUR CRITICISM OF OUR SECURITY AND STORAGE IS APT—
® 1-19-80
BUT WITH BUDGET CUTS, AND A GOVERNMENT— A PUBLIC— UNWILLING TO HELP PROTECT OUR NATIONAL TREASURES— WHAT CAN ONE DO?
"ONE CAN CLEAN UP ONE'S OWN ACT," SAYS TRACY.
WHEN CAN I SEE THE CÉZANNE?
BABY FOOD
© 1980 by Chicago Tribune-N.Y. News Synd. Inc. All Rights Reserved
GOULD Fletcher COLLINS

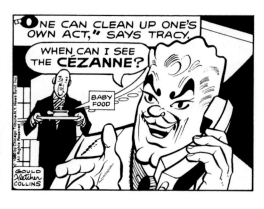

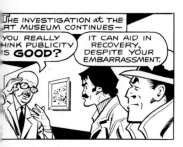

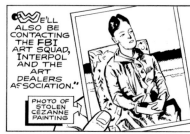

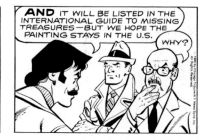

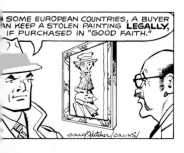

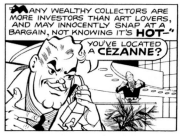

HE INVESTIGATION at THE RT MUSEUM CONTINUES—
YOU REALLY HINK PUBLICITY S GOOD?
IT CAN AID IN RECOVERY, DESPITE YOUR EMBARRASSMENT.
"WE'LL ALSO BE CONTACTING THE FBI ART SQUAD, INTERPOL AND THE ART DEALERS ASSOCIATION."
PHOTO OF STOLEN CÉZANNE PAINTING
AND IT WILL BE LISTED IN THE INTERNATIONAL GUIDE TO MISSING TREASURES—BUT WE HOPE THE PAINTING STAYS IN THE U.S.
WHY?

SOME EUROPEAN COUNTRIES, A BUYER AN KEEP A STOLEN PAINTING LEGALLY, IF PURCHASED IN "GOOD FAITH."
GOULD/Fletcher/COLLINS/
"MANY WEALTHY COLLECTORS ARE MORE INVESTORS THAN ART LOVERS, AND MAY INNOCENTLY SNAP AT A BARGAIN, NOT KNOWING IT'S HOT—"
YOU'VE LOCATED A CÉZANNE?
THAT'S RIGHT, MR. SMITH— AT $750,000, IT'S A STEAL.
1-20-80

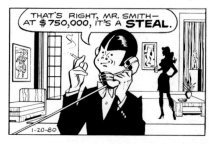

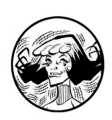

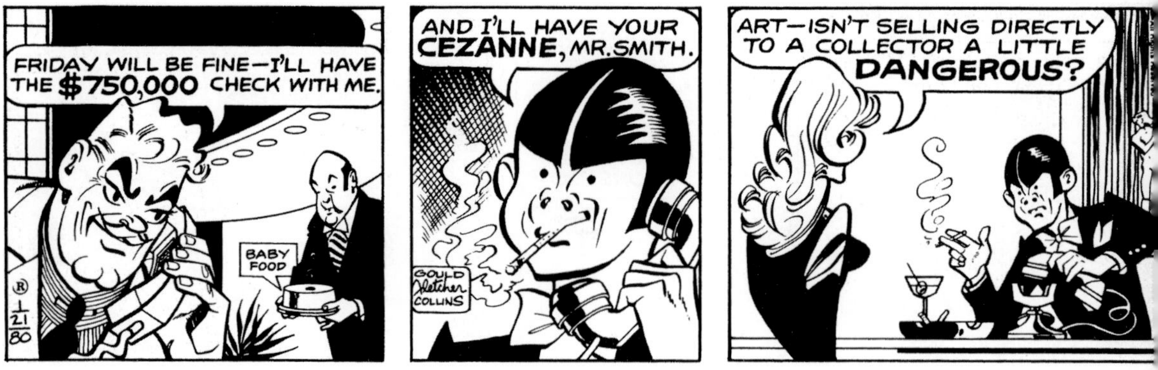
FRIDAY WILL BE FINE—I'LL HAVE THE $750,000 CHECK WITH ME.
BABY FOOD
®
1/21/80
AND I'LL HAVE YOUR CEZANNE, MR. SMITH.
GOULD Fletcher COLLINS
ART—ISN'T SELLING DIRECTLY TO A COLLECTOR A LITTLE DANGEROUS?

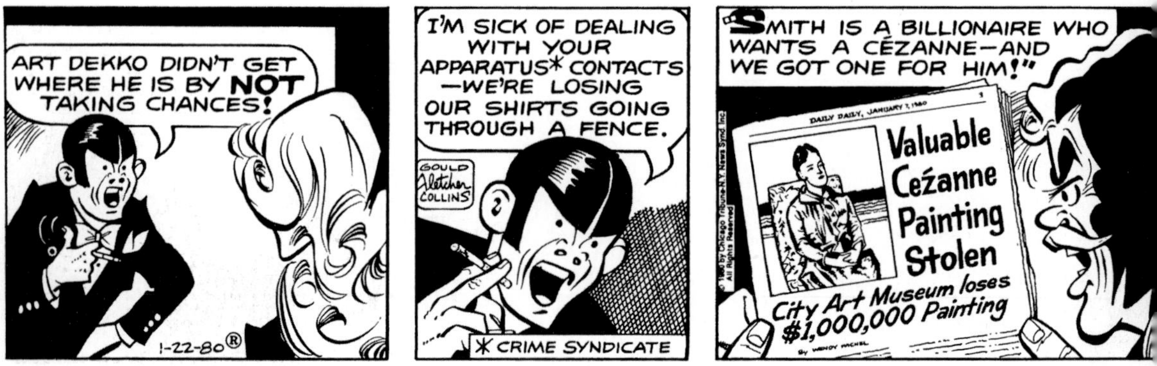
ART DEKKO DIDN'T GET WHERE HE IS BY NOT TAKING CHANCES!
1-22-80®
I'M SICK OF DEALING WITH YOUR APPARATUS* CONTACTS —WE'RE LOSING OUR SHIRTS GOING THROUGH A FENCE.
GOULD Fletcher COLLINS
*CRIME SYNDICATE
"SMITH IS A BILLIONAIRE WHO WANTS A CÉZANNE—AND WE GOT ONE FOR HIM!"
Valuable Cezanne Painting Stolen
City Art Museum loses $1,000,000 Painting

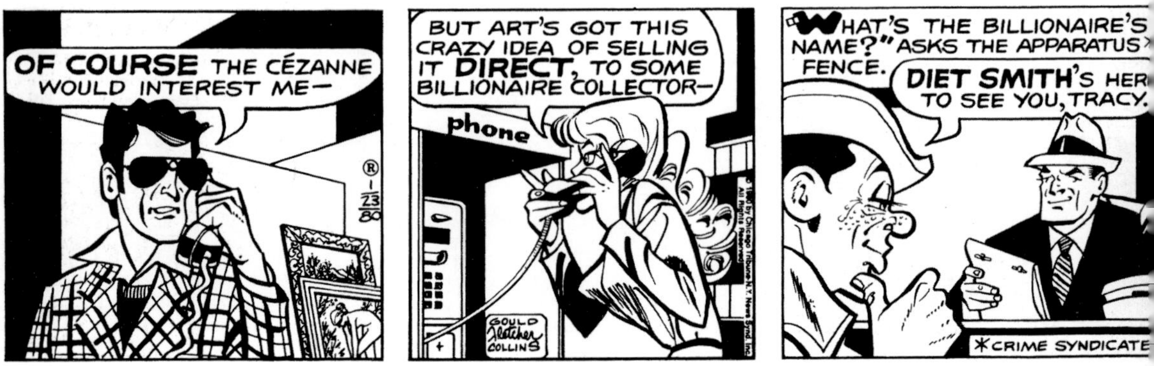
OF COURSE THE CÉZANNE WOULD INTEREST ME—
®
1/23/80
BUT ART'S GOT THIS CRAZY IDEA OF SELLING IT DIRECT, TO SOME BILLIONAIRE COLLECTOR—
phone
GOULD Fletcher COLLINS
"WHAT'S THE BILLIONAIRE'S NAME?" ASKS THE APPARATUS* FENCE.
DIET SMITH'S HERE TO SEE YOU, TRACY.
*CRIME SYNDICATE

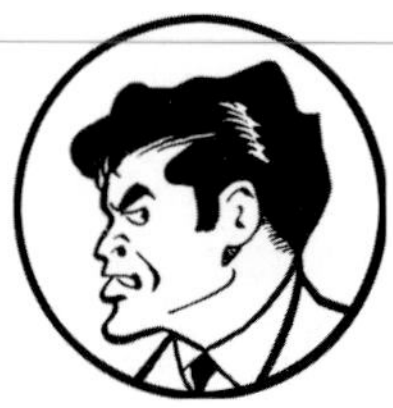

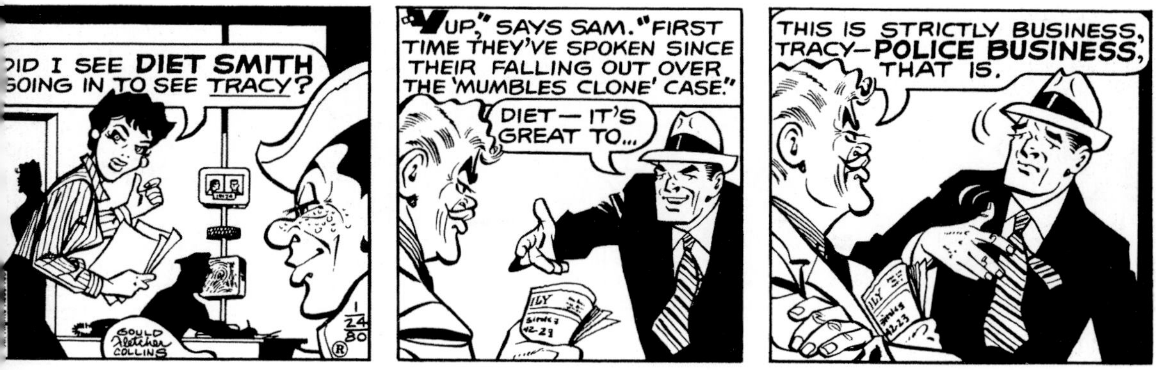
ID I SEE DIET SMITH
OING IN TO SEE TRACY?
GOULD Fletcher COLLINS
1 24 80
"YUP," SAYS SAM. "FIRST TIME THEY'VE SPOKEN SINCE THEIR FALLING OUT OVER THE 'MUMBLES CLONE' CASE."
DIET — IT'S GREAT TO...
THIS IS STRICTLY BUSINESS, TRACY—POLICE BUSINESS, THAT IS.

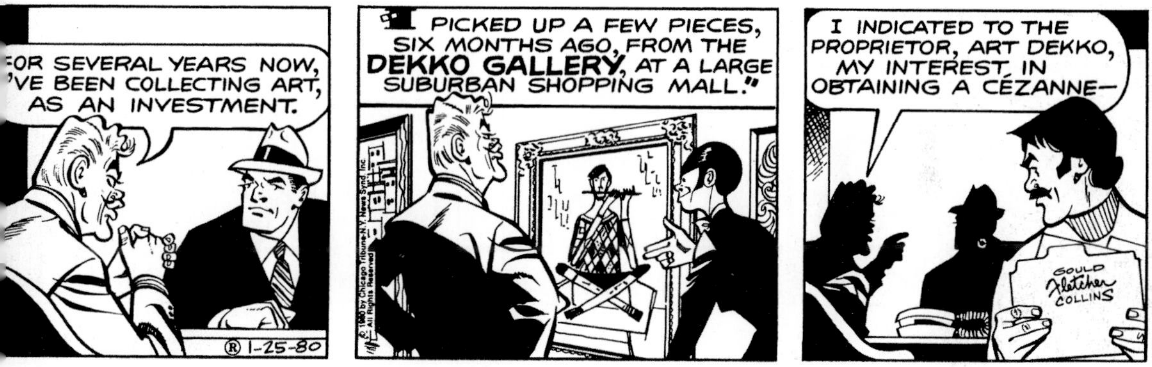
OR SEVERAL YEARS NOW, 'VE BEEN COLLECTING ART, AS AN INVESTMENT.
1-25-80
"I PICKED UP A FEW PIECES, SIX MONTHS AGO, FROM THE DEKKO GALLERY, AT A LARGE SUBURBAN SHOPPING MALL."
© 1980 by Chicago Tribune-N.Y. News Synd. Inc. All Rights Reserved
I INDICATED TO THE PROPRIETOR, ART DEKKO, MY INTEREST, IN OBTAINING A CÉZANNE—
GOULD Fletcher COLLINS

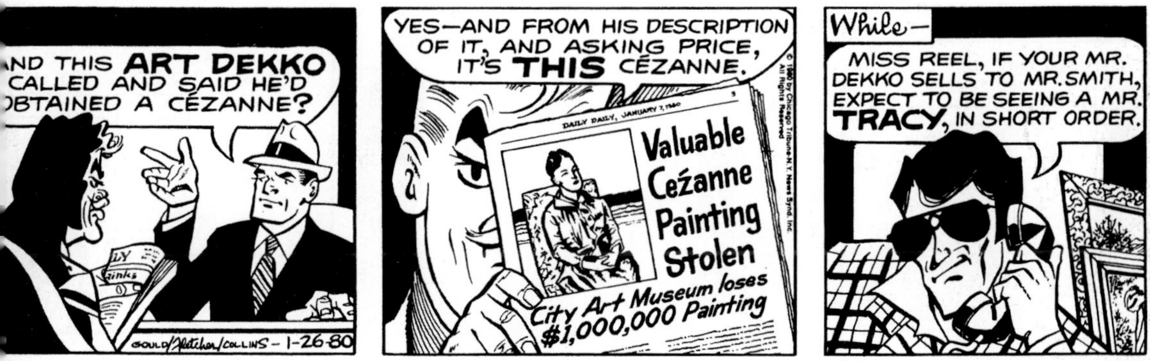
ND THIS ART DEKKO CALLED AND SAID HE'D BTAINED A CÉZANNE?
GOULD/Fletcher/COLLINS - 1-26-80
YES—AND FROM HIS DESCRIPTION OF IT, AND ASKING PRICE, IT'S THIS CÉZANNE.
© 1980 by Chicago Tribune-N.Y. News Synd. Inc. All Rights Reserved
DAILY DAILY, JANUARY 7, 1980
Valuable Cezanne Painting Stolen
City Art Museum loses $1,000,000 Painting
While—
MISS REEL, IF YOUR MR. DEKKO SELLS TO MR. SMITH, EXPECT TO BE SEEING A MR. TRACY, IN SHORT ORDER.

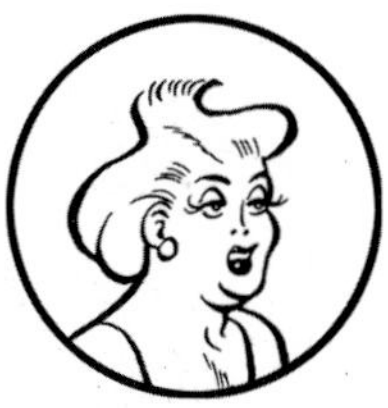

WHAT'S THIS? A RECONCILIATION BETWEEN TRACY AND DIET SMITH?
DON'T THINK SO, CHIEF— SOMETHING TO DO WITH THE CÉZANNE HEIST.
YOU'RE **SURE** THE PAINTING ART DEKKO HAS OFFERED YOU IS THIS ONE?
I'M NOT **POSITIVE**
"BUT IT ADDS UP THAT WAY: THE SUDDEN AVAILABILITY OF A CÉZANNE, HIS DESCRIPTION OF IT, HIS ASKING PRICE—"
Valuable Cézanne Painting Stolen
City Art Museum lose
$1,000,000 Paintin

TRACY, THIS **ART DEKKO** IS A PRIME SUSPECT IN THE ONGOING INTERNATIONAL ART THEFT INVESTIGATION...
BUT THIS DOESN'T FIT HIS PATTERN—HE'S NEVER TRIED TO SELL DIRECT TO A CUSTOMER BEFORE—
GOULD/FLETCHER/COLLINS
"APPARENTLY HE AND HIS ACCOMPLICE **SUE REEL** HAVE BEEN USING AN APPARATUS* FENCE—"
DIET SMITH IS A FRIEND OF **DICK TRACY?** THE COP?
THAT'S RIGHT, ART.
*CRIME SYNDICATE

I'M TO PICK UP THE CÉZANNE PAINTING AT DEKKO'S ART GALLERY.
Ⓡ1-28-80
"WHEN?" ASKS TRACY. "FRIDAY NIGHT," SAYS DIET. "JUST AFTER CLOSING."
SUE REEL, ARE YOU **SURE?**
© 1980 by Chicago Tribune-N.Y. News Synd. Inc. All Rights Reserved
GOULD/FLETCHER COLLINS
ABSOLUTELY—MY CONNECTION SAYS SELLING TO DIET SMITH IS LIKE SELLING TO **TRACY.**

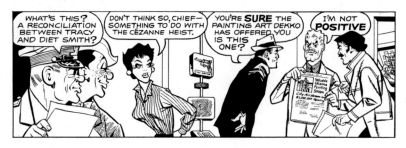

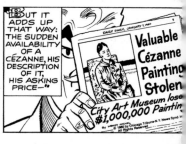

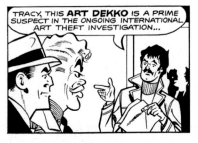

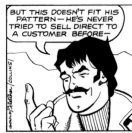

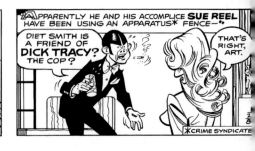

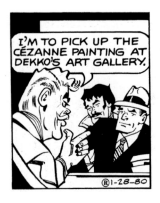

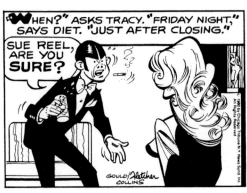

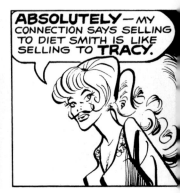

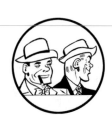

WE'D LIKE YOU TO GO AHEAD WITH THE CÉZANNE BUY.

I'LL BE GLAD TO HELP.

1-29-80

WE CAN WORK OUT THE PARTICULARS FRIDAY MORNING— IF THAT'S ACCEPTABLE.

AND LET US KNOW IF DEKKO CONTACTS YOU AGAIN, IN THE MEANTIME."

MR. SMITH IS OUT?

GOULD
Fletcher
COLLINS

DEKKO'S ONLY RECORD IS A SUSPENDED SENTENCE FOR POSSESSION IN CALIFORNIA.

-30-80

SUSPECTED OF HAVING BEEN A NARCOTICS DEALER, ON THE FRINGES OF THE HOLLYWOOD SCENE, FOR SEVERAL YEARS."

L.A.P.D.
83308
12 AUG 77

DEALING DOPE—DEALING ART —IT'S ALL THE SAME TO HIM."

DON'T WORRY, ART.

ART DEKKO DIDN'T GET WHERE HE IS BY NOT WORRYING.

1980 by Chicago Tribune N Y News Synd Inc

GOULD
Fletcher
COLLINS

DEKKO FANCIES HIMSELF A "LONE WOLF"—

R 1-31-80

PERHAPS HE WANTS TO CUT OUT THE MIDDLEMAN—EVEN IF IT IS AN APPARATUS FENCE WITH INTERNATIONAL CONNECTIONS.

STILL," SAYS TRACY, "SELLING DIRECT TO DIET SMITH IS A BIG BLUNDER."

A MR. DEKKO CALLED WHILE YOU WERE OUT, SIR.

GOULD
Fletcher
COLLINS

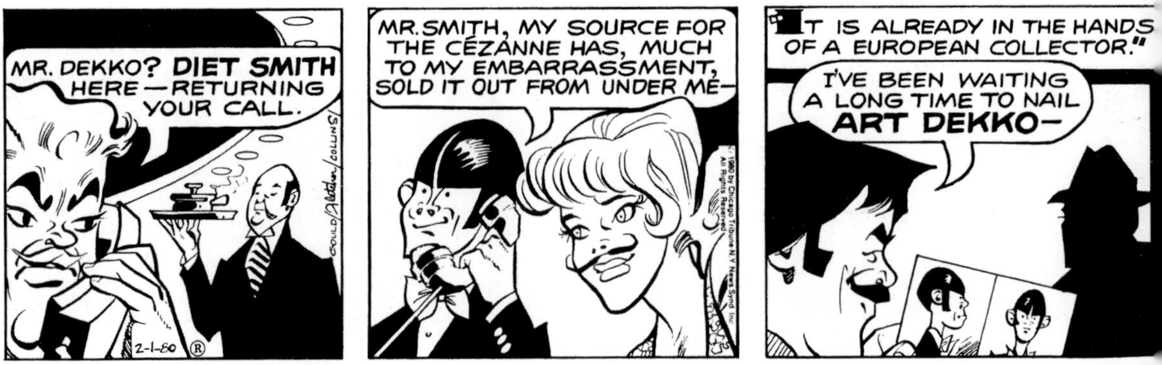
MR. DEKKO? **DIET SMITH** HERE—RETURNING YOUR CALL.
GOULD/Fletcher/COLLINS/
2-1-80
MR. SMITH, MY SOURCE FOR THE CÉZANNE HAS, MUCH TO MY EMBARRASSMENT, SOLD IT OUT FROM UNDER ME—
©1980 by Chicago Tribune-N.Y. News Synd. Inc. All Rights Reserved
"IT IS ALREADY IN THE HAND
OF A EUROPEAN COLLECTOR."
I'VE BEEN WAITING A LONG TIME TO NAIL **ART DEKKO**—

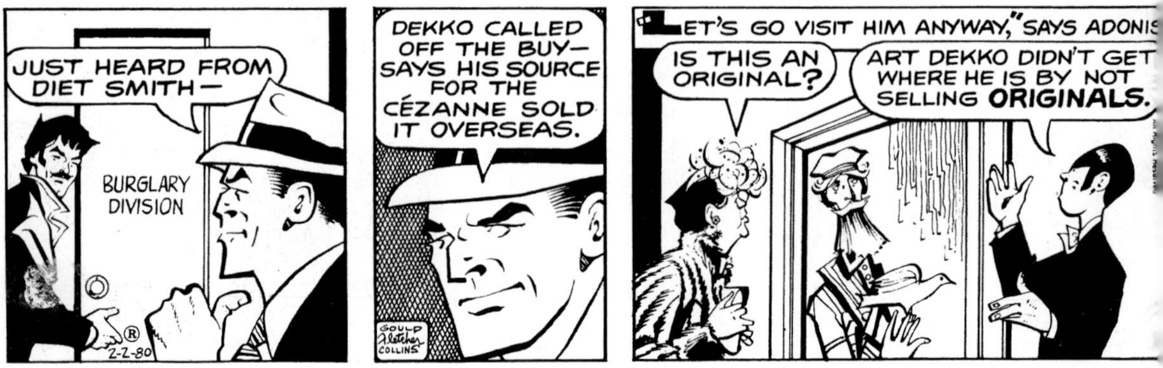
JUST HEARD FROM DIET SMITH—
BURGLARY DIVISION
2-2-80
DEKKO CALLED OFF THE BUY— SAYS HIS SOURCE FOR THE CÉZANNE SOLD IT OVERSEAS.
GOULD Fletcher COLLINS
"LET'S GO VISIT HIM ANYWAY," SAYS ADONI
IS THIS AN ORIGINAL?
ART DEKKO DIDN'T GET WHERE HE IS BY NOT SELLING **ORIGINALS.**

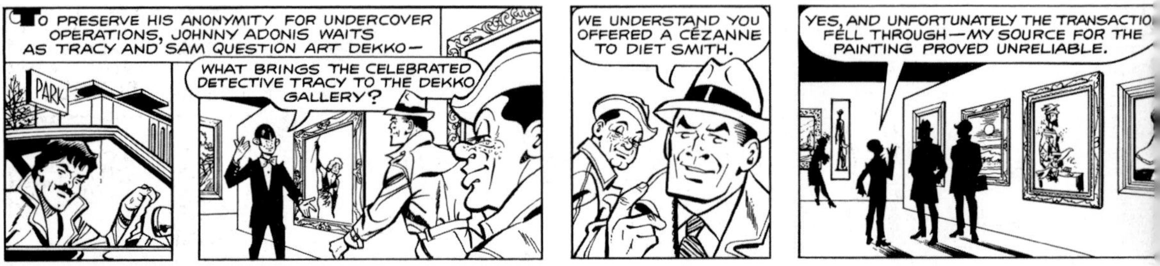
TO PRESERVE HIS ANONYMITY FOR UNDERCOVER OPERATIONS, JOHNNY ADONIS WAITS AS TRACY AND SAM QUESTION ART DEKKO—
PARK
WHAT BRINGS THE CELEBRATED DETECTIVE TRACY TO THE DEKKO GALLERY?
WE UNDERSTAND YOU OFFERED A CÉZANNE TO DIET SMITH.
YES, AND UNFORTUNATELY THE TRANSACTI
FELL THROUGH—MY SOURCE FOR THE PAINTING PROVED UNRELIABLE.

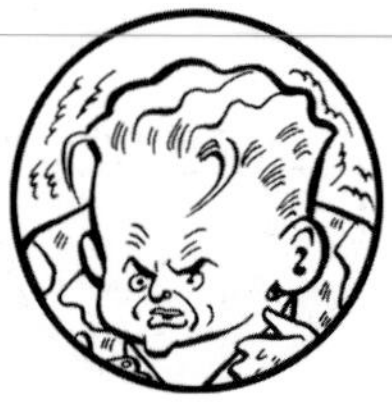

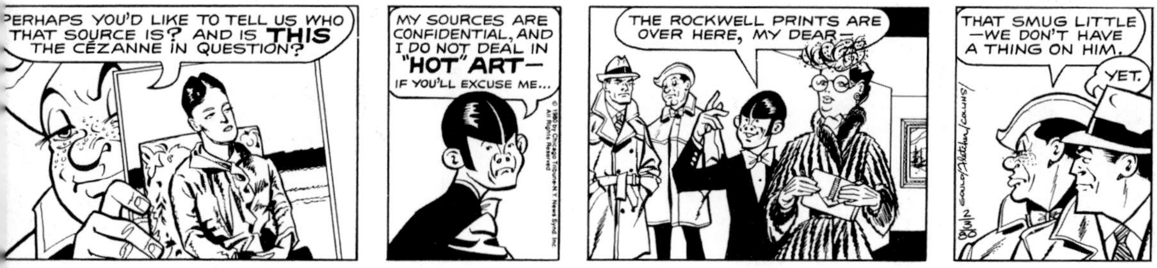
PERHAPS YOU'D LIKE TO TELL US WHO THAT SOURCE IS? AND IS **THIS** THE CÉZANNE IN QUESTION?
MY SOURCES ARE CONFIDENTIAL, AND I DO NOT DEAL IN "HOT" ART— IF YOU'LL EXCUSE ME...
© 1980 by Chicago Tribune-N.Y. News Synd. Inc. All Rights Reserved
THE ROCKWELL PRINTS ARE OVER HERE, MY DEAR—
THAT SMUG LITTLE —WE DON'T HAVE A THING ON HIM.
YET.

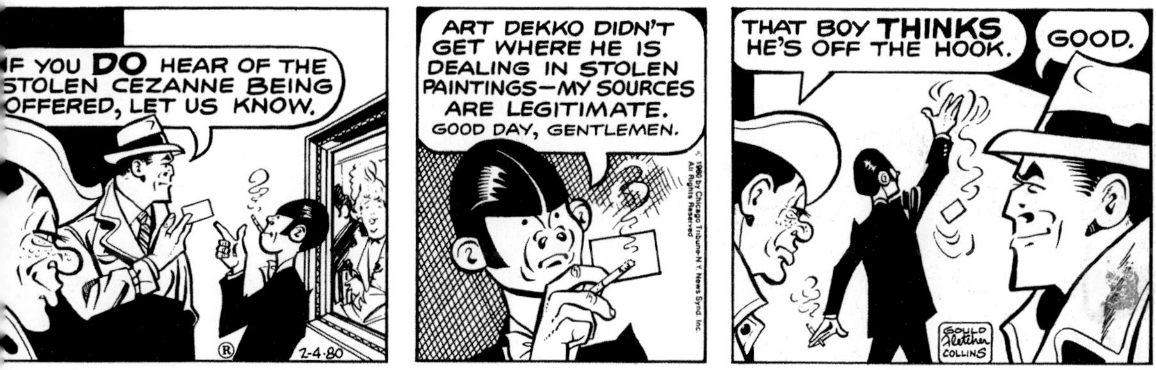
IF YOU **DO** HEAR OF THE STOLEN CEZANNE BEING OFFERED, LET US KNOW.
2-4-80
ART DEKKO DIDN'T GET WHERE HE IS DEALING IN STOLEN PAINTINGS—MY SOURCES ARE LEGITIMATE. GOOD DAY, GENTLEMEN.
© 1980 by Chicago Tribune-N.Y. News Synd. Inc. All Rights Reserved
THAT BOY **THINKS** HE'S OFF THE HOOK.
GOOD.
GOULD Fletcher COLLINS

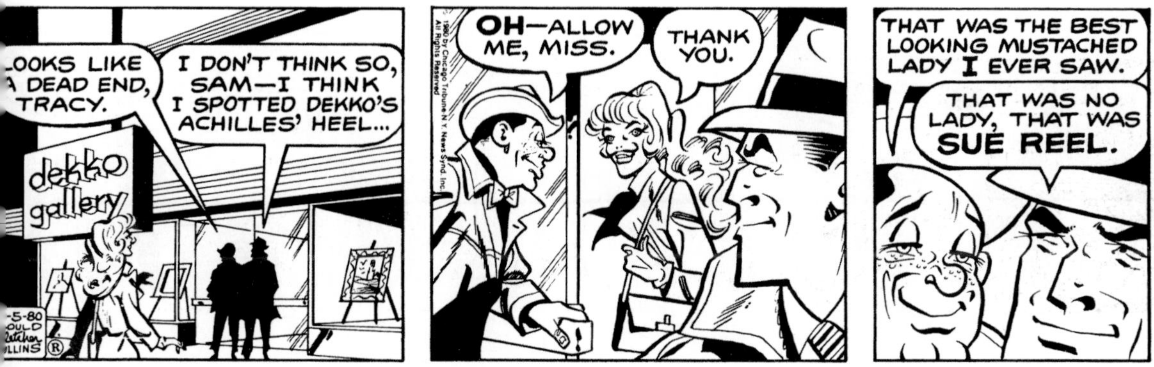
LOOKS LIKE A DEAD END, TRACY.
I DON'T THINK SO, SAM—I THINK I SPOTTED DEKKO'S ACHILLES' HEEL...
dekko gallery
© 1980 by Chicago Tribune-N.Y. News Synd. Inc. All Rights Reserved
OH—ALLOW ME, MISS.
THANK YOU.
THAT WAS THE BEST LOOKING MUSTACHED LADY **I** EVER SAW.
THAT WAS NO LADY, THAT WAS **SUE REEL**.

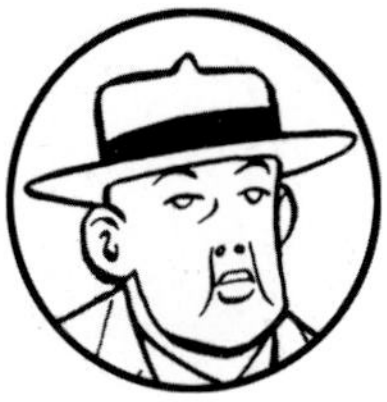

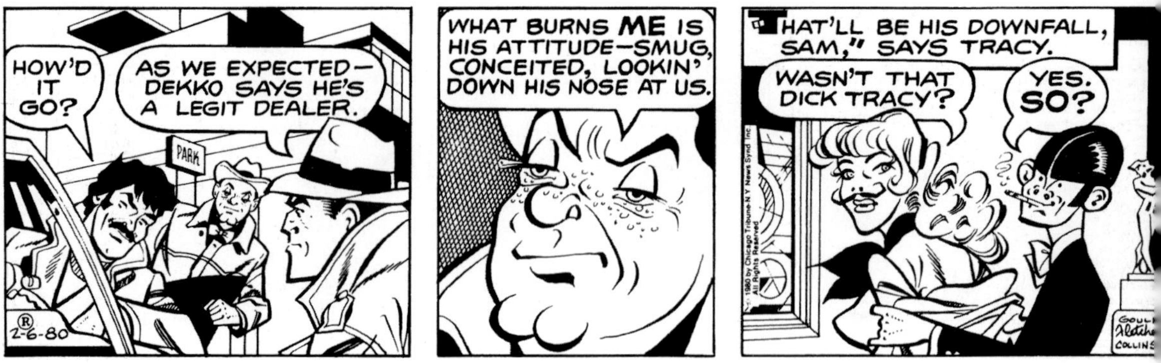
HOW'D IT GO?
AS WE EXPECTED—DEKKO SAYS HE'S A LEGIT DEALER.
PARK
® 2-6-80
WHAT BURNS ME IS HIS ATTITUDE—SMUG, CONCEITED, LOOKIN' DOWN HIS NOSE AT US.
"THAT'LL BE HIS DOWNFALL, SAM," SAYS TRACY.
WASN'T THAT DICK TRACY?
YES. SO?
© 1980 by Chicago Tribune-N.Y. News Synd Inc. All Rights Reserved
GOULD Fletcher COLLINS

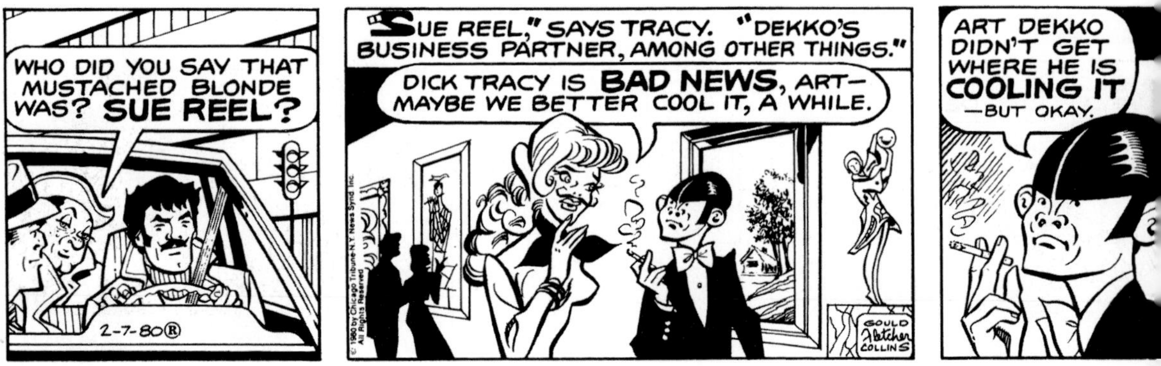
WHO DID YOU SAY THAT MUSTACHED BLONDE WAS? SUE REEL?
2-7-80®
"SUE REEL," SAYS TRACY. "DEKKO'S BUSINESS PARTNER, AMONG OTHER THINGS."
DICK TRACY IS BAD NEWS, ART—MAYBE WE BETTER COOL IT, A WHILE.
© 1980 by Chicago Tribune-N.Y. News Synd Inc. All Rights Reserved
GOULD Fletcher COLLINS
ART DEKKO DIDN'T GET WHERE HE IS COOLING IT —BUT OKAY.

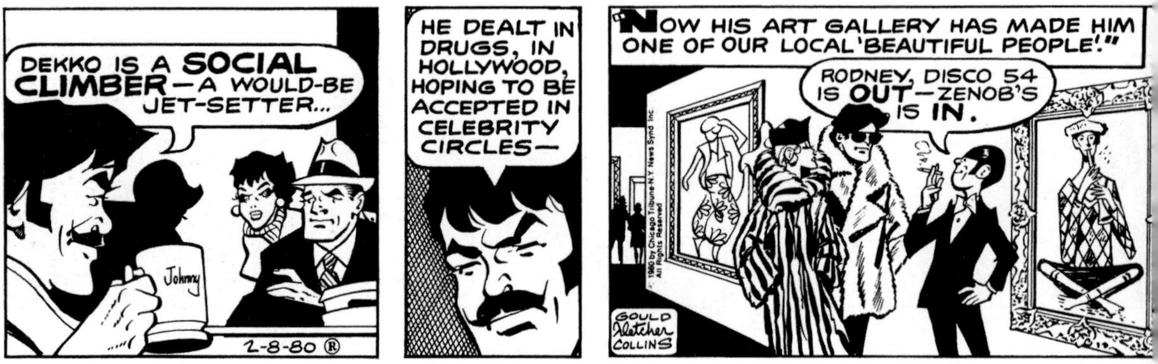
DEKKO IS A SOCIAL CLIMBER—A WOULD-BE JET-SETTER...
Johnny
2-8-80 ®
HE DEALT IN DRUGS, IN HOLLYWOOD, HOPING TO BE ACCEPTED IN CELEBRITY CIRCLES—
"NOW HIS ART GALLERY HAS MADE HIM ONE OF OUR LOCAL 'BEAUTIFUL PEOPLE!'"
RODNEY, DISCO 54 IS OUT—ZENOB'S IS IN.
© 1980 by Chicago Tribune-N.Y. News Synd Inc. All Rights Reserved
GOULD Fletcher COLLINS

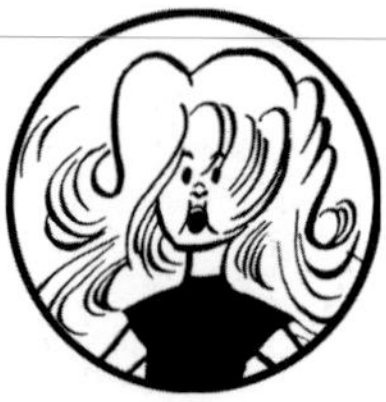

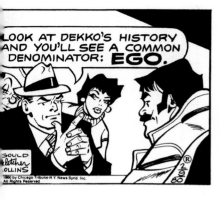

LOOK AT DEKKO'S HISTORY AND YOU'LL SEE A COMMON DENOMINATOR: EGO.
GOULD Fletcher COLLINS
1980 by Chicago Tribune-N.Y. News Synd. Inc. All Rights Reserved
2 9 80
FORMER DRUG-TRAFFICKER TO CELEBRITIES—A SOCIAL CLIMBER RUNNING AN ART GALLERY— "LONE WOLF" ART THIEF—
"THE KEY TO THIS CASE IS DEKKO'S ENORMOUS EGO— AND IT'S A KEY WE'LL USE TO LOCK HIM UP!"

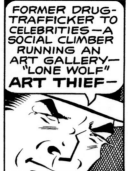

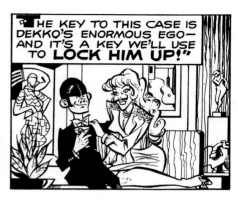

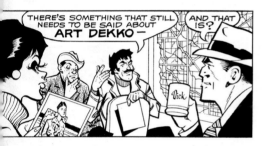

THERE'S SOMETHING THAT STILL NEEDS TO BE SAID ABOUT ART DEKKO—
AND THAT IS?
Dick
HE'S DANGEROUS. THERE'S REASON TO BELIEVE HE MAY HAVE MURDERED A FORMER ACCOMPLICE.
THIS IS CANDY NOZE—DEKKO'S PARTNER WHEN HE WAS TRAFFICKING DRUGS IN CALIFORNIA, SEVERAL YEARS BACK...
disco

'VE HEARD OF HER—WASN'T SHE VEALTHY? TRIED TO BUY HER WAY INTO A HOLLYWOOD CAREER?
1980 by Chicago Tribune-N.Y. News Synd. Inc. All Rights Reserved
disco
YES, ONLY IT DIDN'T WORK OUT—SO SHE TRIED TO GET IN THE BACK DOOR, BY SUPPLYING DOPE TO "CELEBRITIES."
GOULD Fletcher COLLINS
"SHE AND DEKKO, HER PARTNER, WERE SUCCESSFUL, UNTIL AN LAPD INVESTIGATION STARTED CLOSING IN— THEN CANDY TURNED UP DEAD, AN OVERDOSE VICTIM, AND DEKKO TURNED UP HERE."
2 10 80

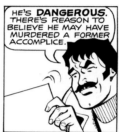

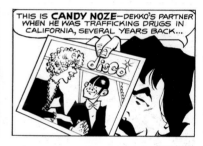

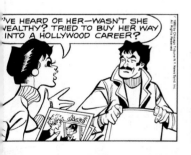

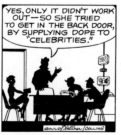

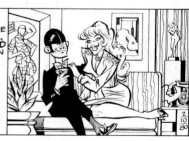

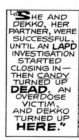

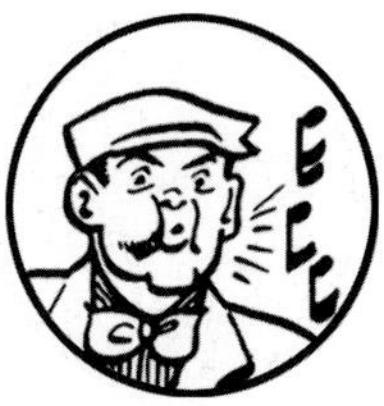

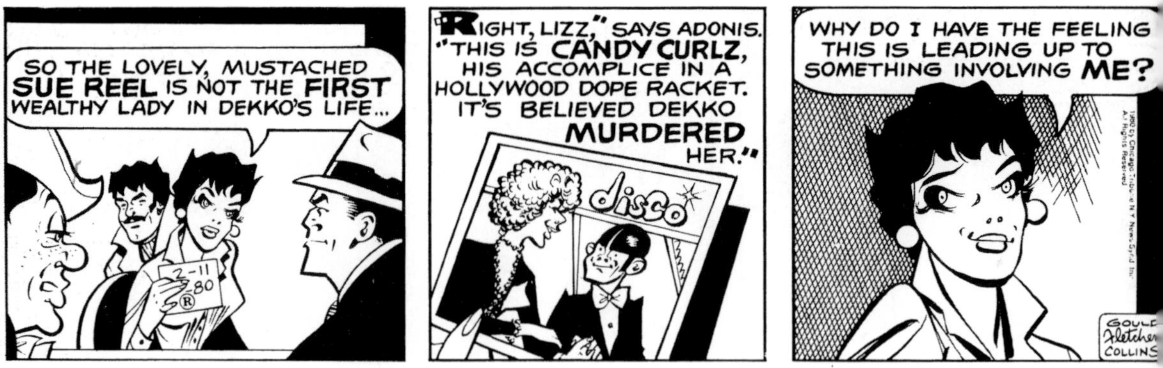
SO THE LOVELY, MUSTACHED SUE REEL IS NOT THE FIRST WEALTHY LADY IN DEKKO'S LIFE...
2-11 80 ®
"RIGHT, LIZZ," SAYS ADONIS. "THIS IS CANDY CURLZ, HIS ACCOMPLICE IN A HOLLYWOOD DOPE RACKET. IT'S BELIEVED DEKKO MURDERED HER."
disco
WHY DO I HAVE THE FEELING THIS IS LEADING UP TO SOMETHING INVOLVING ME?
GOULD Fletcher COLLINS

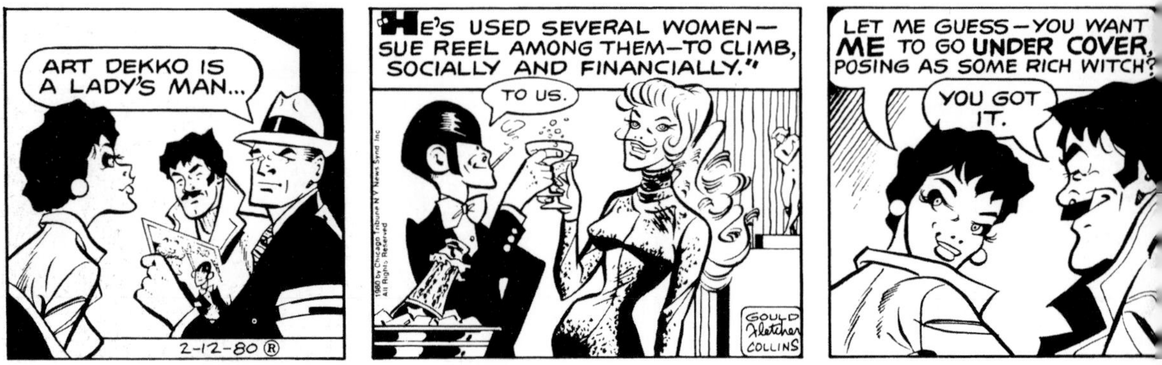
ART DEKKO IS A LADY'S MAN...
2-12-80 ®
"HE'S USED SEVERAL WOMEN—SUE REEL AMONG THEM—TO CLIMB, SOCIALLY AND FINANCIALLY."
TO US.
GOULD Fletcher COLLINS
LET ME GUESS—YOU WANT ME TO GO UNDER COVER, POSING AS SOME RICH WITCH?
YOU GOT IT.

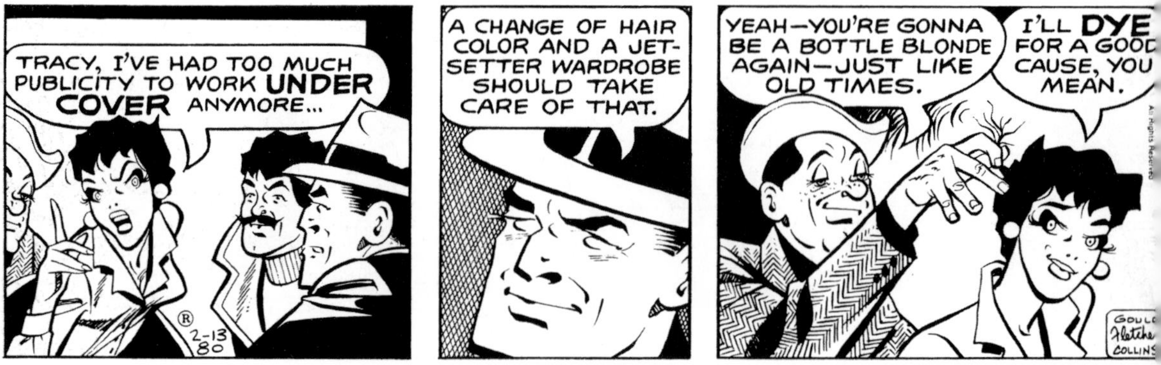
TRACY, I'VE HAD TOO MUCH PUBLICITY TO WORK UNDER COVER ANYMORE...
® 2-13 80
A CHANGE OF HAIR COLOR AND A JET-SETTER WARDROBE SHOULD TAKE CARE OF THAT.
YEAH—YOU'RE GONNA BE A BOTTLE BLONDE AGAIN—JUST LIKE OLD TIMES.
I'LL DYE FOR A GOOD CAUSE, YOU MEAN.
GOULD Fletcher COLLINS

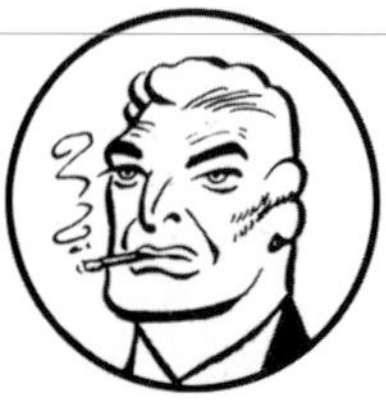

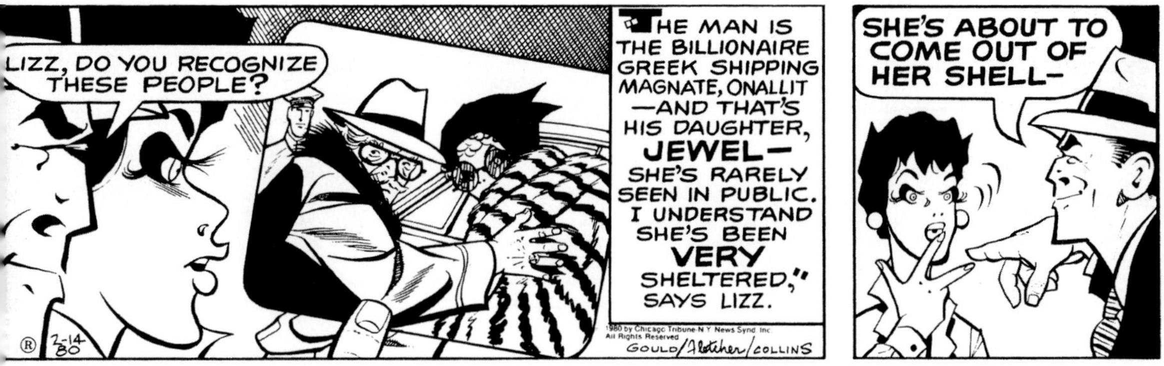
LIZZ, DO YOU RECOGNIZE THESE PEOPLE?
2-14-80
"THE MAN IS THE BILLIONAIRE GREEK SHIPPING MAGNATE, ONALLIT —AND THAT'S HIS DAUGHTER, JEWEL— SHE'S RARELY SEEN IN PUBLIC. I UNDERSTAND SHE'S BEEN VERY SHELTERED," SAYS LIZZ.
©1980 by Chicago Tribune-N.Y. News Synd. Inc All Rights Reserved
GOULD/Fletcher/COLLINS
SHE'S ABOUT TO COME OUT OF HER SHELL—

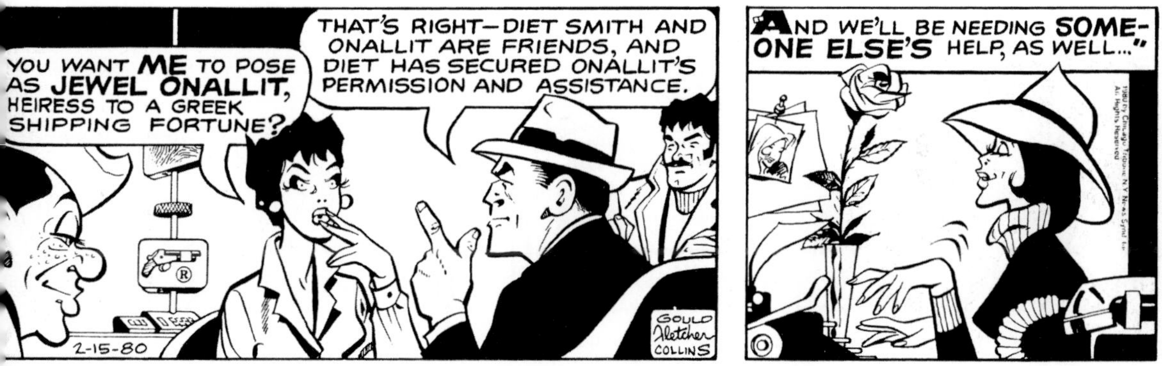
YOU WANT ME TO POSE AS JEWEL ONALLIT, HEIRESS TO A GREEK SHIPPING FORTUNE?
THAT'S RIGHT—DIET SMITH AND ONALLIT ARE FRIENDS, AND DIET HAS SECURED ONALLIT'S PERMISSION AND ASSISTANCE.
2-15-80
GOULD Fletcher COLLINS
"AND WE'LL BE NEEDING SOME-ONE ELSE'S HELP, AS WELL..."

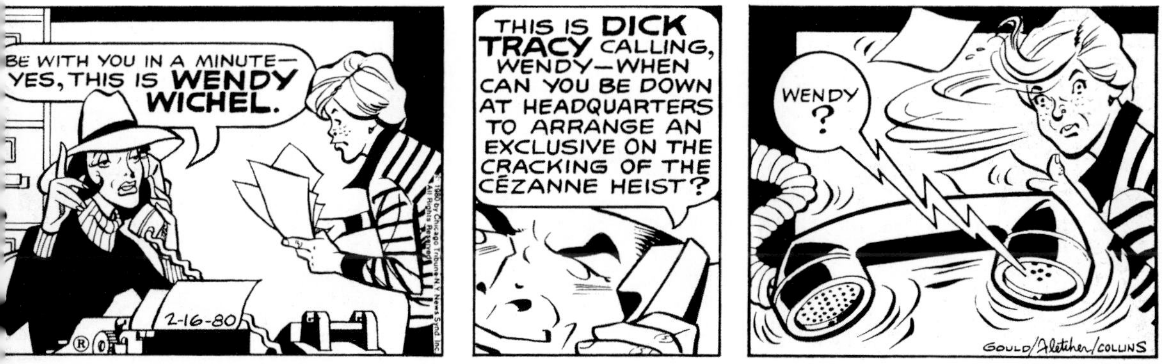
BE WITH YOU IN A MINUTE— YES, THIS IS WENDY WICHEL.
2-16-80
THIS IS DICK TRACY CALLING, WENDY—WHEN CAN YOU BE DOWN AT HEADQUARTERS TO ARRANGE AN EXCLUSIVE ON THE CRACKING OF THE CÉZANNE HEIST?
WENDY ?
GOULD/Fletcher/COLLINS

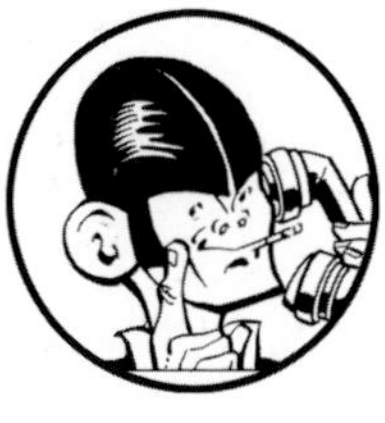

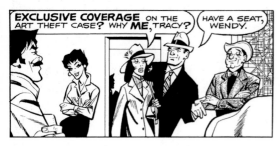

EXCLUSIVE COVERAGE ON THE ART THEFT CASE? WHY ME, TRACY?
HAVE A SEAT, WENDY.
WE NEED TO SEND A POLICEWOMAN—LIZZ, HERE— UNDER COVER. WE NEED HELP IN MAKING HER COVER STORY STICK.
"RECOGNIZE THEM, WENDY?" "SURE-GREEK TYCOON ONALLIT AND HIS SELDOM SEEN, SHELTERED DAUGHTER, JEWEL."
GOULD Fletcher COLLINS

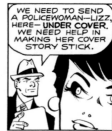

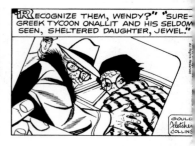

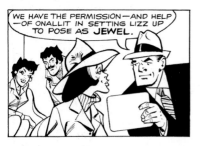

WE HAVE THE PERMISSION—AND HELP —OF ONALLIT IN SETTING LIZZ UP TO POSE AS JEWEL.
ONALLIT WAS SOLD SOME STOLEN PAINTINGS LAST YEAR —THOUGH NOT LEGALLY BOUND, HE RETURNED THEM TO THE RIGHTFUL OWNERS.
BUT HE'D LIKE TO HELP BUST UP THE INTERNATIONAL ART THEFT RING RESPONSIBLE..."
MY APPARATUS CONNECTION WANTS THE CÉZANNE—
HE WANTS IT TOO CHEAP!
2-17-80

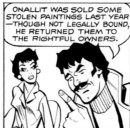

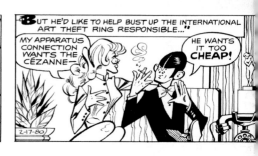

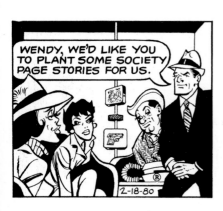

WENDY, WE'D LIKE YOU TO PLANT SOME SOCIETY PAGE STORIES FOR US.
2-18-80
SHOWING LIZZ AS HEIRESS JEWEL ONALLIT? WHAT MAKES YOU THINK I'D HELP YOU HOAX THE PUBLIC?
GOULD Fletcher COLLINS
"IT'S NOT THE PUBLIC WE WANT TO FOOL," SAYS TRACY. "IT'S A THIEF AND MURDERER NAMED ART DEKKO—"

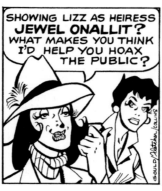

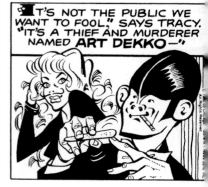

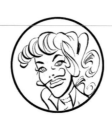

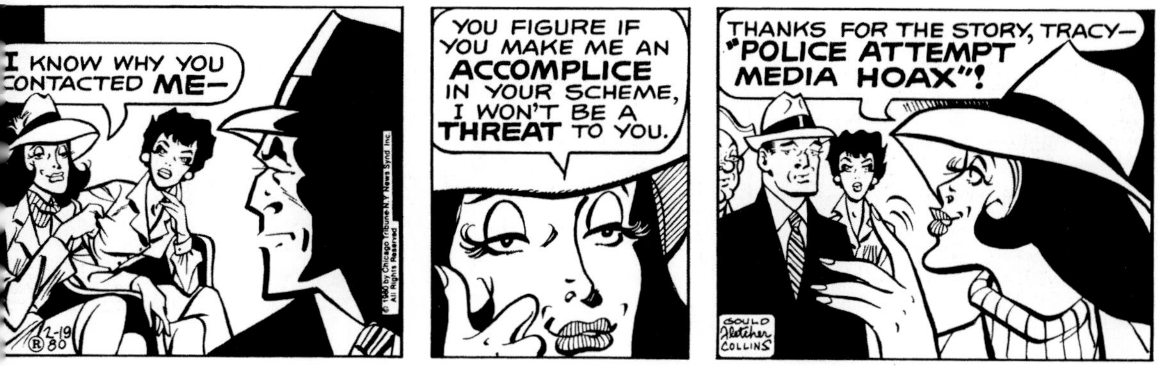
I KNOW WHY YOU CONTACTED ME—
© 1980 by Chicago Tribune-N.Y. News Synd. Inc. All Rights Reserved
2-19 80
YOU FIGURE IF YOU MAKE ME AN ACCOMPLICE IN YOUR SCHEME, I WON'T BE A THREAT TO YOU.
THANKS FOR THE STORY, TRACY— "POLICE ATTEMPT MEDIA HOAX"!
GOULD Fletcher COLLINS

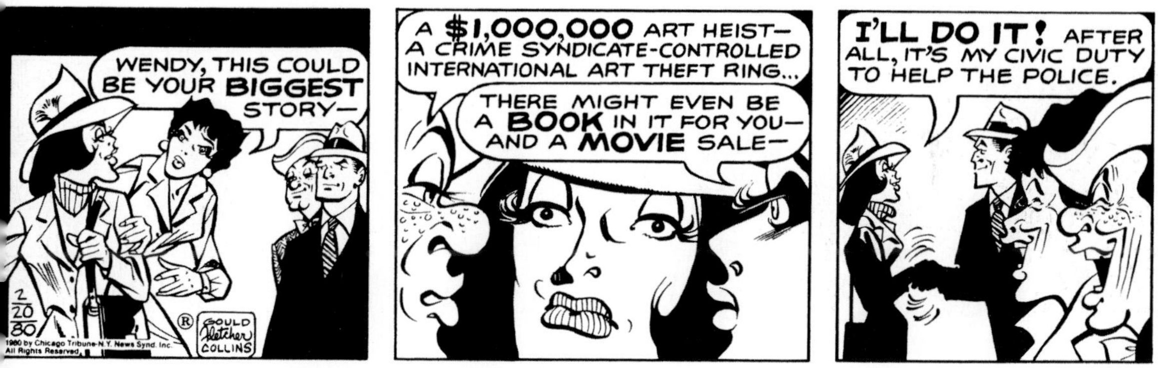
WENDY, THIS COULD BE YOUR BIGGEST STORY—
2 20 80
1980 by Chicago Tribune-N.Y. News Synd. Inc. All Rights Reserved
GOULD Fletcher COLLINS
A $1,000,000 ART HEIST— A CRIME SYNDICATE-CONTROLLED INTERNATIONAL ART THEFT RING...
THERE MIGHT EVEN BE A BOOK IN IT FOR YOU— AND A MOVIE SALE—
I'LL DO IT! AFTER ALL, IT'S MY CIVIC DUTY TO HELP THE POLICE.

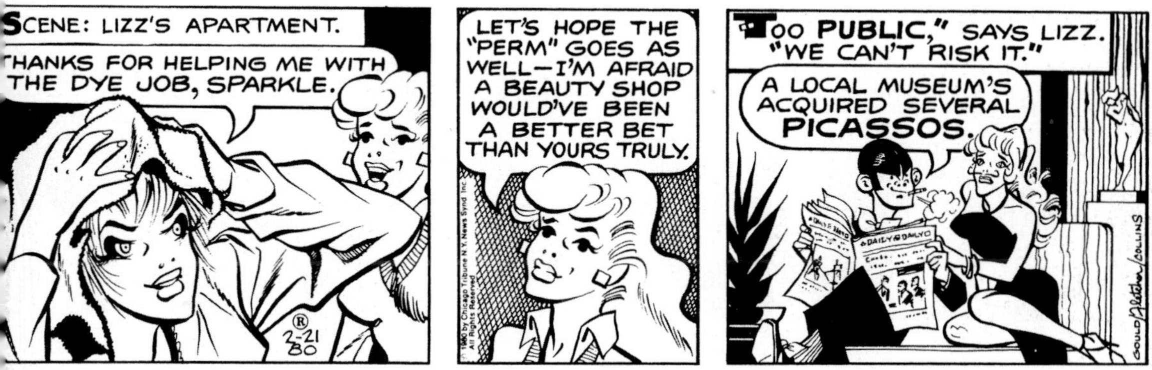
SCENE: LIZZ'S APARTMENT.
THANKS FOR HELPING ME WITH THE DYE JOB, SPARKLE.
2-21 80
LET'S HOPE THE "PERM" GOES AS WELL—I'M AFRAID A BEAUTY SHOP WOULD'VE BEEN A BETTER BET THAN YOURS TRULY.
1980 Chicago Tribune-N.Y. News Synd. Inc. All Rights Reserved
"TOO PUBLIC," SAYS LIZZ. "WE CAN'T RISK IT."
A LOCAL MUSEUM'S ACQUIRED SEVERAL PICASSOS.
GOULD Fletcher COLLINS

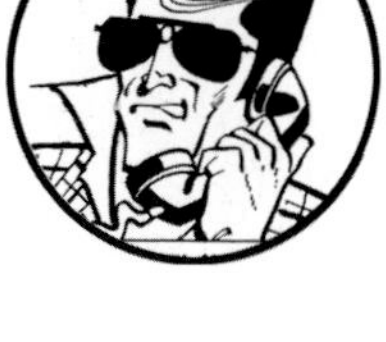

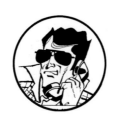

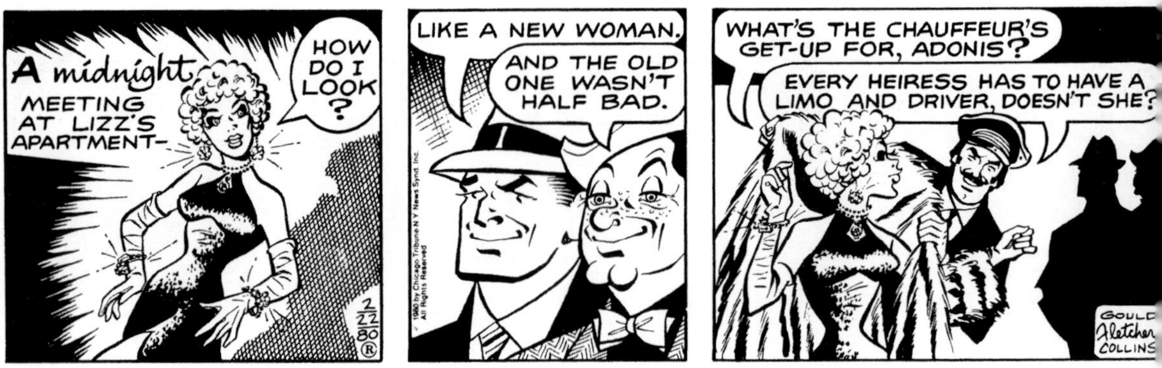
A midnight MEETING AT LIZZ'S APARTMENT—
HOW DO I LOOK?
2/22/80 ®
LIKE A NEW WOMAN.
AND THE OLD ONE WASN'T HALF BAD.
© 1980 by Chicago Tribune-N.Y. News Synd. Inc. All Rights Reserved
WHAT'S THE CHAUFFEUR'S GET-UP FOR, ADONIS?
EVERY HEIRESS HAS TO HAVE A LIMO AND DRIVER, DOESN'T SHE?
GOULD Fletcher COLLINS

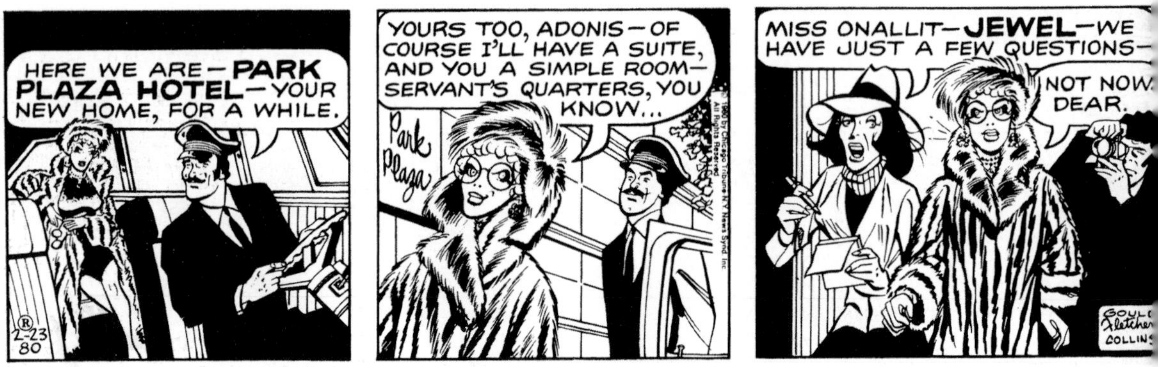
HERE WE ARE—PARK PLAZA HOTEL—YOUR NEW HOME, FOR A WHILE.
® 2-23 80
YOURS TOO, ADONIS—OF COURSE I'LL HAVE A SUITE, AND YOU A SIMPLE ROOM—SERVANT'S QUARTERS, YOU KNOW...
Park Plaza
© 1980 by Chicago Tribune-N.Y. News Synd. Inc. All Rights Reserved
MISS ONALLIT—JEWEL—WE HAVE JUST A FEW QUESTIONS—
NOT NOW. DEAR.
GOULD Fletcher COLLINS

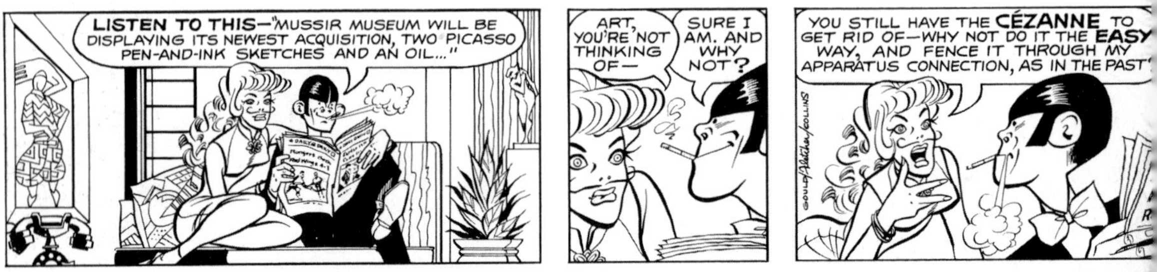
LISTEN TO THIS—"MUSSIR MUSEUM WILL BE DISPLAYING ITS NEWEST ACQUISITION, TWO PICASSO PEN-AND-INK SKETCHES AND AN OIL..."
ART, YOU'RE NOT THINKING OF—
SURE I AM. AND WHY NOT?
YOU STILL HAVE THE CÉZANNE TO GET RID OF—WHY NOT DO IT THE EASY WAY, AND FENCE IT THROUGH MY APPARATUS CONNECTION, AS IN THE PAST?
GOULD/Fletcher/COLLINS

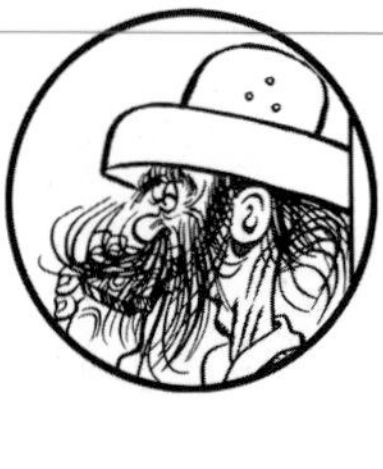

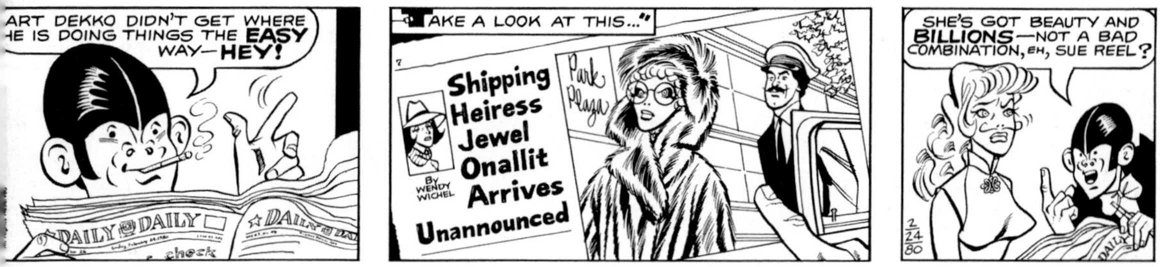
ART DEKKO DIDN'T GET WHERE HE IS DOING THINGS THE **EASY** WAY—**HEY!**
DAILY DAILY
"TAKE A LOOK AT THIS..."
Shipping Heiress Jewel Onallit Arrives Unannounced
By WENDY WICHEL
Park Plaza
SHE'S GOT BEAUTY AND **BILLIONS**—NOT A BAD COMBINATION, EH, SUE REEL?
2/24/80

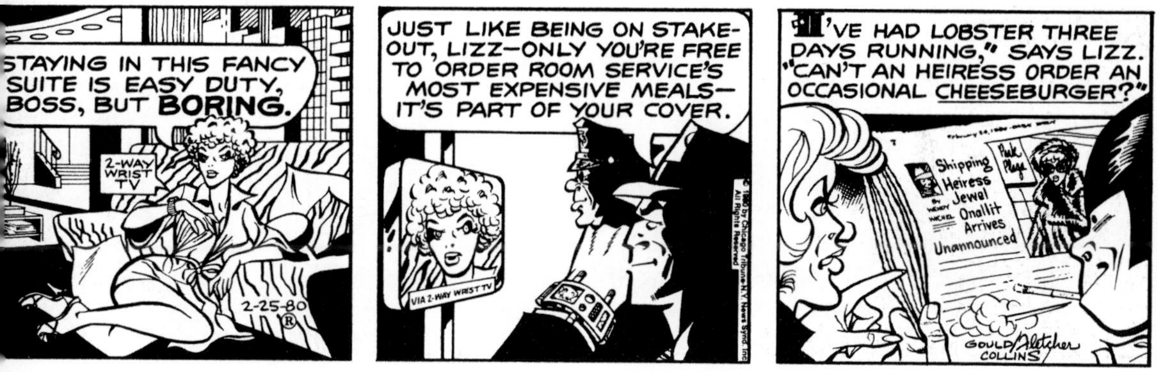
STAYING IN THIS FANCY SUITE IS EASY DUTY, BOSS, BUT **BORING**.
2-WAY WRIST TV
2-25-80
JUST LIKE BEING ON STAKE-OUT, LIZZ—ONLY YOU'RE FREE TO ORDER ROOM SERVICE'S MOST EXPENSIVE MEALS—IT'S PART OF YOUR COVER.
VIA 2-WAY WRIST TV
© 1980 by Chicago Tribune-N.Y. News Synd. Inc. All Rights Reserved
"I'VE HAD LOBSTER THREE DAYS RUNNING," SAYS LIZZ. "CAN'T AN HEIRESS ORDER AN OCCASIONAL CHEESEBURGER?"
Shipping Heiress Jewel Onallit Arrives Unannounced
Park Plaza
GOULD/Fletcher COLLINS

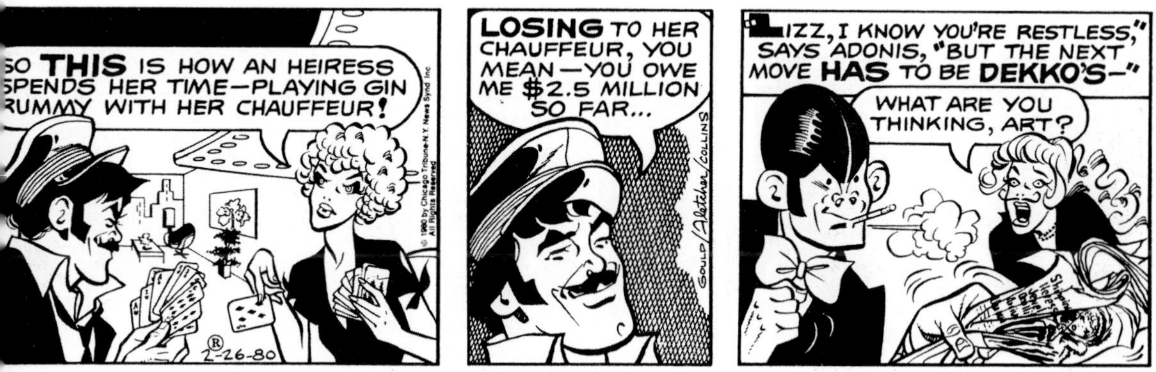
SO **THIS** IS HOW AN HEIRESS SPENDS HER TIME—PLAYING GIN RUMMY WITH HER CHAUFFEUR!
© 1980 by Chicago Tribune-N.Y. News Synd. Inc. All Rights Reserved
2-26-80
LOSING TO HER CHAUFFEUR, YOU MEAN—YOU OWE ME $2.5 MILLION SO FAR...
GOULD/Fletcher/COLLINS
"LIZZ, I KNOW YOU'RE RESTLESS," SAYS ADONIS, "BUT THE NEXT MOVE **HAS** TO BE **DEKKO'S**—"
WHAT ARE YOU THINKING, ART?

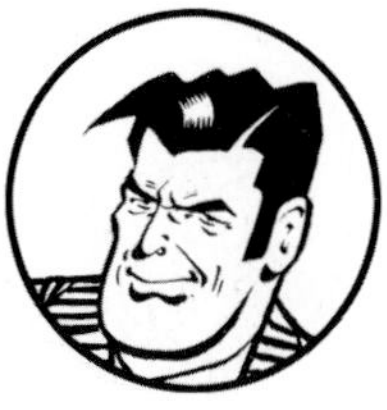

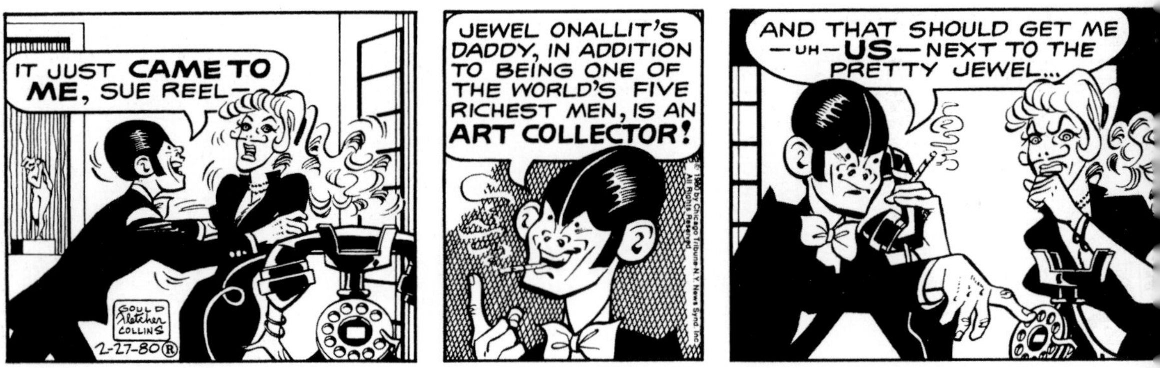
IT JUST CAME TO ME, SUE REEL—
GOULD Fletcher COLLINS
2-27-80 ®
JEWEL ONALLIT'S DADDY, IN ADDITION TO BEING ONE OF THE WORLD'S FIVE RICHEST MEN, IS AN ART COLLECTOR!
© 1980 by Chicago Tribune-N.Y. News Synd. Inc. All Rights Reserved
AND THAT SHOULD GET ME —UH—US—NEXT TO THE PRETTY JEWEL...

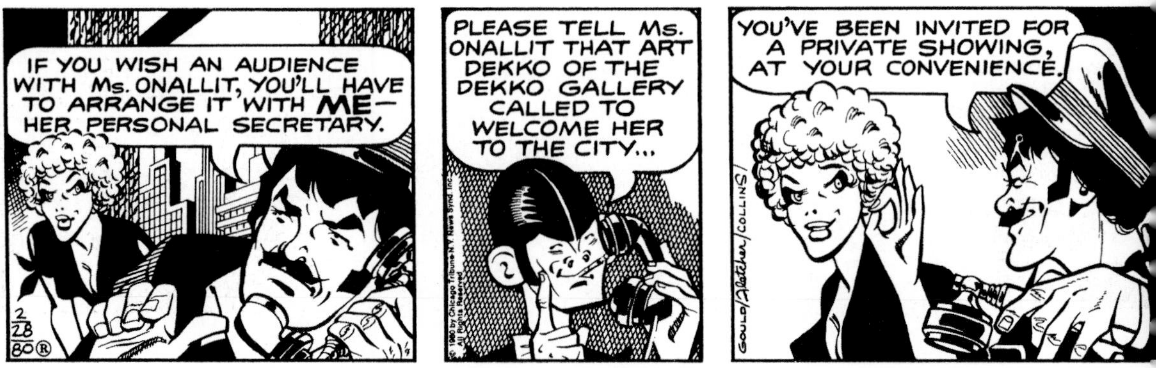
IF YOU WISH AN AUDIENCE WITH Ms. ONALLIT, YOU'LL HAVE TO ARRANGE IT WITH ME—HER PERSONAL SECRETARY.
2/28/80 ®
PLEASE TELL Ms. ONALLIT THAT ART DEKKO OF THE DEKKO GALLERY CALLED TO WELCOME HER TO THE CITY...
© 1980 by Chicago Tribune-N.Y. News Synd. Inc. All Rights Reserved
YOU'VE BEEN INVITED FOR A PRIVATE SHOWING, AT YOUR CONVENIENCE.
GOULD/Fletcher/COLLINS

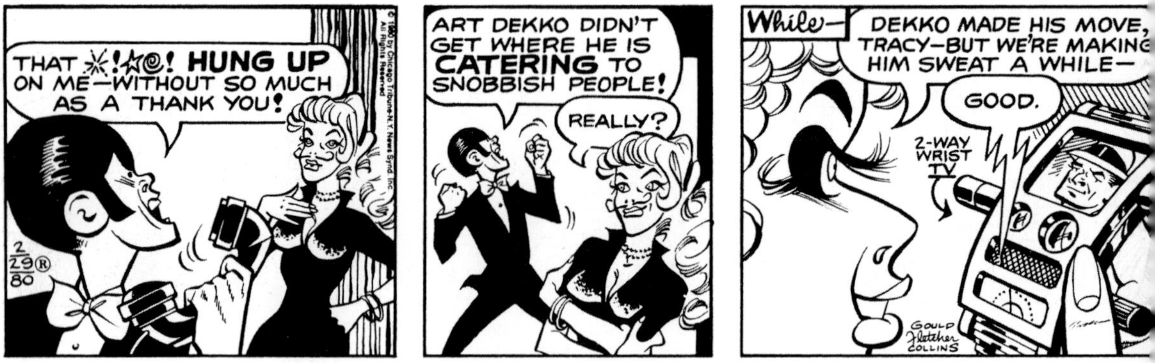
THAT ✳!✩@! HUNG UP ON ME—WITHOUT SO MUCH AS A THANK YOU!
© 1980 by Chicago Tribune-N.Y. News Synd. Inc. All Rights Reserved
2/29/80 ®
ART DEKKO DIDN'T GET WHERE HE IS CATERING TO SNOBBISH PEOPLE!
REALLY?
While—
DEKKO MADE HIS MOVE, TRACY—BUT WE'RE MAKING HIM SWEAT A WHILE—
GOOD.
2-WAY WRIST TV
GOULD Fletcher COLLINS

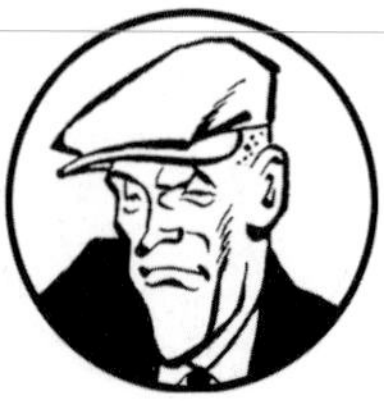

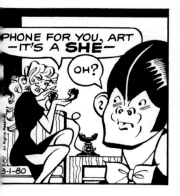

PHONE FOR YOU, ART —IT'S A **SHE**—
OH?
3-1-80
All Rights Reserved
MR. DEKKO? THIS IS JEWEL ONALLIT. MY SECRETARY INFORMS ME YOU HAVE A GALLERY, AND HAVE GENEROUSLY OFFERED TO—
GOULD Fletcher COLLINS
A PRIVATE SHOWING —TOMORROW MORNING? CERTAINLY, Ms. ONALLIT!

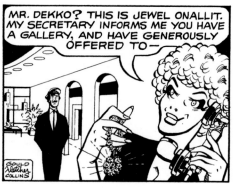

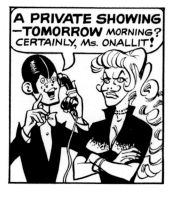

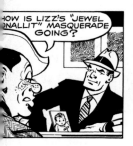

HOW IS LIZZ'S "JEWEL ONALLIT" MASQUERADE GOING?
"NOT BAD," SAYS TRACY. "SHE'S GETTING A PRIVATE SHOWING AT THE DEKKO GALLERY NOW."
I'M GRATEFUL FOR THE OPPORTUNITY TO SHOW OUR LITTLE GALLERY OFF TO YOU, Ms. ONALLIT.
IT'S THOUGHTFUL OF YOU TO INVITE ME. MY FATHER ASKED ME, WHILE IN AMERICA, TO KEEP AN EYE OUT FOR THE UNUSUAL.
GOULD/Fletcher/COLLINS/

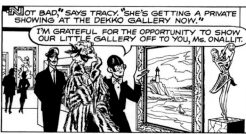

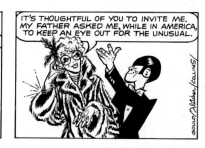

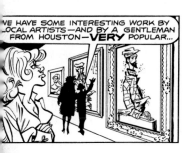

WE HAVE SOME INTERESTING WORK BY LOCAL ARTISTS—AND BY A GENTLEMAN FROM HOUSTON—**VERY** POPULAR...
I KNOW MY FATHER WOULD **LOVE** SOME OF THESE!
DO YOU HAVE AN INTEREST IN ART **YOURSELF**, Ms. ONALLIT?
© 1980 by Chicago Tribune-N.Y. News Synd. Inc. All Rights Reserved
YES—I'VE ALWAYS **DREAMED** OF OWNING A **PICASSO**—
3/2/80

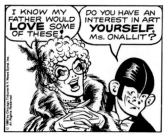

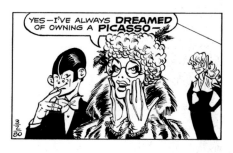

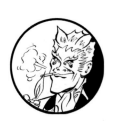

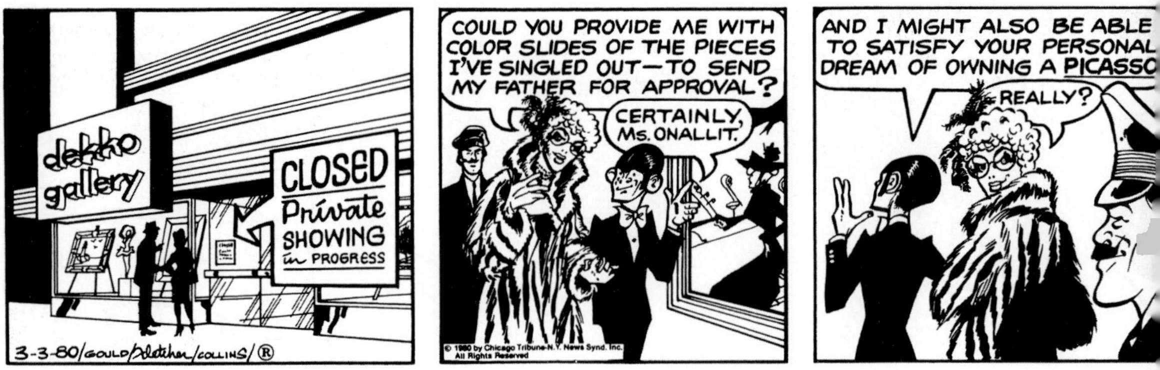
dekko gallery
CLOSED
Private
SHOWING
in PROGRESS
3-3-80/GOULD/Fletcher/COLLINS/®
COULD YOU PROVIDE ME WITH COLOR SLIDES OF THE PIECES I'VE SINGLED OUT—TO SEND MY FATHER FOR APPROVAL?
CERTAINLY, Ms. ONALLIT.
© 1980 by Chicago Tribune-N.Y. News Synd. Inc. All Rights Reserved
AND I MIGHT ALSO BE ABLE TO SATISFY YOUR PERSONAL DREAM OF OWNING A PICASSO
REALLY?

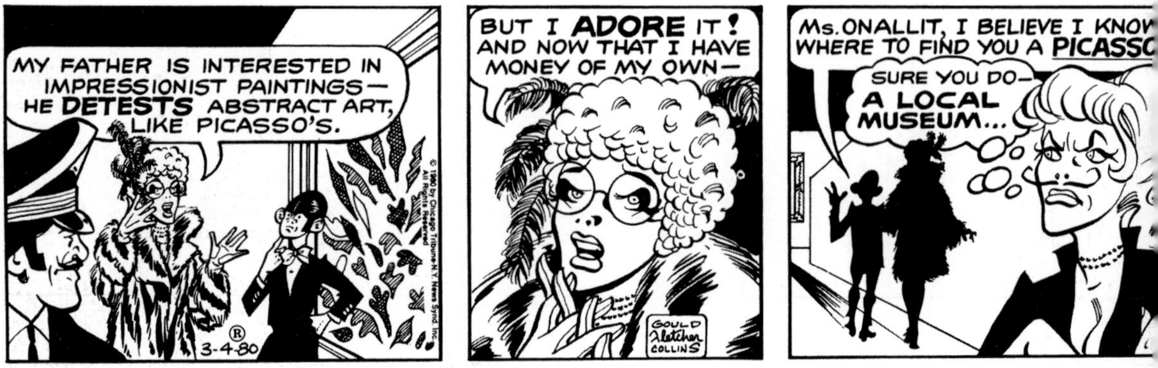
MY FATHER IS INTERESTED IN IMPRESSIONIST PAINTINGS— HE DETESTS ABSTRACT ART, LIKE PICASSO'S.
® 3-4-80
© 1980 by Chicago Tribune-N.Y. News Synd. Inc. All Rights Reserved
BUT I ADORE IT! AND NOW THAT I HAVE MONEY OF MY OWN—
GOULD Fletcher COLLINS
Ms. ONALLIT, I BELIEVE I KNOW WHERE TO FIND YOU A PICASSO
SURE YOU DO— A LOCAL MUSEUM...

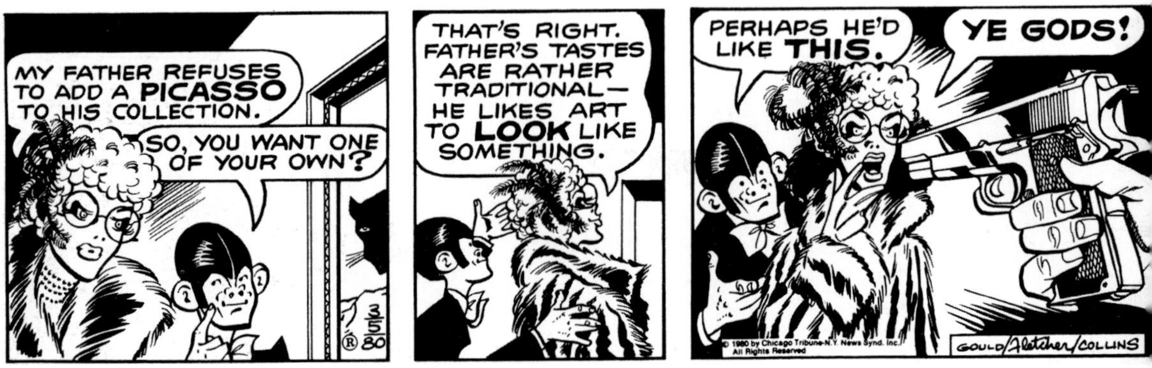
MY FATHER REFUSES TO ADD A PICASSO TO HIS COLLECTION.
SO, YOU WANT ONE OF YOUR OWN?
3/5/80 ®
THAT'S RIGHT. FATHER'S TASTES ARE RATHER TRADITIONAL— HE LIKES ART TO LOOK LIKE SOMETHING.
PERHAPS HE'D LIKE THIS.
YE GODS!
© 1980 by Chicago Tribune-N.Y. News Synd. Inc. All Rights Reserved
GOULD/Fletcher/COLLINS

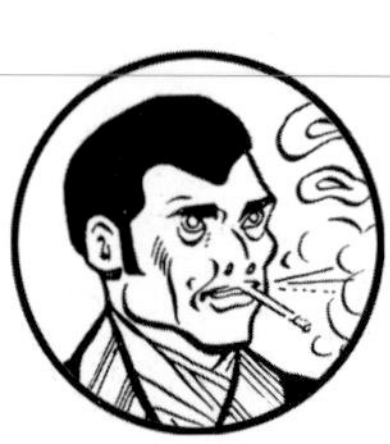

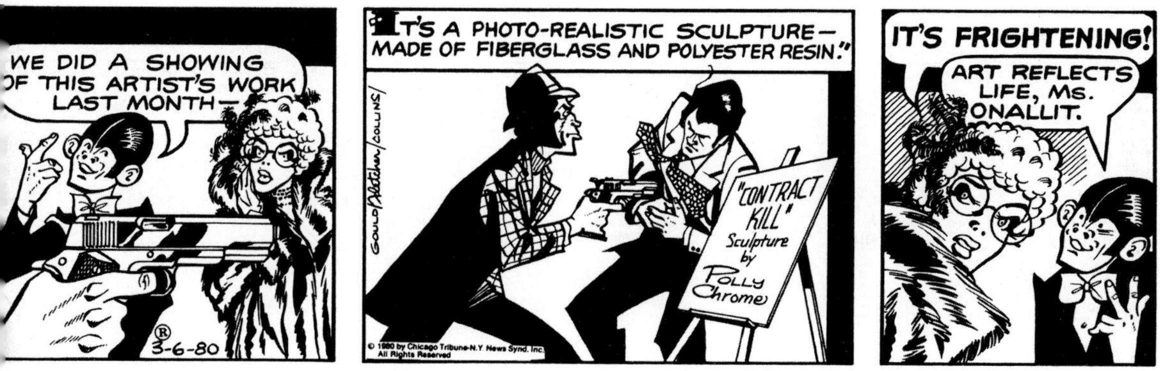
WE DID A SHOWING OF THIS ARTIST'S WORK LAST MONTH—
3-6-80
IT'S A PHOTO-REALISTIC SCULPTURE—MADE OF FIBERGLASS AND POLYESTER RESIN."
GOULD/FLETCHER/COLLINS
"CONTRACT KILL" Sculpture by POLLY Chrome
© 1980 by Chicago Tribune-N.Y. News Synd. Inc. All Rights Reserved
IT'S FRIGHTENING!
ART REFLECTS LIFE, MS. ONALLIT.

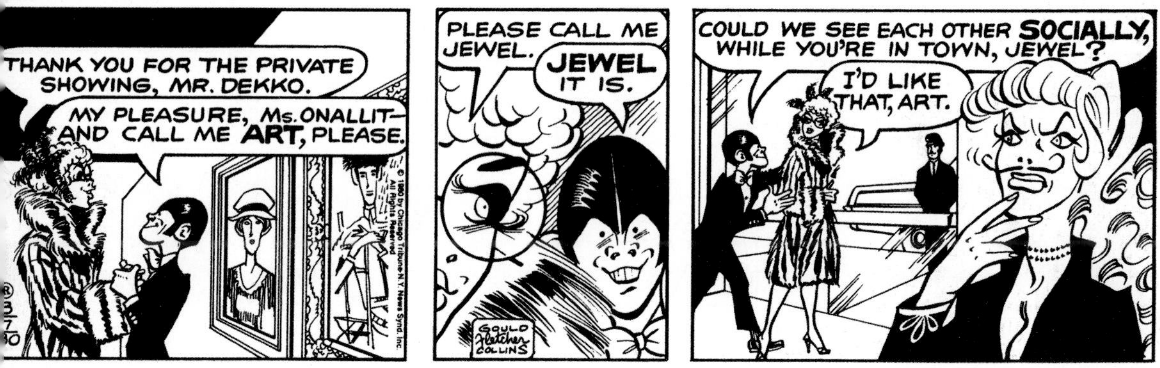
THANK YOU FOR THE PRIVATE SHOWING, MR. DEKKO.
MY PLEASURE, Ms. ONALLIT—AND CALL ME ART, PLEASE.
© 1980 by Chicago Tribune-N.Y. News Synd. Inc. All Rights Reserved
3/7/80
PLEASE CALL ME JEWEL.
JEWEL IT IS.
GOULD FLETCHER COLLINS
COULD WE SEE EACH OTHER SOCIALLY, WHILE YOU'RE IN TOWN, JEWEL?
I'D LIKE THAT, ART.

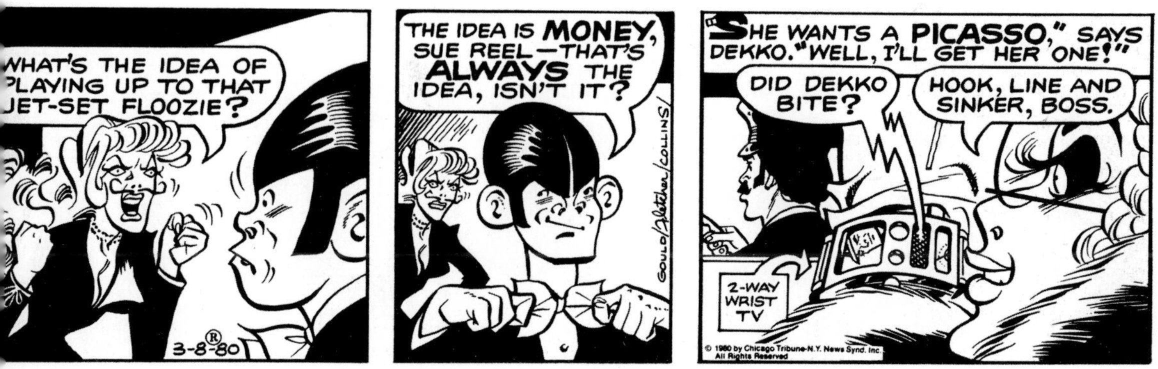
WHAT'S THE IDEA OF PLAYING UP TO THAT JET-SET FLOOZIE?
3-8-80
THE IDEA IS MONEY, SUE REEL—THAT'S ALWAYS THE IDEA, ISN'T IT?
GOULD/FLETCHER/COLLINS
"SHE WANTS A PICASSO," SAYS DEKKO. "WELL, I'LL GET HER ONE!"
DID DEKKO BITE?
HOOK, LINE AND SINKER, BOSS.
2-WAY WRIST TV
© 1980 by Chicago Tribune-N.Y. News Synd. Inc. All Rights Reserved

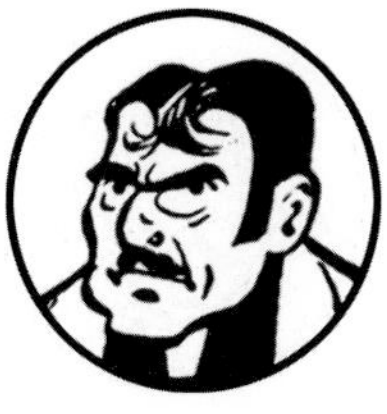

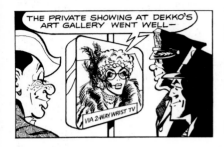

THE PRIVATE SHOWING AT DEKKO'S ART GALLERY WENT WELL—
VIA 2-WAY WRIST TV
I INDICATED MY INTEREST IN A PICASSO, AND DEKKO INDICATED HIS INTEREST IN ME.
2-WAY WRIST TV
"WAS SUE REEL ON HAND?" ASKS TRACY. "OH YES," SAYS LIZZ. "IN THE BACKGROUND, BUT EVER PRESENT—"
I DON'T LIKE IT!

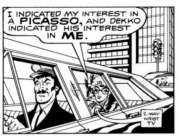

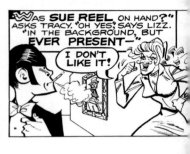

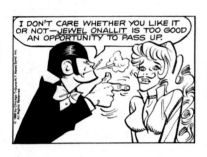

I DON'T CARE WHETHER YOU LIKE IT OR NOT—JEWEL ONALLIT IS TOO GOOD AN OPPORTUNITY TO PASS UP.
© 1980 by Chicago Tribune-N.Y. News Synd. Inc. All Rights Reserved
TOO PRETTY AN OPPORTUNITY, YOU MEAN.
GOULD/FLETCHER/COLLINS/
"SHE'S HEIRESS TO THE WORLD'S FIFTH LARGEST FORTUNE, SUE REEL... NOW, WHERE IS THAT CRAZY PHOTO-REALIST SCULPTOR, POLLY CHROME? SHE WAS SUPPOSED TO MEET ME HERE—"
"CONTRACT KILL" Sculpture by POLLY Chrome

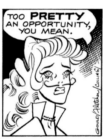

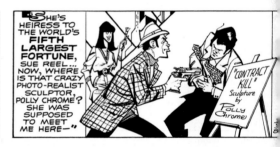

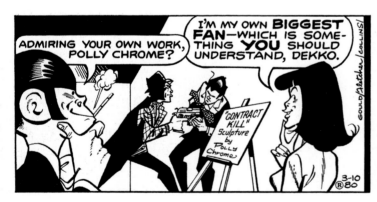

ADMIRING YOUR OWN WORK, POLLY CHROME?
I'M MY OWN BIGGEST FAN—WHICH IS SOMETHING YOU SHOULD UNDERSTAND, DEKKO.
"CONTRACT KILL" Sculpture by POLLY Chrome
GOULD/FLETCHER/COLLINS/
3-10 80
"NEVER MIND THE WISECRACKS," SAYS DEKKO. "IS MY 'SPECIAL ORDER' READY?"
THIS IS SUE REEL—I NEED A FAVOR.
© 1980 by Chicago Tribune-N.Y. News Synd. Inc. All Rights Reserved

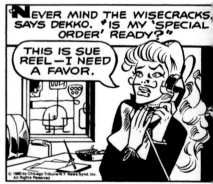

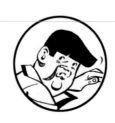

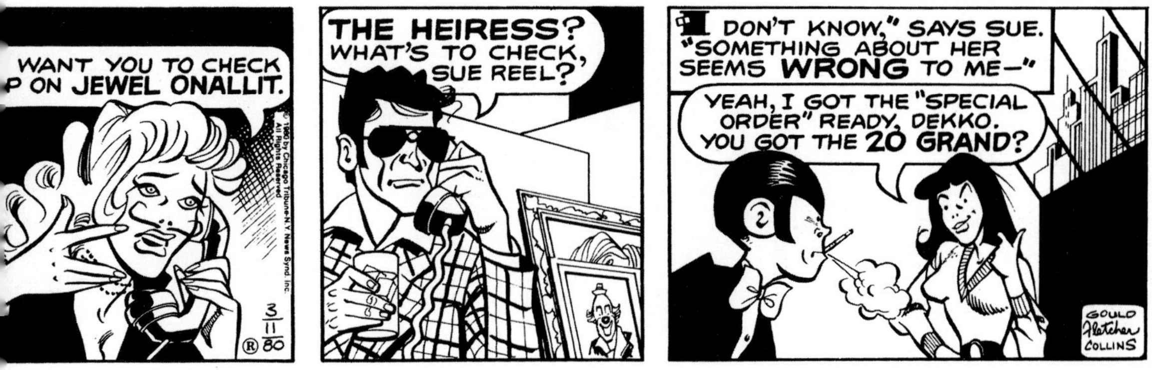
WANT YOU TO CHECK
P ON JEWEL ONALLIT.
© 1980 by Chicago Tribune-N.Y. News Synd. Inc. All Rights Reserved
3/11/80
THE HEIRESS? WHAT'S TO CHECK, SUE REEL?
"I DON'T KNOW," SAYS SUE. "SOMETHING ABOUT HER SEEMS WRONG TO ME—"
YEAH, I GOT THE "SPECIAL ORDER" READY, DEKKO. YOU GOT THE 20 GRAND?
GOULD Fletcher COLLINS

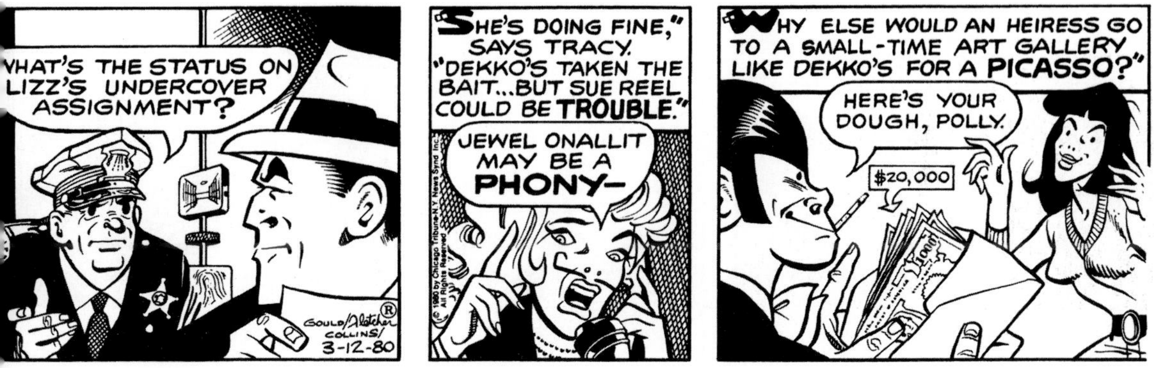
WHAT'S THE STATUS ON LIZZ'S UNDERCOVER ASSIGNMENT?
GOULD/Fletcher COLLINS/ 3-12-80
"SHE'S DOING FINE," SAYS TRACY. "DEKKO'S TAKEN THE BAIT...BUT SUE REEL COULD BE TROUBLE."
JEWEL ONALLIT MAY BE A PHONY—
© 1980 by Chicago Tribune-N.Y. News Synd. Inc. All Rights Reserved
"WHY ELSE WOULD AN HEIRESS GO TO A SMALL-TIME ART GALLERY LIKE DEKKO'S FOR A PICASSO?"
HERE'S YOUR DOUGH, POLLY.
$20,000

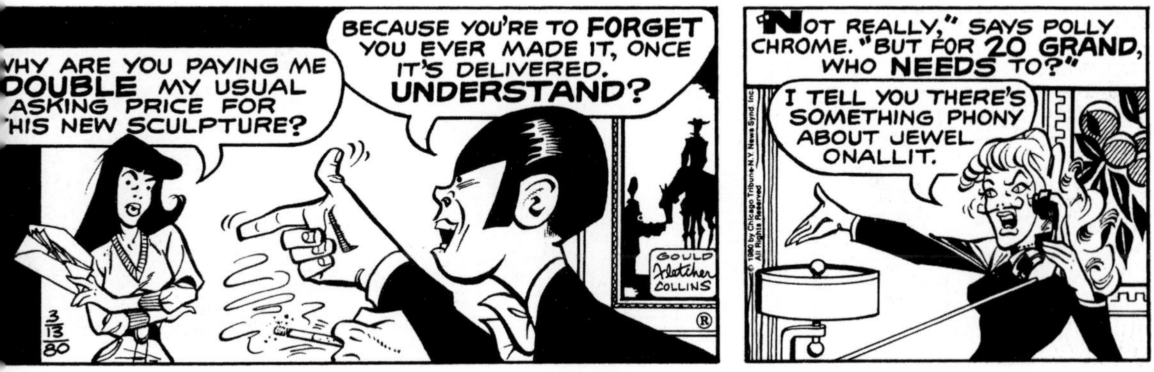
WHY ARE YOU PAYING ME DOUBLE MY USUAL ASKING PRICE FOR THIS NEW SCULPTURE?
BECAUSE YOU'RE TO FORGET YOU EVER MADE IT, ONCE IT'S DELIVERED. UNDERSTAND?
3/13/80
GOULD Fletcher COLLINS
"NOT REALLY," SAYS POLLY CHROME. "BUT FOR 20 GRAND, WHO NEEDS TO?"
I TELL YOU THERE'S SOMETHING PHONY ABOUT JEWEL ONALLIT.
© 1980 by Chicago Tribune-N.Y. News Synd. Inc. All Rights Reserved

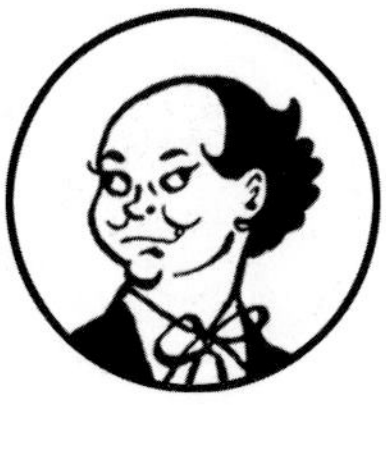

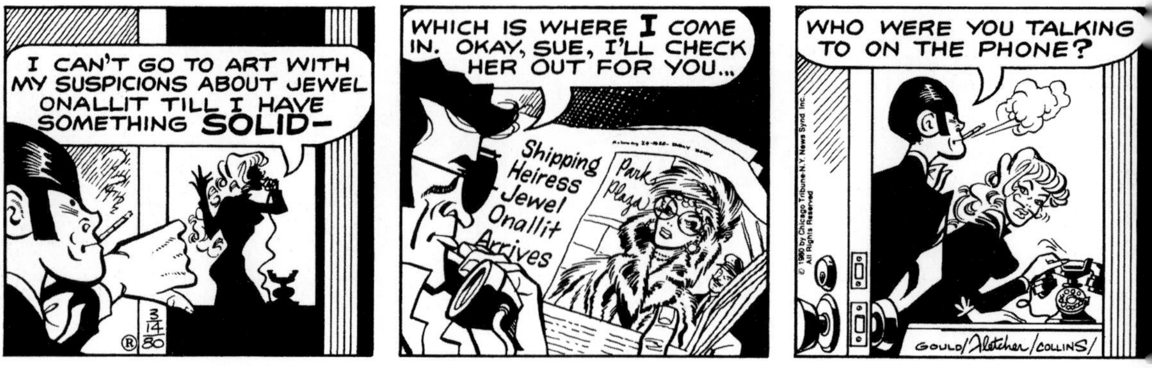
I CAN'T GO TO ART WITH MY SUSPICIONS ABOUT JEWEL ONALLIT TILL I HAVE SOMETHING **SOLID**—
3/14/80
WHICH IS WHERE **I** COME IN. OKAY, SUE, I'LL CHECK HER OUT FOR YOU...
Shipping Heiress Jewel Onallit Arrives
Park Plaza
WHO WERE YOU TALKING TO ON THE PHONE?
© 1980 by Chicago Tribune-N.Y. News Synd. Inc. All Rights Reserved
GOULD/Fletcher/COLLINS/

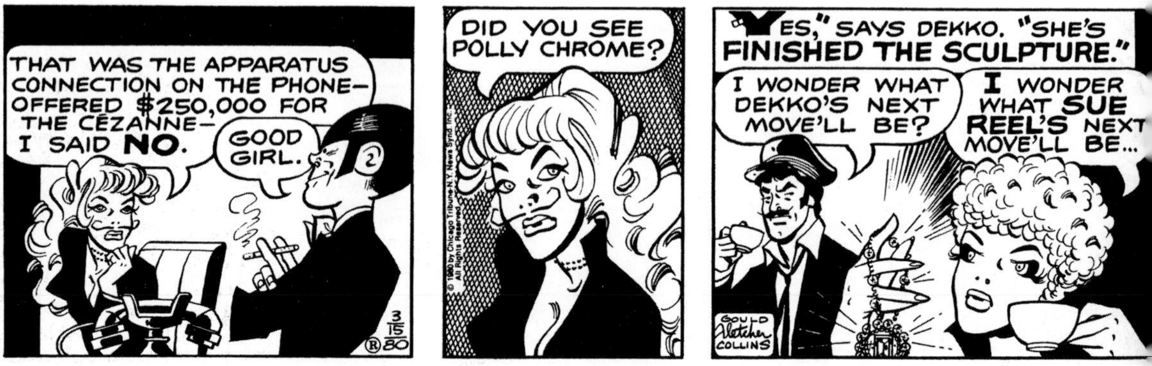
THAT WAS THE APPARATUS CONNECTION ON THE PHONE—OFFERED $250,000 FOR THE CÉZANNE—I SAID **NO**.
GOOD GIRL.
3/15/80
DID YOU SEE POLLY CHROME?
© 1980 by Chicago Tribune-N.Y. News Synd. Inc. All Rights Reserved
"YES," SAYS DEKKO. "SHE'S **FINISHED THE SCULPTURE.**"
I WONDER WHAT DEKKO'S NEXT MOVE'LL BE?
I WONDER WHAT **SUE REEL'S** NEXT MOVE'LL BE...
GOULD Fletcher COLLINS

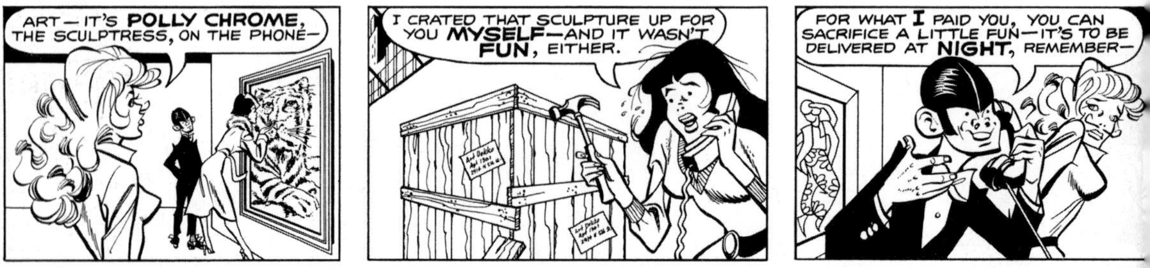
ART—IT'S **POLLY CHROME**, THE SCULPTRESS, ON THE PHONE—
I CRATED THAT SCULPTURE UP FOR YOU **MYSELF**—AND IT WASN'T **FUN**, EITHER.
FOR WHAT **I** PAID YOU, YOU CAN SACRIFICE A LITTLE FUN—IT'S TO BE DELIVERED AT **NIGHT**, REMEMBER—

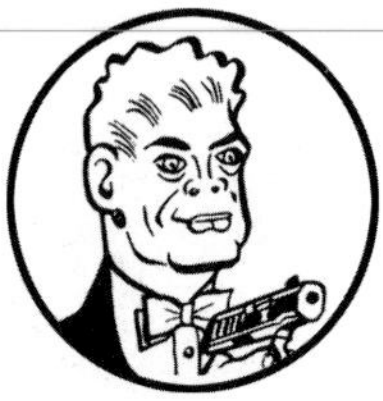

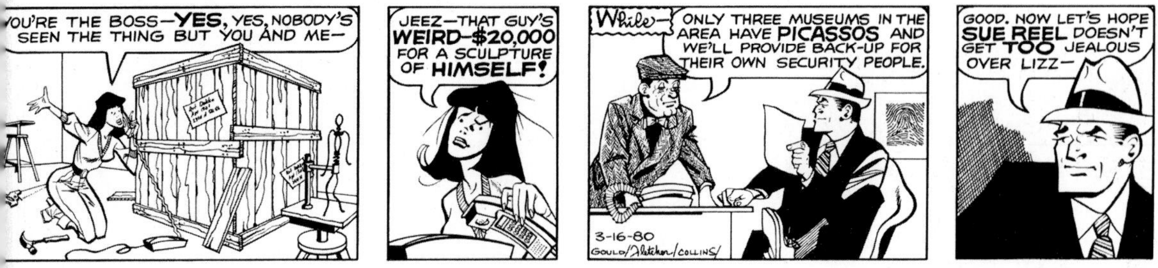
YOU'RE THE BOSS—YES, YES, NOBODY'S SEEN THE THING BUT YOU AND ME—
JEEZ—THAT GUY'S WEIRD—$20,000 FOR A SCULPTURE OF HIMSELF!
While—
ONLY THREE MUSEUMS IN THE AREA HAVE PICASSOS AND WE'LL PROVIDE BACK-UP FOR THEIR OWN SECURITY PEOPLE.
3-16-80
GOULD/Fletcher/COLLINS
GOOD. NOW LET'S HOPE SUE REEL DOESN'T GET TOO JEALOUS OVER LIZZ—

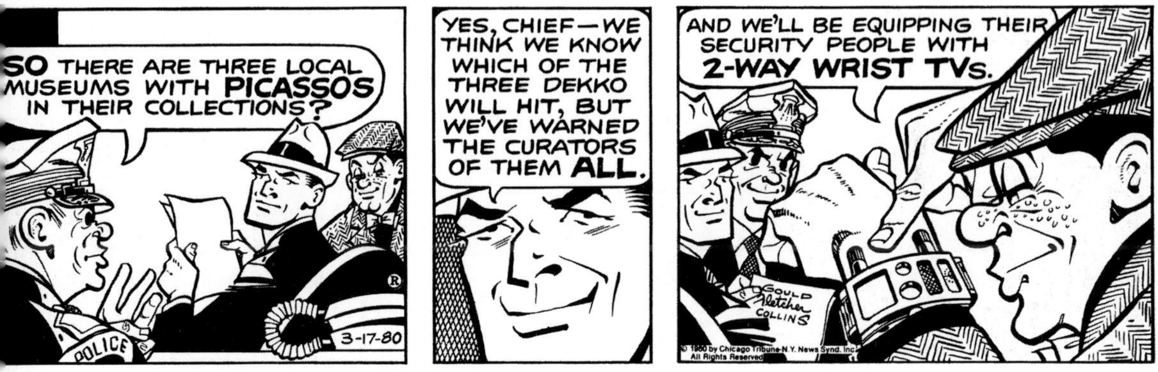
SO THERE ARE THREE LOCAL MUSEUMS WITH PICASSOS IN THEIR COLLECTIONS?
POLICE
3-17-80
YES, CHIEF—WE THINK WE KNOW WHICH OF THE THREE DEKKO WILL HIT, BUT WE'VE WARNED THE CURATORS OF THEM ALL.
AND WE'LL BE EQUIPPING THEIR SECURITY PEOPLE WITH 2-WAY WRIST TVs.
GOULD Fletcher COLLINS
© 1980 by Chicago Tribune-N.Y. News Synd. Inc. All Rights Reserved

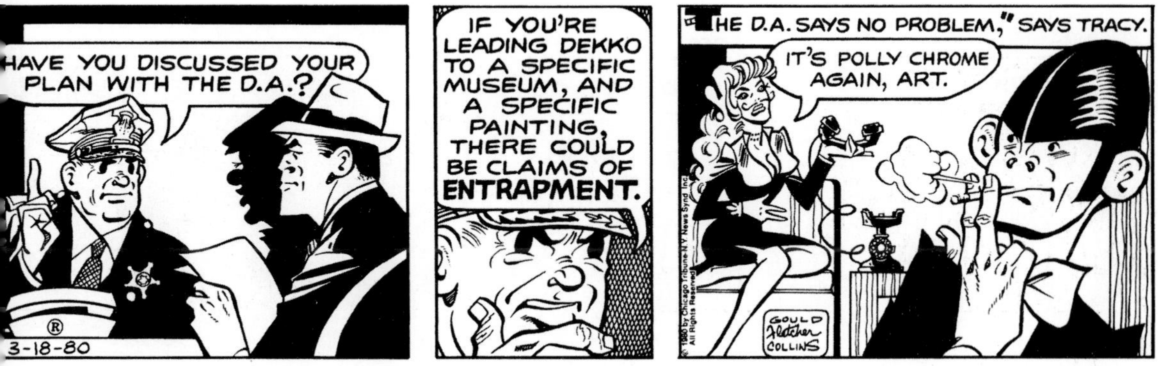
HAVE YOU DISCUSSED YOUR PLAN WITH THE D.A.?
3-18-80
IF YOU'RE LEADING DEKKO TO A SPECIFIC MUSEUM, AND A SPECIFIC PAINTING, THERE COULD BE CLAIMS OF ENTRAPMENT.
"THE D.A. SAYS NO PROBLEM," SAYS TRACY.
IT'S POLLY CHROME AGAIN, ART.
GOULD Fletcher COLLINS

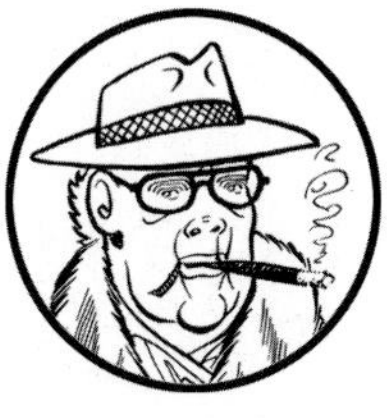

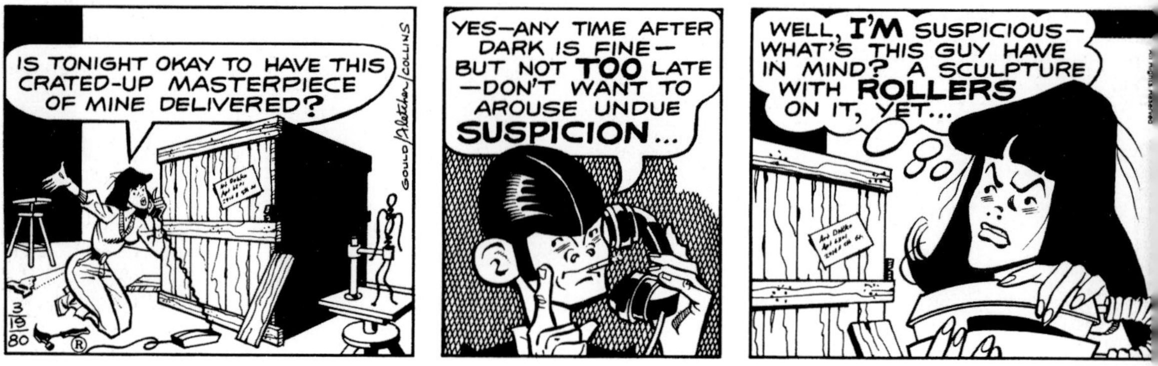
IS TONIGHT OKAY TO HAVE THIS CRATED-UP MASTERPIECE OF MINE DELIVERED?
3/19/80
GOULD/Fletcher/COLLINS
YES—ANY TIME AFTER DARK IS FINE—BUT NOT TOO LATE—DON'T WANT TO AROUSE UNDUE SUSPICION...
WELL, I'M SUSPICIOUS—WHAT'S THIS GUY HAVE IN MIND? A SCULPTURE WITH ROLLERS ON IT, YET...

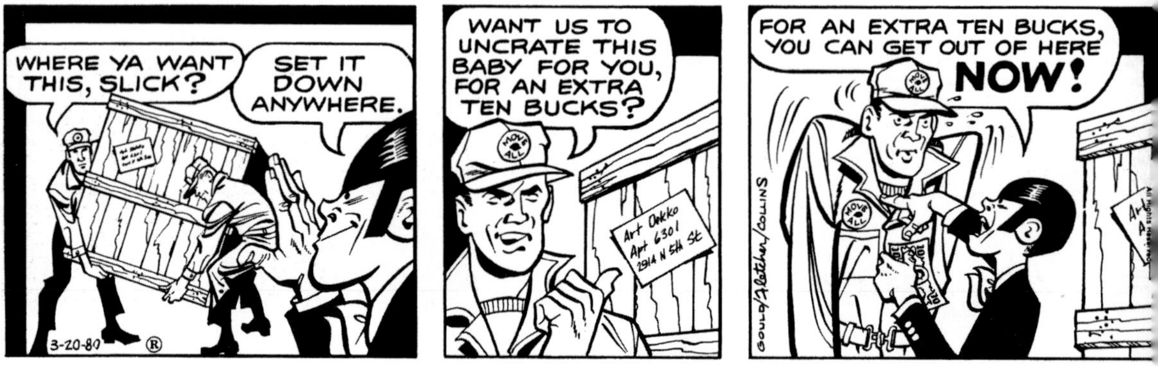
WHERE YA WANT THIS, SLICK?
SET IT DOWN ANYWHERE.
3-20-80
WANT US TO UNCRATE THIS BABY FOR YOU, FOR AN EXTRA TEN BUCKS?
Art Dekko
Apt 6301
2914 N 5th St
FOR AN EXTRA TEN BUCKS, YOU CAN GET OUT OF HERE NOW!
GOULD/Fletcher/COLLINS

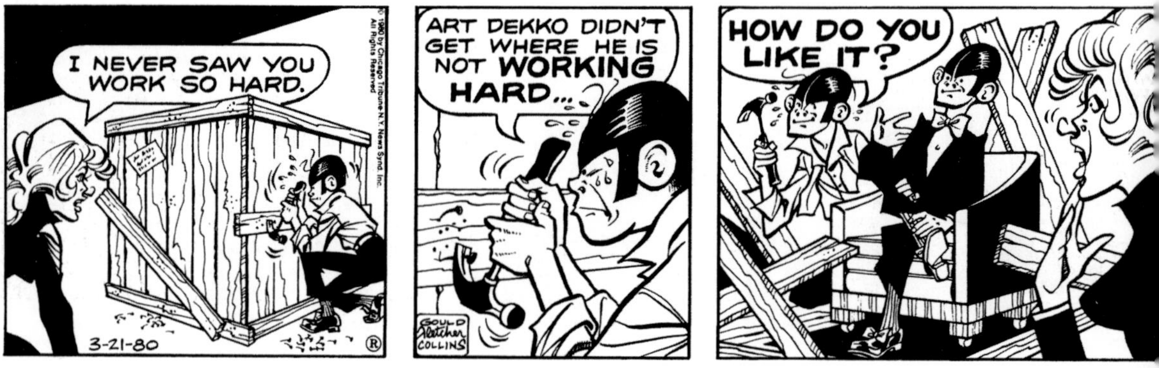
© 1980 by Chicago Tribune-N.Y. News Synd. Inc.
All Rights Reserved
I NEVER SAW YOU WORK SO HARD.
3-21-80
ART DEKKO DIDN'T GET WHERE HE IS NOT WORKING HARD...
GOULD Fletcher COLLINS
HOW DO YOU LIKE IT?

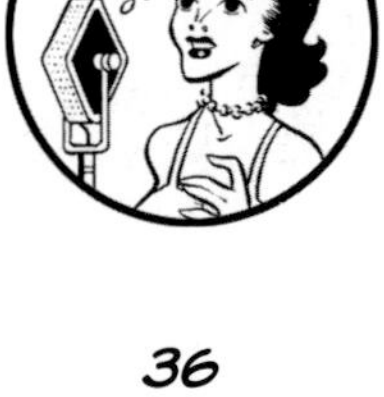
LOVE, YOU'VE.....

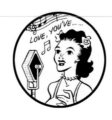

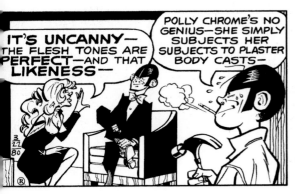

IT'S UNCANNY— THE FLESH TONES ARE PERFECT—AND THAT LIKENESS—
POLLY CHROME'S NO GENIUS—SHE SIMPLY SUBJECTS HER SUBJECTS TO PLASTER BODY CASTS—
"ART DEKKO DOESN'T GO THROUGH SUCH DISCOMFORT WITHOUT A REASON," SAYS DEKKO.
WE HAVEN'T HEARD FROM DEKKO IN DAYS...
© 1980 by Chicago Tribune-N.Y. News Synd. Inc. All Rights Reserved
GOULD Fletcher COLLINS

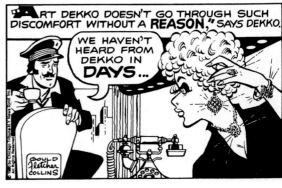

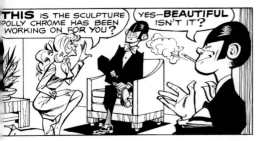

THIS IS THE SCULPTURE POLLY CHROME HAS BEEN WORKING ON FOR YOU?
YES—BEAUTIFUL ISN'T IT?
IT'S INCREDIBLY LIFE-LIKE—YOU HAVE TO GET RIGHT UP AND TOUCH IT TO KNOW IT'S NOT REAL—
IT BETTER LOOK REAL—AFTER $20,000 AND THREE PLASTER BODY CASTS—WHAT A PAIN!

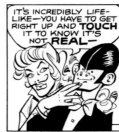

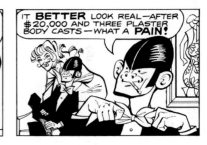

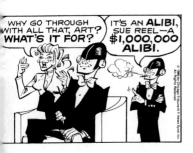

WHY GO THROUGH WITH ALL THAT, ART? WHAT'S IT FOR?
IT'S AN ALIBI, SUE REEL—A $1,000,000 ALIBI.
© 1980 by Chicago Tribune-N.Y. News Synd. Inc. All Rights Reserved
Soon
IT'S DEKKO —ARE YOU IN, "JEWEL"?
Ms. ONALLIT TO YOU, SLAVE—AND AFTER WAITING A WEEK TO HEAR FROM HIM, YOU BET I'M IN...
A PARTY, ART? AT YOUR PENTHOUSE? I'D LOVE TO.
GOULD Fletcher COLLINS

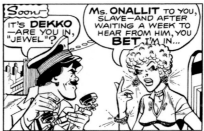

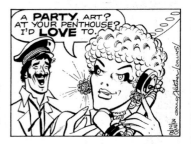

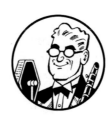

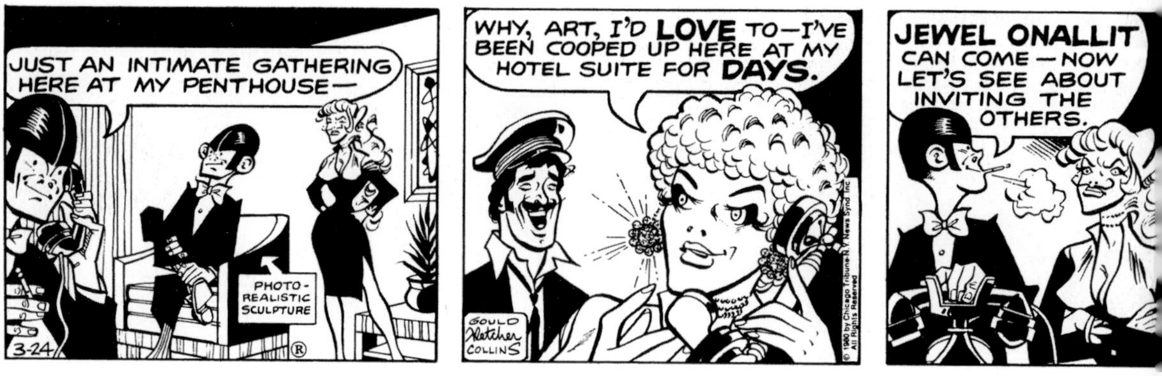
JUST AN INTIMATE GATHERING HERE AT MY PENTHOUSE—
PHOTO-REALISTIC SCULPTURE
3-24
WHY, ART, I'D LOVE TO—I'VE BEEN COOPED UP HERE AT MY HOTEL SUITE FOR DAYS.
GOULD Fletcher COLLINS
© 1980 by Chicago Tribune-N.Y. News Synd. Inc. All Rights Reserved
JEWEL ONALLIT CAN COME—NOW LET'S SEE ABOUT INVITING THE OTHERS.

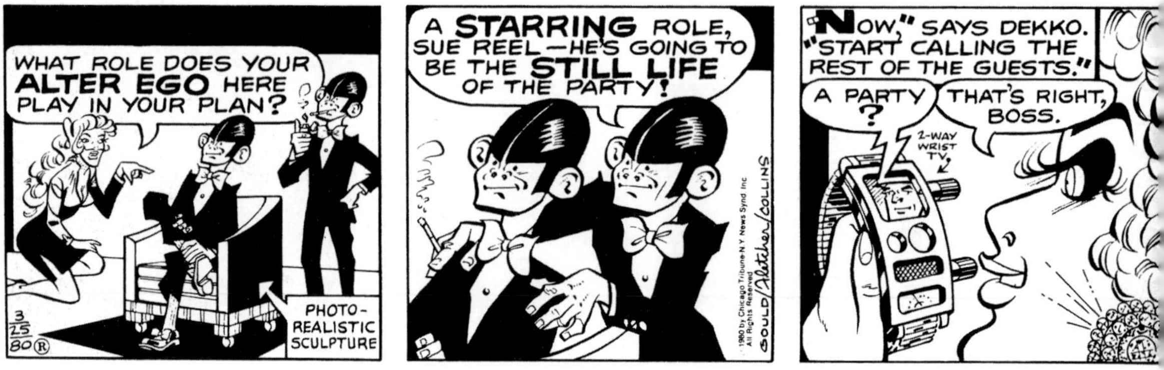
WHAT ROLE DOES YOUR ALTER EGO HERE PLAY IN YOUR PLAN?
PHOTO-REALISTIC SCULPTURE
3 25 80
A STARRING ROLE, SUE REEL—HE'S GOING TO BE THE STILL LIFE OF THE PARTY!
1980 by Chicago Tribune-N.Y. News Synd Inc All Rights Reserved
GOULD/Fletcher/COLLINS
"NOW," SAYS DEKKO. "START CALLING THE REST OF THE GUESTS."
A PARTY?
THAT'S RIGHT, BOSS.
2-WAY WRIST TV

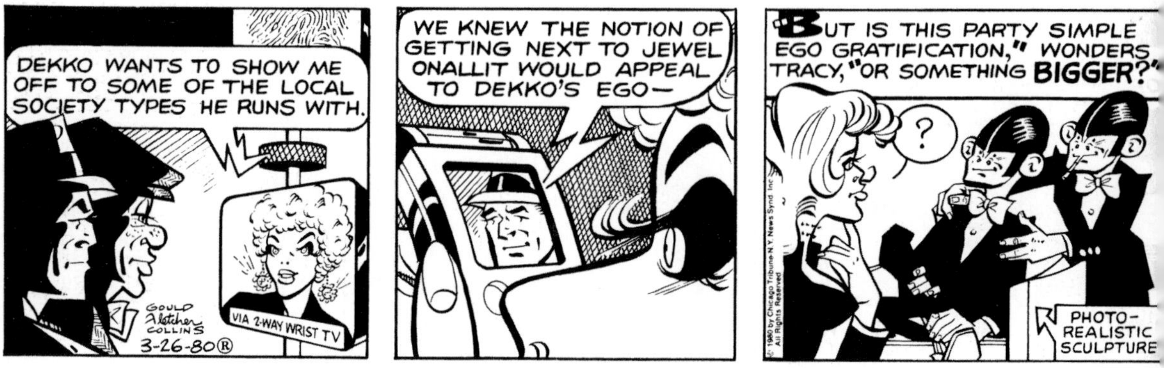
DEKKO WANTS TO SHOW ME OFF TO SOME OF THE LOCAL SOCIETY TYPES HE RUNS WITH.
GOULD Fletcher COLLINS
3-26-80
VIA 2-WAY WRIST TV
WE KNEW THE NOTION OF GETTING NEXT TO JEWEL ONALLIT WOULD APPEAL TO DEKKO'S EGO—
"BUT IS THIS PARTY SIMPLE EGO GRATIFICATION," WONDERS TRACY, "OR SOMETHING BIGGER?"
?
© 1980 by Chicago Tribune-N.Y. News Synd. Inc. All Rights Reserved
PHOTO-REALISTIC SCULPTURE

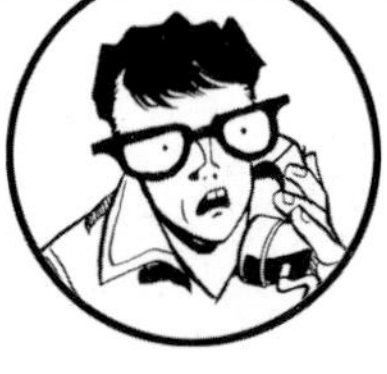

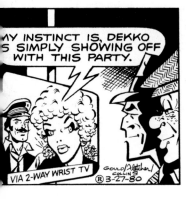

MY INSTINCT IS, DEKKO
S SIMPLY SHOWING OFF
WITH THIS PARTY.
VIA 2-WAY WRIST TV
GOULD/Fletcher/COLLINS
® 3-27-80
AFTER ALL, HE HASN'T EVEN FORMALLY APPROACHED ME ABOUT ACQUIRING A PICASSO FOR ME.
"I'D SAY ANY ART HEIST HE'S PLANNING IS WEEKS AWAY," CONCLUDES LIZZ.
ART—DON'T TELL ME THAT THING MOVES—
© 1980 by Chicago Tribune-N.Y. News Synd. Inc. All Rights Reserved

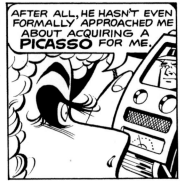

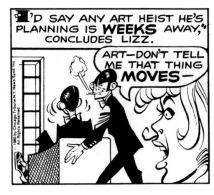

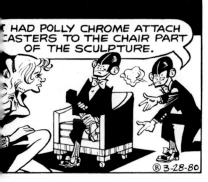

I HAD POLLY CHROME ATTACH
CASTERS TO THE CHAIR PART
OF THE SCULPTURE.
® 3-28-80
THEN MOBILITY FOR THIS THING IS A KEY PART OF YOUR PLAN?
OF COURSE, SUE REEL...
GOULD Fletcher COLLINS
"ART DEKKO DIDN'T GET WHERE HE IS BY NOT GETTING AROUND."
IS LIZZ RIGHT, TRACY? IS THIS PARTY JUST A PARTY?
© 1980 Chicago Tribune-N.Y. News Synd. Inc. All Rights Reserved

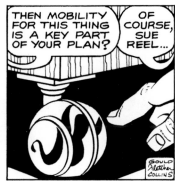

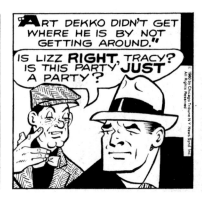

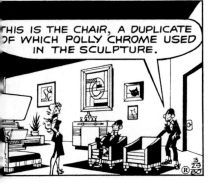

THIS IS THE CHAIR, A DUPLICATE
OF WHICH POLLY CHROME USED
IN THE SCULPTURE.
® 3 29 80
TO IT, ALSO, I'VE HAD CASTERS AFFIXED—
© 1980 by Chicago Tribune-N.Y. News Synd. Inc. All Rights Reserved
GOULD/Fletcher/COLLINS
"BUT WHY, ART?" SUE WONDERS.
WANT TO WAIT A WHILE BEFORE STEPPING UP SECURITY AT THE ART MUSEUMS?
DEKKO DOES SEEM TO BE LYING LOW.

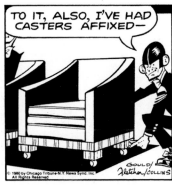

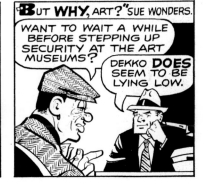

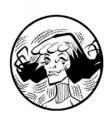

NOBODY WANTS TO BUST UP THIS ART HEIST RING ANY MORE THAN I DO—
HANDMADE .22 ZIP GUN
CASE #A 308
BUT IT APPEARS ANY HEIST DEKKO IS PLANNING REGARDING THE PICASSO LIZZ HAS REQUESTED IS WEEKS AWAY—
CHIEF, THIS PARTY HE'S INVITED LIZZ TO TO SHOW OFF "JEWEL ONALLIT" TO HIS SOCIETY PALS, COULD BE A COVER—

I DON'T THINK SO. I'M AFRAID, OUR BUDGET BEING WHAT IT IS, YOU'LL HAVE TO HOLD OFF STEPPING UP MUSEUM SECURITY A GOOD WEEK."
EVERYONE'S ACCEPTED OUR INVITATION, ART—
THAT'S FINE—BUT ONLY TWO GUESTS REALLY COUNT—
"...Ms. JEWEL ONALLIT..."
© 1980 by Chicago Tribune-N.Y. News Synd. Inc. All Rights Reserved
...AND MY HANDSOME FRIEND HERE—
PHOTO-REALIST SCULPTURE

I'VE TALKED TO THE CURATORS OF THE THREE ART MUSEUMS INVOLVED—
3-31-80
WE'RE SETTING UP TIMES FOR ME TO FAMILIARIZE THEIR SECURITY PEOPLE WITH THE USE OF THE 2-WAY WRIST TV.
While—
WHERE ARE YOU GOING, SUE REEL?
UH—TO THE GOURMET SHOP —FOR THE PARTY—
GOULD Fletcher COLLINS
All Rights Reserved

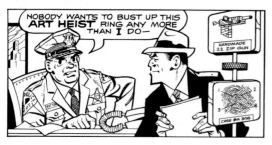

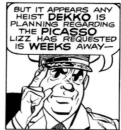

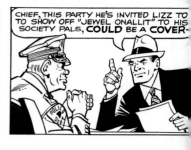

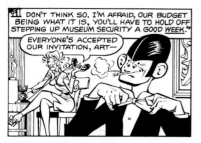

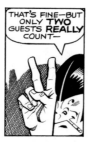

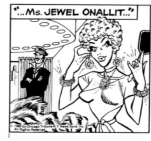

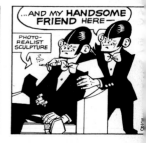

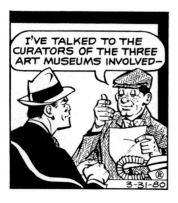

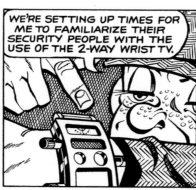

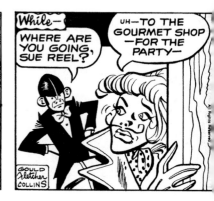

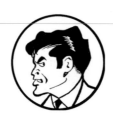

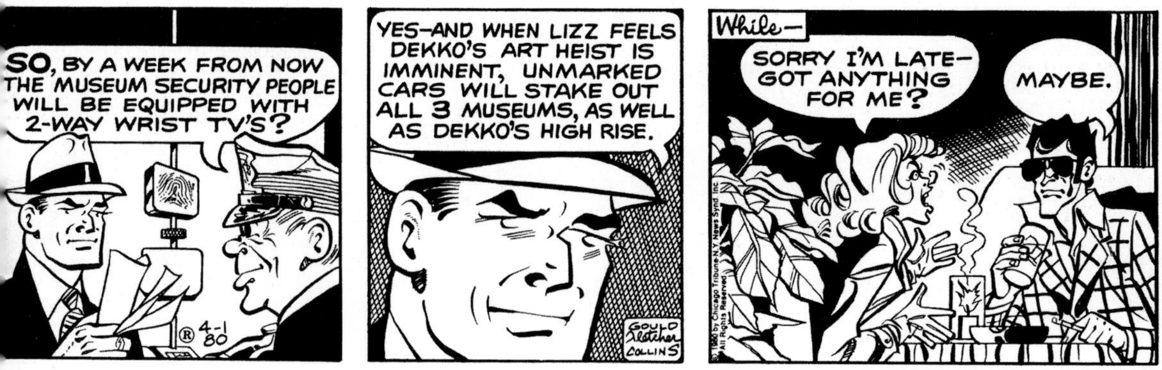
SO, BY A WEEK FROM NOW THE MUSEUM SECURITY PEOPLE WILL BE EQUIPPED WITH 2-WAY WRIST TV'S?
4-1 80
YES—AND WHEN LIZZ FEELS DEKKO'S ART HEIST IS IMMINENT, UNMARKED CARS WILL STAKE OUT ALL 3 MUSEUMS, AS WELL AS DEKKO'S HIGH RISE.
GOULD Fletcher COLLINS
While—
SORRY I'M LATE—GOT ANYTHING FOR ME?
MAYBE.
© 1980 by Chicago Tribune-N.Y. News Synd. Inc. All Rights Reserved

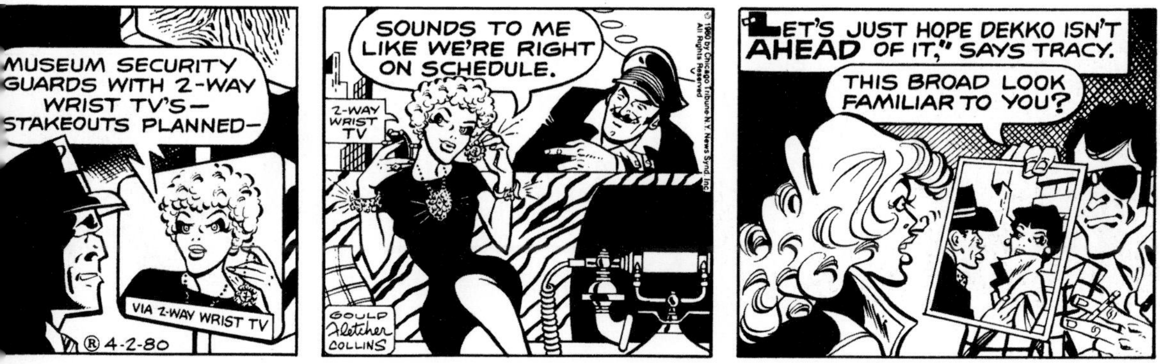
MUSEUM SECURITY GUARDS WITH 2-WAY WRIST TV'S—STAKEOUTS PLANNED—
VIA 2-WAY WRIST TV
4-2-80
SOUNDS TO ME LIKE WE'RE RIGHT ON SCHEDULE.
2-WAY WRIST TV
© 1980 by Chicago Tribune-N.Y. News Synd. Inc. All Rights Reserved
GOULD Fletcher COLLINS
"LET'S JUST HOPE DEKKO ISN'T AHEAD OF IT," SAYS TRACY.
THIS BROAD LOOK FAMILIAR TO YOU?

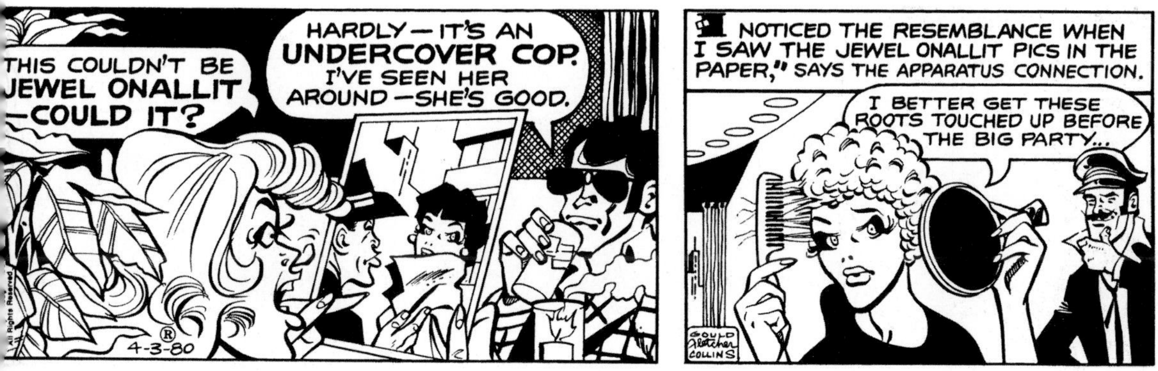
THIS COULDN'T BE JEWEL ONALLIT—COULD IT?
HARDLY—IT'S AN UNDERCOVER COP. I'VE SEEN HER AROUND—SHE'S GOOD.
4-3-80
All Rights Reserved
"I NOTICED THE RESEMBLANCE WHEN I SAW THE JEWEL ONALLIT PICS IN THE PAPER," SAYS THE APPARATUS CONNECTION.
I BETTER GET THESE ROOTS TOUCHED UP BEFORE THE BIG PARTY...
GOULD Fletcher COLLINS

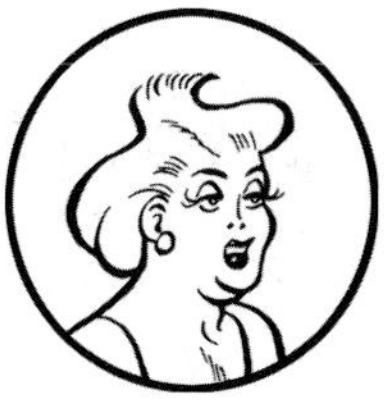

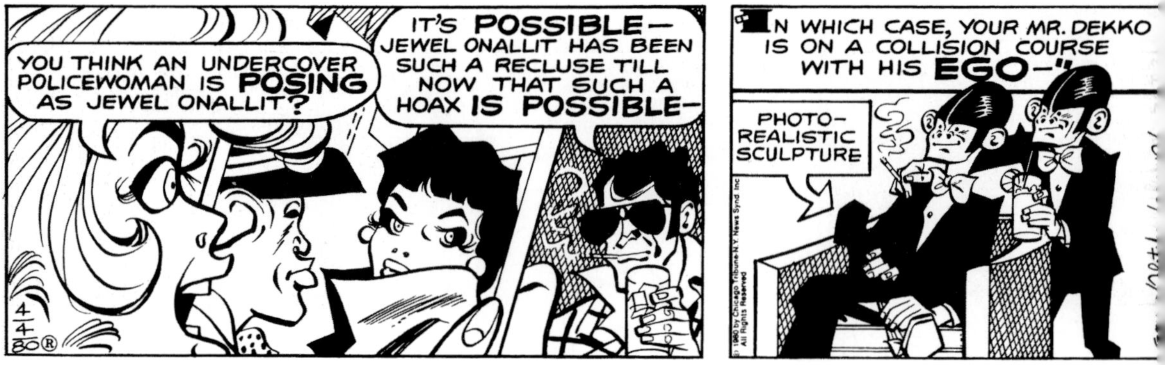
YOU THINK AN UNDERCOVER POLICEWOMAN IS POSING AS JEWEL ONALLIT?
IT'S POSSIBLE— JEWEL ONALLIT HAS BEEN SUCH A RECLUSE TILL NOW THAT SUCH A HOAX IS POSSIBLE—
4/4/80 ®
IN WHICH CASE, YOUR MR. DEKKO IS ON A COLLISION COURSE WITH HIS EGO—"
PHOTO-REALISTIC SCULPTURE
© 1980 by Chicago Tribune-N.Y. News Synd Inc All Rights Reserved

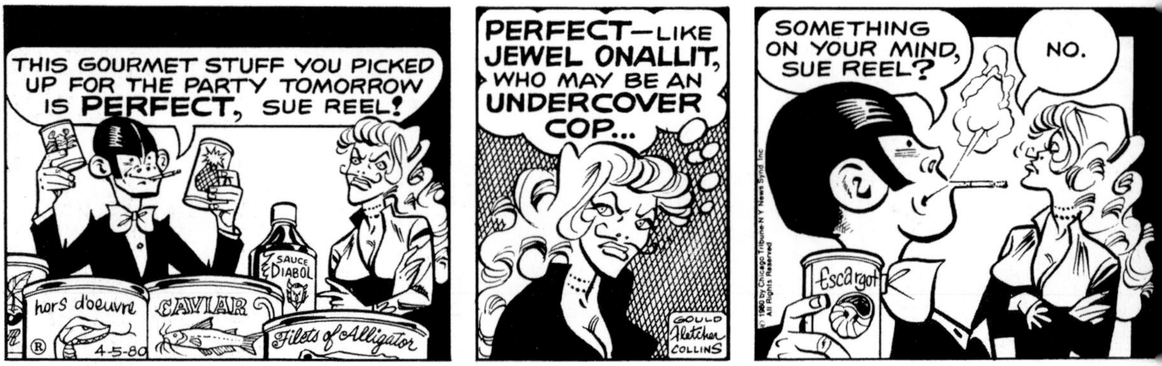
THIS GOURMET STUFF YOU PICKED UP FOR THE PARTY TOMORROW IS PERFECT, SUE REEL!
SAUCE DIABOL
hors d'oeuvre
CAVIAR
Filets of Alligator
® 4-5-80
PERFECT—LIKE JEWEL ONALLIT, WHO MAY BE AN UNDERCOVER COP...
GOULD Fletcher COLLINS
SOMETHING ON YOUR MIND, SUE REEL?
NO.
Escargot
© 1980 by Chicago Tribune-N.Y. News Synd Inc All Rights Reserved

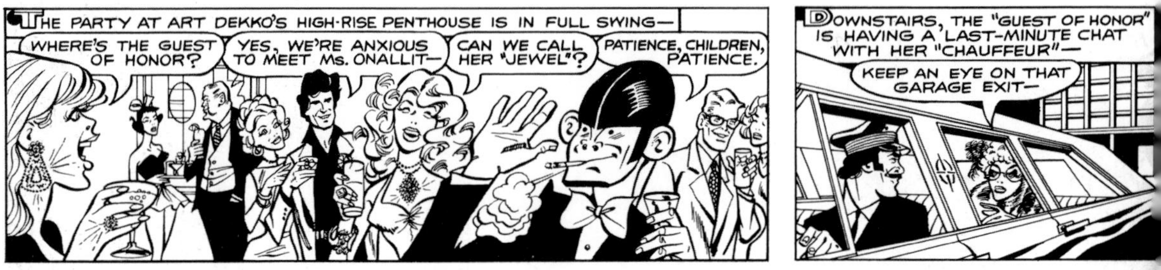
THE PARTY AT ART DEKKO'S HIGH-RISE PENTHOUSE IS IN FULL SWING—
WHERE'S THE GUEST OF HONOR?
YES, WE'RE ANXIOUS TO MEET Ms. ONALLIT—
CAN WE CALL HER "JEWEL"?
PATIENCE, CHILDREN, PATIENCE.
DOWNSTAIRS, THE "GUEST OF HONOR" IS HAVING A LAST-MINUTE CHAT WITH HER "CHAUFFEUR"—
KEEP AN EYE ON THAT GARAGE EXIT—

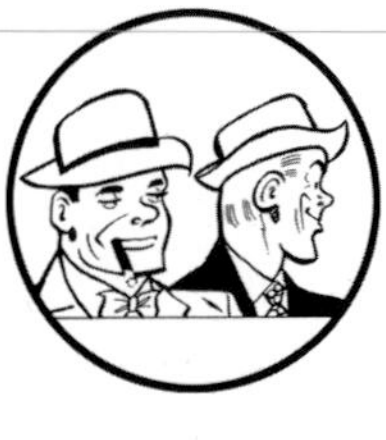

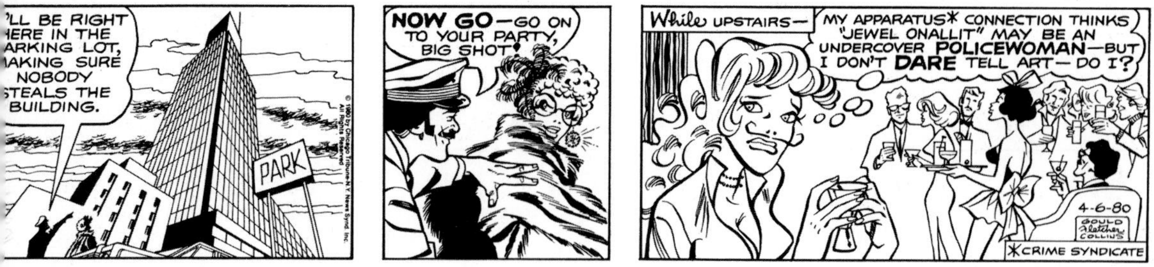
'LL BE RIGHT HERE IN THE ARKING LOT, AKING SURE NOBODY TEALS THE BUILDING.
PARK
NOW GO—GO ON TO YOUR PARTY, BIG SHOT!
While UPSTAIRS—
MY APPARATUS✻ CONNECTION THINKS "JEWEL ONALLIT" MAY BE AN UNDERCOVER POLICEWOMAN—BUT I DON'T DARE TELL ART—DO I?
4-6-80
✻CRIME SYNDICATE

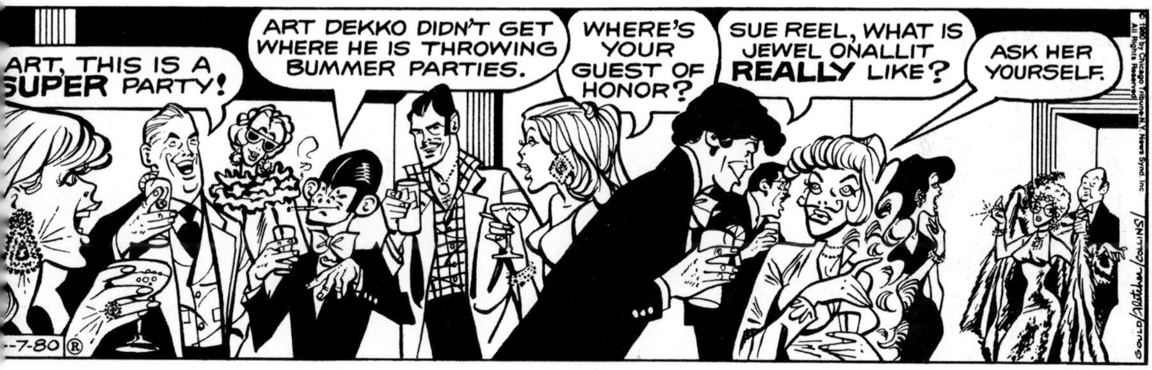
ART, THIS IS A SUPER PARTY!
ART DEKKO DIDN'T GET WHERE HE IS THROWING BUMMER PARTIES.
WHERE'S YOUR GUEST OF HONOR?
SUE REEL, WHAT IS JEWEL ONALLIT REALLY LIKE?
ASK HER YOURSELF.
-7-80

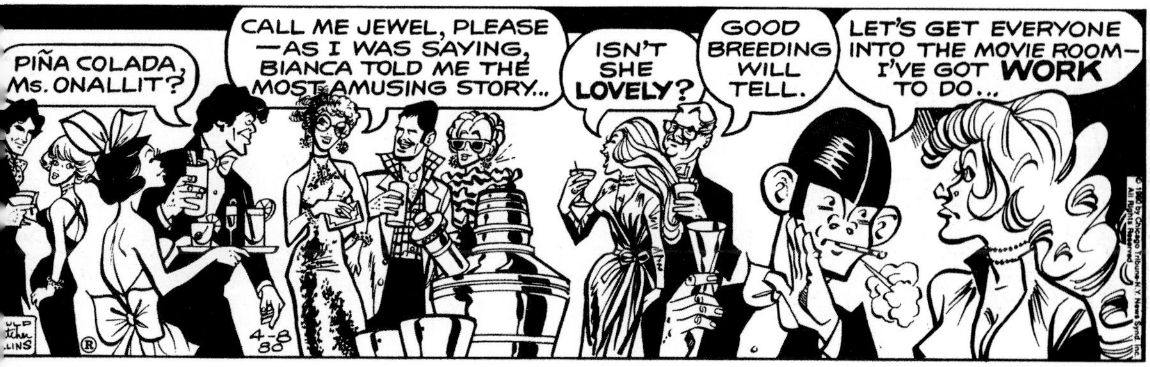
PIÑA COLADA, Ms. ONALLIT?
CALL ME JEWEL, PLEASE —AS I WAS SAYING, BIANCA TOLD ME THE MOST AMUSING STORY...
ISN'T SHE LOVELY?
GOOD BREEDING WILL TELL.
LET'S GET EVERYONE INTO THE MOVIE ROOM—I'VE GOT WORK TO DO...
4-8 80

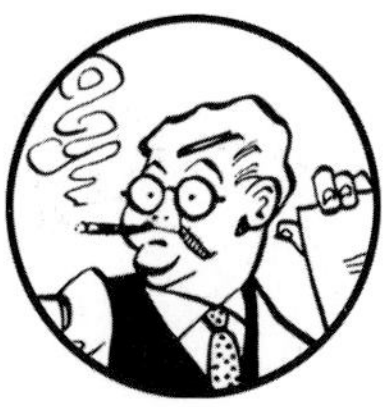

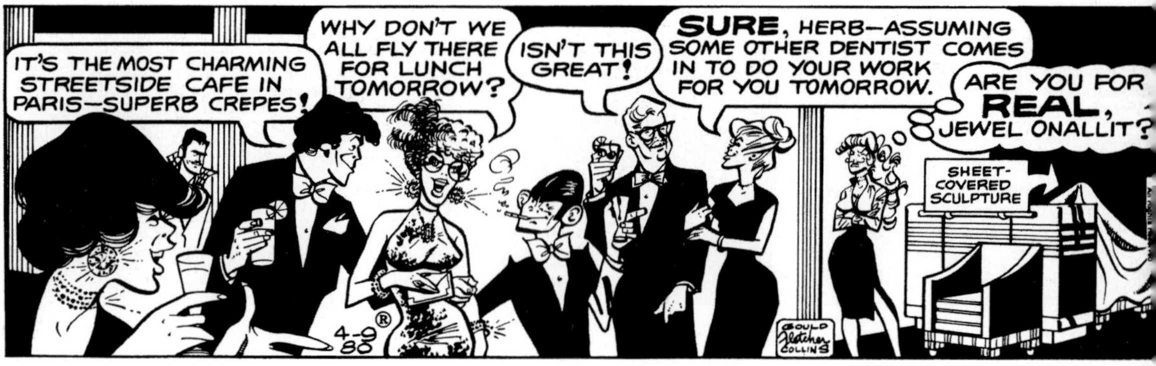
IT'S THE MOST CHARMING STREETSIDE CAFE IN PARIS—SUPERB CREPES!
WHY DON'T WE ALL FLY THERE FOR LUNCH TOMORROW?
ISN'T THIS GREAT!
SURE, HERB—ASSUMING SOME OTHER DENTIST COMES IN TO DO YOUR WORK FOR YOU TOMORROW.
ARE YOU FOR REAL, JEWEL ONALLIT?
SHEET-COVERED SCULPTURE
4-9 80
GOULD Fletcher COLLINS

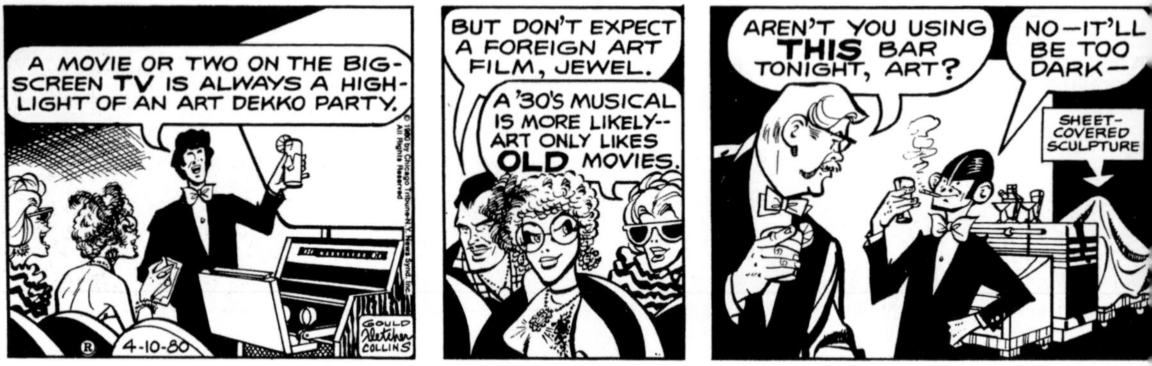
A MOVIE OR TWO ON THE BIG-SCREEN TV IS ALWAYS A HIGH-LIGHT OF AN ART DEKKO PARTY.
© 1980 by Chicago Tribune-N.Y. News Synd. Inc. All Rights Reserved
4-10-80
GOULD Fletcher COLLINS
BUT DON'T EXPECT A FOREIGN ART FILM, JEWEL.
A '30'S MUSICAL IS MORE LIKELY-- ART ONLY LIKES OLD MOVIES.
AREN'T YOU USING THIS BAR TONIGHT, ART?
NO—IT'LL BE TOO DARK—
SHEET-COVERED SCULPTURE

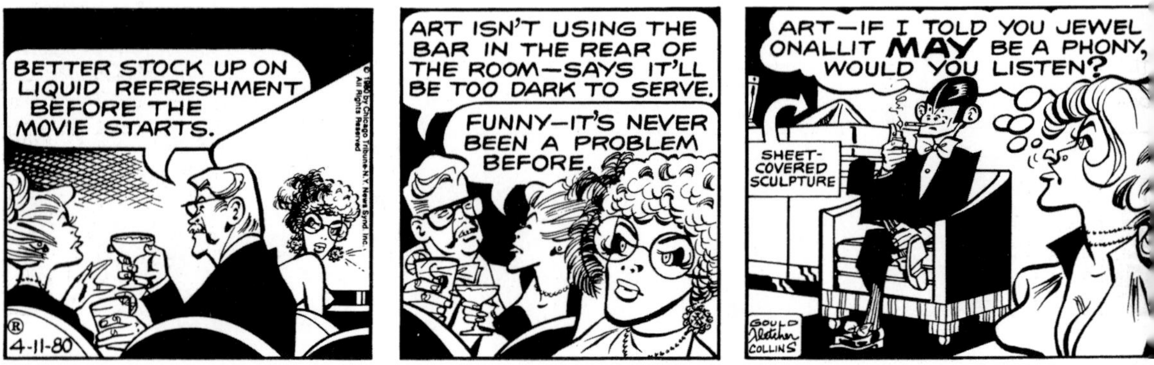
BETTER STOCK UP ON LIQUID REFRESHMENT BEFORE THE MOVIE STARTS.
© 1980 by Chicago Tribune-N.Y. News Synd. Inc. All Rights Reserved
4-11-80
ART ISN'T USING THE BAR IN THE REAR OF THE ROOM—SAYS IT'LL BE TOO DARK TO SERVE.
FUNNY—IT'S NEVER BEEN A PROBLEM BEFORE.
ART—IF I TOLD YOU JEWEL ONALLIT MAY BE A PHONY, WOULD YOU LISTEN?
SHEET-COVERED SCULPTURE
GOULD Fletcher COLLINS

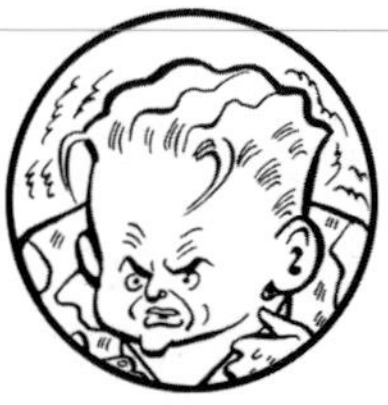

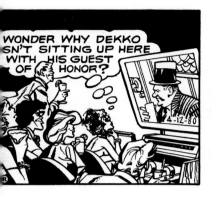

WONDER WHY DEKKO
SN'T SITTING UP HERE
WITH HIS GUEST
OF HONOR?
4-12-80
ART — THERE'S SOMETHING I SHOULD SAY...
SAVE IT— IT'S TIME TO **MOVE!**
PHOTO-REALISTIC SCULPTURE
© 1980 by Chicago Tribune-N.Y. News Synd. Inc. All Rights Reserved
GOULD Fletcher COLLINS

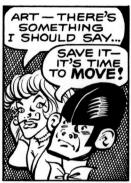

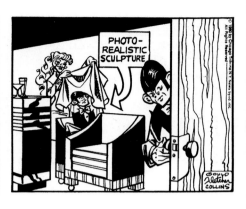

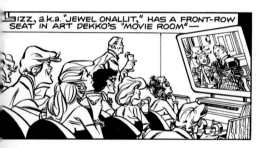

LIZZ, a.k.a. "JEWEL ONALLIT," HAS A FRONT-ROW SEAT IN ART DEKKO'S "MOVIE ROOM"—
DEKKO WAS AT MY SIDE ALL EVENING—
BUT SUDDENLY HE OPTS FOR A SEAT AT THE REAR OF THE ROOM," LIZZ MUSES. **"WHY?"**

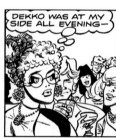

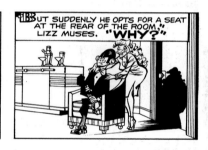

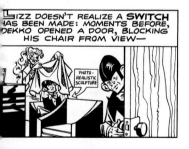

LIZZ DOESN'T REALIZE A **SWITCH** HAS BEEN MADE: MOMENTS BEFORE, DEKKO OPENED A DOOR, BLOCKING HIS CHAIR FROM VIEW—
PHOTO-REALISTIC SCULPTURE
SO THAT HE, AND THE CHAIR, COULD DISAPPEAR INTO THE ADJOINING ROOM, WHILE SUE REEL PUSHED HIS SCULPTURE INTO PLACE—
© 1980 by Chicago Tribune-N.Y. News Synd. Inc. All Rights Reserved
GOULD Fletcher COLLINS
WITH THE DOOR SHUT, THE PARTY'S "HOST" APPEARS TO BE ENJOYING THE MOVIE —BUT WHERE IS THE **REAL** DEKKO?
PHOTO-REALISTIC SCULPTURE
4 13 80

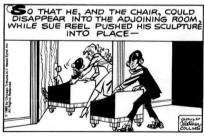

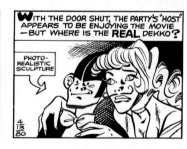

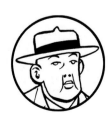

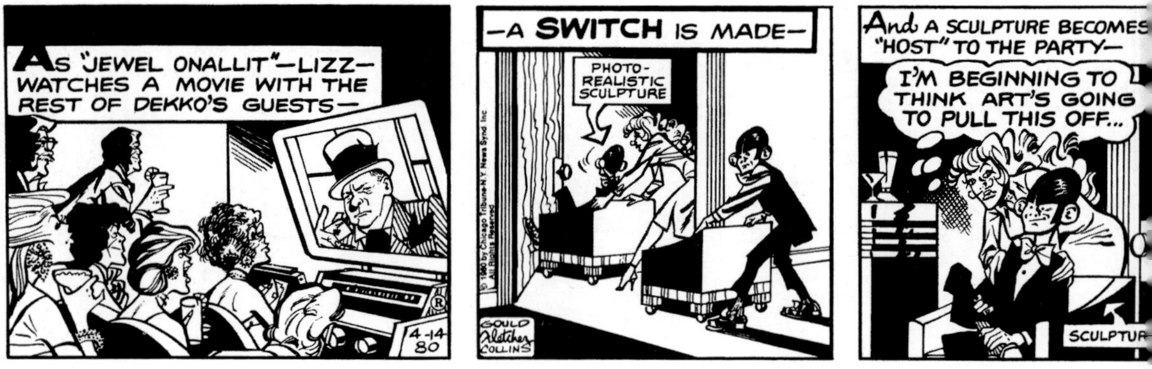
AS "JEWEL ONALLIT"—LIZZ—WATCHES A MOVIE WITH THE REST OF DEKKO'S GUESTS—
4-14 80
—A SWITCH IS MADE—
PHOTO-REALISTIC SCULPTURE
© 1980 by Chicago Tribune-N.Y. News Synd Inc All Rights Reserved
GOULD Fletcher COLLINS
And A SCULPTURE BECOMES "HOST" TO THE PARTY—
I'M BEGINNING TO THINK ART'S GOING TO PULL THIS OFF...
SCULPTUR

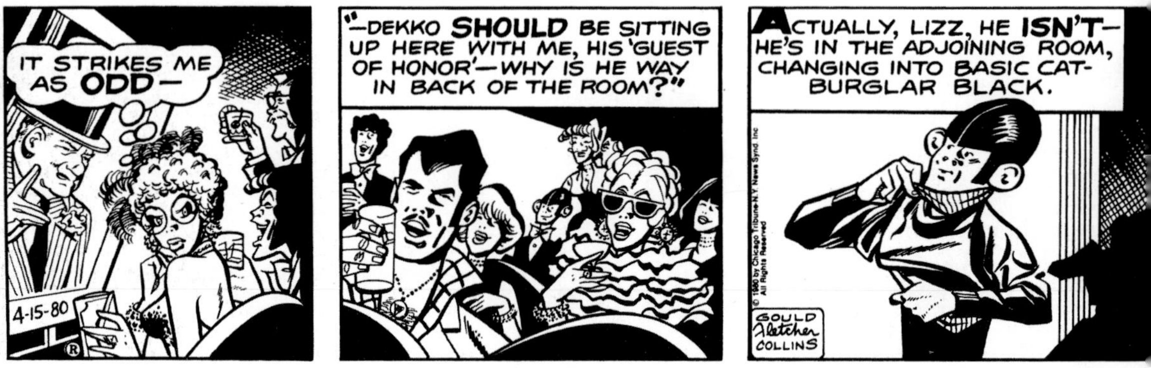
IT STRIKES ME AS ODD—
4-15-80
"—DEKKO SHOULD BE SITTING UP HERE WITH ME, HIS 'GUEST OF HONOR'—WHY IS HE WAY IN BACK OF THE ROOM?"
ACTUALLY, LIZZ, HE ISN'T—HE'S IN THE ADJOINING ROOM, CHANGING INTO BASIC CAT-BURGLAR BLACK.
© 1980 by Chicago Tribune-N.Y. News Synd Inc All Rights Reserved
GOULD Fletcher COLLINS

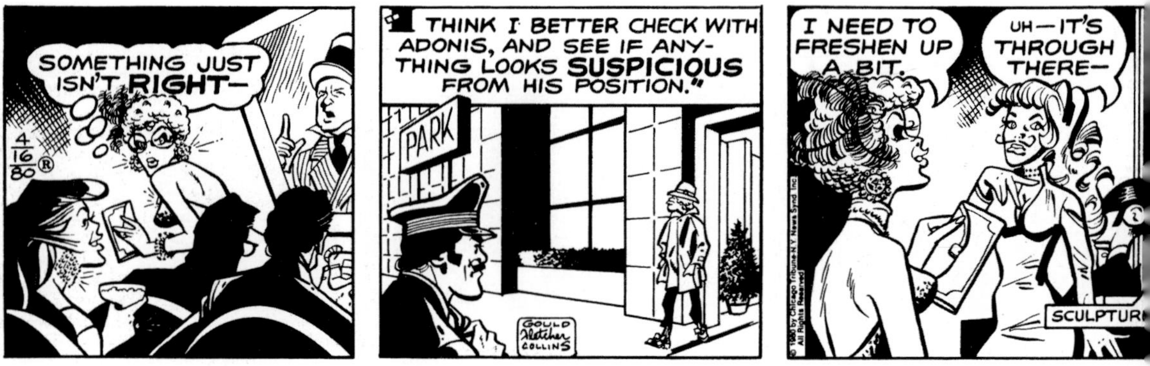
SOMETHING JUST ISN'T RIGHT—
4/16/80
"I THINK I BETTER CHECK WITH ADONIS, AND SEE IF ANYTHING LOOKS SUSPICIOUS FROM HIS POSITION."
PARK
GOULD Fletcher COLLINS
I NEED TO FRESHEN UP A BIT.
UH—IT'S THROUGH THERE—
© 1980 by Chicago Tribune-N.Y. News Synd Inc All Rights Reserved
SCULPTUR

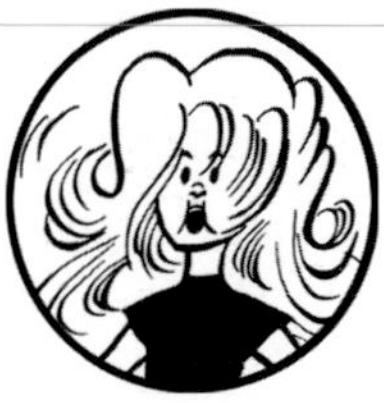

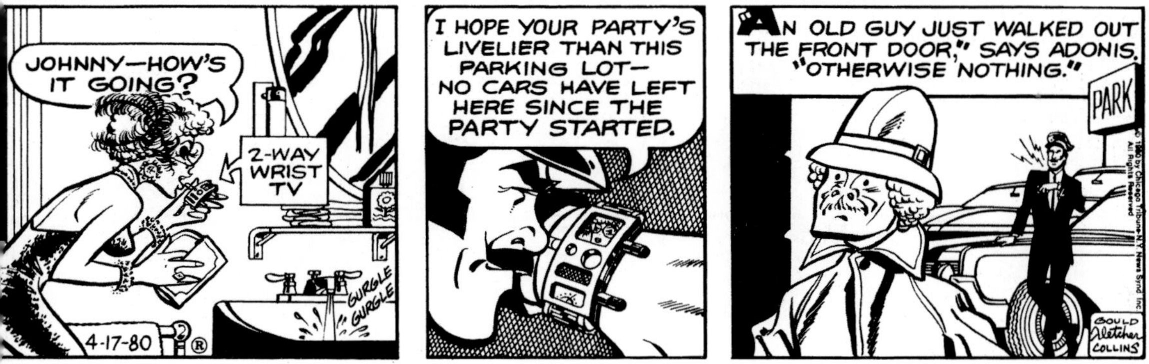
JOHNNY—HOW'S IT GOING?
2-WAY WRIST TV
GURGLE GURGLE
4-17-80
I HOPE YOUR PARTY'S LIVELIER THAN THIS PARKING LOT— NO CARS HAVE LEFT HERE SINCE THE PARTY STARTED.
"AN OLD GUY JUST WALKED OUT THE FRONT DOOR," SAYS ADONIS. "OTHERWISE NOTHING."
PARK
© 1980 by Chicago Tribune-N.Y. News Synd. Inc. All Rights Reserved
GOULD Fletcher COLLINS

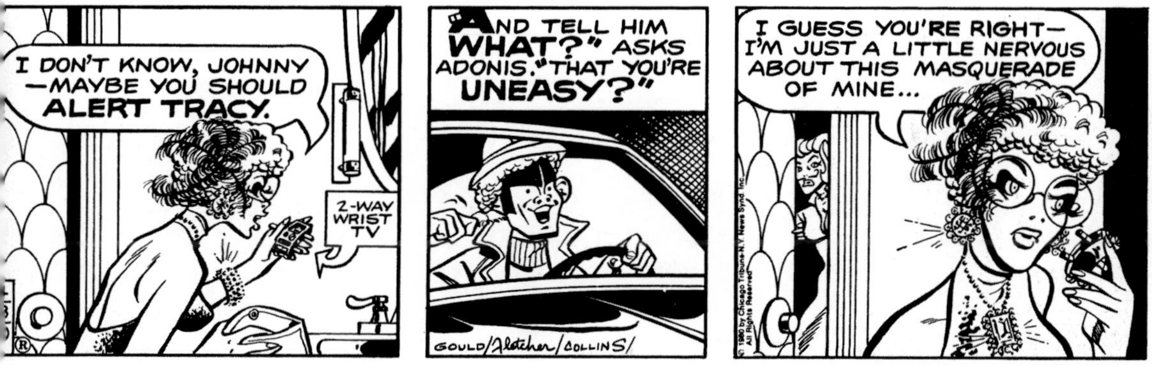
I DON'T KNOW, JOHNNY —MAYBE YOU SHOULD ALERT TRACY.
2-WAY WRIST TV
"AND TELL HIM WHAT?" ASKS ADONIS. "THAT YOU'RE UNEASY?"
GOULD/Fletcher/COLLINS/
I GUESS YOU'RE RIGHT— I'M JUST A LITTLE NERVOUS ABOUT THIS MASQUERADE OF MINE...
© 1980 by Chicago Tribune-N.Y. News Synd. Inc. All Rights Reserved

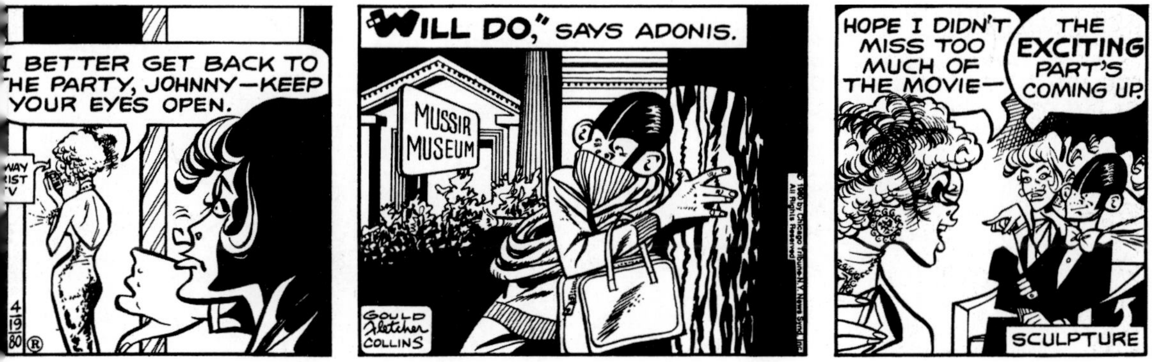
I BETTER GET BACK TO THE PARTY, JOHNNY—KEEP YOUR EYES OPEN.
4 19 80
"WILL DO," SAYS ADONIS.
MUSSIR MUSEUM
GOULD Fletcher COLLINS
© 1980 by Chicago Tribune-N.Y. News Synd. Inc. All Rights Reserved
HOPE I DIDN'T MISS TOO MUCH OF THE MOVIE—
THE EXCITING PART'S COMING UP.
SCULPTURE

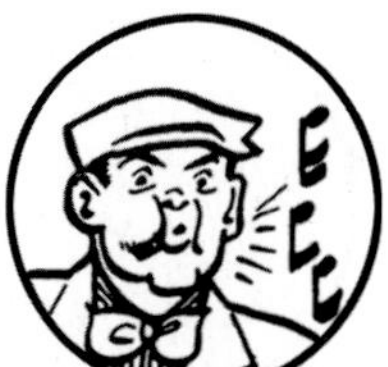

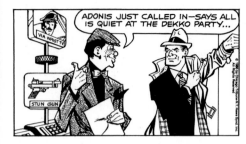

VIA WRIST TV
STUN GUN
ADONIS JUST CALLED IN—SAYS ALL IS QUIET AT THE DEKKO PARTY...
© 1980 by Chicago Tribune-N.Y. News Synd. Inc. All Rights Reserved
I DON'T KNOW—MAYBE I SHOULD HANG AROUND—JUST IN CASE.
LET ME—YOU GOT SOMETHING TO DO, DON'T YOU?
"GOT TO PICK SOMETHING UP," SAYS TRACY. "AT MY GUNSMITH'S."

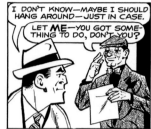

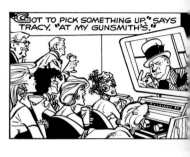

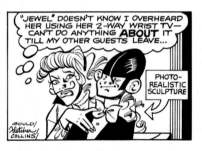

"JEWEL" DOESN'T KNOW I OVERHEARD HER USING HER 2-WAY WRIST TV—CAN'T DO ANYTHING ABOUT IT TILL MY OTHER GUESTS LEAVE...
PHOTO-REALISTIC SCULPTURE
GOULD/ Fletcher/ COLLINS/
"IF ONLY I COULD WARN ART SHE'S A COP—BUT IT'S TOO LATE—"
MUSSIR MUSEUM
4/20/80

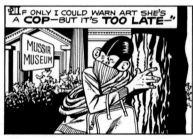

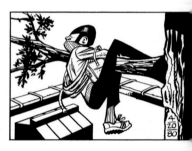

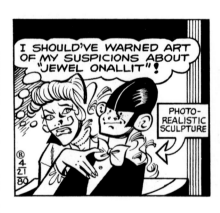

I SHOULD'VE WARNED ART OF MY SUSPICIONS ABOUT "JEWEL ONALLIT"!
PHOTO-REALISTIC SCULPTURE
® 4/21/80
"NOW I KNOW SHE'S A COP, AND I CAN'T TELL HIM—HE'S PROBABLY AT THE MUSEUM BY NOW—"
1980 by Chicago Tribune-N.Y. News Synd. Inc. All Rights Reserved
GOULD Fletcher COLLINS
RIGHT, SUE REEL—ON THE ROOF, TO BE EXACT—

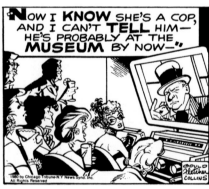

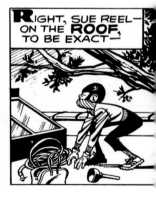

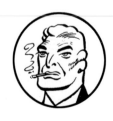

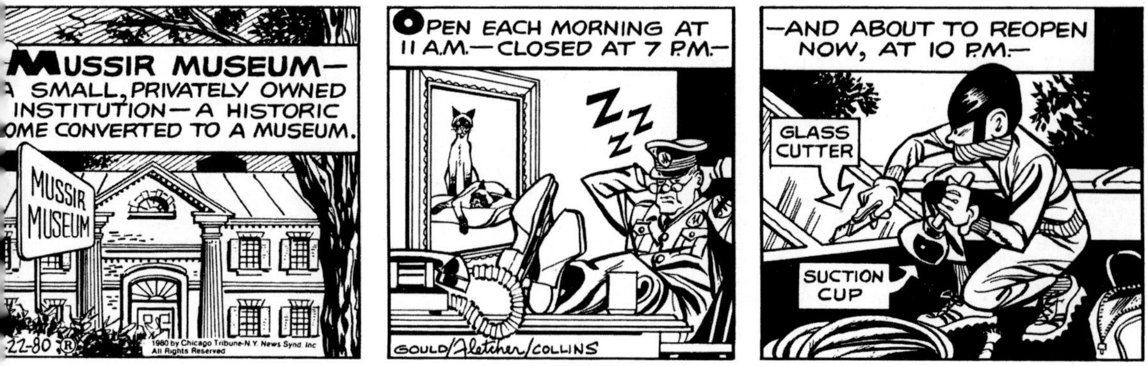
MUSSIR MUSEUM—
A SMALL, PRIVATELY OWNED INSTITUTION—A HISTORIC
OME CONVERTED TO A MUSEUM.
MUSSIR MUSEUM
22-80
1980 by Chicago Tribune-N.Y. News Synd. Inc All Rights Reserved
OPEN EACH MORNING AT 11 A.M.—CLOSED AT 7 P.M.—
ZZZ
GOULD/Fletcher/COLLINS
—AND ABOUT TO REOPEN NOW, AT 10 P.M.—
GLASS CUTTER
SUCTION CUP

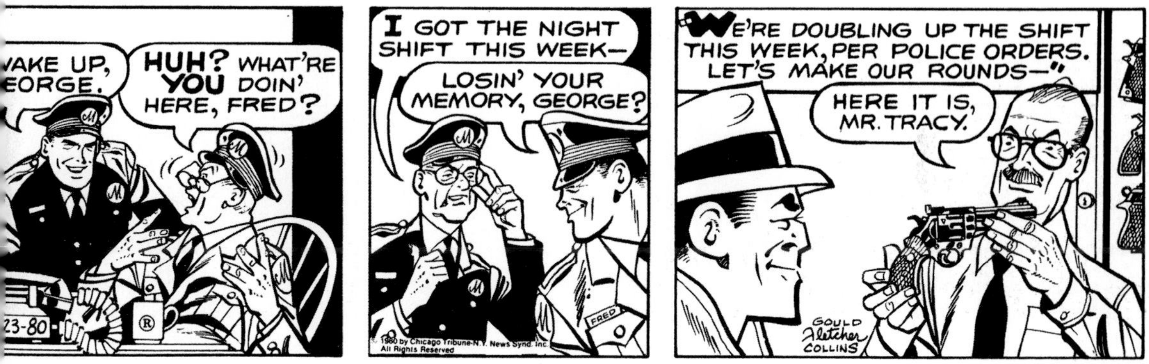
AKE UP, EORGE.
HUH? WHAT'RE YOU DOIN' HERE, FRED?
23-80
I GOT THE NIGHT SHIFT THIS WEEK—
LOSIN' YOUR MEMORY, GEORGE?
FRED
1980 by Chicago Tribune-N.Y. News Synd. Inc All Rights Reserved
"WE'RE DOUBLING UP THE SHIFT THIS WEEK, PER POLICE ORDERS. LET'S MAKE OUR ROUNDS—"
HERE IT IS, MR. TRACY.
GOULD Fletcher COLLINS

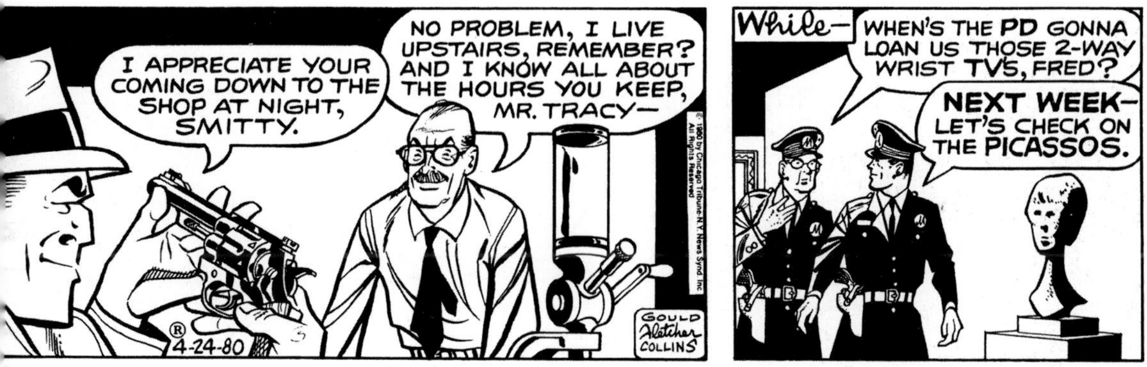
I APPRECIATE YOUR COMING DOWN TO THE SHOP AT NIGHT, SMITTY.
NO PROBLEM, I LIVE UPSTAIRS, REMEMBER? AND I KNOW ALL ABOUT THE HOURS YOU KEEP, MR. TRACY—
4-24-80
1980 by Chicago Tribune-N.Y. News Synd. Inc All Rights Reserved
GOULD Fletcher COLLINS
While—
WHEN'S THE PD GONNA LOAN US THOSE 2-WAY WRIST TV'S, FRED?
NEXT WEEK—LET'S CHECK ON THE PICASSOS.

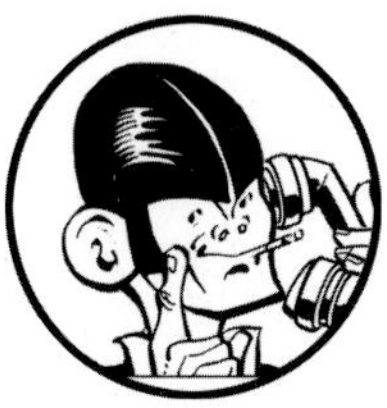

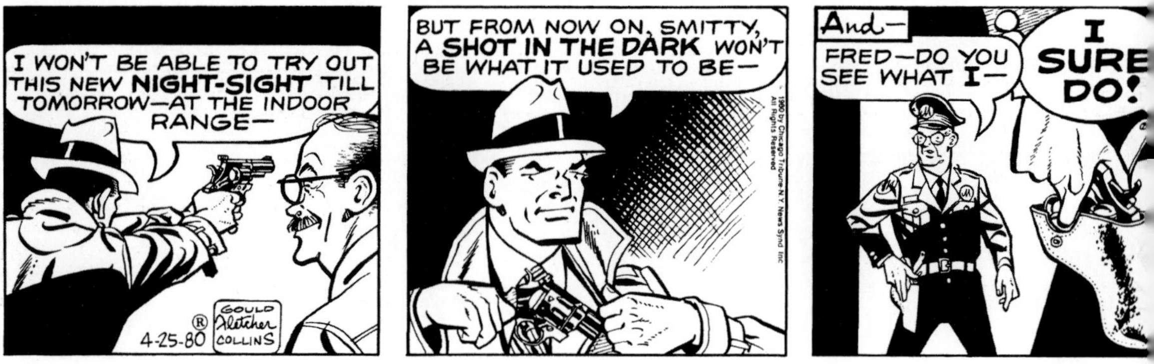
I WON'T BE ABLE TO TRY OUT THIS NEW NIGHT-SIGHT TILL TOMORROW—AT THE INDOOR RANGE—
4-25-80
GOULD Fletcher COLLINS
BUT FROM NOW ON, SMITTY, A SHOT IN THE DARK WON'T BE WHAT IT USED TO BE—
1980 by Chicago Tribune-N.Y. News Synd. Inc All Rights Reserved
And—
FRED—DO YOU SEE WHAT I—
I SURE DO!

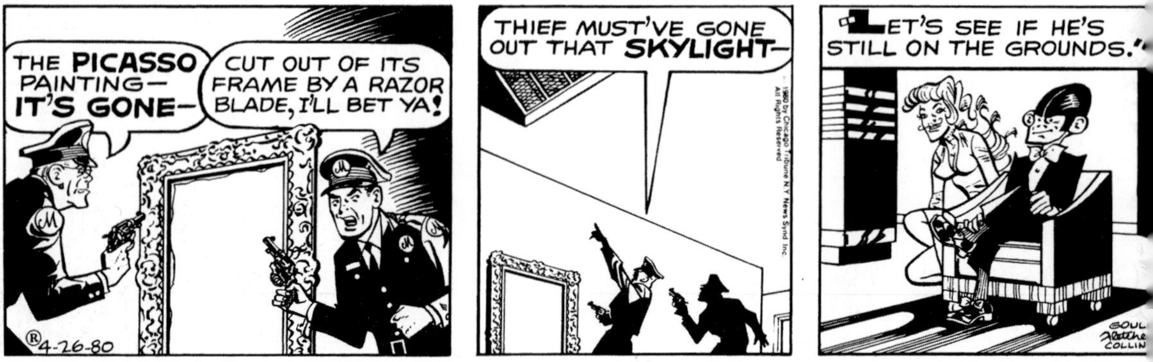
THE PICASSO PAINTING— IT'S GONE—
CUT OUT OF ITS FRAME BY A RAZOR BLADE, I'LL BET YA!
4-26-80
THIEF MUST'VE GONE OUT THAT SKYLIGHT—
1980 by Chicago Tribune-N.Y. News Synd. Inc All Rights Reserved
"LET'S SEE IF HE'S STILL ON THE GROUNDS."

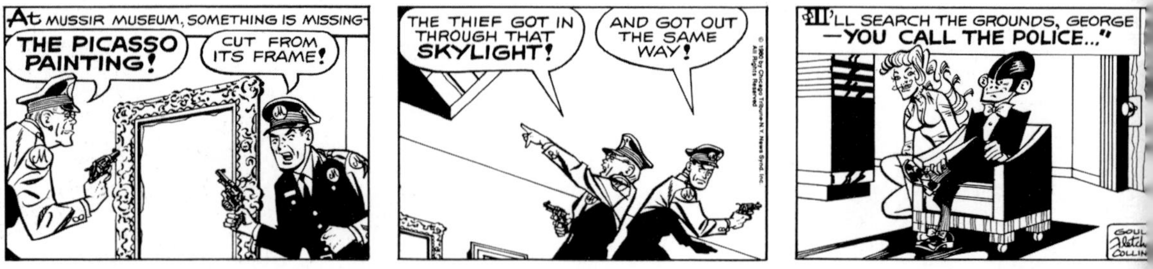
At MUSSIR MUSEUM, SOMETHING IS MISSING—
THE PICASSO PAINTING!
CUT FROM ITS FRAME!
THE THIEF GOT IN THROUGH THAT SKYLIGHT!
AND GOT OUT THE SAME WAY!
"I'LL SEARCH THE GROUNDS, GEORGE —YOU CALL THE POLICE..."

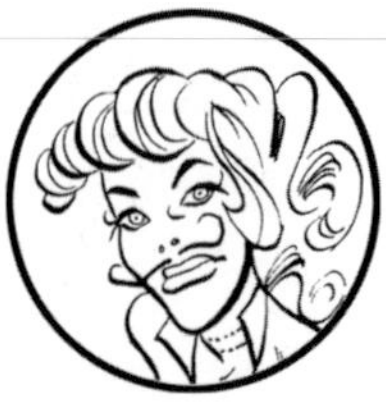

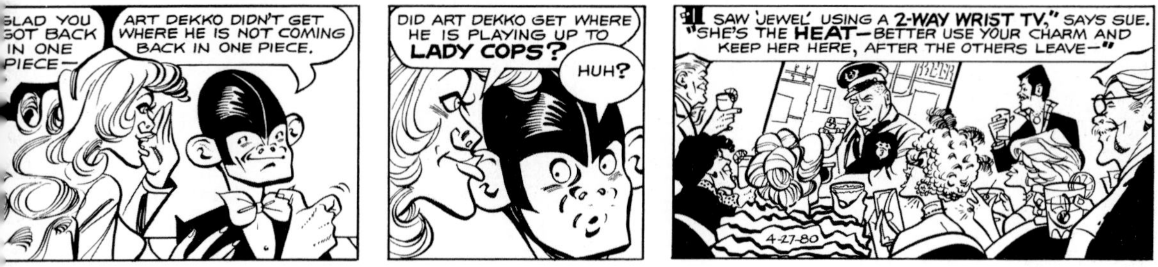
LAD YOU OT BACK IN ONE PIECE—
ART DEKKO DIDN'T GET WHERE HE IS NOT COMING BACK IN ONE PIECE.
DID ART DEKKO GET WHERE HE IS PLAYING UP TO LADY COPS?
HUH?
"I SAW 'JEWEL' USING A 2-WAY WRIST TV," SAYS SUE. "SHE'S THE HEAT—BETTER USE YOUR CHARM AND KEEP HER HERE, AFTER THE OTHERS LEAVE—"
4-27-80

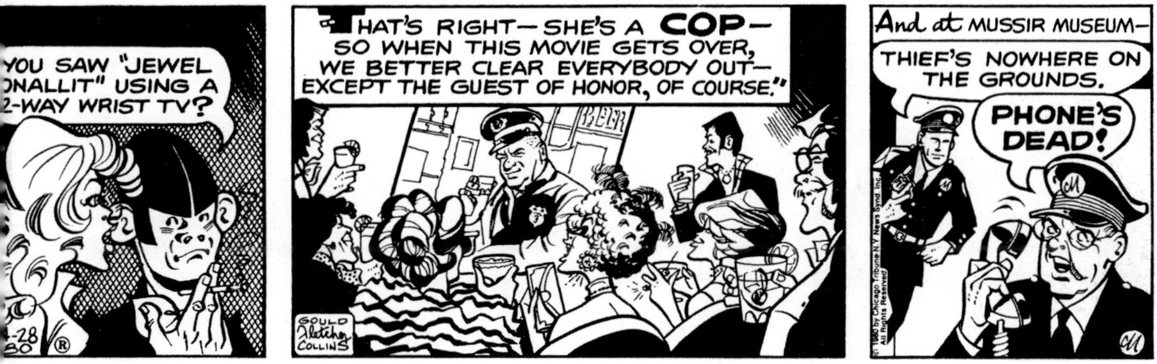
YOU SAW "JEWEL NALLIT" USING A -WAY WRIST TV?
4-28 80
"THAT'S RIGHT—SHE'S A COP—SO WHEN THIS MOVIE GETS OVER, WE BETTER CLEAR EVERYBODY OUT—EXCEPT THE GUEST OF HONOR, OF COURSE."
GOULD Fletcher COLLINS
And at MUSSIR MUSEUM—
THIEF'S NOWHERE ON THE GROUNDS.
PHONE'S DEAD!
© 1980 by Chicago Tribune-N.Y. News Synd. Inc. All Rights Reserved

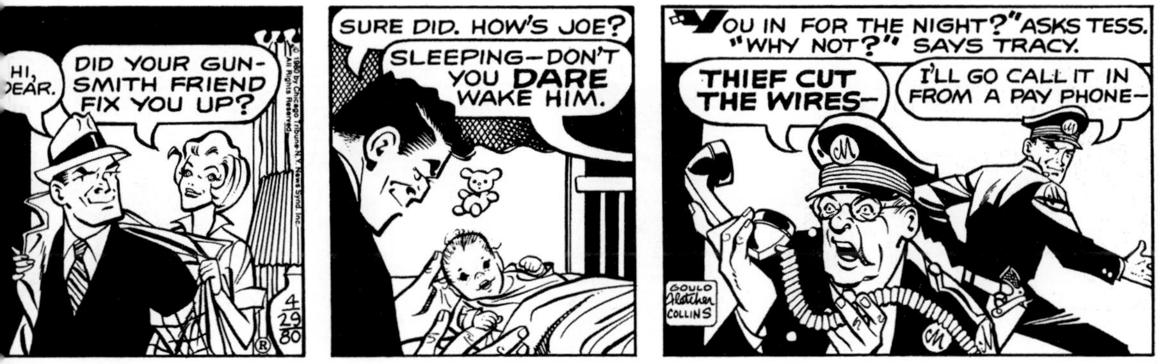
HI, EAR.
DID YOUR GUN-SMITH FRIEND FIX YOU UP?
© 1980 by Chicago Tribune-N.Y. News Synd. Inc. All Rights Reserved
4 29 80
SURE DID. HOW'S JOE?
SLEEPING—DON'T YOU DARE WAKE HIM.
"YOU IN FOR THE NIGHT?" ASKS TESS. "WHY NOT?" SAYS TRACY.
THIEF CUT THE WIRES—
I'LL GO CALL IT IN FROM A PAY PHONE—
GOULD Fletcher COLLINS

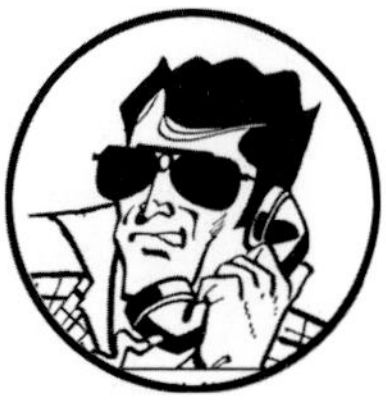

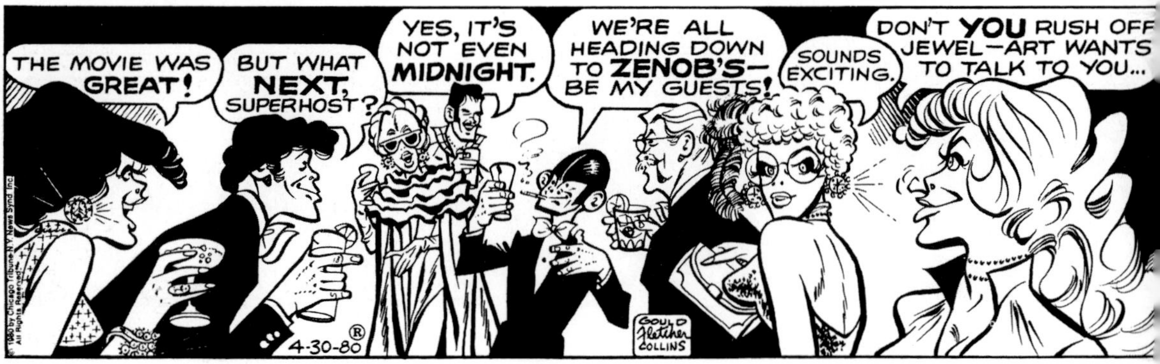
THE MOVIE WAS GREAT!
BUT WHAT NEXT, SUPERHOST?
YES, IT'S NOT EVEN MIDNIGHT.
WE'RE ALL HEADING DOWN TO ZENOB'S—BE MY GUESTS!
SOUNDS EXCITING.
DON'T YOU RUSH OFF JEWEL—ART WANTS TO TALK TO YOU...
4-30-80
GOULD Fletcher COLLINS

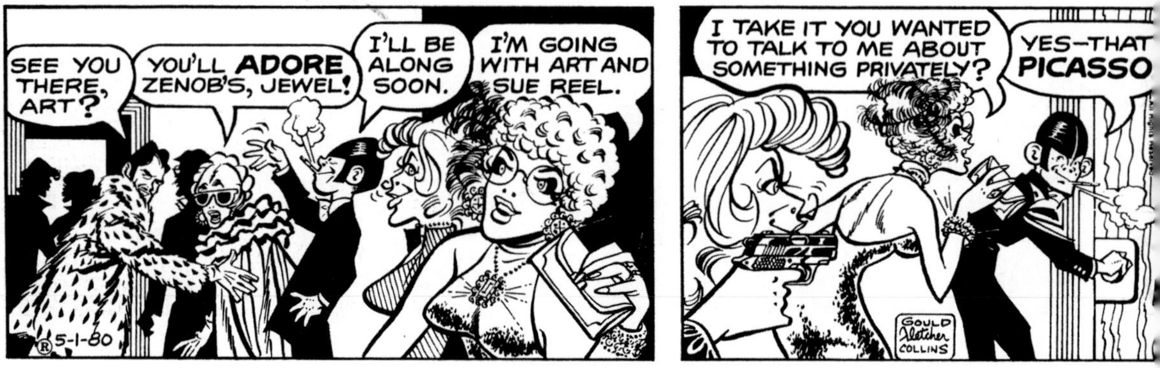
SEE YOU THERE, ART?
YOU'LL ADORE ZENOB'S, JEWEL!
I'LL BE ALONG SOON.
I'M GOING WITH ART AND SUE REEL.
5-1-80
I TAKE IT YOU WANTED TO TALK TO ME ABOUT SOMETHING PRIVATELY?
YES—THAT PICASSO
GOULD Fletcher COLLINS

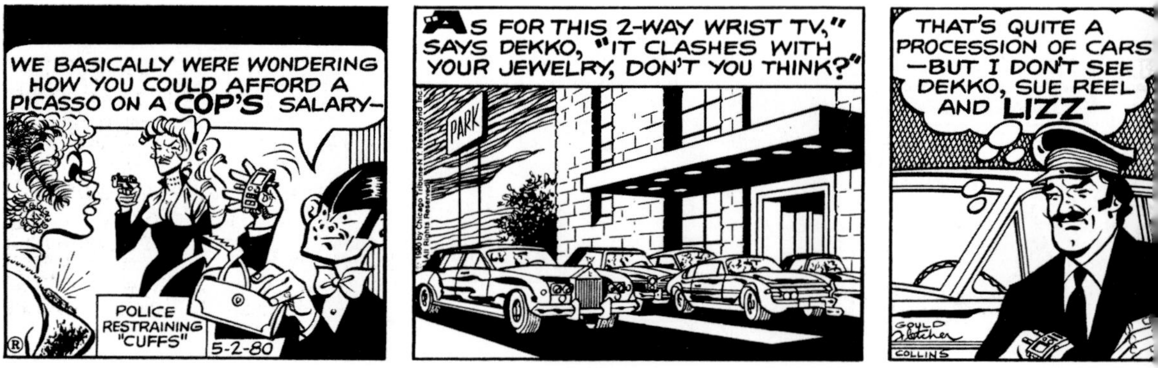
WE BASICALLY WERE WONDERING HOW YOU COULD AFFORD A PICASSO ON A COP'S SALARY—
POLICE RESTRAINING "CUFFS"
5-2-80
AS FOR THIS 2-WAY WRIST TV," SAYS DEKKO, "IT CLASHES WITH YOUR JEWELRY, DON'T YOU THINK?"
PARK
THAT'S QUITE A PROCESSION OF CARS—BUT I DON'T SEE DEKKO, SUE REEL AND LIZZ—
GOULD Fletcher COLLINS

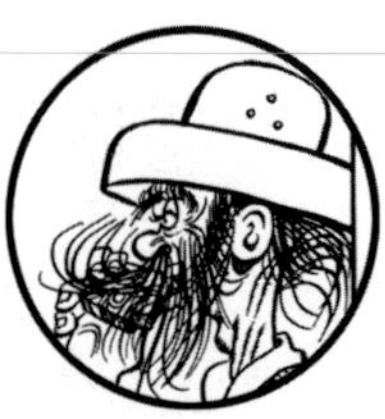

PUT ME THROUGH TO TRACY OR CATCHEM—

2-WAY WRIST TV

1980 by Chicago Tribune-N.Y. News Synd. Inc.
All Rights Reserved

5-3-80
GOULD
Fletcher
COLLINS

"TRACY'S OFF DUTY," SAYS THE DISPATCHER. "CATCHEM IS EN ROUTE TO A CRIME SCENE."

HAS SOMEBODY OTHER THAN DEKKO HIT THE MUSSIR MUSEUM?

"PATCH ME THROUGH TO SAM," SAYS ADONIS.

THE PARTY'S OVER, "JEWEL"...

POLICE RESTRAINING "CUFFS"

SAM, THIS IS ADONIS—KEEPING WATCH IN DEKKO'S PARKING LOT.

2-WAY WRIST TV

PARK

"A PROCESSION OF CARS IS LEAVING DEKKO'S PARTY—BUT WITHOUT DEKKO, SUE OR LIZZ, SO FAR—"

PARK

JOHNNY, SOMETHING MAY BE UP—THE MUSSIR MUSEUM'S BEEN HIT... A PICASSO STOLEN...

"I'M EN ROUTE NOW," SAYS SAM, "AND TRACY'S BEING CONTACTED."

DICK—IT'S HQ—MESSAGE FROM SAM...

DEKKO COULDN'T HAVE HIT THAT MUSEUM, SAM —WAIT!

GOULD/Fletcher/COLLINS

"THERE'S DEKKO'S CAR NOW—WITH SUE AND LIZZ—GOING TO WHEREVER THE PARTY'S MOVED TO, I GUESS—"

CORVETTE

5-4-80

IN THE '30s THEY CALLED THIS GOING FOR A RIDE, "JEWEL."

53

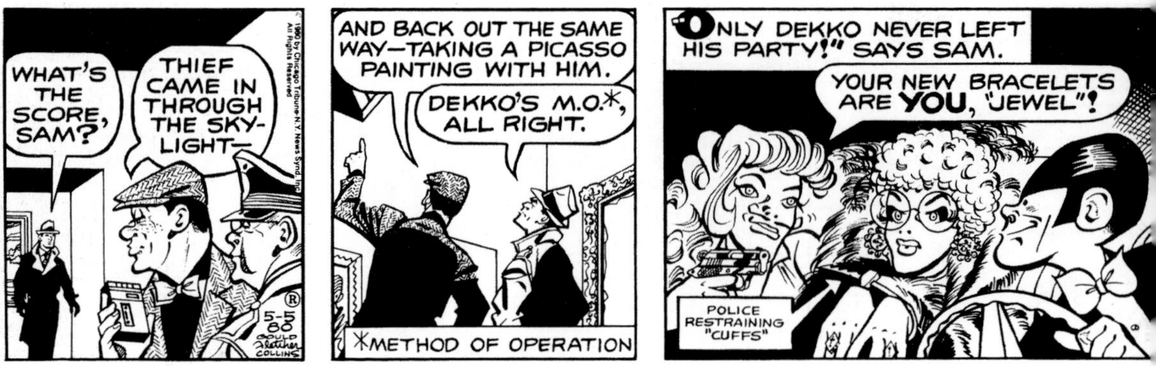
WHAT'S THE SCORE, SAM?
THIEF CAME IN THROUGH THE SKY-LIGHT—
AND BACK OUT THE SAME WAY—TAKING A PICASSO PAINTING WITH HIM.
DEKKO'S M.O.*, ALL RIGHT.
*METHOD OF OPERATION
"ONLY DEKKO NEVER LEFT HIS PARTY!" SAYS SAM.
YOUR NEW BRACELETS ARE YOU, "JEWEL"!
POLICE RESTRAINING "CUFFS"
5-5 80
GOULD Fletcher COLLINS

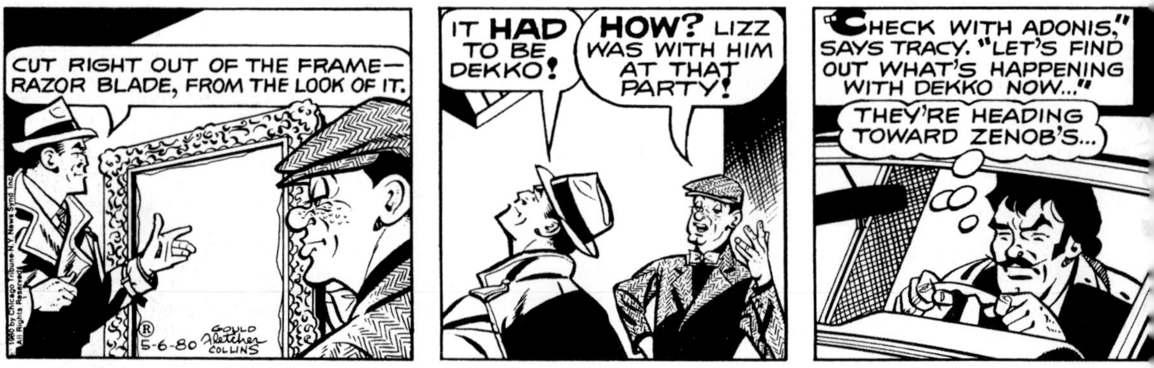
CUT RIGHT OUT OF THE FRAME— RAZOR BLADE, FROM THE LOOK OF IT.
5-6-80
GOULD Fletcher COLLINS
IT HAD TO BE DEKKO!
HOW? LIZZ WAS WITH HIM AT THAT PARTY!
"CHECK WITH ADONIS," SAYS TRACY. "LET'S FIND OUT WHAT'S HAPPENING WITH DEKKO NOW..."
THEY'RE HEADING TOWARD ZENOB'S...

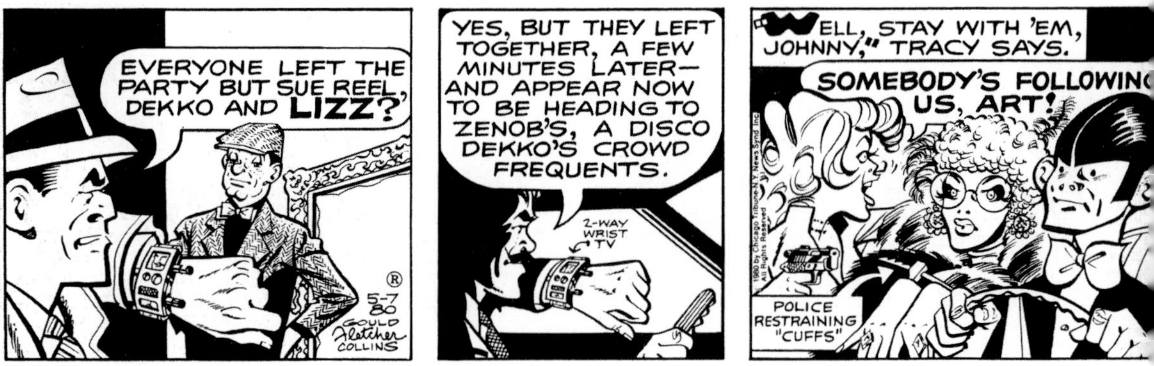
EVERYONE LEFT THE PARTY BUT SUE REEL, DEKKO AND LIZZ?
5-7 80
GOULD Fletcher COLLINS
YES, BUT THEY LEFT TOGETHER, A FEW MINUTES LATER— AND APPEAR NOW TO BE HEADING TO ZENOB'S, A DISCO DEKKO'S CROWD FREQUENTS.
2-WAY WRIST TV
"WELL, STAY WITH 'EM, JOHNNY," TRACY SAYS.
SOMEBODY'S FOLLOWIN
US, ART!
POLICE RESTRAINING "CUFFS"

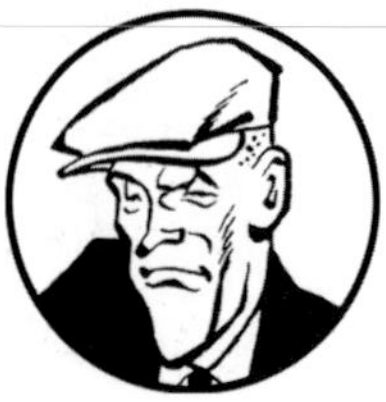

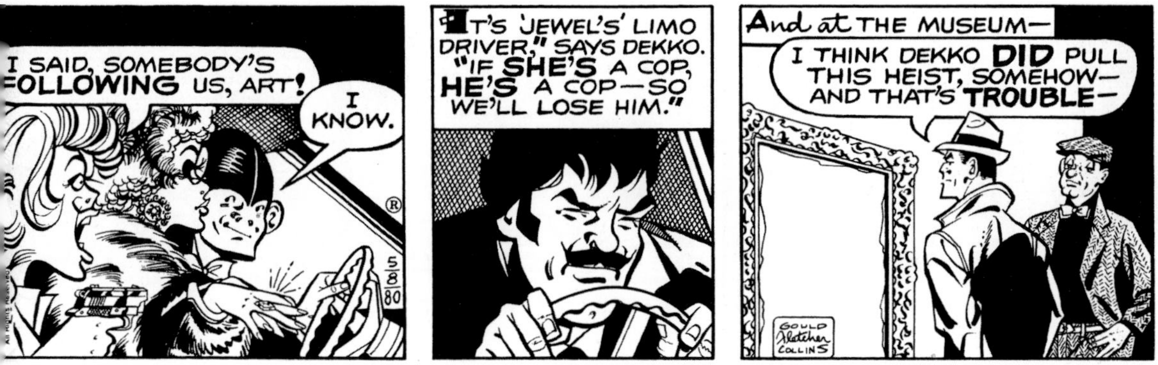
I SAID, SOMEBODY'S FOLLOWING US, ART!
I KNOW.
5/8/80
"IT'S 'JEWEL'S' LIMO DRIVER," SAYS DEKKO. "IF SHE'S A COP, HE'S A COP—SO WE'LL LOSE HIM."
And at THE MUSEUM—
I THINK DEKKO DID PULL THIS HEIST, SOMEHOW—AND THAT'S TROUBLE—
GOULD Fletcher COLLINS

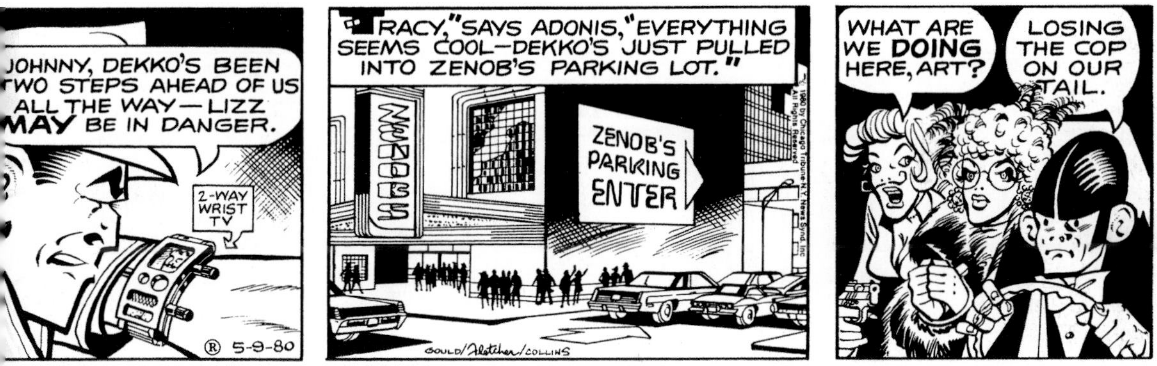
JOHNNY, DEKKO'S BEEN TWO STEPS AHEAD OF US ALL THE WAY—LIZZ MAY BE IN DANGER.
2-WAY WRIST TV
5-9-80
"TRACY," SAYS ADONIS, "EVERYTHING SEEMS COOL—DEKKO'S JUST PULLED INTO ZENOB'S PARKING LOT."
ZENOB'S
ZENOB'S PARKING ENTER
© 1980 by Chicago Tribune-N.Y. News Synd. Inc All Rights Reserved
GOULD/Fletcher/COLLINS
WHAT ARE WE DOING HERE, ART?
LOSING THE COP ON OUR TAIL.

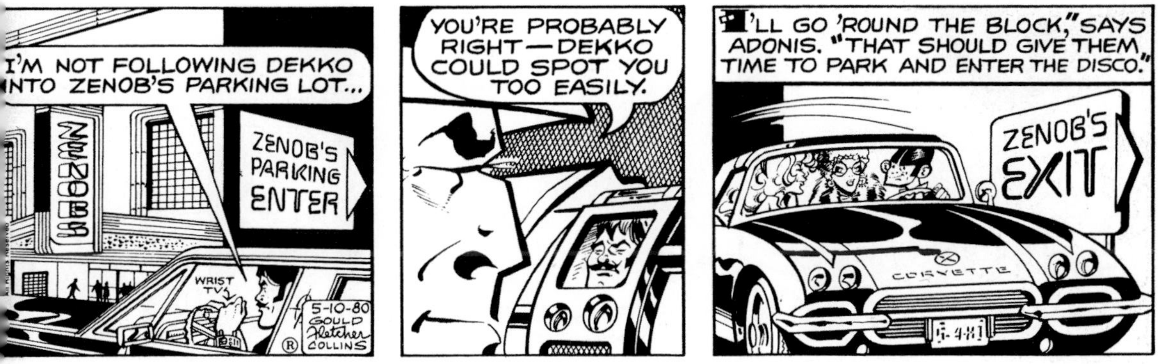
I'M NOT FOLLOWING DEKKO INTO ZENOB'S PARKING LOT...
ZENOB'S
ZENOB'S PARKING ENTER
WRIST TV
5-10-80 GOULD Fletcher COLLINS
YOU'RE PROBABLY RIGHT—DEKKO COULD SPOT YOU TOO EASILY.
"I'LL GO 'ROUND THE BLOCK," SAYS ADONIS. "THAT SHOULD GIVE THEM TIME TO PARK AND ENTER THE DISCO."
ZENOB'S EXIT
CORVETTE

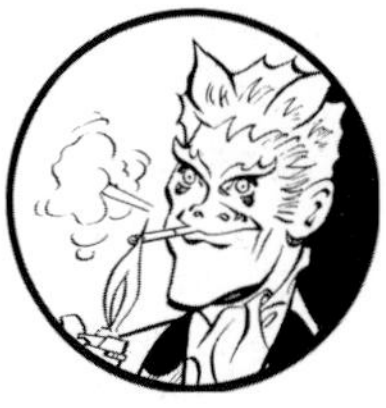

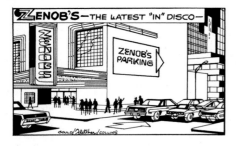

ZENOB'S—THE LATEST "IN" DISCO—
ZENOB'S
ZENOB'S PARKING
GOULD/Fletcher/COLLINS
DEKKO PULLED HIS CAR INTO THEIR PARKING LOT, BUT I DON'T DARE FOLLOW HIM IN...
© 1980 by Chicago Tribune-N.Y. News Synd. Inc All Rights Reserved
AT MUSSIR MUSEUM—
ADONIS IS GOING AROUND THE BLOCK —HE'LL PARK DOWN THE STREET FROM THE DISCO, THEN GO ON IN—

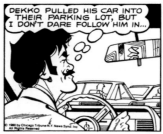

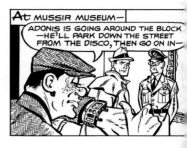

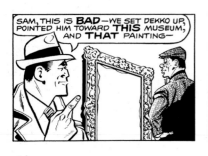

SAM, THIS IS BAD—WE SET DEKKO UP, POINTED HIM TOWARD THIS MUSEUM, AND THAT PAINTING—
BUT HE WAS TWO WEEKS AHEAD OF US—CAUGHT US UNPREPARED IN OUR OWN GAME—
5 11 80
WHICH PUTS LIZZ IN THE THICK OF IT."
WE LOST YOUR "CHAUFFEUR" PAL BACK AT ZENOB'S, "JEWEL"—
AND HE DOESN'T EVEN KNOW YOUR COVER'S BLOWN...
POLICE RESTRAINING "CUFFS"

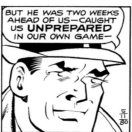

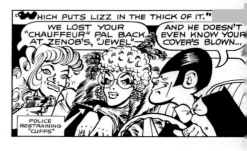

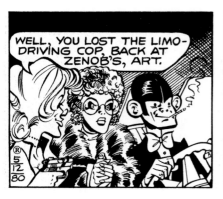

WELL, YOU LOST THE LIMO-DRIVING COP, BACK AT ZENOB'S, ART.
® 5 12 80
ART DEKKO DIDN'T GET WHERE HE IS NOT BEING ABLE TO LOSE A COP—
Meanwhile, ADONIS HAS PARKED, LEAVING HIS CHAUFFEUR'S CAP AND JACKET BEHIND—
SORRY, PAL—NOT JUST ANYBODY GETS IN AT ZENOB'S!

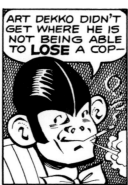

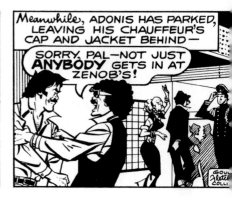

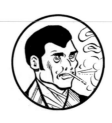

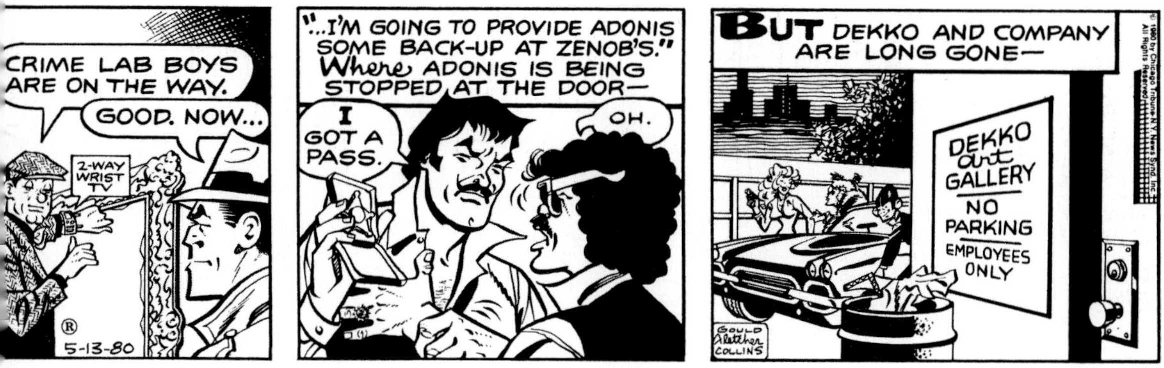

CRIME LAB BOYS ARE ON THE WAY.
GOOD. NOW...
2-WAY WRIST TV
5-13-80
"...I'M GOING TO PROVIDE ADONIS SOME BACK-UP AT ZENOB'S." Where ADONIS IS BEING STOPPED AT THE DOOR—
I GOT A PASS.
OH.
BUT DEKKO AND COMPANY ARE LONG GONE—
DEKKO Art GALLERY
NO PARKING
EMPLOYEES ONLY
GOULD Fletcher COLLINS
© 1980 by Chicago Tribune-N.Y. News Synd. Inc. All Rights Reserved

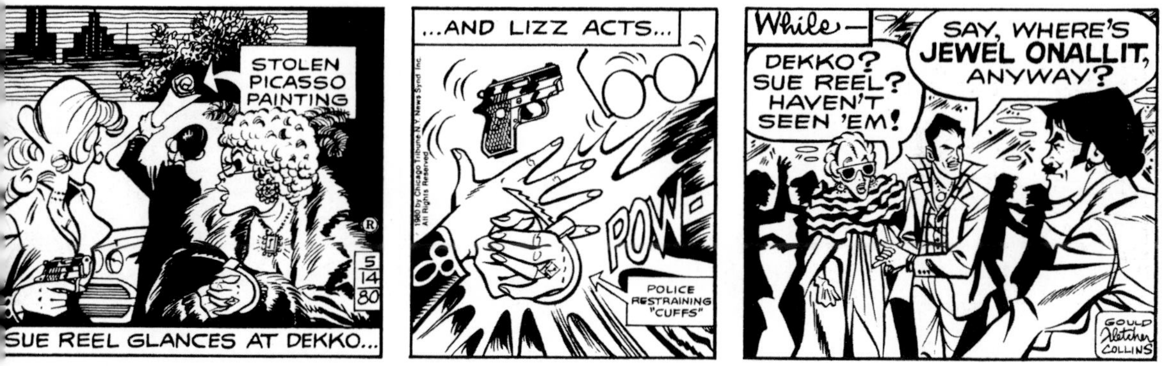

STOLEN PICASSO PAINTING
5 14 80
SUE REEL GLANCES AT DEKKO...
...AND LIZZ ACTS...
© 1980 by Chicago Tribune-N.Y. News Synd. Inc. All Rights Reserved
POW
POLICE RESTRAINING "CUFFS"
While—
DEKKO? SUE REEL? HAVEN'T SEEN 'EM!
SAY, WHERE'S JEWEL ONALLIT, ANYWAY?
GOULD Fletcher COLLINS

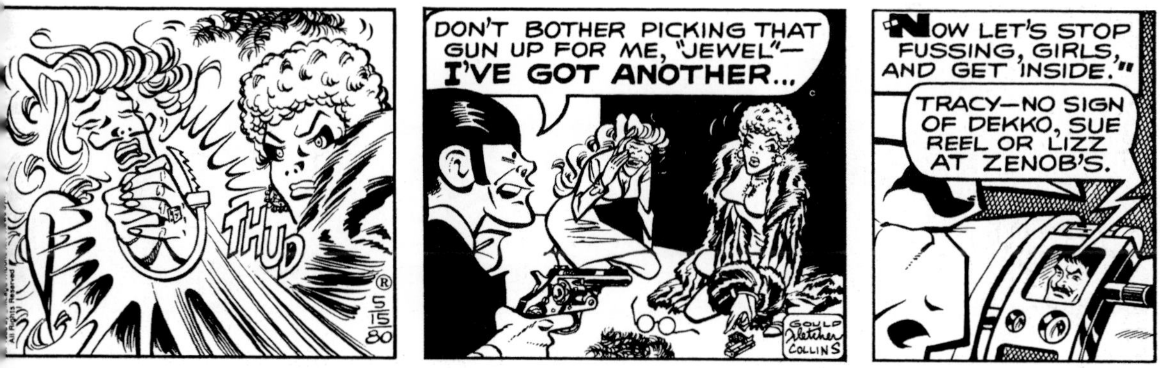

THUD
5 15 80
DON'T BOTHER PICKING THAT GUN UP FOR ME, "JEWEL"— I'VE GOT ANOTHER...
GOULD Fletcher COLLINS
"NOW LET'S STOP FUSSING, GIRLS, AND GET INSIDE."
TRACY—NO SIGN OF DEKKO, SUE REEL OR LIZZ AT ZENOB'S.

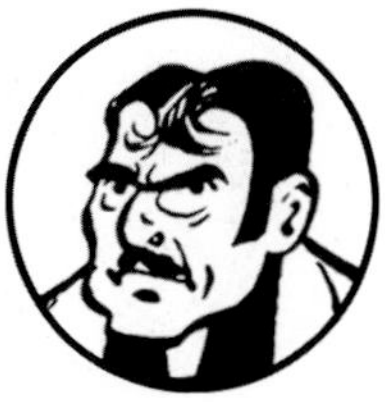

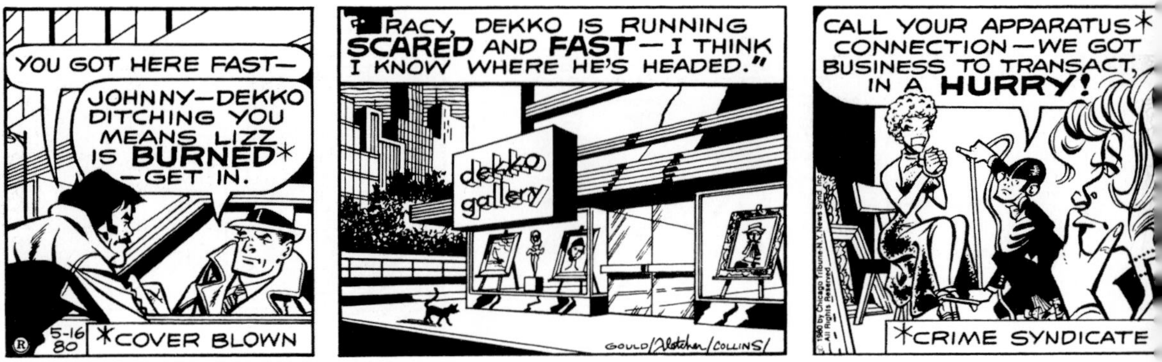
YOU GOT HERE FAST—
JOHNNY—DEKKO DITCHING YOU MEANS LIZZ IS BURNED*—GET IN.
5-16 80
*COVER BLOWN
"TRACY, DEKKO IS RUNNING SCARED AND FAST—I THINK I KNOW WHERE HE'S HEADED."
dekko gallery
GOULD/Fletcher/COLLINS/
CALL YOUR APPARATUS* CONNECTION—WE GOT BUSINESS TO TRANSACT, IN A HURRY!
© 1980 by Chicago Tribune-N.Y. News Synd. Inc. All Rights Reserved
*CRIME SYNDICATE

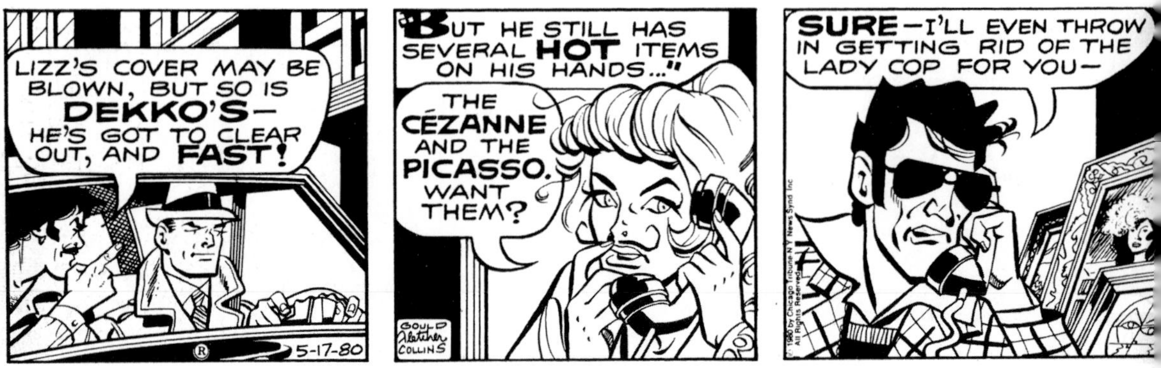
LIZZ'S COVER MAY BE BLOWN, BUT SO IS DEKKO'S—HE'S GOT TO CLEAR OUT, AND FAST!
5-17-80
"BUT HE STILL HAS SEVERAL HOT ITEMS ON HIS HANDS..."
THE CÉZANNE AND THE PICASSO. WANT THEM?
GOULD Fletcher COLLINS
SURE—I'LL EVEN THROW IN GETTING RID OF THE LADY COP FOR YOU—
© 1980 by Chicago Tribune-N.Y. News Synd. Inc. All Rights Reserved

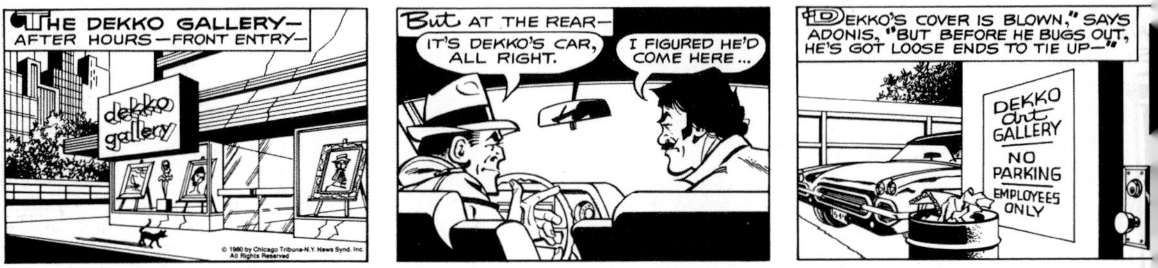
THE DEKKO GALLERY—AFTER HOURS—FRONT ENTRY—
dekko gallery
© 1980 by Chicago Tribune-N.Y. News Synd. Inc. All Rights Reserved
But AT THE REAR—
IT'S DEKKO'S CAR, ALL RIGHT.
I FIGURED HE'D COME HERE...
"DEKKO'S COVER IS BLOWN," SAYS ADONIS, "BUT BEFORE HE BUGS OUT, HE'S GOT LOOSE ENDS TO TIE UP—"
DEKKO art GALLERY
NO PARKING
EMPLOYEES ONLY

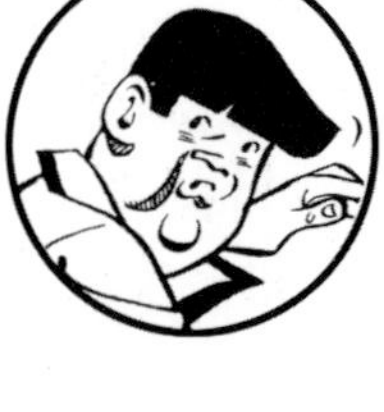

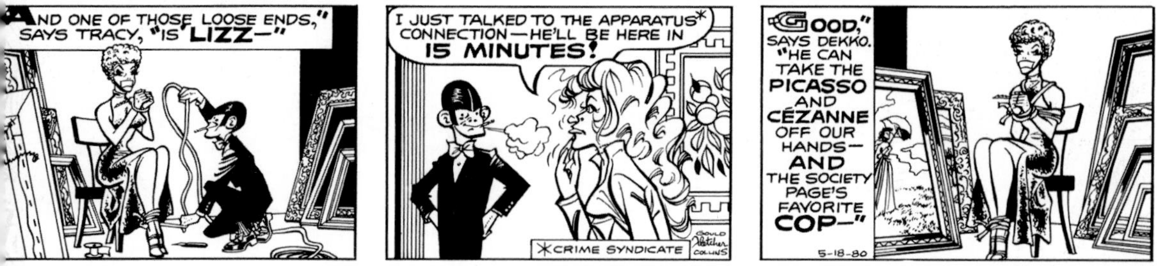
"AND ONE OF THOSE LOOSE ENDS," SAYS TRACY, "IS "LIZZ—"
I JUST TALKED TO THE APPARATUS* CONNECTION—HE'LL BE HERE IN 15 MINUTES!
*CRIME SYNDICATE
GOULD Fletcher COLLINS
"GOOD," SAYS DEKKO. "HE CAN TAKE THE PICASSO AND CÉZANNE OFF OUR HANDS—AND THE SOCIETY PAGE'S FAVORITE COP—"
5-18-80

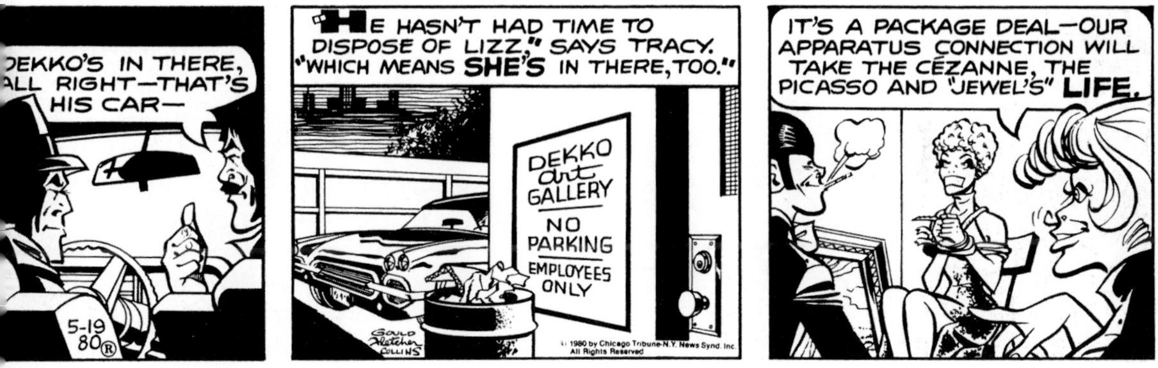
EKKO'S IN THERE, LL RIGHT—THAT'S HIS CAR—
5-19 80 ®
"HE HASN'T HAD TIME TO DISPOSE OF LIZZ," SAYS TRACY. "WHICH MEANS SHE'S IN THERE, TOO."
DEKKO Art GALLERY
NO PARKING
EMPLOYEES ONLY
GOULD Fletcher COLLINS
© 1980 by Chicago Tribune-N.Y. News Synd. Inc. All Rights Reserved
IT'S A PACKAGE DEAL—OUR APPARATUS CONNECTION WILL TAKE THE CÉZANNE, THE PICASSO AND "JEWEL'S" LIFE.

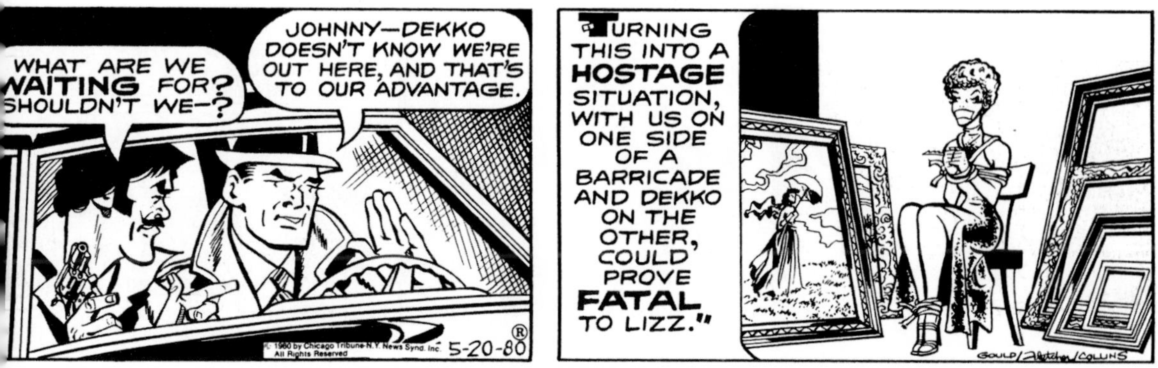
WHAT ARE WE AITING FOR? HOULDN'T WE—?
JOHNNY—DEKKO DOESN'T KNOW WE'RE OUT HERE, AND THAT'S TO OUR ADVANTAGE.
© 1980 by Chicago Tribune-N.Y. News Synd. Inc. All Rights Reserved
5-20-80 ®
"TURNING THIS INTO A HOSTAGE SITUATION, WITH US ON ONE SIDE OF A BARRICADE AND DEKKO ON THE OTHER, COULD PROVE FATAL TO LIZZ."
GOULD/Fletcher/COLLINS

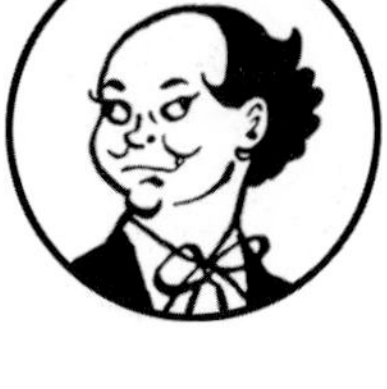

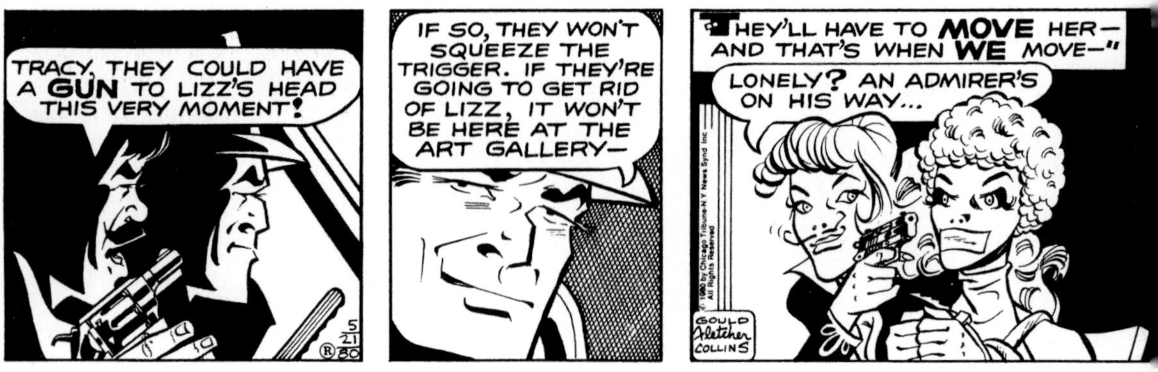
TRACY, THEY COULD HAVE A GUN TO LIZZ'S HEAD THIS VERY MOMENT!
IF SO, THEY WON'T SQUEEZE THE TRIGGER. IF THEY'RE GOING TO GET RID OF LIZZ, IT WON'T BE HERE AT THE ART GALLERY—
"THEY'LL HAVE TO MOVE HER— AND THAT'S WHEN WE MOVE—"
LONELY? AN ADMIRER'S ON HIS WAY...
© 1980 by Chicago Tribune-N.Y. News Synd. Inc. All Rights Reserved
GOULD Fletcher COLLINS
5/21/80

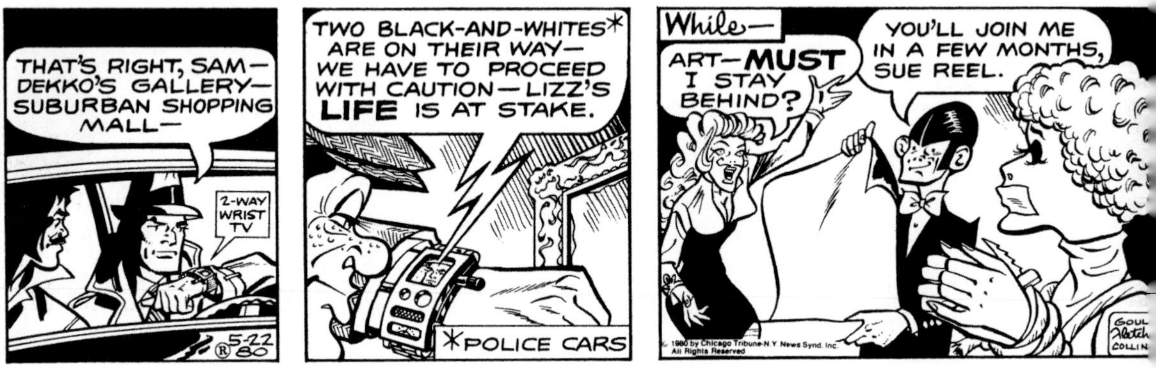
THAT'S RIGHT, SAM— DEKKO'S GALLERY— SUBURBAN SHOPPING MALL—
2-WAY WRIST TV
5-22-80
TWO BLACK-AND-WHITES* ARE ON THEIR WAY— WE HAVE TO PROCEED WITH CAUTION—LIZZ'S LIFE IS AT STAKE.
*POLICE CARS
While—
ART—MUST I STAY BEHIND?
YOU'LL JOIN ME IN A FEW MONTHS, SUE REEL.
© 1980 by Chicago Tribune-N.Y. News Synd. Inc. All Rights Reserved

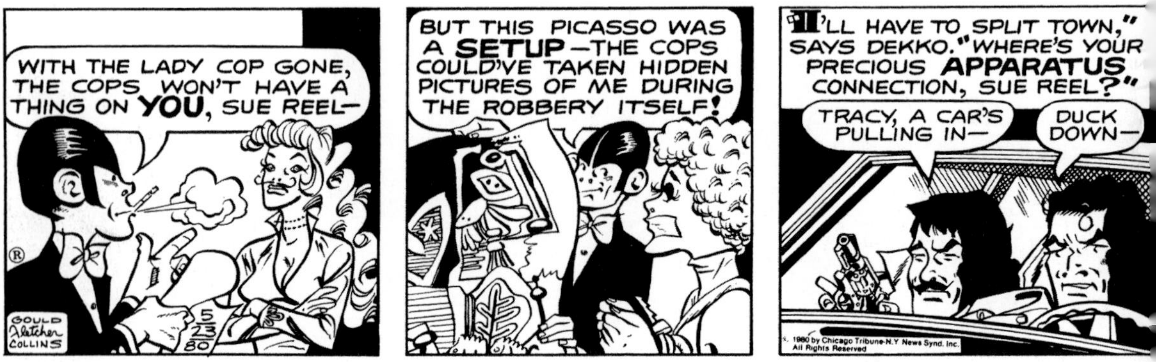
WITH THE LADY COP GONE, THE COPS WON'T HAVE A THING ON YOU, SUE REEL—
GOULD Fletcher COLLINS
5/23/80
BUT THIS PICASSO WAS A SETUP—THE COPS COULD'VE TAKEN HIDDEN PICTURES OF ME DURING THE ROBBERY ITSELF!
"I'LL HAVE TO SPLIT TOWN," SAYS DEKKO. "WHERE'S YOUR PRECIOUS APPARATUS CONNECTION, SUE REEL?"
TRACY, A CAR'S PULLING IN—
DUCK DOWN—
© 1980 by Chicago Tribune-N.Y. News Synd. Inc. All Rights Reserved

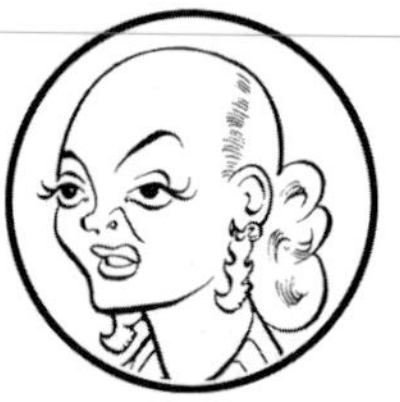

THINK HE
POTTED US, TRACY?
NOT IN THIS UNMARKED CAR...
5/24 ®/80
"RECOGNIZE HIM?" ASKS TRACY. "I SURE DO," SAYS ADONIS.
© 1980 by Chicago Tribune-N.Y. News Synd. Inc. All Rights Reserved
"HE'S A FORMER APPARATUS HIT MAN WHO GOT 'RESPECTABLE'—FENCING STOLEN ART."
DEKK
KNOCK
KNOCK
GOULD Fletcher COLLINS

HE APPARATUS CONNECTION
RRIVES AT the DEKKO GALLERY—
IT'S ABOUT TIME!
COME ON IN.
IN THE SHOPPING MALL PARKING LOT, ACROSS THE WAY—
HE DIDN'T NOTICE US.
HERE COMES ANOTHER CAR—I THINK IT'S SAM...
Inside—
HERE'S YOUR $750,000.
HERE'S YOUR CÉZANNE AND PICASSO...
BARGAIN DAY.

ND THIS WORK OF ART APPEARS TO BE A FORGERY!
DON'T DO IT HERE—TAKE HER OUT—
GOULD Fletcher COLLINS
5/25/80
And OUTSIDE—
DID I MISS ANYTHING?
AN APPARATUS BOY JUST WENT IN—
TAKE THE BACK—I'M COVERING THE FRONT—

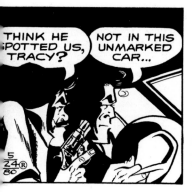

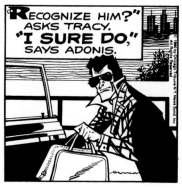

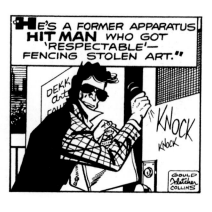

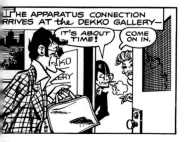

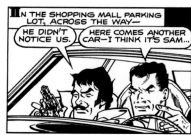

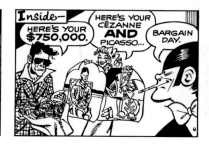

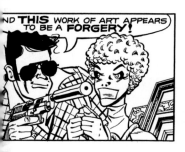

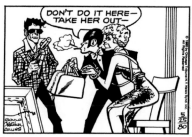

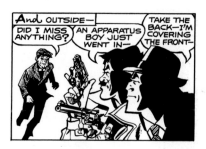

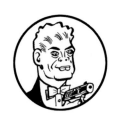

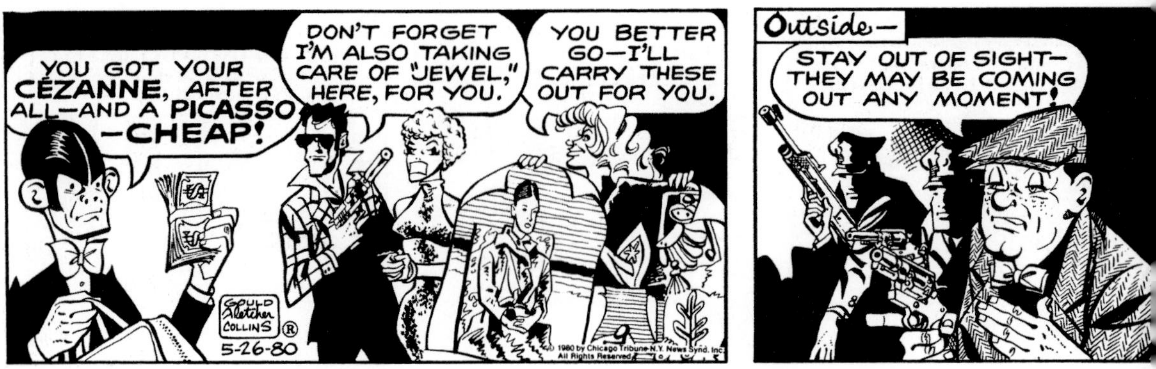
YOU GOT YOUR CÉZANNE, AFTER ALL—AND A PICASSO —CHEAP!
DON'T FORGET I'M ALSO TAKING CARE OF "JEWEL," HERE, FOR YOU.
YOU BETTER GO—I'LL CARRY THESE OUT FOR YOU.
GOULD Fletcher COLLINS ®
5-26-80
© 1980 by Chicago Tribune-N.Y. News Synd. Inc. All Rights Reserved
Outside—
STAY OUT OF SIGHT— THEY MAY BE COMING OUT ANY MOMENT!

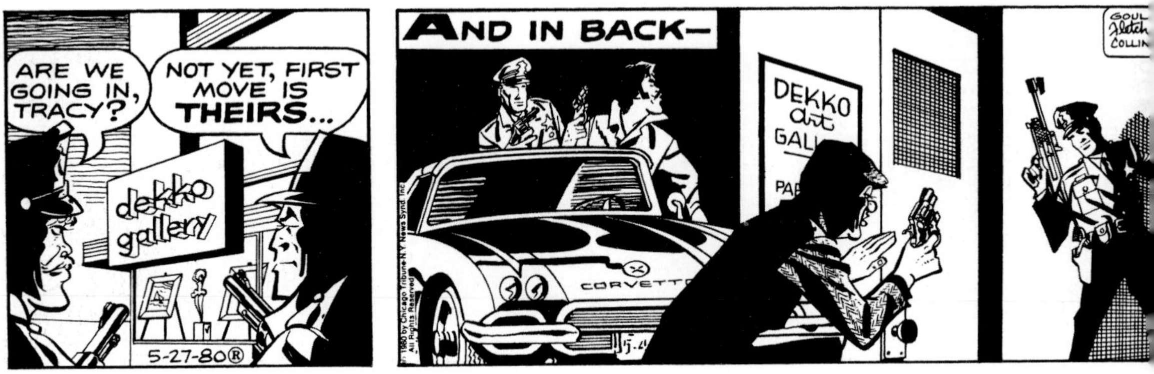
ARE WE GOING IN, TRACY?
NOT YET, FIRST MOVE IS THEIRS...
dekko gallery
5-27-80®
AND IN BACK—
© 1980 by Chicago Tribune-N.Y. News Synd. Inc. All Rights Reserved
CORVETTE
DEKKO Art GALL
GOULD Fletcher COLLINS

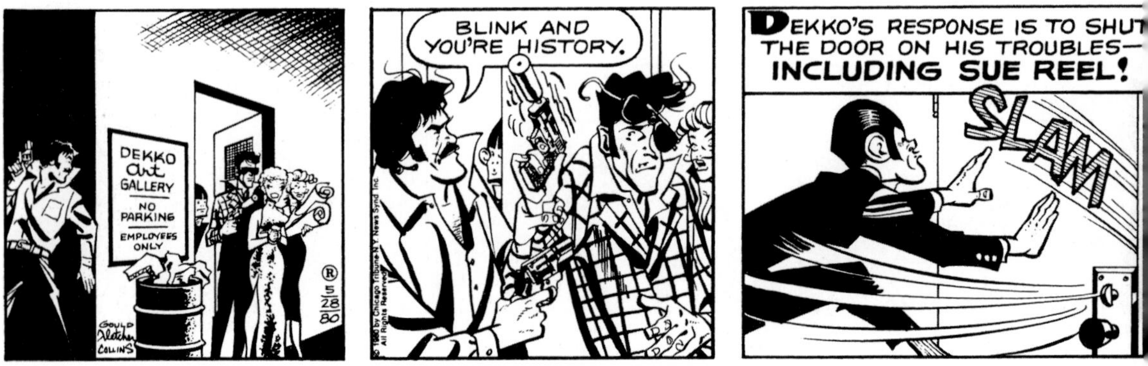
DEKKO Art GALLERY
NO PARKING
EMPLOYEES ONLY
® 5/28/80
GOULD Fletcher COLLINS
BLINK AND YOU'RE HISTORY.
© 1980 by Chicago Tribune-N.Y. News Synd. Inc. All Rights Reserved
DEKKO'S RESPONSE IS TO SHUT THE DOOR ON HIS TROUBLES— INCLUDING SUE REEL!
SLAM

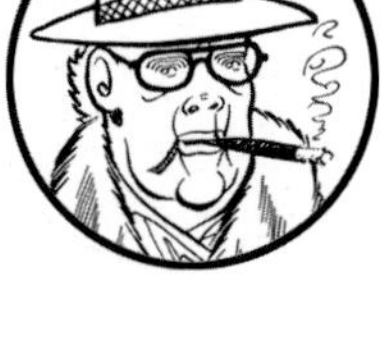

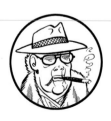

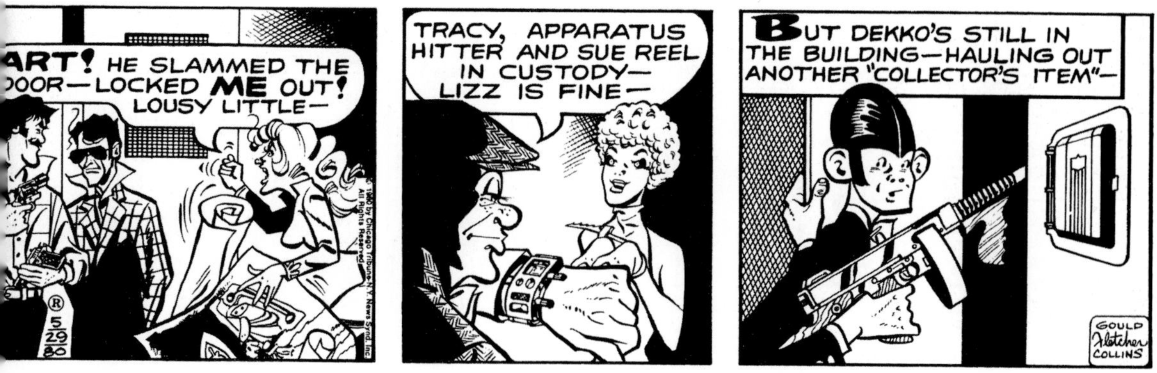
ART! HE SLAMMED THE
DOOR—LOCKED ME OUT!
LOUSY LITTLE—
© 1980 by Chicago Tribune-N.Y. News Synd. Inc.
All Rights Reserved
® 5 29 80
TRACY, APPARATUS HITTER AND SUE REEL IN CUSTODY— LIZZ IS FINE—
BUT DEKKO'S STILL IN THE BUILDING—HAULING OUT ANOTHER "COLLECTOR'S ITEM"—
GOULD Fletcher COLLINS

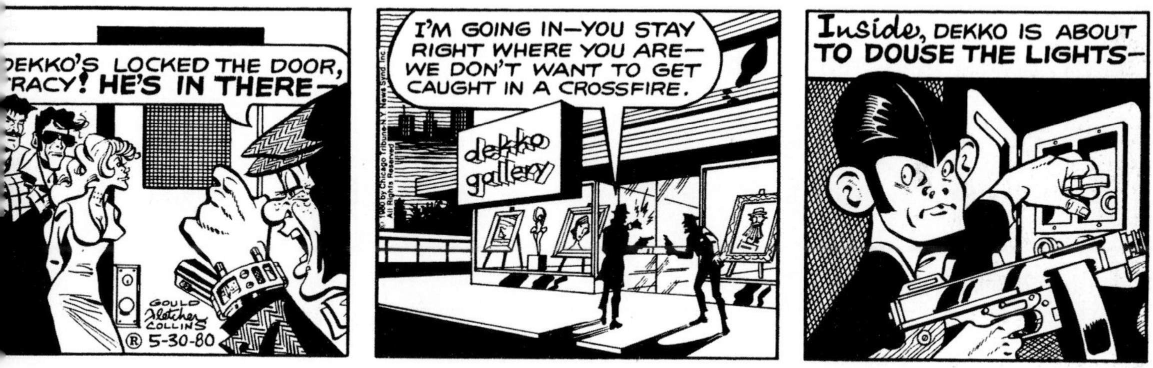
DEKKO'S LOCKED THE DOOR, TRACY! HE'S IN THERE—
GOULD Fletcher COLLINS
® 5-30-80
I'M GOING IN—YOU STAY RIGHT WHERE YOU ARE— WE DON'T WANT TO GET CAUGHT IN A CROSSFIRE.
dekko gallery
© 1980 by Chicago Tribune-N.Y. News Synd. Inc.
All Rights Reserved
Inside, DEKKO IS ABOUT TO DOUSE THE LIGHTS—

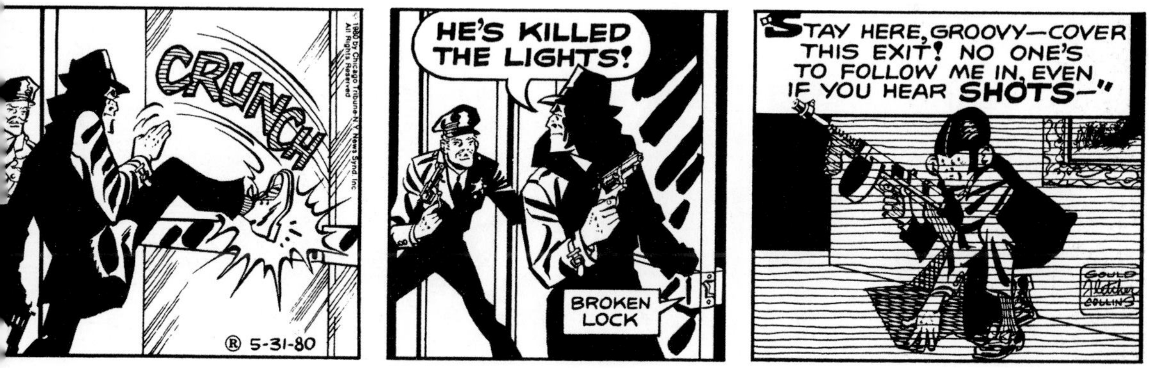
CRUNCH
© 1980 by Chicago Tribune-N.Y. News Synd. Inc.
All Rights Reserved
® 5-31-80
HE'S KILLED THE LIGHTS!
BROKEN LOCK
"STAY HERE, GROOVY—COVER THIS EXIT! NO ONE'S TO FOLLOW ME IN, EVEN IF YOU HEAR SHOTS—"
GOULD Fletcher COLLINS

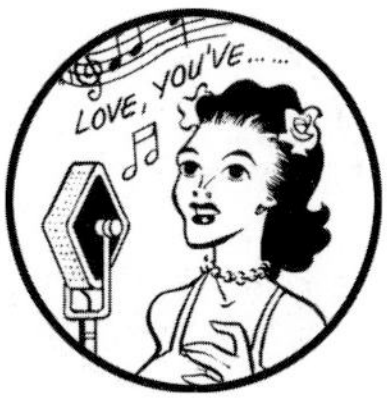
LOVE, YOU'VE.....

LIZZ IS SAFE—THE APPARATUS CONNECTION IS IN CUSTODY, AS IS SUE REEL, But—
DEKKO'S STILL IN THERE!
HE SLAMMED THE DOOR! LOCKED IT! LEFT ME OUT HERE FOR YOU—
WELL, TRACY'S IN THERE WITH HIM, BY NOW—
YES, HE IS—BUT DEKKO TURNED OUT THE LIGHTS IN THE GALLERY—
HE KNOWS HIS WAY AROUND IN HERE, AND I DON'T—

DEKKO! GIVE IT UP! YOU MAY FEEL SAFE IN THE DARK, BUT YOU CAN'T ESCAPE!
THAT'S DICK TRACY...
© 1980 by Chicago Tribune-N.Y. News Synd. Inc. All Rights Reserved
DEKKO FIRES IN THE DIRECTION OF TRACY'S VOICE—
RATTATATATAT--
GOULD/Fletcher/COLLINS
BUT TRACY HAS ALREADY MOVED—
THANKS, DEKKO— THAT'S JUST WHAT I HOPED YOU'D DO...
6-1-80

YOU CAN'T HIDE, DEKKO—
6-2-80
I SHOULDN'T HAVE FIRED AT TRACY—NOW HE KNOWS WHICH PART OF THE ROOM I'M IN...
© 1980 by Chicago Tribune-N.Y. News Synd. Inc. All Rights Reserved
GOULD Fletcher COLLINS

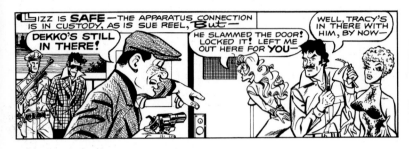

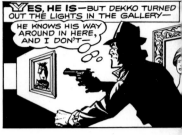

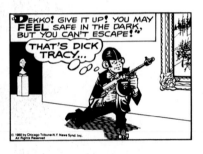

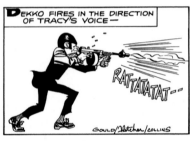

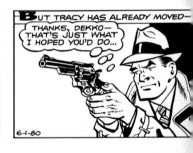

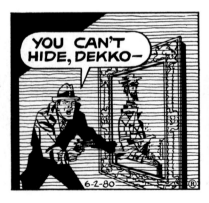

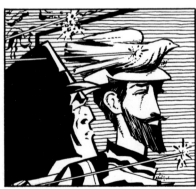

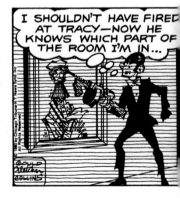

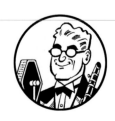

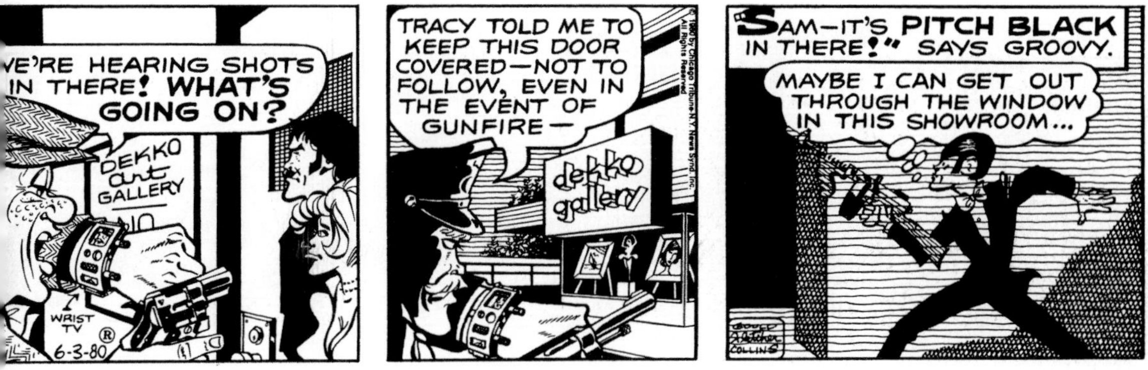
VE'RE HEARING SHOTS IN THERE! WHAT'S GOING ON?
DEKKO Art GALLERY
WRIST TV
6-3-80
TRACY TOLD ME TO KEEP THIS DOOR COVERED—NOT TO FOLLOW, EVEN IN THE EVENT OF GUNFIRE—
dekko gallery
© 1980 by Chicago Tribune-N.Y. News Synd. Inc. All Rights Reserved
SAM—IT'S PITCH BLACK IN THERE!" SAYS GROOVY.
MAYBE I CAN GET OUT THROUGH THE WINDOW IN THIS SHOWROOM...
GOULD Fletcher COLLINS

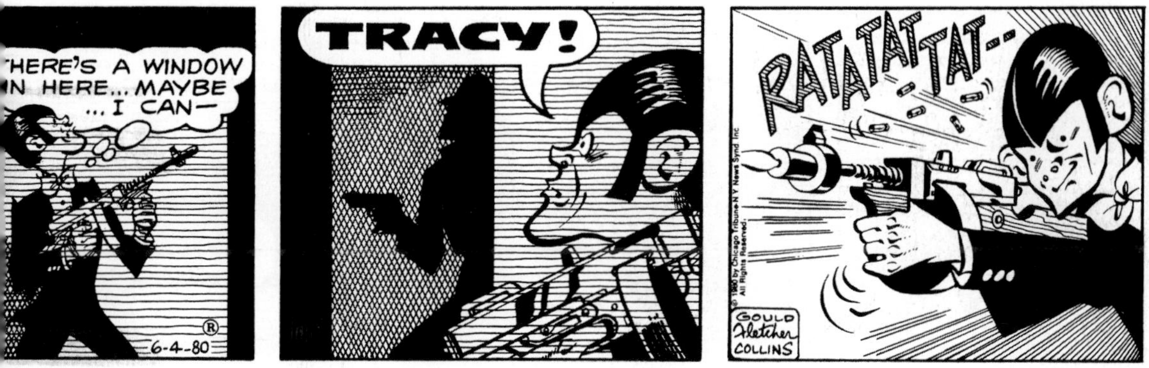
'HERE'S A WINDOW IN HERE... MAYBE ...I CAN—
6-4-80
TRACY!
RATATATTAT--
© 1980 by Chicago Tribune-N.Y. News Synd. Inc. All Rights Reserved.
GOULD Fletcher COLLINS

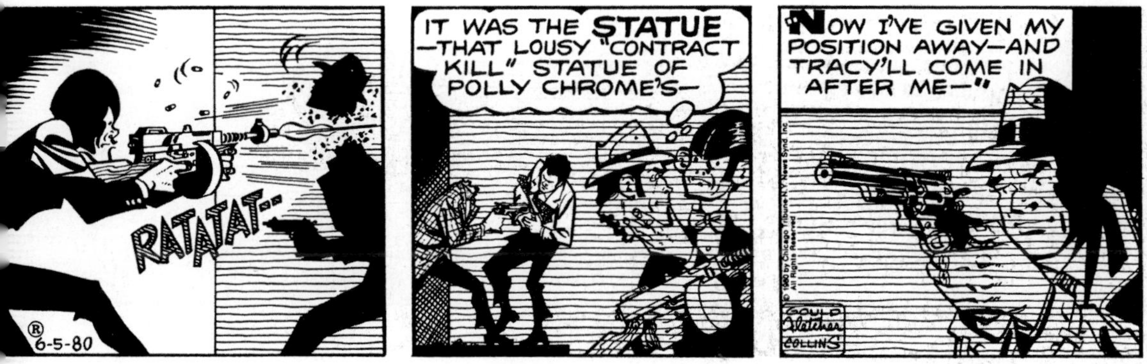
RATATAT--
6-5-80
IT WAS THE STATUE —THAT LOUSY "CONTRACT KILL" STATUE OF POLLY CHROME'S—
NOW I'VE GIVEN MY POSITION AWAY—AND TRACY'LL COME IN AFTER ME—"
© 1980 by Chicago Tribune-N.Y. News Synd. Inc. All Rights Reserved
GOULD Fletcher COLLINS

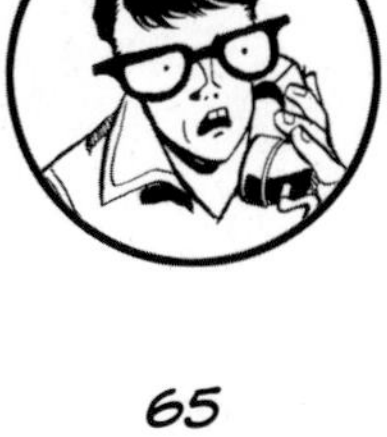

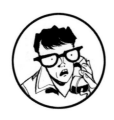

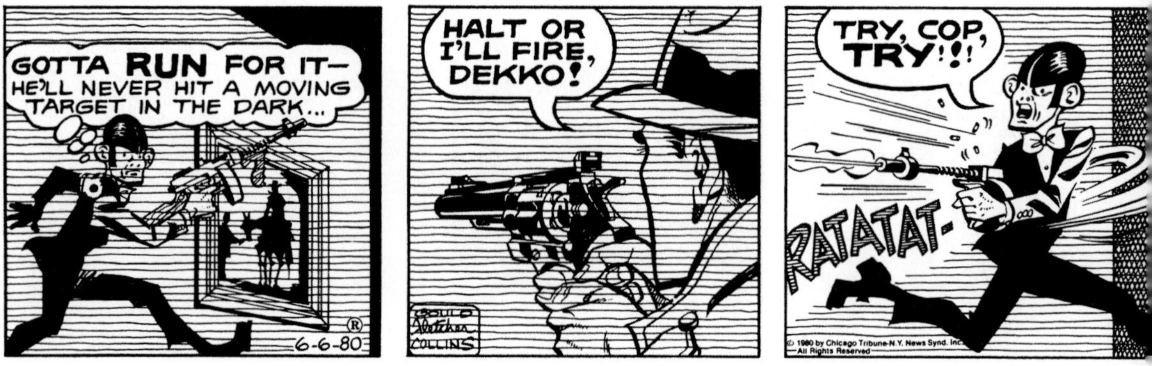
GOTTA RUN FOR IT— HE'LL NEVER HIT A MOVING TARGET IN THE DARK...
6-6-80
HALT OR I'LL FIRE, DEKKO!
GOULD Fletcher COLLINS
TRY, COP, TRY!!!
RATATAT-
© 1980 by Chicago Tribune-N.Y. News Synd. Inc. —All Rights Reserved—

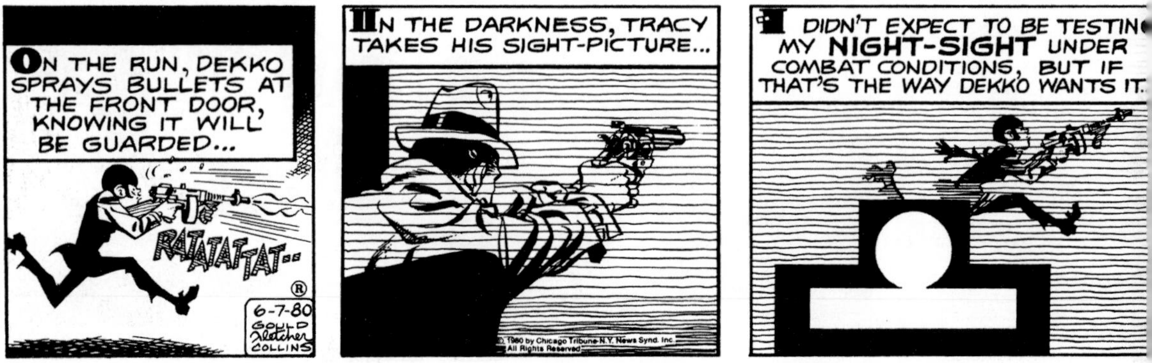
ON THE RUN, DEKKO SPRAYS BULLETS AT THE FRONT DOOR, KNOWING IT WILL BE GUARDED...
RATATATTAT--
6-7-80 GOULD Fletcher COLLINS
IN THE DARKNESS, TRACY TAKES HIS SIGHT-PICTURE...
© 1980 by Chicago Tribune-N.Y. News Synd. Inc. —All Rights Reserved—
I DIDN'T EXPECT TO BE TESTIN MY NIGHT-SIGHT UNDER COMBAT CONDITIONS, BUT IF THAT'S THE WAY DEKKO WANTS IT..

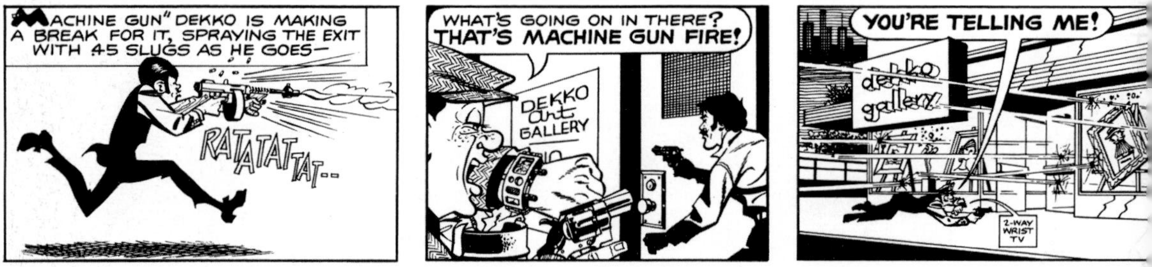
"MACHINE GUN" DEKKO IS MAKING A BREAK FOR IT, SPRAYING THE EXIT WITH 45 SLUGS AS HE GOES—
RATATATTAT--
WHAT'S GOING ON IN THERE? THAT'S MACHINE GUN FIRE!
DEKKO Art GALLERY
YOU'RE TELLING ME!
2-WAY WRIST TV

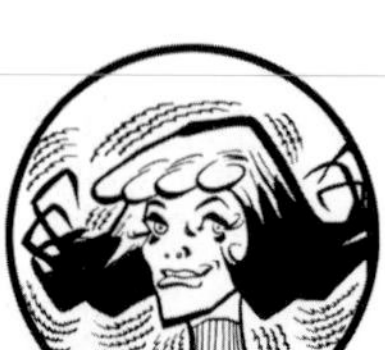

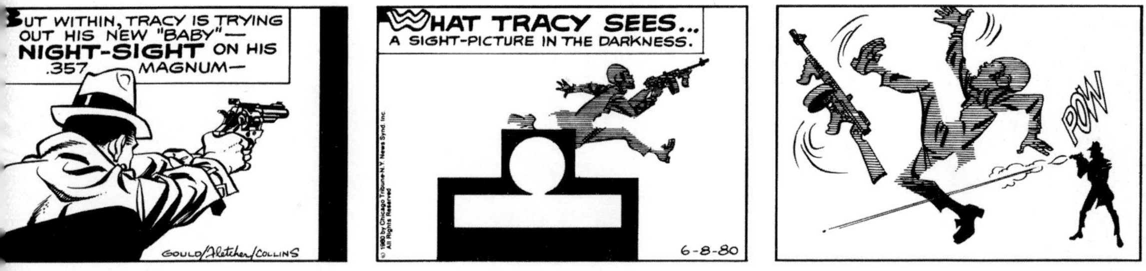
BUT WITHIN, TRACY IS TRYING OUT HIS NEW "BABY"— NIGHT-SIGHT ON HIS .357 MAGNUM—
GOULD/Fletcher/COLLINS
WHAT TRACY SEES... A SIGHT-PICTURE IN THE DARKNESS.
© 1980 by Chicago Tribune-N.Y. News Synd. Inc. All Rights Reserved
6-8-80
POW

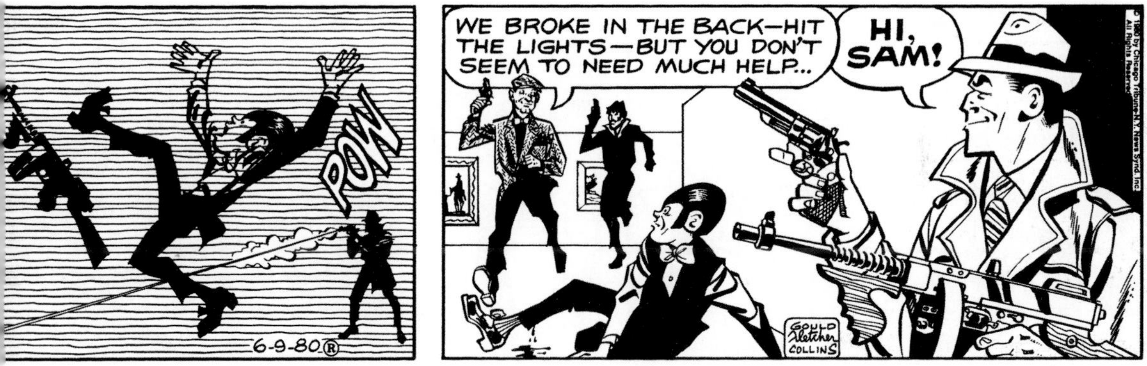
POW
6-9-80 ®
WE BROKE IN THE BACK—HIT THE LIGHTS—BUT YOU DON'T SEEM TO NEED MUCH HELP...
HI, SAM!
© 1980 by Chicago Tribune-N.Y. News Synd. Inc. All Rights Reserved
GOULD Fletcher COLLINS

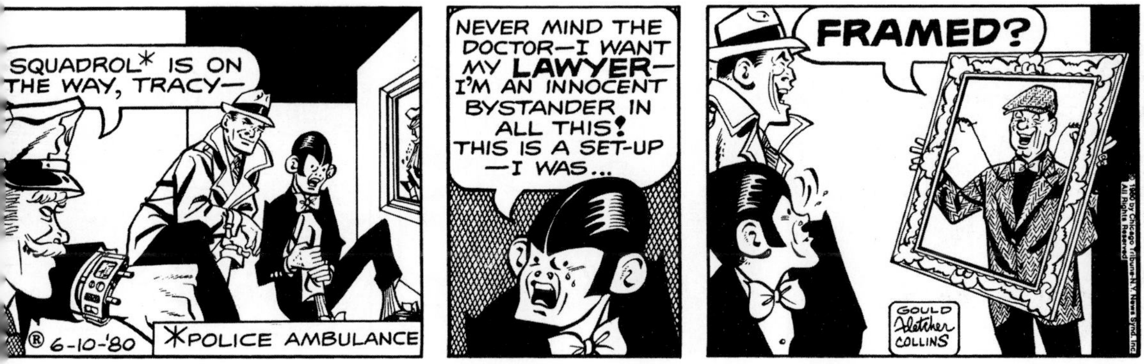
SQUADROL* IS ON THE WAY, TRACY—
® 6-10-'80
*POLICE AMBULANCE
NEVER MIND THE DOCTOR—I WANT MY LAWYER—I'M AN INNOCENT BYSTANDER IN ALL THIS! THIS IS A SET-UP —I WAS...
FRAMED?
© 1980 by Chicago Tribune-N.Y. News Synd. Inc. All Rights Reserved
GOULD Fletcher COLLINS

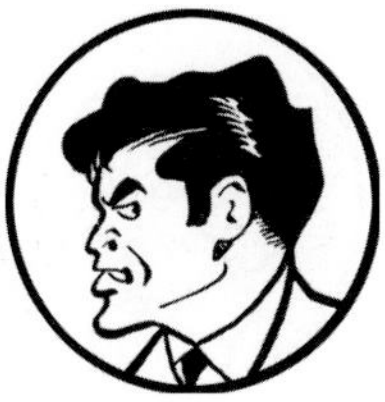

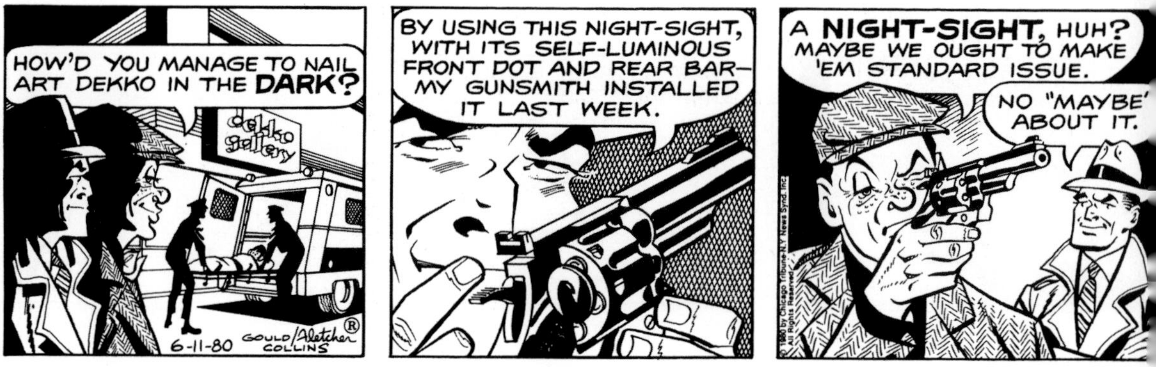
HOW'D YOU MANAGE TO NAIL ART DEKKO IN THE DARK?
dekko gallery
6-11-80
GOULD/Fletcher COLLINS
BY USING THIS NIGHT-SIGHT, WITH ITS SELF-LUMINOUS FRONT DOT AND REAR BAR— MY GUNSMITH INSTALLED IT LAST WEEK.
A NIGHT-SIGHT, HUH? MAYBE WE OUGHT TO MAKE 'EM STANDARD ISSUE.
NO "MAYBE" ABOUT IT.

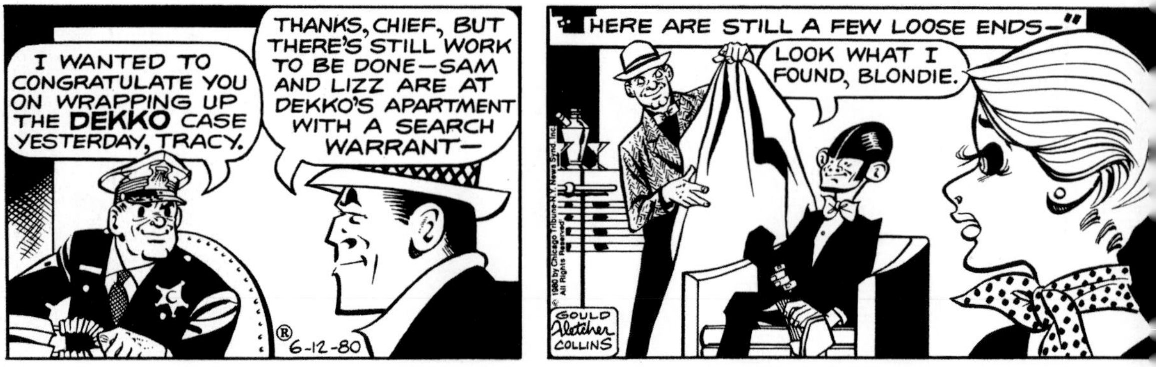
I WANTED TO CONGRATULATE YOU ON WRAPPING UP THE DEKKO CASE YESTERDAY, TRACY.
THANKS, CHIEF, BUT THERE'S STILL WORK TO BE DONE—SAM AND LIZZ ARE AT DEKKO'S APARTMENT WITH A SEARCH WARRANT—
6-12-80
"THERE ARE STILL A FEW LOOSE ENDS—"
LOOK WHAT I FOUND, BLONDIE.
GOULD Fletcher COLLINS

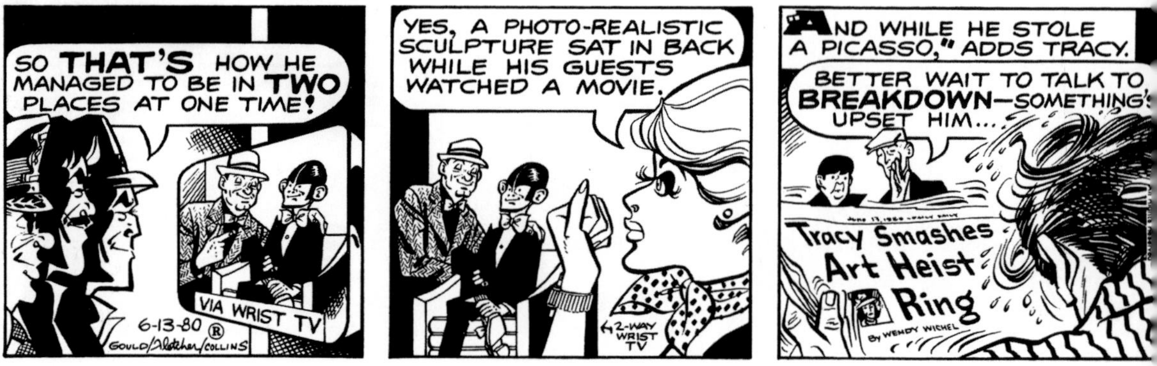
SO THAT'S HOW HE MANAGED TO BE IN TWO PLACES AT ONE TIME!
VIA WRIST TV
6-13-80
GOULD/Fletcher/COLLINS
YES, A PHOTO-REALISTIC SCULPTURE SAT IN BACK WHILE HIS GUESTS WATCHED A MOVIE.
2-WAY WRIST TV
"AND WHILE HE STOLE A PICASSO," ADDS TRACY.
BETTER WAIT TO TALK TO BREAKDOWN—SOMETHING'S UPSET HIM...
Tracy Smashes Art Heist Ring
BY WENDY WICHEL

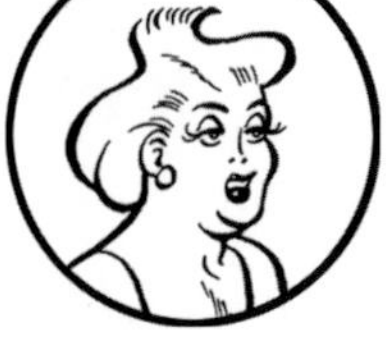

DICK TRACY

THE COLLINS CASEFILES, VOLUME 3

CHAPTER 2
DICK TRACY MEETS BREAKDOWN

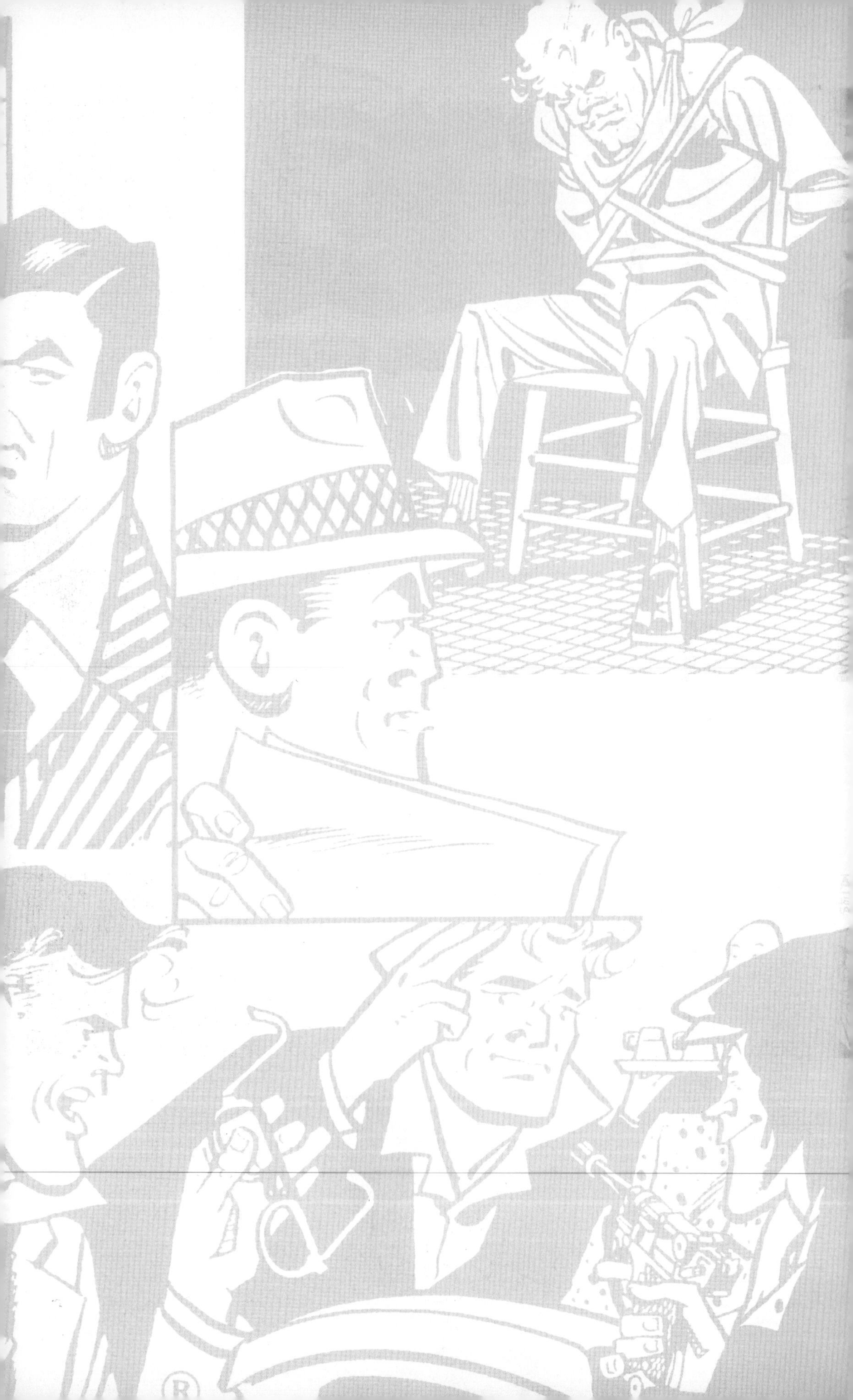

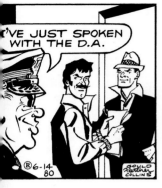

I'VE JUST SPOKEN WITH THE D.A.
®6-14-80
GOULD Fletcher COLLINS
WITH THE APPARATUS CONNECTION TURNING STATE'S EVIDENCE, THE INTERNATIONAL ART HEIST RING DEKKO'S BEEN SELLING TO WILL BE EFFECTIVELY DESTROYED!
"INTERPOL AND SEVERAL OTHER AGENCIES HAVE ALREADY WIRED US THEIR THANKS."
I GOT THE "STUN GUNS," BREAKDOWN.
GOOD.
© 1980 by Chicago Tribune-N.Y. News Synd. Inc. All Rights Reserved

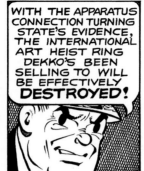

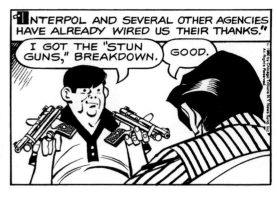

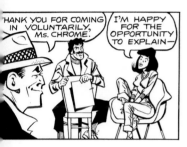

THANK YOU FOR COMING IN VOLUNTARILY, Ms. CHROME.
I'M HAPPY FOR THE OPPORTUNITY TO EXPLAIN—
"I HAD NO IDEA," SAYS POLLY CHROME, "THAT THE PHOTO-REALISTIC SCULPTURE I DID OF DEKKO WOULD BE USED BY HIM AS AN 'ALIBI.'"
FILE CASE #C-73390
GOULD/Fletcher/COLLINS
THANK YOU FOR YOUR STATEMENT, Ms. CHROME —YOU'LL BE CALLED UPON TO TESTIFY—
TRACY— DEKKO WANTS TO TALK TO YOU.
© 1980 by Chicago Tribune-N.Y. News Synd. Inc. All Rights Reserved

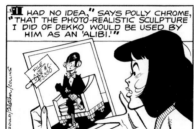

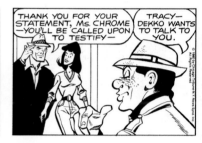

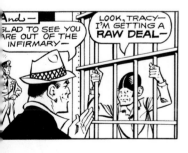

And—
GLAD TO SEE YOU ARE OUT OF THE INFIRMARY—
LOOK, TRACY— I'M GETTING A RAW DEAL—
"IT'S SUE REEL WHO'S THE REAL GUILTY PARTY— LET ME TURN STATE'S EVIDENCE AGAINST HER!"
I'M INNOCENT, I TELL YOU!
ART DEKKO DIDN'T GET WHERE HE IS BY BEING INNOCENT.
6-15-80

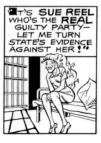

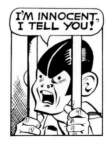

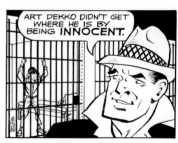

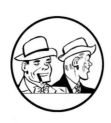

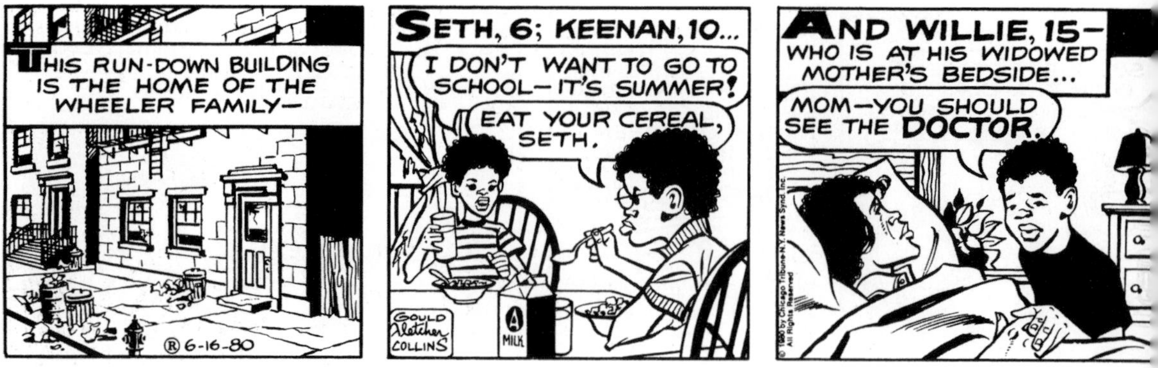
THIS RUN-DOWN BUILDING IS THE HOME OF THE WHEELER FAMILY—
6-16-80
SETH, 6; KEENAN, 10...
I DON'T WANT TO GO TO SCHOOL—IT'S SUMMER!
EAT YOUR CEREAL, SETH.
GOULD Fletcher COLLINS
MILK
AND WILLIE, 15—
WHO IS AT HIS WIDOWED MOTHER'S BEDSIDE...
MOM—YOU SHOULD SEE THE DOCTOR.

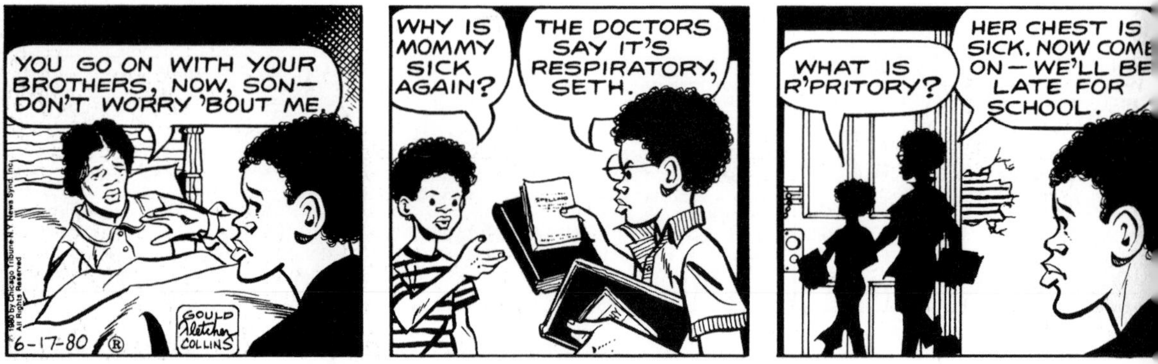
YOU GO ON WITH YOUR BROTHERS, NOW, SON—DON'T WORRY 'BOUT ME.
6-17-80
GOULD Fletcher COLLINS
WHY IS MOMMY SICK AGAIN?
THE DOCTORS SAY IT'S RESPIRATORY, SETH.
WHAT IS R'PRITORY?
HER CHEST IS SICK. NOW COME ON—WE'LL BE LATE FOR SCHOOL.

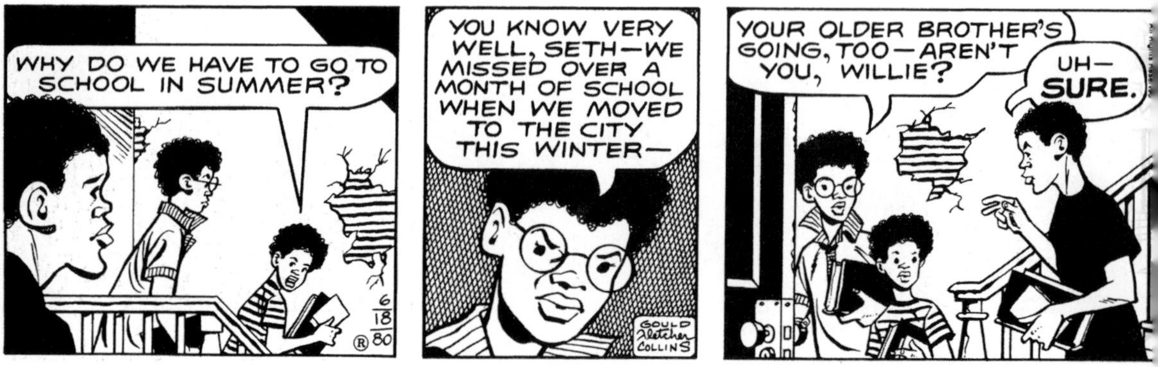
WHY DO WE HAVE TO GO TO SCHOOL IN SUMMER?
6/18/80
YOU KNOW VERY WELL, SETH—WE MISSED OVER A MONTH OF SCHOOL WHEN WE MOVED TO THE CITY THIS WINTER—
GOULD Fletcher COLLINS
YOUR OLDER BROTHER'S GOING, TOO—AREN'T YOU, WILLIE?
UH—SURE.

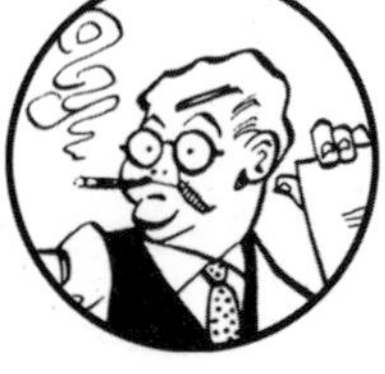

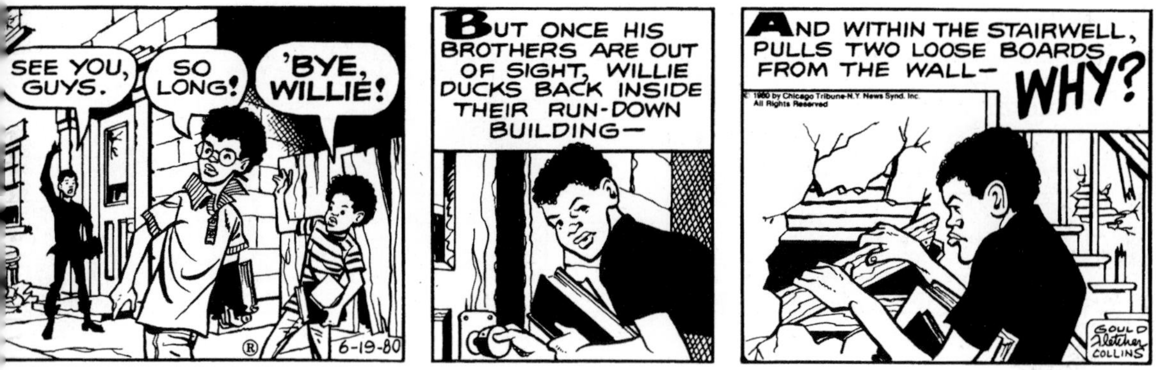
SEE YOU, GUYS.
SO LONG!
'BYE, WILLIE!
6-19-80
BUT ONCE HIS BROTHERS ARE OUT OF SIGHT, WILLIE DUCKS BACK INSIDE THEIR RUN-DOWN BUILDING—
AND WITHIN THE STAIRWELL, PULLS TWO LOOSE BOARDS FROM THE WALL— WHY?
© 1980 by Chicago Tribune-N.Y. News Synd. Inc. All Rights Reserved
GOULD
Fletcher
COLLINS

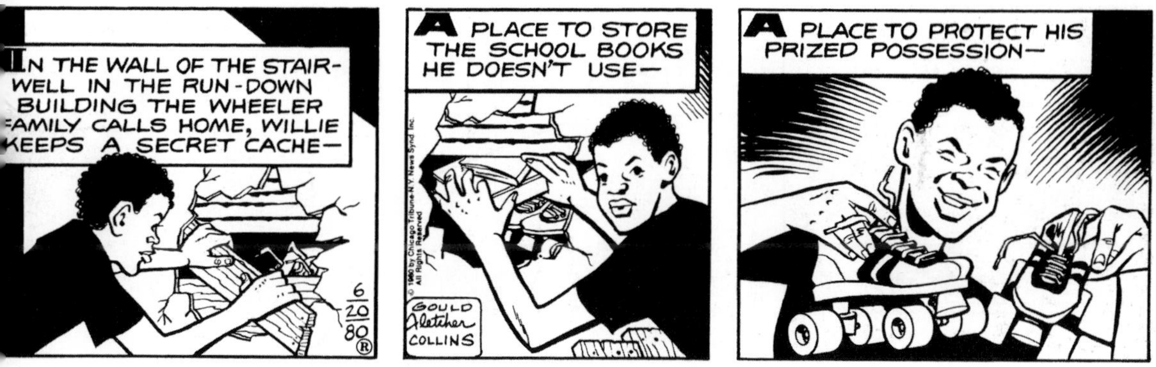
IN THE WALL OF THE STAIRWELL IN THE RUN-DOWN BUILDING THE WHEELER FAMILY CALLS HOME, WILLIE KEEPS A SECRET CACHE—
6 20 80
A PLACE TO STORE THE SCHOOL BOOKS HE DOESN'T USE—
© 1980 by Chicago Tribune-N.Y. News Synd. Inc. All Rights Reserved
GOULD
Fletcher
COLLINS
A PLACE TO PROTECT HIS PRIZED POSSESSION—

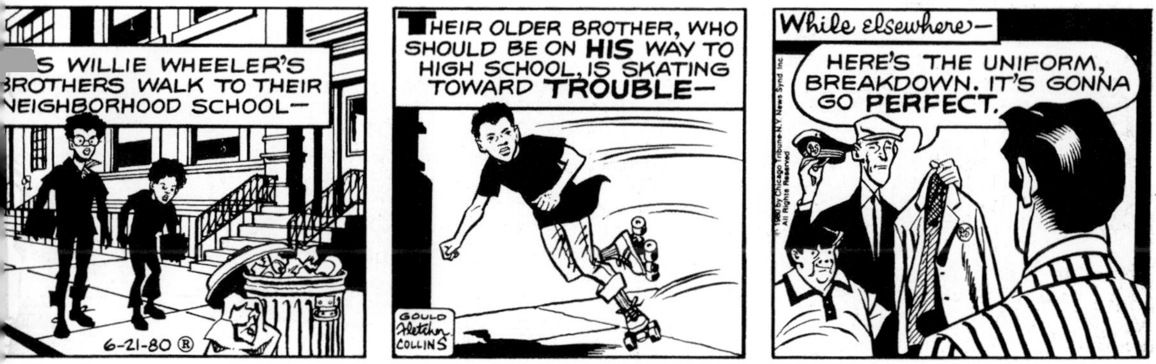
AS WILLIE WHEELER'S BROTHERS WALK TO THEIR NEIGHBORHOOD SCHOOL—
6-21-80
THEIR OLDER BROTHER, WHO SHOULD BE ON HIS WAY TO HIGH SCHOOL, IS SKATING TOWARD TROUBLE—
GOULD
Fletcher
COLLINS
While elsewhere—
© 1980 by Chicago Tribune-N.Y. News Synd. Inc. All Rights Reserved
HERE'S THE UNIFORM, BREAKDOWN. IT'S GONNA GO PERFECT.

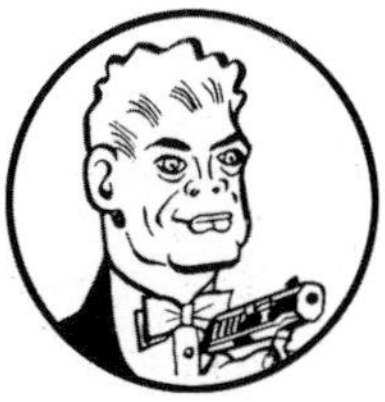

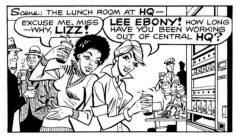

Scene: THE LUNCH ROOM AT HQ—
EXCUSE ME, MISS —WHY, LIZZ!
LEE EBONY! HOW LONG HAVE YOU BEEN WORKING OUT OF CENTRAL HQ?
NOT LONG—TRANSFERRED IN FROM THE 84th. HOW LONG HAVE YOU BEEN A BLONDE?
© 1980 by Chicago Tribune-N.Y. News Synd. Inc.
All Rights Reserved
THIS IS LEFT OVER FROM AN UNDER-COVER ASSIGNMENT—THE ART DEKKO CASE. HAVEN'T DYED IT BACK YET.
I'M WORKING UNDER COVER MYSELF.

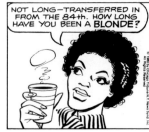

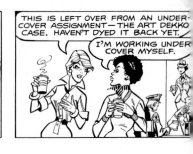

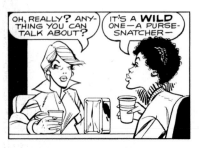

OH, REALLY? ANY-THING YOU CAN TALK ABOUT?
IT'S A WILD ONE—A PURSE-SNATCHER—
"IS THAT ALL?" ASKS LIZZ. "WHAT MAKES A PURSE SNATCHER SO SPECIAL?"
CRIPPLED CREEK
Leather
STONE'S Gifts
"WELL, FOR ONE THING," SAYS LEE, HE'S A ROLLER-SKATING PURSE SNATCHER."
6-22-80
GOULD/Fletcher/COLLINS

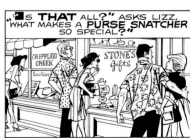

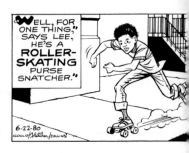

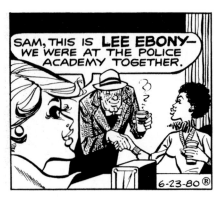

SAM, THIS IS LEE EBONY—WE WERE AT THE POLICE ACADEMY TOGETHER.
6-23-80 ®
THE BOYS FROM THE 84th SAY GOOD THINGS ABOUT YOU, LEE—WORKING OUT OF CENTRAL HQ NOW?
"YES," SAYS LEE. "DOING DECOY DUTY —WE'VE GOT AN UNUSUAL PURSE SNATCHER WE'RE TRYING TO COLLAR."
GOULD
Fletcher
COLLINS

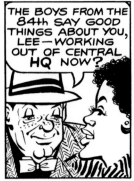

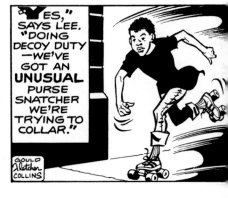

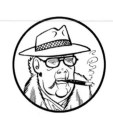

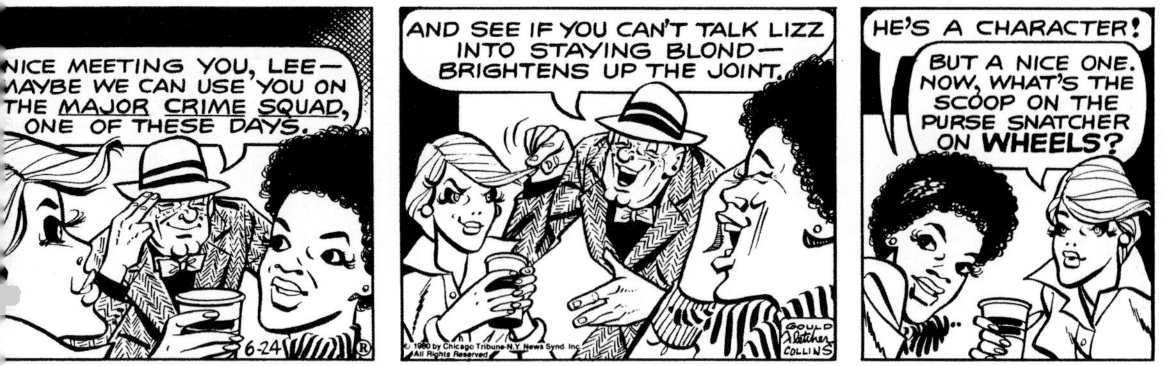
NICE MEETING YOU, LEE—MAYBE WE CAN USE YOU ON THE MAJOR CRIME SQUAD, ONE OF THESE DAYS.
6-24
AND SEE IF YOU CAN'T TALK LIZZ INTO STAYING BLOND—BRIGHTENS UP THE JOINT.
© 1980 by Chicago Tribune-N.Y. News Synd. Inc. All Rights Reserved
GOULD Fletcher COLLINS
HE'S A CHARACTER!
BUT A NICE ONE. NOW, WHAT'S THE SCOOP ON THE PURSE SNATCHER ON WHEELS?

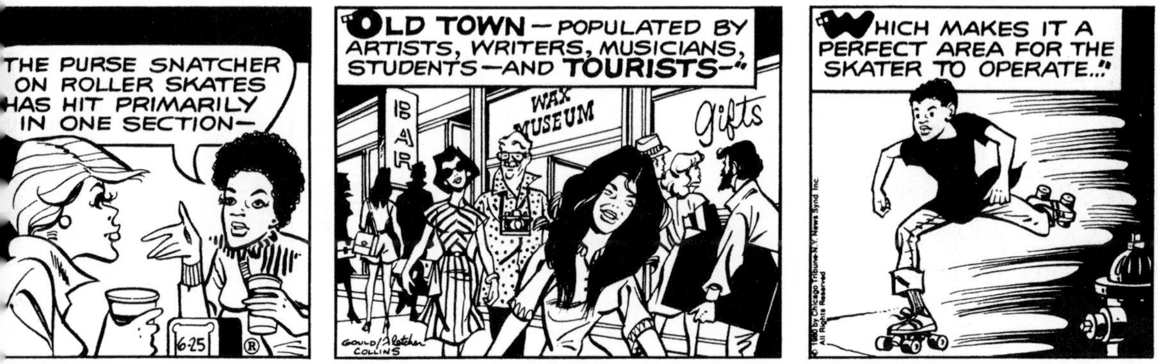
THE PURSE SNATCHER ON ROLLER SKATES HAS HIT PRIMARILY IN ONE SECTION—
6-25
"OLD TOWN—POPULATED BY ARTISTS, WRITERS, MUSICIANS, STUDENTS—AND TOURISTS—
BAR
WAX MUSEUM
Gifts
GOULD/Fletcher COLLINS
"WHICH MAKES IT A PERFECT AREA FOR THE SKATER TO OPERATE..."
© 1980 by Chicago Tribune-N.Y. News Synd. Inc. All Rights Reserved

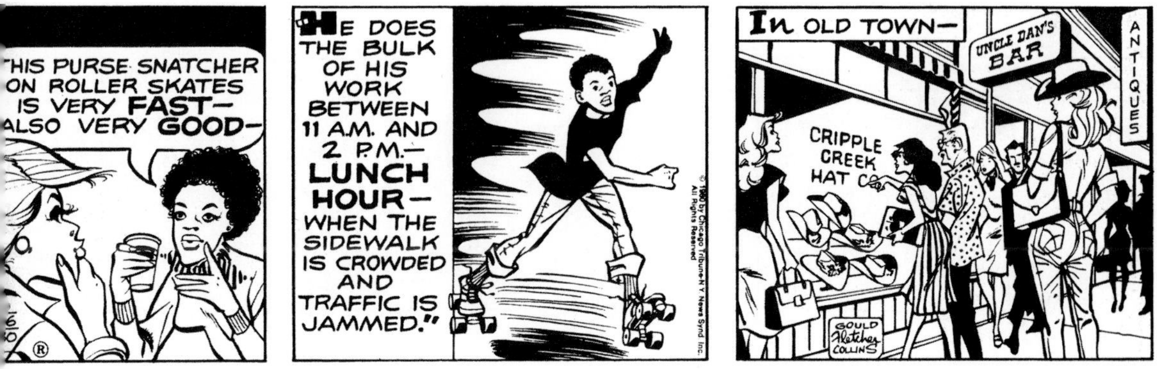
THIS PURSE SNATCHER ON ROLLER SKATES IS VERY FAST—ALSO VERY GOOD—
"HE DOES THE BULK OF HIS WORK BETWEEN 11 A.M. AND 2 P.M.—LUNCH HOUR—WHEN THE SIDEWALK IS CROWDED AND TRAFFIC IS JAMMED."
© 1980 by Chicago Tribune-N.Y. News Synd. Inc. All Rights Reserved
IN OLD TOWN—
UNCLE DAN'S BAR
ANTIQUES
CRIPPLE CREEK HAT CO
GOULD Fletcher COLLINS

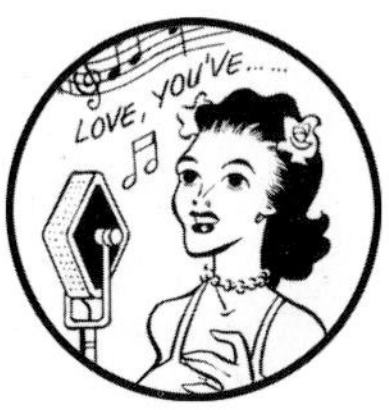
LOVE, YOU'VE.....

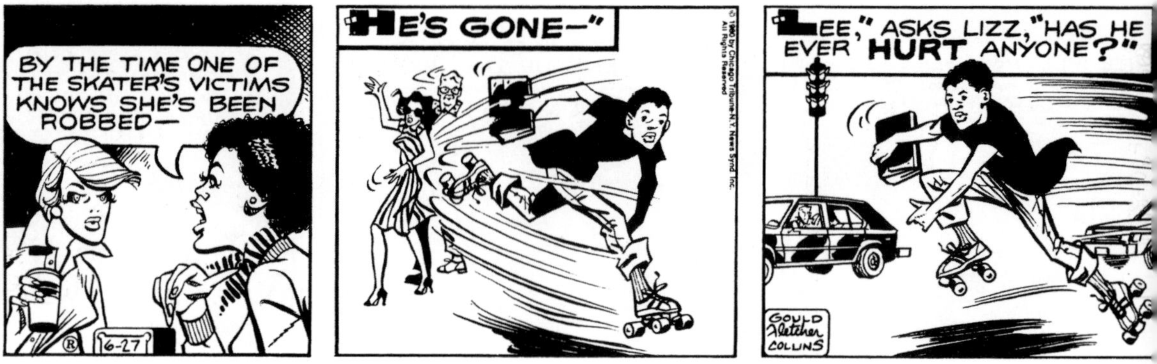

BY THE TIME ONE OF THE SKATER'S VICTIMS KNOWS SHE'S BEEN ROBBED—
6-27
"HE'S GONE—"
© 1980 by Chicago Tribune-N.Y. News Synd. Inc. All Rights Reserved
"LEE," ASKS LIZZ, "HAS HE EVER HURT ANYONE?"
GOULD Fletcher COLLINS

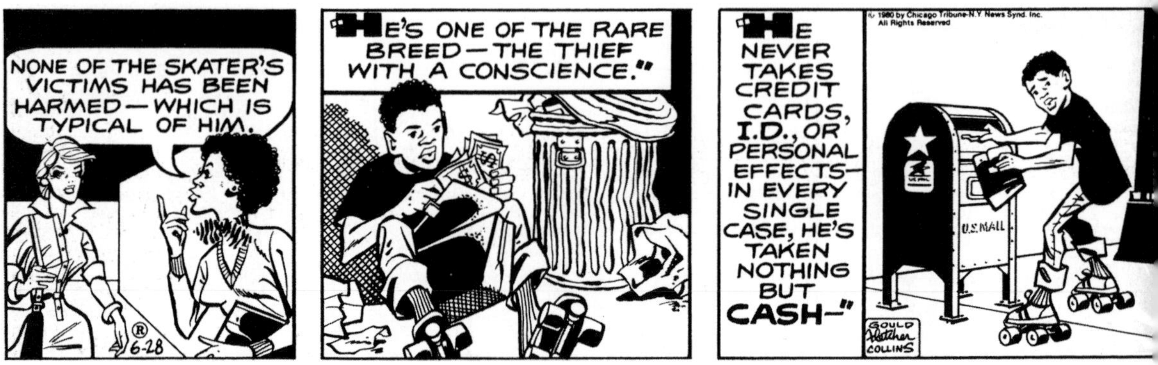

NONE OF THE SKATER'S VICTIMS HAS BEEN HARMED—WHICH IS TYPICAL OF HIM.
6-28
"HE'S ONE OF THE RARE BREED—THE THIEF WITH A CONSCIENCE."
"HE NEVER TAKES CREDIT CARDS, I.D., OR PERSONAL EFFECTS—IN EVERY SINGLE CASE, HE'S TAKEN NOTHING BUT CASH—"
© 1980 by Chicago Tribune-N.Y. News Synd. Inc. All Rights Reserved
U.S. MAIL
GOULD Fletcher COLLINS

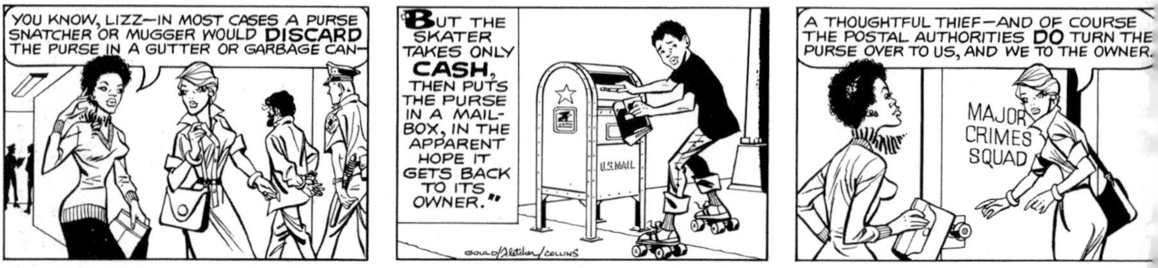

YOU KNOW, LIZZ—IN MOST CASES A PURSE SNATCHER OR MUGGER WOULD DISCARD THE PURSE IN A GUTTER OR GARBAGE CAN—
"BUT THE SKATER TAKES ONLY CASH, THEN PUTS THE PURSE IN A MAIL-BOX, IN THE APPARENT HOPE IT GETS BACK TO ITS OWNER."
U.S. MAIL
GOULD/Fletcher/COLLINS
A THOUGHTFUL THIEF—AND OF COURSE THE POSTAL AUTHORITIES DO TURN THE PURSE OVER TO US, AND WE TO THE OWNER.
MAJOR CRIMES SQUAD

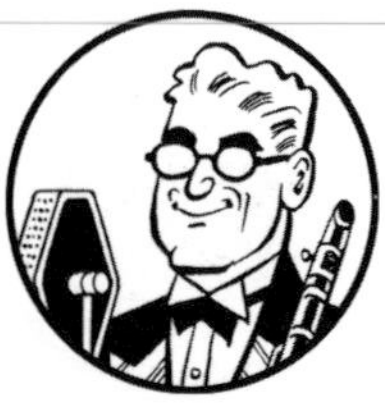

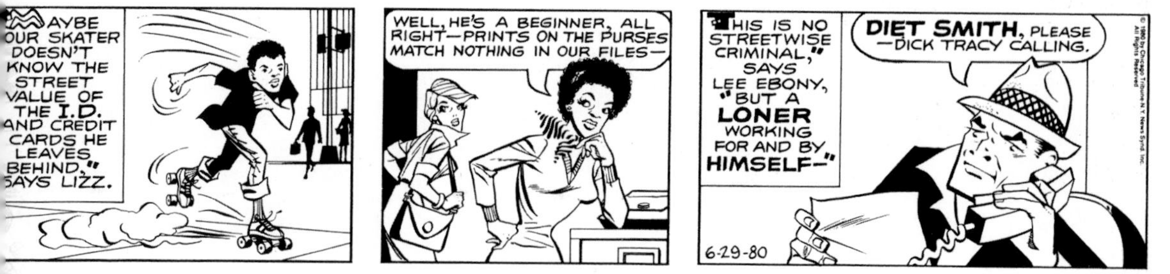
"MAYBE OUR SKATER DOESN'T KNOW THE STREET VALUE OF THE I.D. AND CREDIT CARDS HE LEAVES BEHIND," SAYS LIZZ.
WELL, HE'S A BEGINNER, ALL RIGHT—PRINTS ON THE PURSES MATCH NOTHING IN OUR FILES—
"THIS IS NO STREETWISE CRIMINAL," SAYS LEE EBONY, "BUT A LONER WORKING FOR AND BY HIMSELF—"
DIET SMITH, PLEASE —DICK TRACY CALLING.
6-29-80

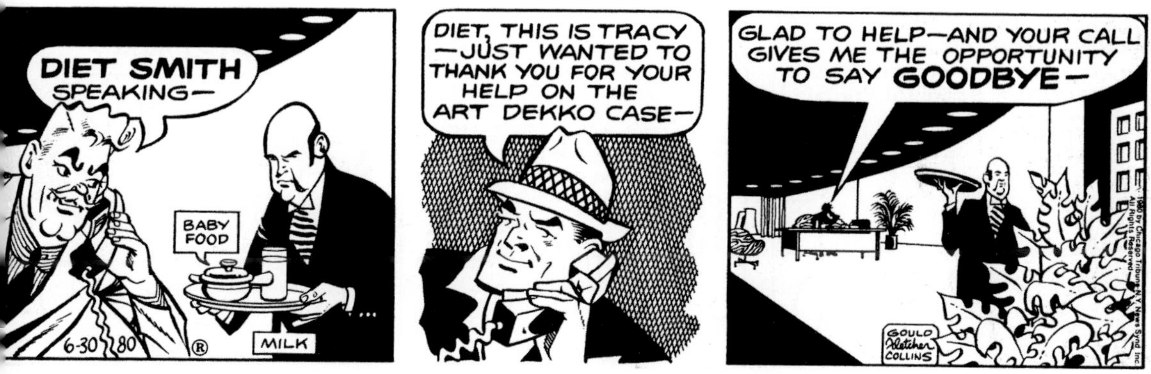
DIET SMITH SPEAKING—
BABY FOOD
MILK
6-30-80
DIET, THIS IS TRACY —JUST WANTED TO THANK YOU FOR YOUR HELP ON THE ART DEKKO CASE—
GLAD TO HELP—AND YOUR CALL GIVES ME THE OPPORTUNITY TO SAY GOODBYE—
GOULD Fletcher COLLINS

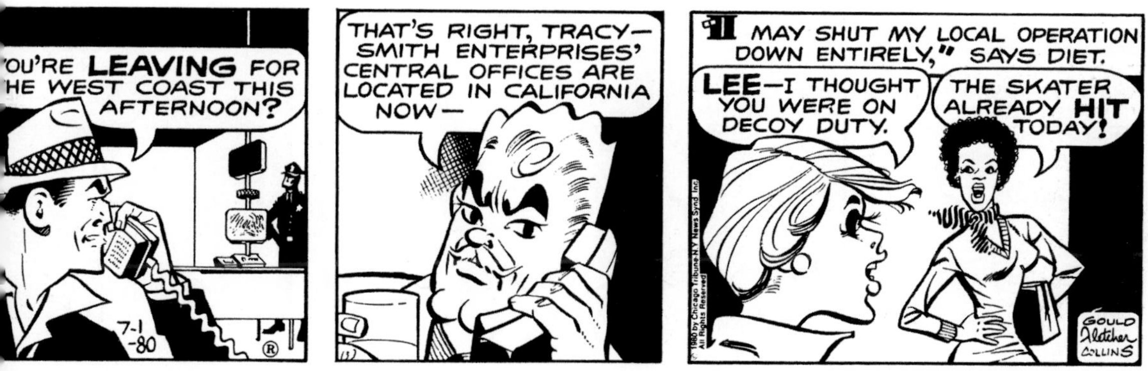
YOU'RE LEAVING FOR THE WEST COAST THIS AFTERNOON?
7-1-80
THAT'S RIGHT, TRACY—SMITH ENTERPRISES' CENTRAL OFFICES ARE LOCATED IN CALIFORNIA NOW—
"I MAY SHUT MY LOCAL OPERATION DOWN ENTIRELY," SAYS DIET.
LEE—I THOUGHT YOU WERE ON DECOY DUTY.
THE SKATER ALREADY HIT TODAY!
GOULD Fletcher COLLINS

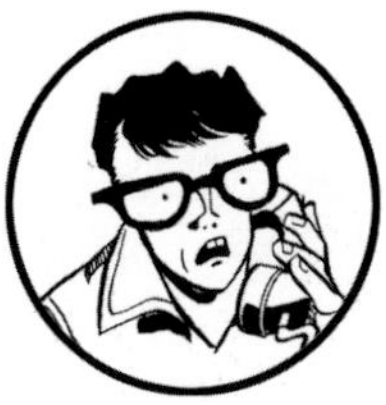

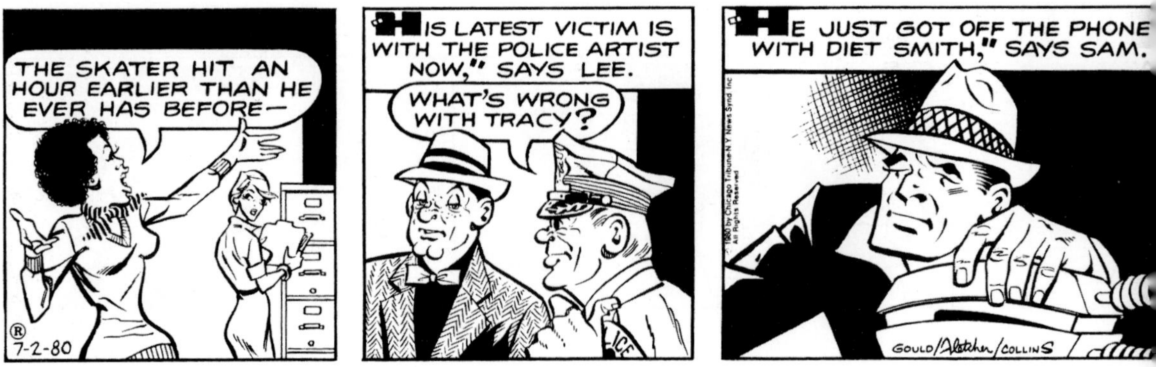
THE SKATER HIT AN HOUR EARLIER THAN HE EVER HAS BEFORE—
7-2-80
"HIS LATEST VICTIM IS WITH THE POLICE ARTIST NOW," SAYS LEE.
WHAT'S WRONG WITH TRACY?
"HE JUST GOT OFF THE PHONE WITH DIET SMITH," SAYS SAM.
GOULD/Fletcher/COLLINS

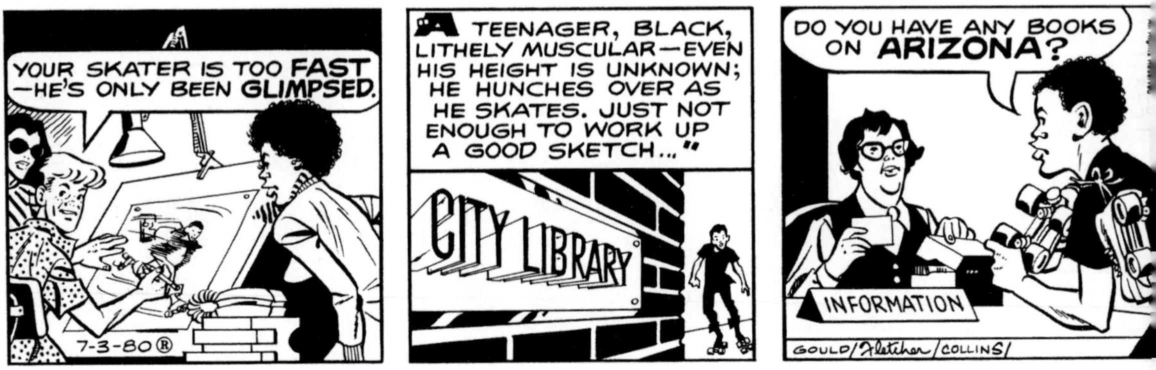
YOUR SKATER IS TOO FAST —HE'S ONLY BEEN GLIMPSED.
7-3-80
"A TEENAGER, BLACK, LITHELY MUSCULAR—EVEN HIS HEIGHT IS UNKNOWN; HE HUNCHES OVER AS HE SKATES. JUST NOT ENOUGH TO WORK UP A GOOD SKETCH..."
CITY LIBRARY
DO YOU HAVE ANY BOOKS ON ARIZONA?
INFORMATION
GOULD/Fletcher/COLLINS/

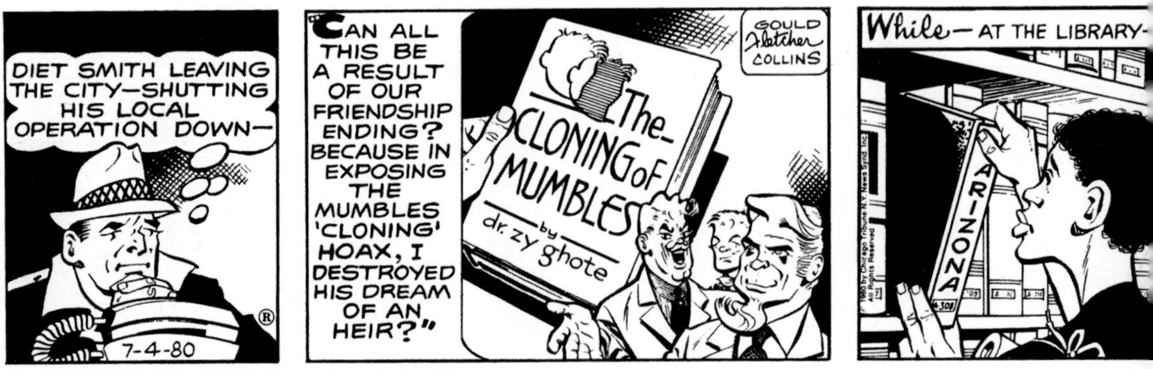
DIET SMITH LEAVING THE CITY—SHUTTING HIS LOCAL OPERATION DOWN—
7-4-80
"CAN ALL THIS BE A RESULT OF OUR FRIENDSHIP ENDING? BECAUSE IN EXPOSING THE MUMBLES 'CLONING' HOAX, I DESTROYED HIS DREAM OF AN HEIR?"
The CLONING OF MUMBLES by dr. zy ghote
GOULD Fletcher COLLINS
While— AT THE LIBRARY-
ARIZONA

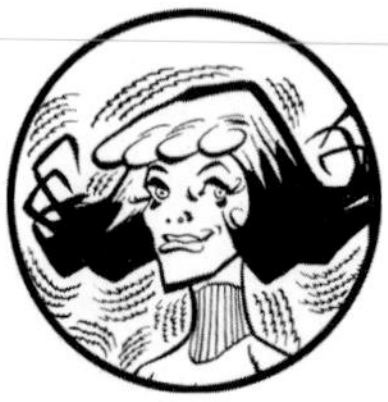

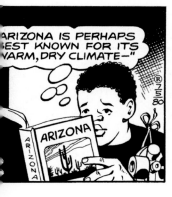

"ARIZONA IS PERHAPS BEST KNOWN FOR ITS WARM, DRY CLIMATE—"

"—WHICH HAS GIVEN HOPE TO THOUSANDS UPON THOUSANDS SUFFERING **RESPIRATORY AILMENTS.**"

Meanwhile, A LIMO ARRIVES AT THE SMITH ENTERPRISES COMPOUND—

I DIDN'T KNOW MR. SMITH HAD A NEW DRIVER...

HERE'S MY I.D. CARD—

I NEED TO ASK TRACY ABOUT ASSIGNING ME TO THE ROLLER-SKATING PURSE SNATCHER CASE.

I WOULDN'T BOTHER HIM RIGHT NOW.

"HE JUST HEARD THAT DIET SMITH'S SHUTTING DOWN HIS LOCAL OPERATION —LEAVING FOR THE WEST COAST **PERMANENTLY.**"

"THAT'S A SHAME," SAYS LIZZ. "THEIR FRIENDSHIP LED TO DIET USING OUR DEPARTMENT TO TEST HIS BRILLIANT POLICE INVENTIONS, LIKE THE 2-WAY WRIST TV."

"I'M SURE TRACY MUST FEEL A DEEP SENSE OF LOSS," SAYS SAM. LIZZ SAYS, "I WONDER HOW **DIET** FEELS."

MR. SMITH? YOUR LIMO IS HERE—

UH, SORRY, JARVIS —I WAS JUST... REMINISCING.

7-6-80

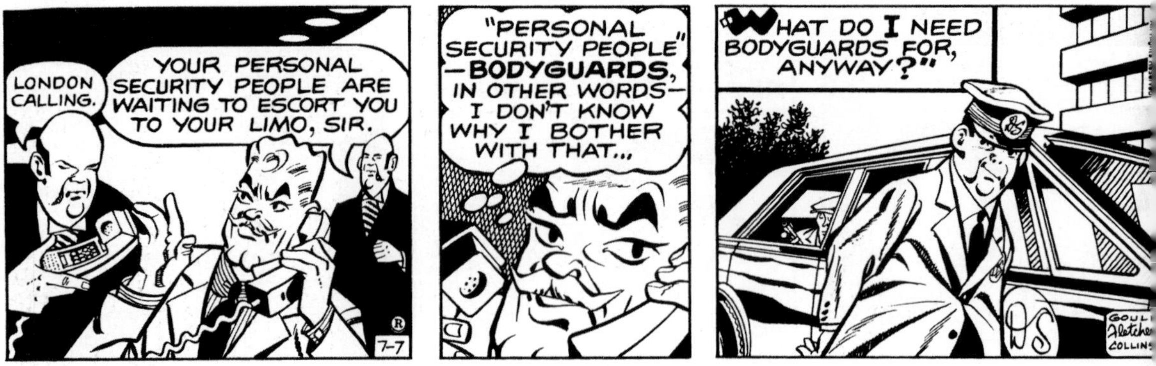
LONDON CALLING.
YOUR PERSONAL SECURITY PEOPLE ARE WAITING TO ESCORT YOU TO YOUR LIMO, SIR.
7-7
"PERSONAL SECURITY PEOPLE" —BODYGUARDS, IN OTHER WORDS— I DON'T KNOW WHY I BOTHER WITH THAT...
WHAT DO I NEED BODYGUARDS FOR, ANYWAY?"

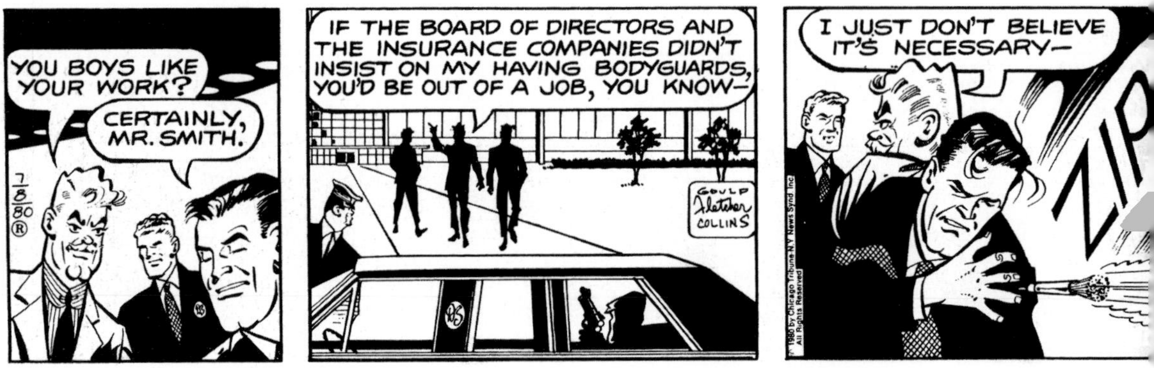
YOU BOYS LIKE YOUR WORK?
CERTAINLY, MR. SMITH!
7/8/80
IF THE BOARD OF DIRECTORS AND THE INSURANCE COMPANIES DIDN'T INSIST ON MY HAVING BODYGUARDS, YOU'D BE OUT OF A JOB, YOU KNOW—
GOULD Fletcher COLLINS
I JUST DON'T BELIEVE IT'S NECESSARY—
ZIP
1980 by Chicago Tribune-N.Y. News Synd. Inc.
All Rights Reserved

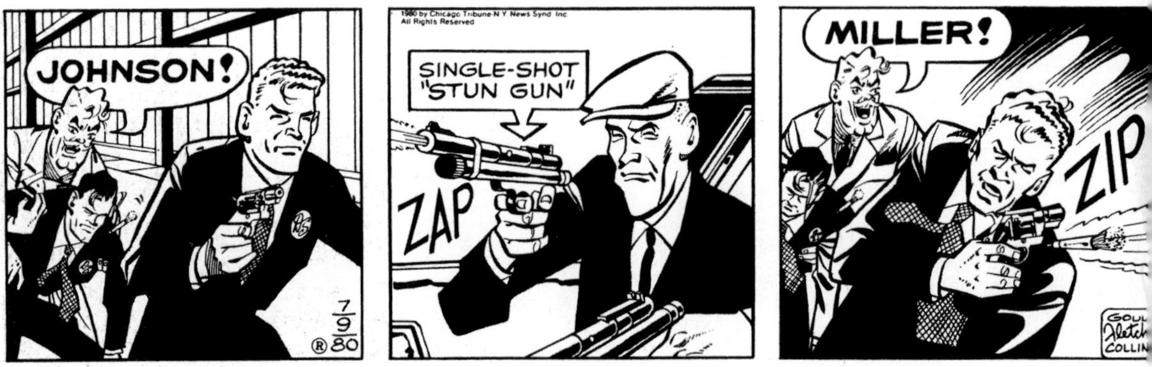
JOHNSON!
7/9/80
1980 by Chicago Tribune-N.Y. News Synd. Inc.
All Rights Reserved
SINGLE-SHOT "STUN GUN"
ZAP
MILLER!
ZIP

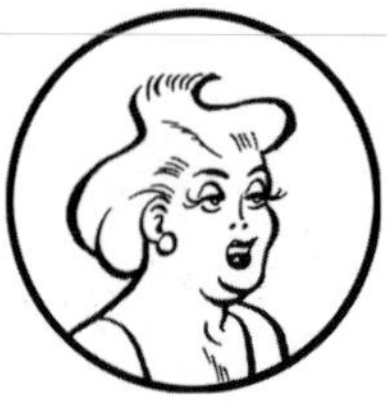

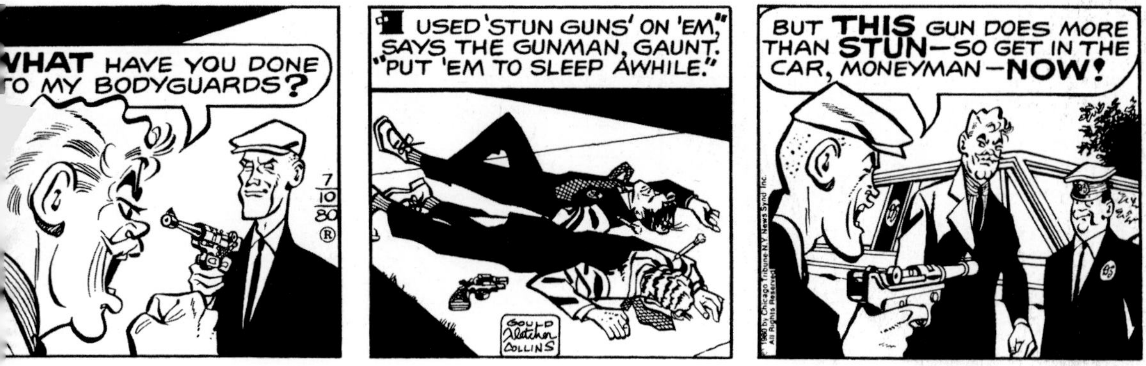
WHAT HAVE YOU DONE TO MY BODYGUARDS?
7/10/80
"I USED 'STUN GUNS' ON 'EM," SAYS THE GUNMAN, GAUNT. "PUT 'EM TO SLEEP AWHILE."
GOULD Fletcher COLLINS
BUT THIS GUN DOES MORE THAN STUN—SO GET IN THE CAR, MONEYMAN—NOW!

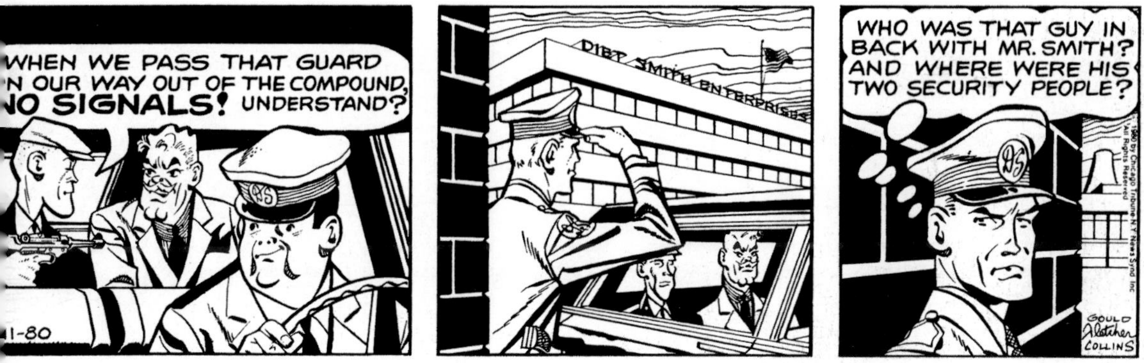
WHEN WE PASS THAT GUARD ON OUR WAY OUT OF THE COMPOUND, NO SIGNALS! UNDERSTAND?
1-80
DIBT SMITH ENTERPRISES
WHO WAS THAT GUY IN BACK WITH MR. SMITH? AND WHERE WERE HIS TWO SECURITY PEOPLE?
GOULD Fletcher COLLINS

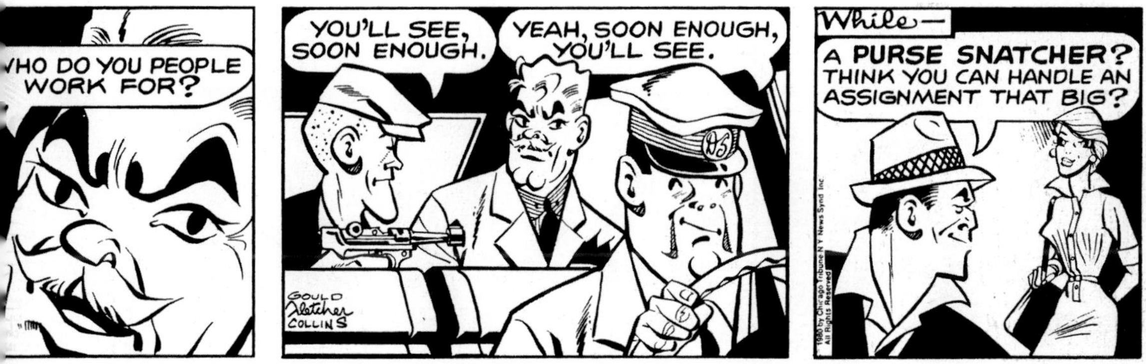
WHO DO YOU PEOPLE WORK FOR?
YOU'LL SEE, SOON ENOUGH.
YEAH, SOON ENOUGH, YOU'LL SEE.
GOULD Fletcher COLLINS
While—
A PURSE SNATCHER? THINK YOU CAN HANDLE AN ASSIGNMENT THAT BIG?

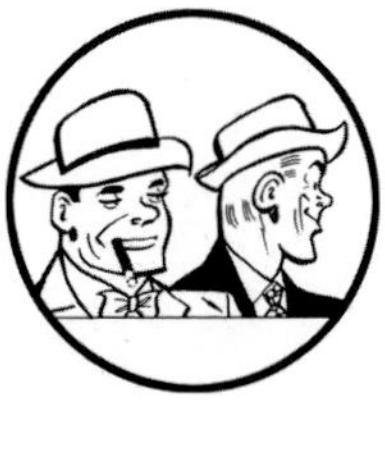

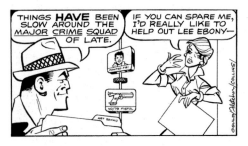

THINGS HAVE BEEN SLOW AROUND THE MAJOR CRIME SQUAD OF LATE.
IF YOU CAN SPARE ME, I'D REALLY LIKE TO HELP OUT LEE EBONY—
WANTED-FBI
VO/79 PISTOL
ART DEKKO
YOU KNOW, THIS YOUNG PURSE SNATCHER ON WHEELS SEEMS TO HAVE A CONSCIENCE.
POLICE DEPT. SKETCH
"IF WE COLLAR HIM SOON ENOUGH, MAYBE THIS IS ONE THIEF WE CAN STRAIGHTEN OUT."
"WARM, DRY CLIMATE"... THAT'D BE PERFECT FOR MOM...
ARIZONA
ARIZONA

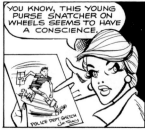

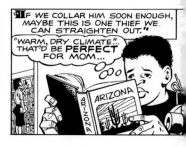

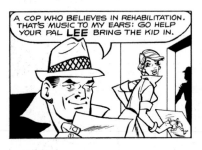

A COP WHO BELIEVES IN REHABILITATION. THAT'S MUSIC TO MY EARS: GO HELP YOUR PAL LEE BRING THE KID IN.
TRACY—DIET SMITH'S BEEN KIDNAPPED!
"'STUN GUNS' WERE USED TO KNOCK OUT HIS BODY-GUARDS, AND A FAKE CHAUFFEUR IN A LIMO DROVE HIM RIGHT OUT OF THE SMITH ENTERPRISES COMPOUND!"
WHO DO YOU WORK FOR?
IT'S A SURPRISE.
7-13-80

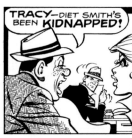

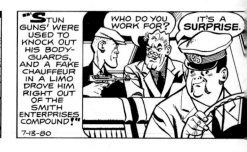

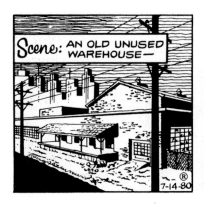

Scene: AN OLD UNUSED WAREHOUSE—
7-14-80
WELL, NOT QUITE UNUSED—
IS THIS WHERE YOU'RE GOING TO HOLD ME?
NO— WE'RE JUST SWITCHING CARS.
YOU'RE GONNA LIKE THIS: YOU'LL HAVE THE TRUNK ALL TO YOURSELF—

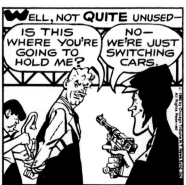

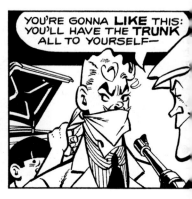

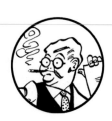

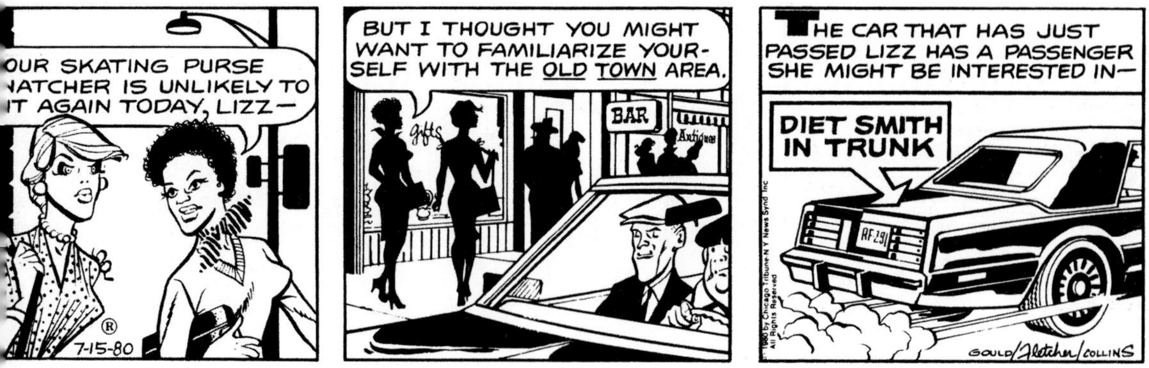
OUR SKATING PURSE
NATCHER IS UNLIKELY TO
IT AGAIN TODAY, LIZZ—
7-15-80
BUT I THOUGHT YOU MIGHT WANT TO FAMILIARIZE YOURSELF WITH THE OLD TOWN AREA.
Gifts
BAR
Antiques
THE CAR THAT HAS JUST PASSED LIZZ HAS A PASSENGER SHE MIGHT BE INTERESTED IN—
DIET SMITH IN TRUNK
RF-291
GOULD/Fletcher/COLLINS

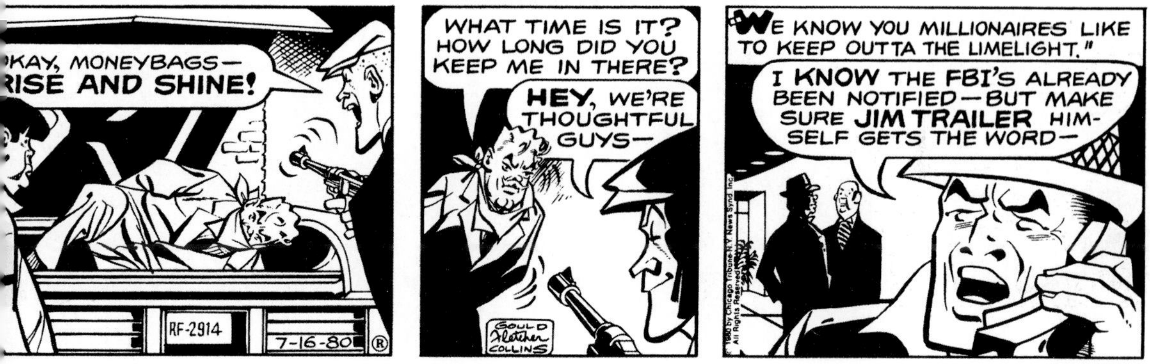
OKAY, MONEYBAGS—
RISE AND SHINE!
RF-2914
7-16-80
WHAT TIME IS IT? HOW LONG DID YOU KEEP ME IN THERE?
HEY, WE'RE THOUGHTFUL GUYS—
GOULD Fletcher COLLINS
"WE KNOW YOU MILLIONAIRES LIKE TO KEEP OUTTA THE LIMELIGHT."
I KNOW THE FBI'S ALREADY BEEN NOTIFIED—BUT MAKE SURE JIM TRAILER HIMSELF GETS THE WORD—

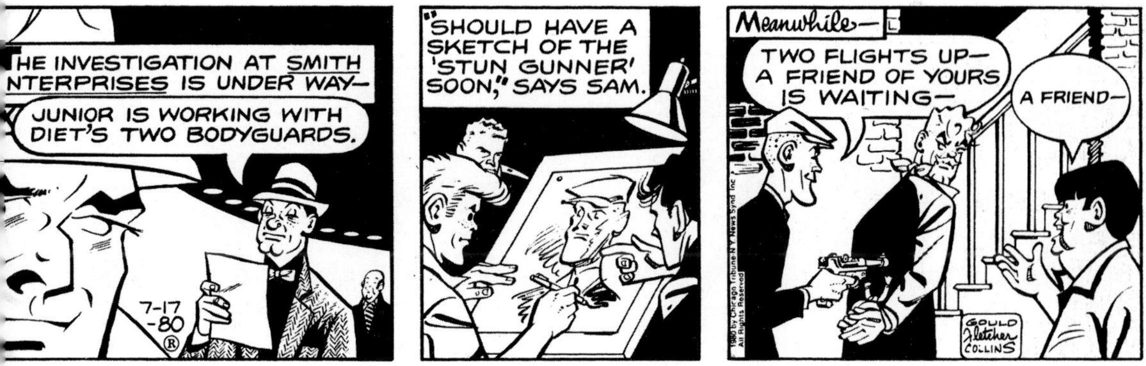
THE INVESTIGATION AT SMITH ENTERPRISES IS UNDER WAY—
JUNIOR IS WORKING WITH DIET'S TWO BODYGUARDS.
7-17-80
"SHOULD HAVE A SKETCH OF THE 'STUN GUNNER' SOON," SAYS SAM.
Meanwhile—
TWO FLIGHTS UP—A FRIEND OF YOURS IS WAITING—
A FRIEND—
GOULD Fletcher COLLINS

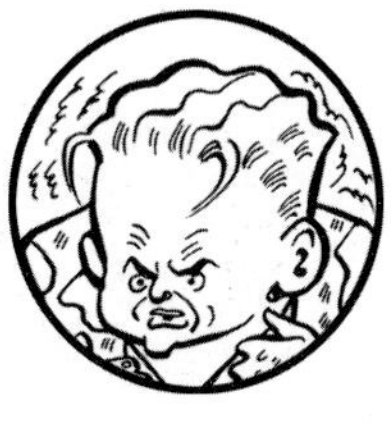

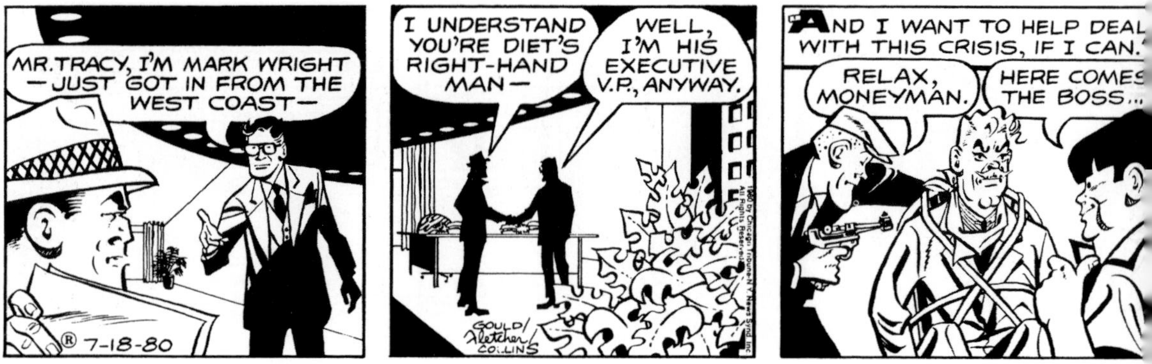

MR. TRACY, I'M MARK WRIGHT —JUST GOT IN FROM THE WEST COAST—
7-18-80
I UNDERSTAND YOU'RE DIET'S RIGHT-HAND MAN—
WELL, I'M HIS EXECUTIVE V.P., ANYWAY.
GOULD/ Fletcher/ COLLINS
©1980 by Chicago Tribune-N.Y. News Synd. Inc. All Rights Reserved
"AND I WANT TO HELP DEAL WITH THIS CRISIS, IF I CAN."
RELAX, MONEYMAN.
HERE COMES THE BOSS...

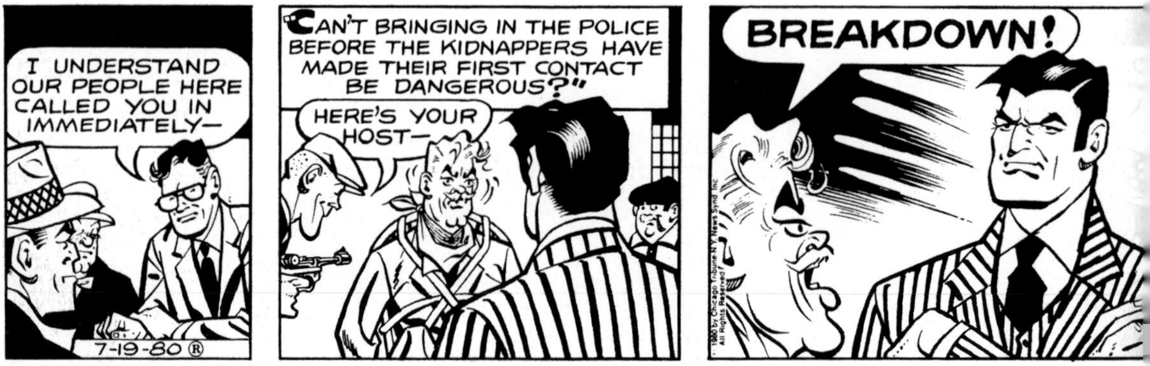

I UNDERSTAND OUR PEOPLE HERE CALLED YOU IN IMMEDIATELY—
7-19-80
"CAN'T BRINGING IN THE POLICE BEFORE THE KIDNAPPERS HAVE MADE THEIR FIRST CONTACT BE DANGEROUS?"
HERE'S YOUR HOST—
BREAKDOWN!
©1980 by Chicago Tribune-N.Y. News Synd. Inc. All Rights Reserved

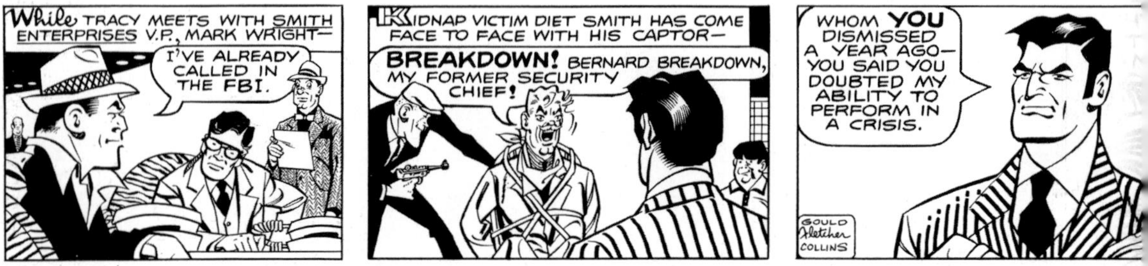

While TRACY MEETS WITH SMITH ENTERPRISES V.P., MARK WRIGHT—
I'VE ALREADY CALLED IN THE FBI.
KIDNAP VICTIM DIET SMITH HAS COME FACE TO FACE WITH HIS CAPTOR—
BREAKDOWN! BERNARD BREAKDOWN, MY FORMER SECURITY CHIEF!
WHOM YOU DISMISSED A YEAR AGO— YOU SAID YOU DOUBTED MY ABILITY TO PERFORM IN A CRISIS.
GOULD Fletcher COLLINS

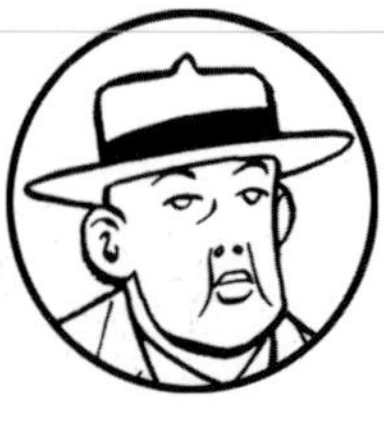

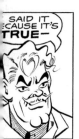

SAID IT ECAUSE IT'S TRUE—
IT ISN'T!
IT IS.
I... I... JUST CAN'T COPE—
TAKE IT EASY, BOSS—
SHUTTUP! WE'LL SOON SEE HOW YOU HOLD UP IN A CRISIS, DIET SMITH!
7-20-80

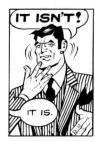

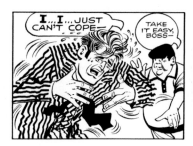

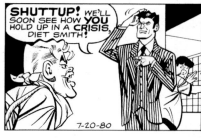

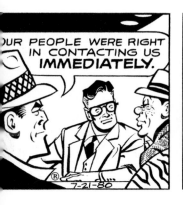

UR PEOPLE WERE RIGHT IN CONTACTING US IMMEDIATELY.
7-21-80
COME TO THINK OF IT —DIET'S STANDING ORDERS, IN SUCH A CASE, ARE TO CALL IN THE AUTHORITIES AT ONCE, NO MATTER WHAT THE KIDNAPPERS DEMAND.
"WHAT NOW, TRACY?"
YOU SHOULD NEVER HAVE FIRED ME, DIET SMITH!
© 1980 by Chicago Tribune N.Y. News Synd. Inc. All Rights Reserved
GOULD Fletcher COLLINS

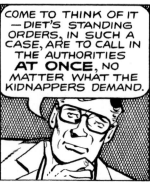

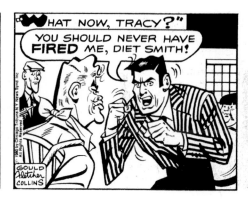

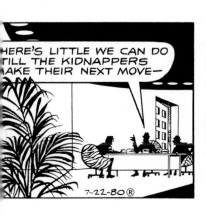

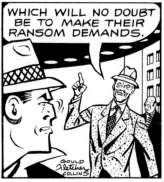

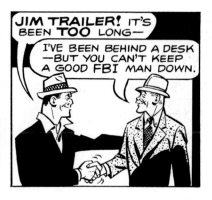

HERE'S LITTLE WE CAN DO TILL THE KIDNAPPERS AKE THEIR NEXT MOVE—
7-22-80
WHICH WILL NO DOUBT BE TO MAKE THEIR RANSOM DEMANDS.
GOULD Fletcher COLLINS
JIM TRAILER! IT'S BEEN TOO LONG—
I'VE BEEN BEHIND A DESK —BUT YOU CAN'T KEEP A GOOD FBI MAN DOWN.

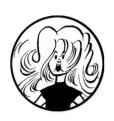

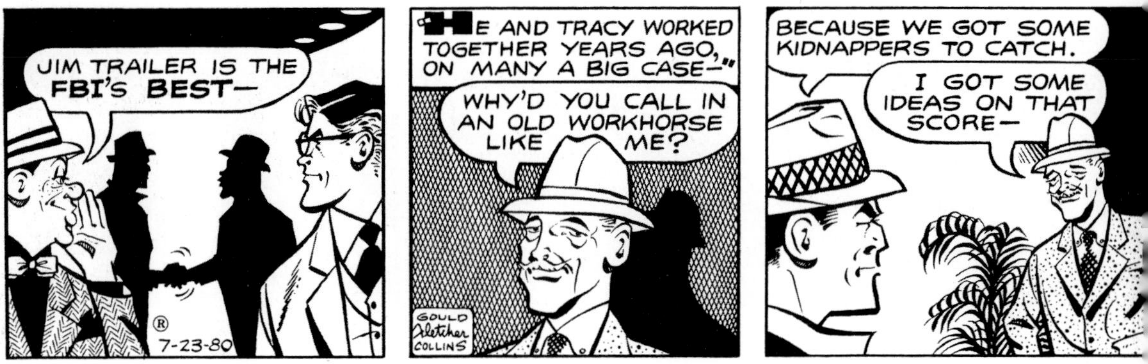
JIM TRAILER IS THE FBI'S BEST—
7-23-80
"HE AND TRACY WORKED TOGETHER YEARS AGO, ON MANY A BIG CASE—"
WHY'D YOU CALL IN AN OLD WORKHORSE LIKE ME?
GOULD Fletcher COLLINS
BECAUSE WE GOT SOME KIDNAPPERS TO CATCH.
I GOT SOME IDEAS ON THAT SCORE—

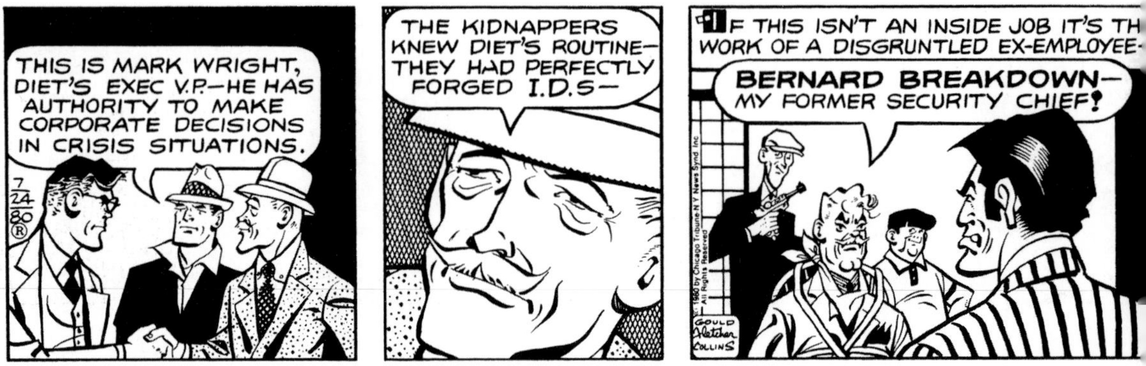
THIS IS MARK WRIGHT, DIET'S EXEC V.P.—HE HAS AUTHORITY TO MAKE CORPORATE DECISIONS IN CRISIS SITUATIONS.
7/24/80
THE KIDNAPPERS KNEW DIET'S ROUTINE—THEY HAD PERFECTLY FORGED I.D.S—
"IF THIS ISN'T AN INSIDE JOB IT'S TH WORK OF A DISGRUNTLED EX-EMPLOYEE-
BERNARD BREAKDOWN—MY FORMER SECURITY CHIEF!
© 1980 by Chicago Tribune-N.Y. News Synd Inc. All Rights Reserved
GOULD Fletcher COLLINS

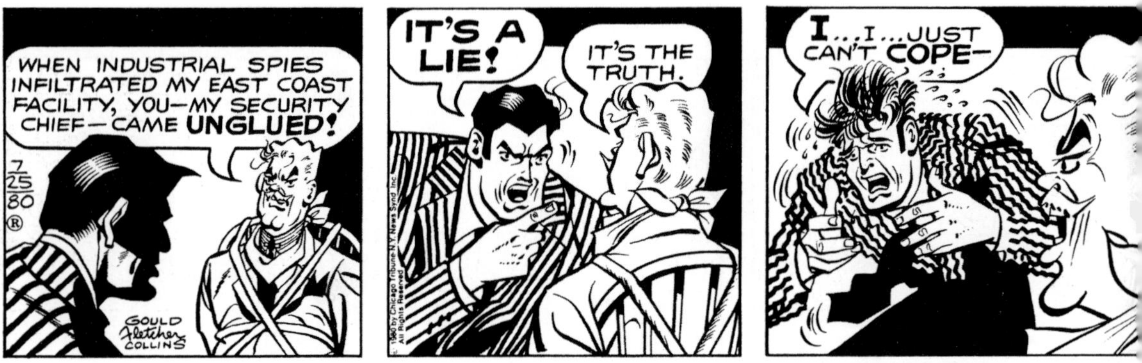
WHEN INDUSTRIAL SPIES INFILTRATED MY EAST COAST FACILITY, YOU—MY SECURITY CHIEF—CAME UNGLUED!
7/25/80
GOULD Fletcher COLLINS
IT'S A LIE!
IT'S THE TRUTH.
© 1980 by Chicago Tribune-N.Y. News Synd Inc. All Rights Reserved
I...I...JUST CAN'T COPE—

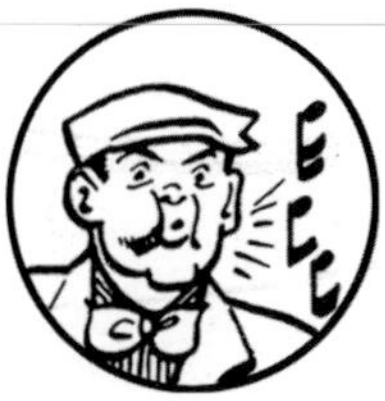

T'LL BE OKAY, BREAKDOWN.
I CAN'T... COPE... CAN'T...
26
SHUTTUP! AS FOR YOU, SMITH...
"STILL COMING UNGLUED IN A CRISIS, I SEE," SAYS DIET.
HOW WAS SCHOOL TODAY, WILLIE?
UH— FINE, MOM.
1980 by Chicago Tribune-N.Y. News Synd. Inc. All Rights Reserved
GOULD Fletcher COLLINS

ELEVEN P.M. AND NO WORD FROM THE KIDNAPPERS— BUT TRACY'S FBI FRIEND M TRAILER IS ON THE CASE—
I WANT YOUR PERSONNEL PEOPLE TO LIST ALL DISMISSALS FOR THE LAST TWO YEARS.
"CONSIDERING THE PERFECTLY FORGED I.D.S AND INSIDE KNOWLEDGE OF DIET'S ROUTINE, OUR KIDNAPPER MAY BE A FORMER EMPLOYEE WITH A GRUDGE—"
BREAKDOWN, THERE WAS NOTHING PERSONAL IN MY FIRING YOU—
NOTHING PERSONAL! WHAT'S MORE PERSONAL THAN TAKING SOMEONE'S JOB AWAY FROM HIM!
GOULD Fletcher COLLINS

OU CAME UNGLUED IN STRESS SITUATIONS—
I DIDN'T!
YOU DID.
I CAN'T... JUST CAN'T... COPE—
EASY, BOSS, EASY...
SHUTTUP!
Elsewhere, WILLIE WHEELER— ROLLER-SKATING PURSE SNATCHER—CAN'T SLEEP...
I SHOULDN'T DO IT... BUT IT'S FOR MOM—
7-27-80

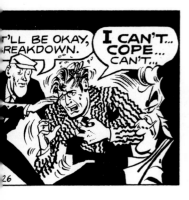

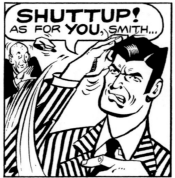

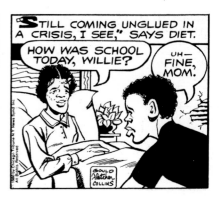

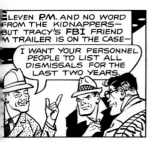

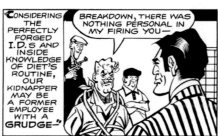

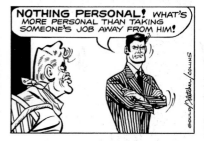

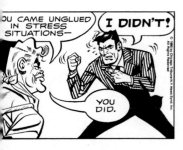

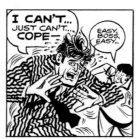

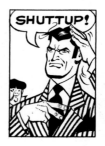

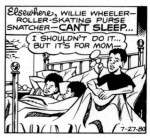

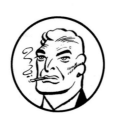

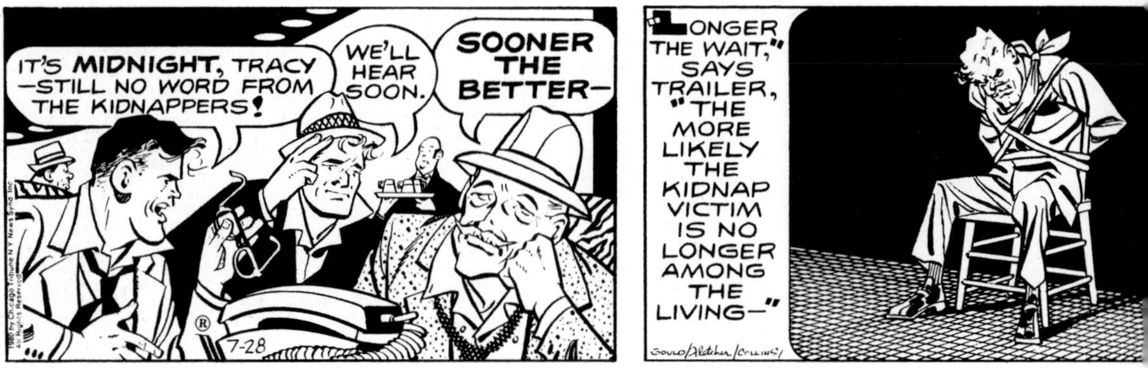
IT'S MIDNIGHT, TRACY —STILL NO WORD FROM THE KIDNAPPERS!
WE'LL HEAR SOON.
SOONER THE BETTER—
"LONGER THE WAIT," SAYS TRAILER, "THE MORE LIKELY THE KIDNAP VICTIM IS NO LONGER AMONG THE LIVING—"
7-28
GOULD/Fletcher/COLLINS

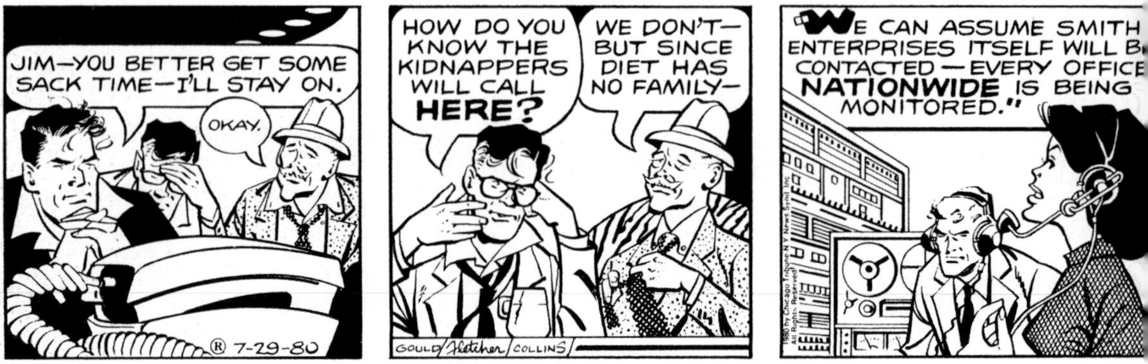
JIM—YOU BETTER GET SOME SACK TIME—I'LL STAY ON.
OKAY.
7-29-80
HOW DO YOU KNOW THE KIDNAPPERS WILL CALL HERE?
WE DON'T— BUT SINCE DIET HAS NO FAMILY—
GOULD/Fletcher/COLLINS
"WE CAN ASSUME SMITH ENTERPRISES ITSELF WILL BE CONTACTED — EVERY OFFICE NATIONWIDE IS BEING MONITORED."

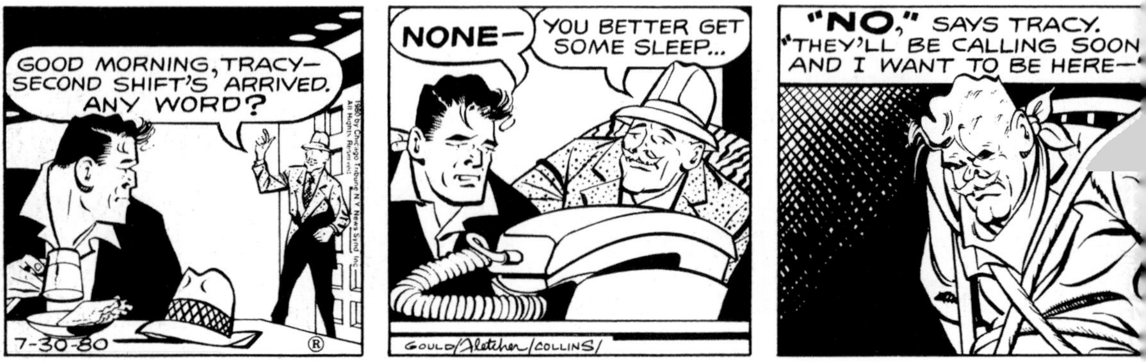
GOOD MORNING, TRACY— SECOND SHIFT'S ARRIVED. ANY WORD?
7-30-80
NONE—
YOU BETTER GET SOME SLEEP...
GOULD/Fletcher/COLLINS
"NO," SAYS TRACY. "THEY'LL BE CALLING SOON AND I WANT TO BE HERE—"

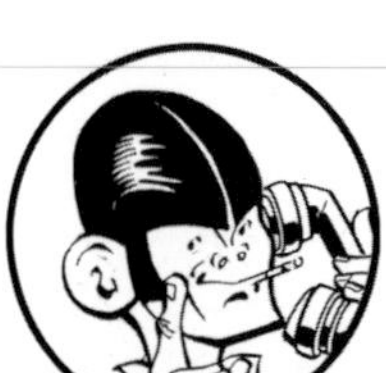

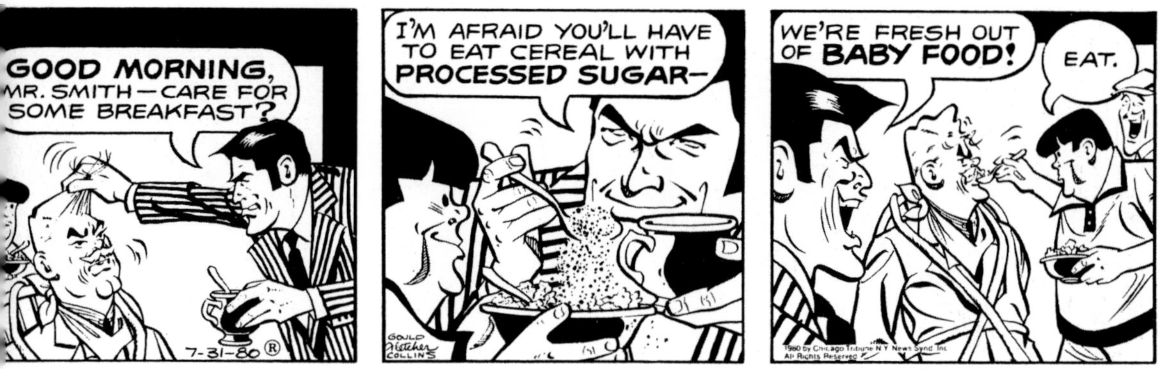
GOOD MORNING, MR. SMITH—CARE FOR SOME BREAKFAST?
7-31-80 ®
I'M AFRAID YOU'LL HAVE TO EAT CEREAL WITH PROCESSED SUGAR—
WE'RE FRESH OUT OF BABY FOOD!
EAT.
1980 by Chicago Tribune N.Y. News Synd. Inc.
All Rights Reserved

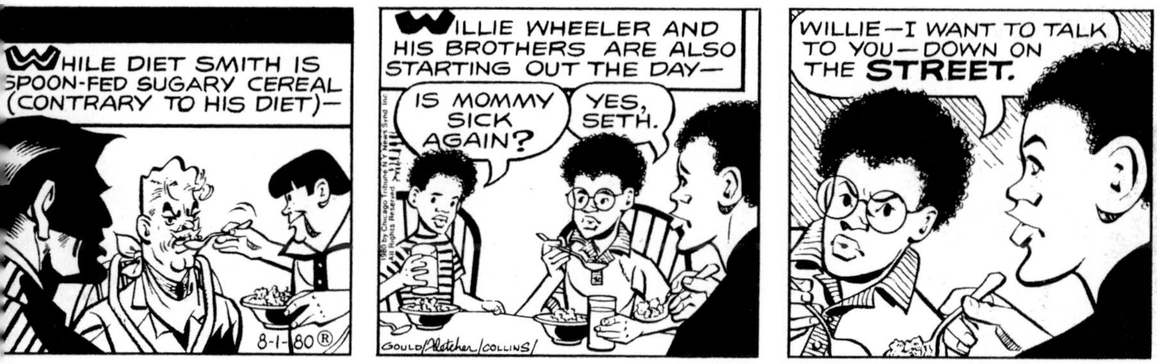
WHILE DIET SMITH IS SPOON-FED SUGARY CEREAL (CONTRARY TO HIS DIET)—
8-1-80 ®
WILLIE WHEELER AND HIS BROTHERS ARE ALSO STARTING OUT THE DAY—
IS MOMMY SICK AGAIN?
YES, SETH.
WILLIE—I WANT TO TALK TO YOU—DOWN ON THE STREET.

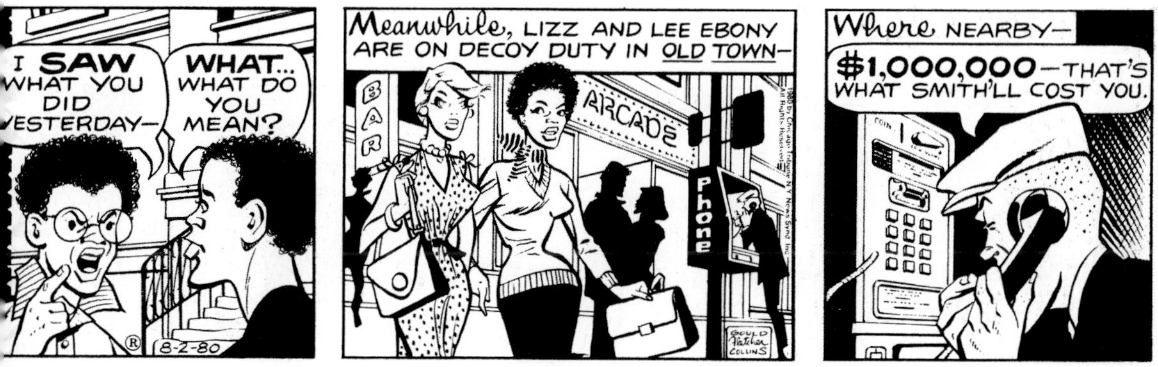
I SAW WHAT YOU DID YESTERDAY—
WHAT... WHAT DO YOU MEAN?
® 8-2-80
Meanwhile, LIZZ AND LEE EBONY ARE ON DECOY DUTY IN OLD TOWN—
BAR
ARCADE
Phone
Where NEARBY—
$1,000,000—THAT'S WHAT SMITH'LL COST YOU.

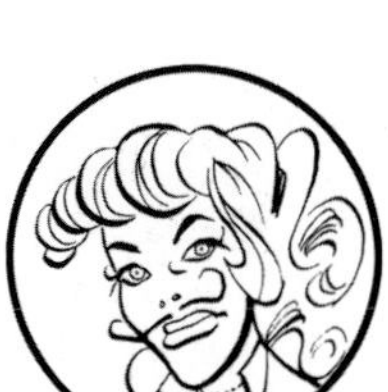

WILLIE WHEELER IS CONFRONTED BY HIS YOUNGER BROTHER KEENAN—
I KNOW WHAT YOU'VE BEEN DOING!
HOW COULD HE KNOW?
THERE WAS A LETTER FOR MOM FROM THE HIGH SCHOOL, YESTERDAY—YOU TORE IT UP AND THREW IT IN THE TRASH!
GOULD/Fletcher/COLLINS
"IS THAT ALL?" WILLIE THINKS, RELIEVED THAT HIS PURSE-SNATCHING IS STILL UNKNOWN TO KEENAN—

YOU BEEN SKIPPING OUT OF SUMMER SCHOOL, HAVEN'T YOU, WILLIE? I KNOW—I CHECKED!
?
"KEEP OUT OF IT!" WILLIE SNAPS. "YOU TELL MOMMA AND I'LL BUST YOU 'LONGSIDE YOUR HEAD."
Elsewhere, A CALL TRACY WAITED FOR ALL NIGHT HAS FINALLY COME IN—
IT'S THE KIDNAPPERS!
8-3-80

IT'S NOT RIGHT, YOU SKIPPING SUMMER SCHOOL, WILLIE!
MIND YOUR OWN BUSINESS!
8-4-80
KEENAN! WILLIE!
GOULD Fletcher COLLINS
Meanwhile—A $1,000,000 RANSOM DEMAND HAS BEEN MADE—
HOW AND WHEN DO WE DELIVER THE MONEY?
1980 by Chicago Tribune-N.Y. News Synd Inc
All Rights Reserved

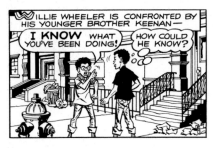

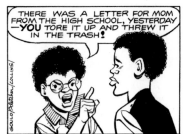

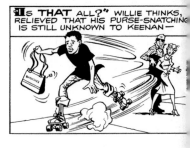

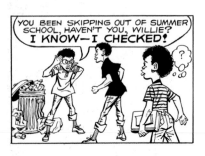

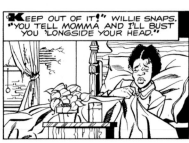

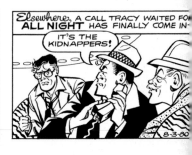

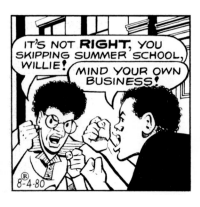

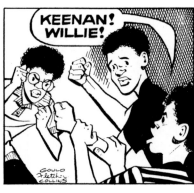

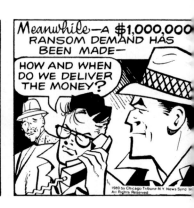

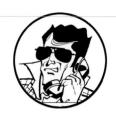

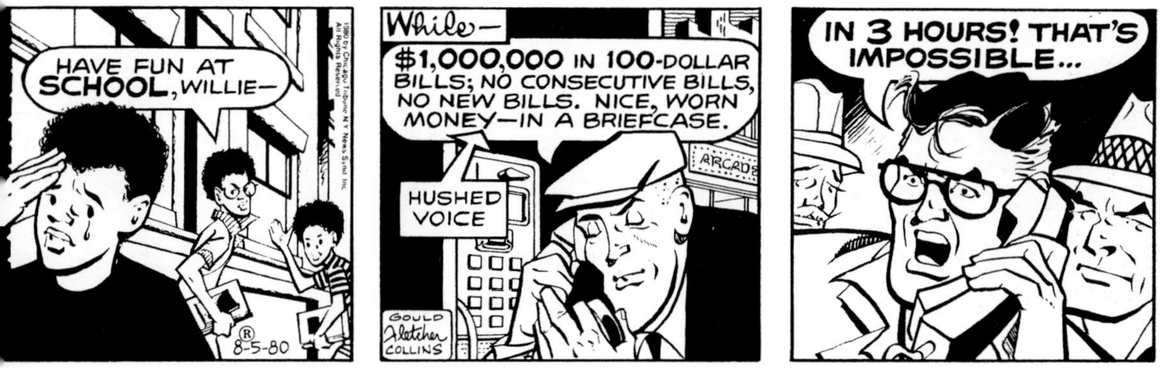
HAVE FUN AT SCHOOL, WILLIE—
8-5-80
While—
$1,000,000 IN 100-DOLLAR BILLS; NO CONSECUTIVE BILLS, NO NEW BILLS. NICE, WORN MONEY—IN A BRIEFCASE.
HUSHED VOICE
ARCADE
GOULD Fletcher COLLINS
IN 3 HOURS! THAT'S IMPOSSIBLE...

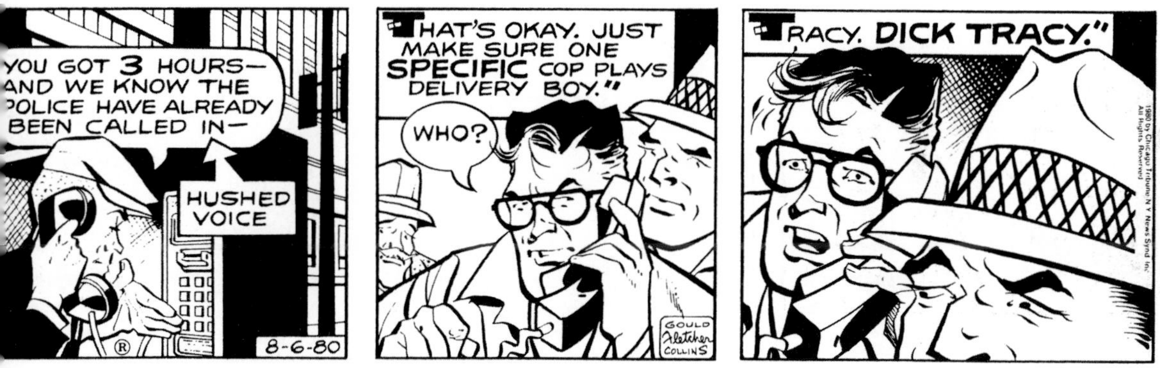
YOU GOT 3 HOURS—AND WE KNOW THE POLICE HAVE ALREADY BEEN CALLED IN—
HUSHED VOICE
8-6-80
"THAT'S OKAY. JUST MAKE SURE ONE SPECIFIC COP PLAYS DELIVERY BOY."
WHO?
GOULD Fletcher COLLINS
"TRACY. DICK TRACY."

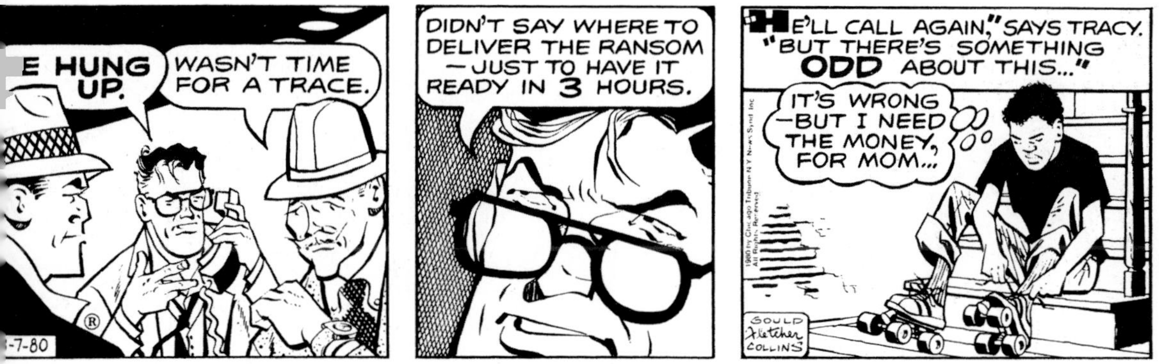
E HUNG UP.
WASN'T TIME FOR A TRACE.
-7-80
DIDN'T SAY WHERE TO DELIVER THE RANSOM —JUST TO HAVE IT READY IN 3 HOURS.
"HE'LL CALL AGAIN," SAYS TRACY. "BUT THERE'S SOMETHING ODD ABOUT THIS..."
IT'S WRONG —BUT I NEED THE MONEY, FOR MOM...
GOULD Fletcher COLLINS

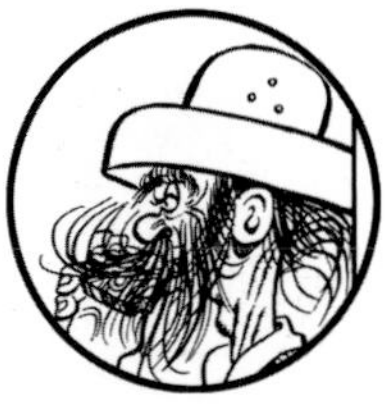

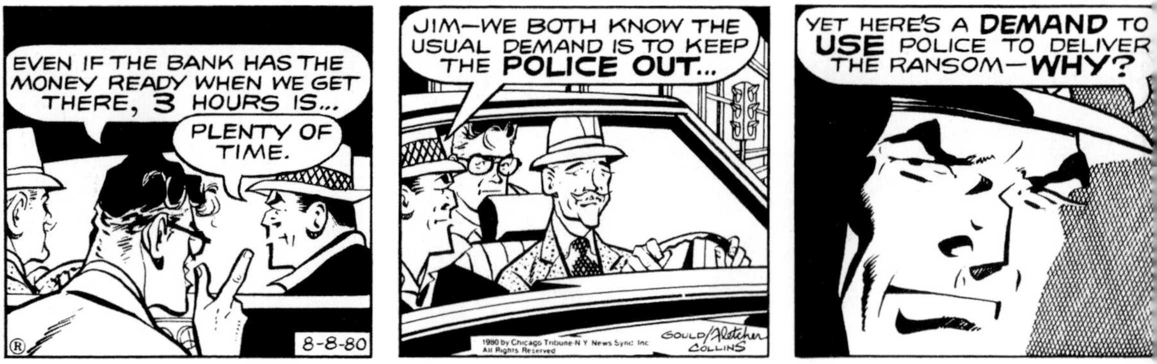

EVEN IF THE BANK HAS THE MONEY READY WHEN WE GET THERE, 3 HOURS IS...
PLENTY OF TIME.
8-8-80
JIM—WE BOTH KNOW THE USUAL DEMAND IS TO KEEP THE POLICE OUT...
1980 by Chicago Tribune-N Y News Sync Inc All Rights Reserved
GOULD/Fletcher COLLINS
YET HERE'S A DEMAND TO USE POLICE TO DELIVER THE RANSOM—WHY?

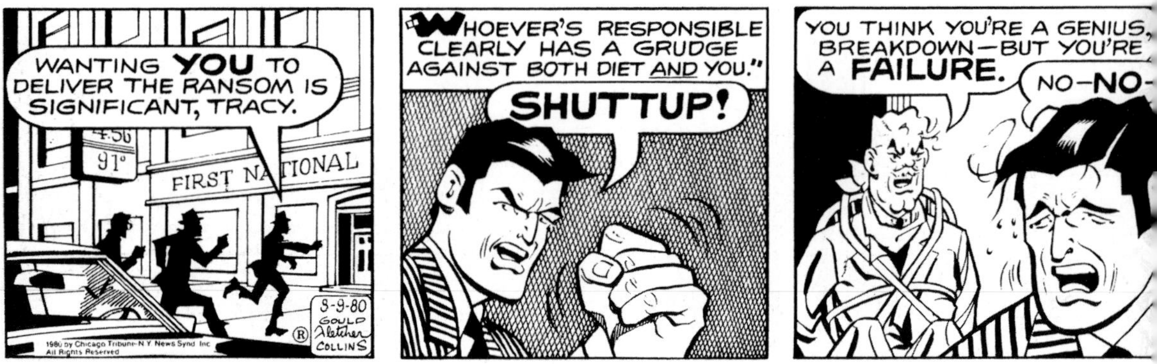

WANTING YOU TO DELIVER THE RANSOM IS SIGNIFICANT, TRACY.
91°
FIRST NATIONAL
8-9-80 GOULD Fletcher COLLINS
1980 by Chicago Tribune-N Y News Synd Inc All Rights Reserved
"WHOEVER'S RESPONSIBLE CLEARLY HAS A GRUDGE AGAINST BOTH DIET AND YOU."
SHUTTUP!
YOU THINK YOU'RE A GENIUS, BREAKDOWN—BUT YOU'RE A FAILURE.
NO—NO—

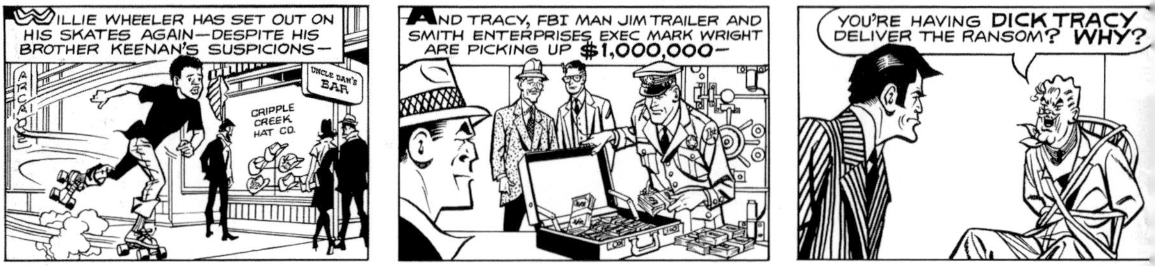

WILLIE WHEELER HAS SET OUT ON HIS SKATES AGAIN—DESPITE HIS BROTHER KEENAN'S SUSPICIONS—
ARCADE
UNCLE DAN'S BAR
CRIPPLE CREEK HAT CO.
AND TRACY, FBI MAN JIM TRAILER AND SMITH ENTERPRISES EXEC MARK WRIGHT ARE PICKING UP $1,000,000—
YOU'RE HAVING DICK TRACY DELIVER THE RANSOM? WHY?

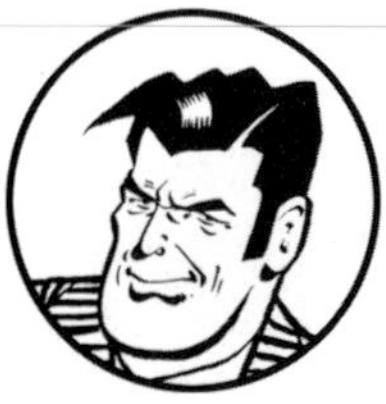

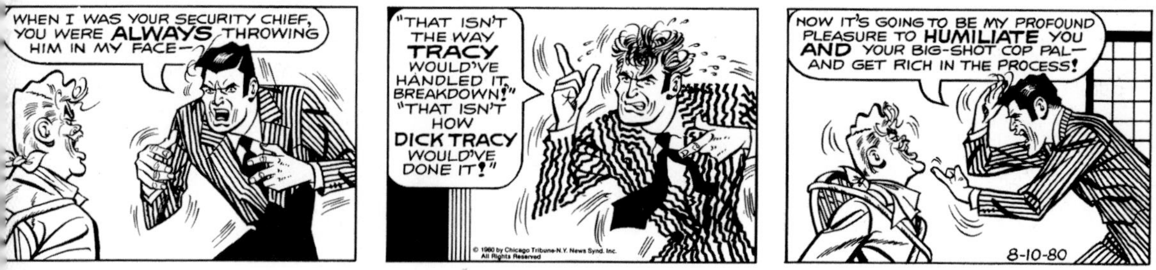
WHEN I WAS YOUR SECURITY CHIEF, YOU WERE ALWAYS THROWING HIM IN MY FACE—
"THAT ISN'T THE WAY TRACY WOULD'VE HANDLED IT, BREAKDOWN!" "THAT ISN'T HOW DICK TRACY WOULD'VE DONE IT!"
© 1980 by Chicago Tribune-N.Y. News Synd. Inc. All Rights Reserved
NOW IT'S GOING TO BE MY PROFOUND PLEASURE TO HUMILIATE YOU AND YOUR BIG-SHOT COP PAL—AND GET RICH IN THE PROCESS!
8-10-80

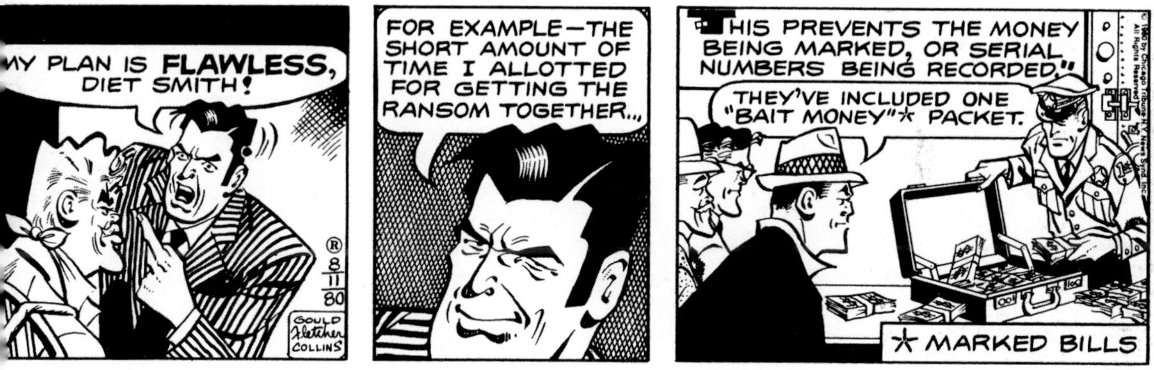
MY PLAN IS FLAWLESS, DIET SMITH!
® 8 11 80
GOULD Fletcher COLLINS
FOR EXAMPLE—THE SHORT AMOUNT OF TIME I ALLOTTED FOR GETTING THE RANSOM TOGETHER...
THIS PREVENTS THE MONEY BEING MARKED, OR SERIAL NUMBERS BEING RECORDED."
"THEY'VE INCLUDED ONE "BAIT MONEY"✯ PACKET.
✯ MARKED BILLS

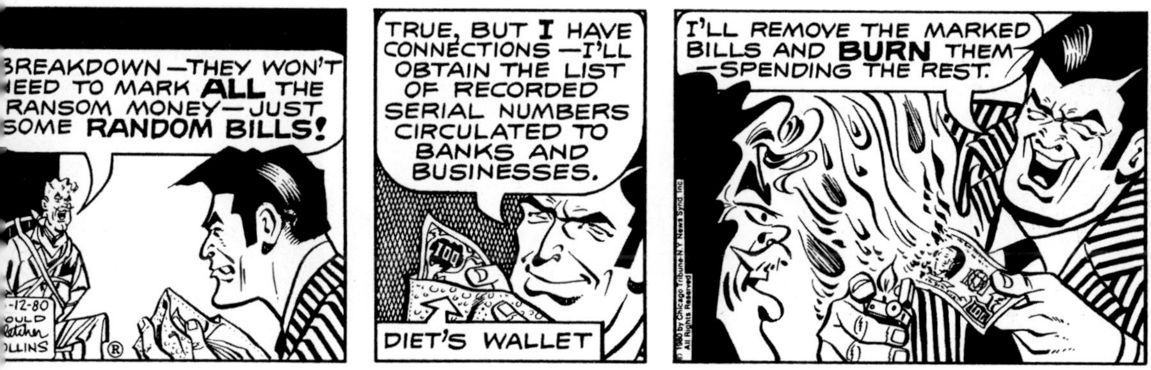
REAKDOWN—THEY WON'T EED TO MARK ALL THE RANSOM MONEY—JUST OME RANDOM BILLS!
TRUE, BUT I HAVE CONNECTIONS—I'LL OBTAIN THE LIST OF RECORDED SERIAL NUMBERS CIRCULATED TO BANKS AND BUSINESSES.
DIET'S WALLET
© 1980 by Chicago Tribune-N.Y. News Synd. Inc. All Rights Reserved
I'LL REMOVE THE MARKED BILLS AND BURN THEM—SPENDING THE REST.

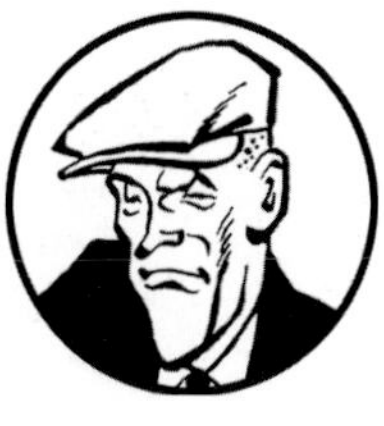

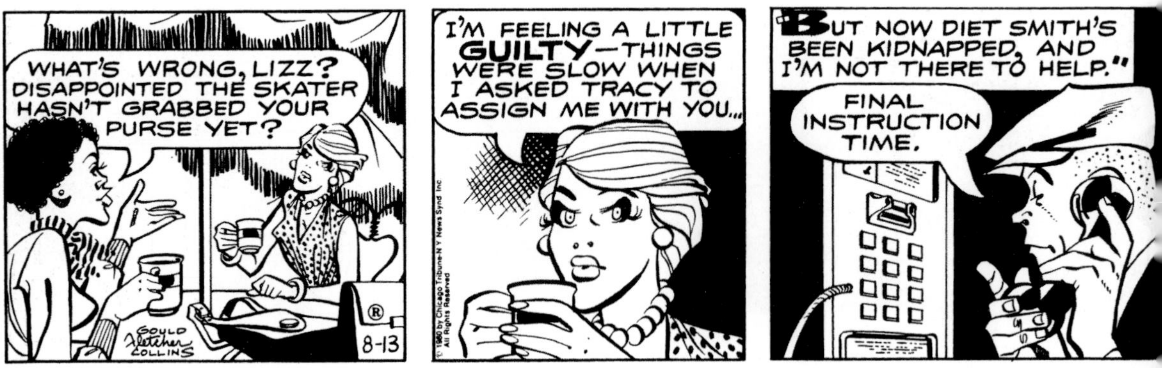
WHAT'S WRONG, LIZZ? DISAPPOINTED THE SKATER HASN'T GRABBED YOUR PURSE YET?
GOULD Fletcher COLLINS
8-13
I'M FEELING A LITTLE GUILTY—THINGS WERE SLOW WHEN I ASKED TRACY TO ASSIGN ME WITH YOU...
© 1980 by Chicago Tribune-N.Y. News Synd. Inc All Rights Reserved
"BUT NOW DIET SMITH'S BEEN KIDNAPPED, AND I'M NOT THERE TO HELP."
FINAL INSTRUCTION TIME.

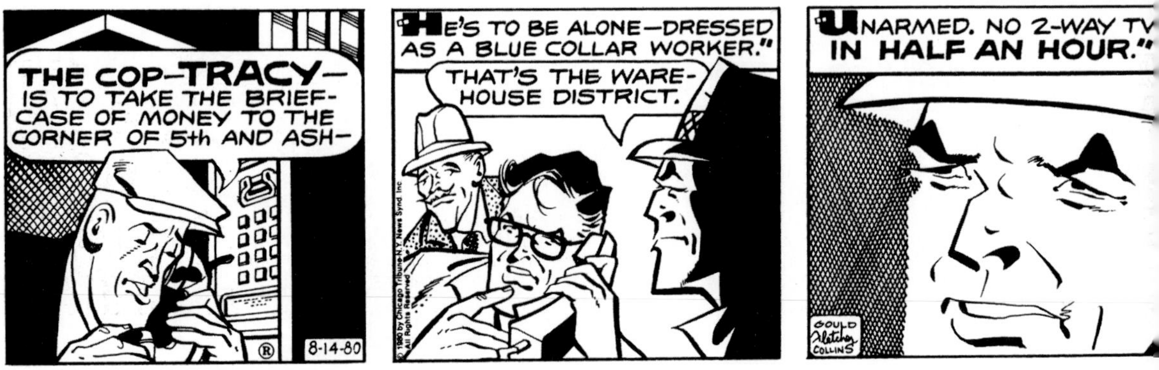
THE COP—TRACY—IS TO TAKE THE BRIEF-CASE OF MONEY TO THE CORNER OF 5th AND ASH—
8-14-80
"HE'S TO BE ALONE—DRESSED AS A BLUE COLLAR WORKER."
THAT'S THE WARE-HOUSE DISTRICT.
© 1980 by Chicago Tribune-N.Y. News Synd. Inc All Rights Reserved
"UNARMED. NO 2-WAY TV IN HALF AN HOUR."
GOULD Fletcher COLLINS

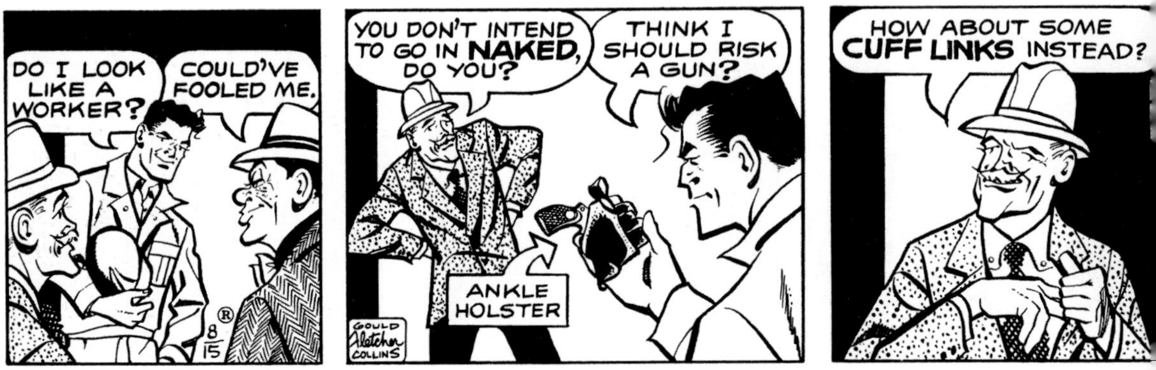
DO I LOOK LIKE A WORKER?
COULD'VE FOOLED ME.
8/15
YOU DON'T INTEND TO GO IN NAKED, DO YOU?
THINK I SHOULD RISK A GUN?
ANKLE HOLSTER
GOULD Fletcher COLLINS
HOW ABOUT SOME CUFF LINKS INSTEAD?

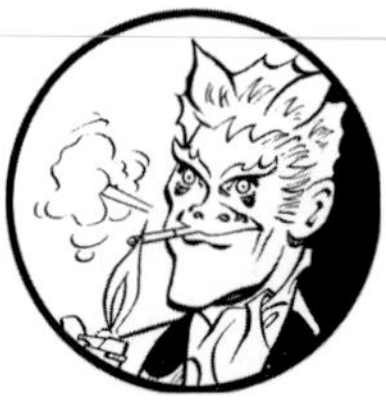

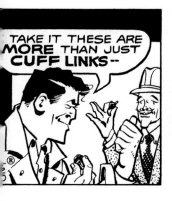

TAKE IT THESE ARE MORE THAN JUST CUFF LINKS--
ONLY IF YOU HURL 'EM AT THE FLOOR—IN WHICH CASE THEY EXPLODE INTO A CLOUD OF TEAR GAS.
"I'LL TRY NOT TO DROP 'EM," TRACY GRINS. While in OLD TOWN—
© 1980 by Chicago Tribune-N.Y. News Synd. Inc. All Rights Reserved
GOULD Fletcher COLLINS

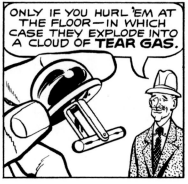

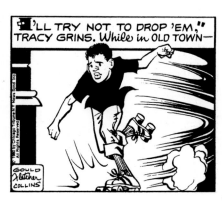

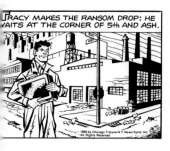

TRACY MAKES THE RANSOM DROP: HE WAITS AT THE CORNER OF 5th AND ASH.
© 1980 by Chicago Tribune-N.Y. News Synd. Inc. All Rights Reserved
GET IN—THE BOSS WANTS BOTH YOU AND THE BRIEFCASE.
YOU BOYS ARE GENIUSES—HAVING ME WAIT IN A WAREHOUSE DISTRICT IN WORKCLOTHES WITH A BRIEFCASE. REAL INCONSPICUOUS.

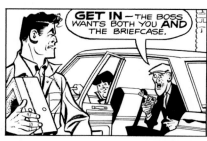

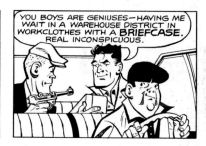

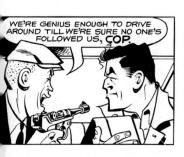

WE'RE GENIUS ENOUGH TO DRIVE AROUND TILL WE'RE SURE NO ONE'S FOLLOWED US, COP.
HALF AN HOUR LATER, IN THE OLD TOWN SECTION—
OKAY, COP—NO FANCY MOVES—
BAR
Pizza Pub
GOULD Fletcher COLLINS
8-17-80

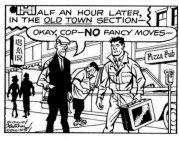

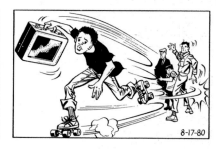

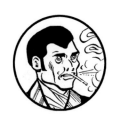

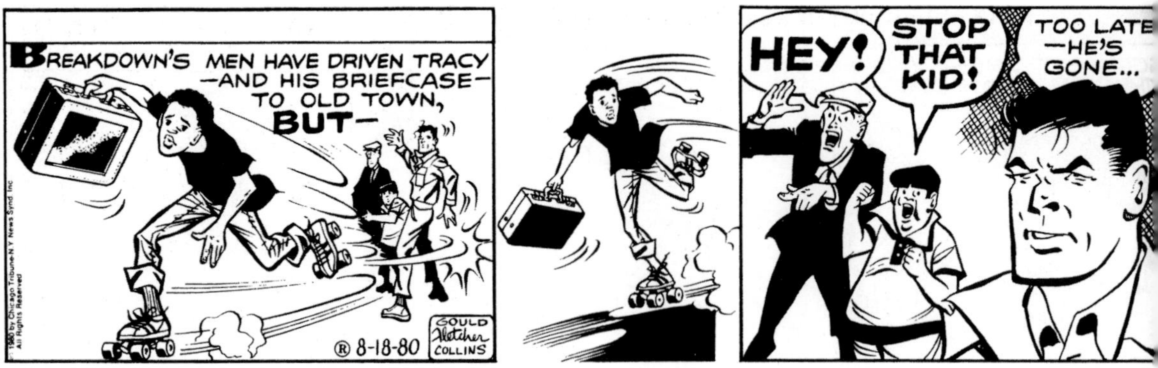
BREAKDOWN'S MEN HAVE DRIVEN TRACY —AND HIS BRIEFCASE— TO OLD TOWN, BUT—
© 1980 by Chicago Tribune-N.Y. News Synd. Inc All Rights Reserved
® 8-18-80
GOULD Fletcher COLLINS
HEY!
STOP THAT KID!
TOO LATE —HE'S GONE...

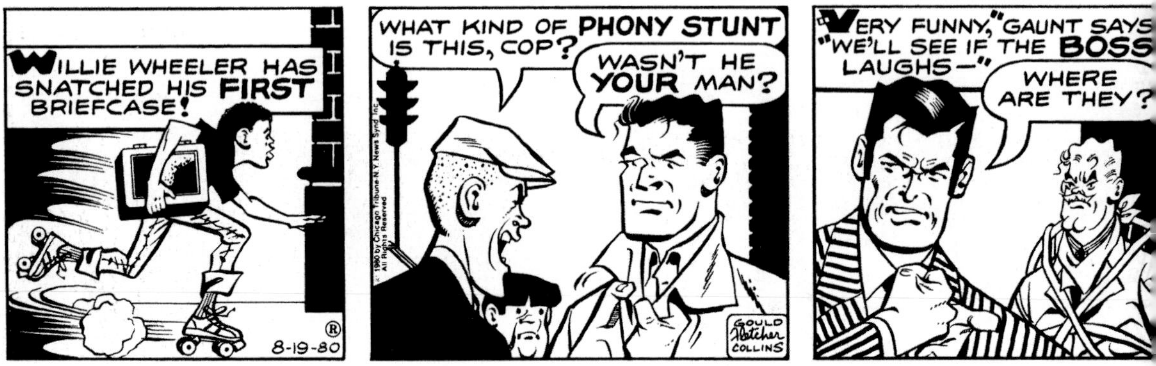
WILLIE WHEELER HAS SNATCHED HIS FIRST BRIEFCASE!
® 8-19-80
WHAT KIND OF PHONY STUNT IS THIS, COP?
WASN'T HE YOUR MAN?
© 1980 by Chicago Tribune-N.Y. News Synd. Inc All Rights Reserved
GOULD Fletcher COLLINS
"VERY FUNNY," GAUNT SAYS "WE'LL SEE IF THE BOSS LAUGHS—"
WHERE ARE THEY?

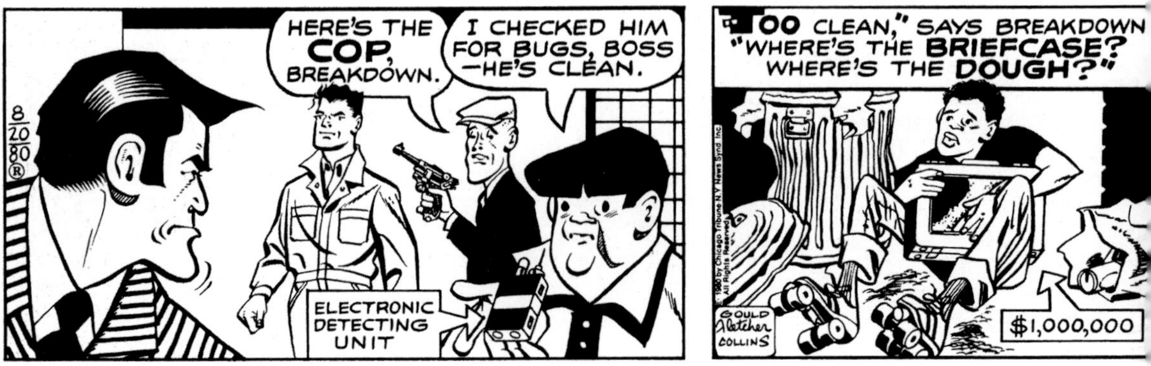
8 20 80 ®
HERE'S THE COP, BREAKDOWN.
I CHECKED HIM FOR BUGS, BOSS —HE'S CLEAN.
ELECTRONIC DETECTING UNIT
"TOO CLEAN," SAYS BREAKDOWN "WHERE'S THE BRIEFCASE? WHERE'S THE DOUGH?"
© 1980 by Chicago Tribune-N.Y. News Synd. Inc All Rights Reserved
GOULD Fletcher COLLINS
$1,000,000

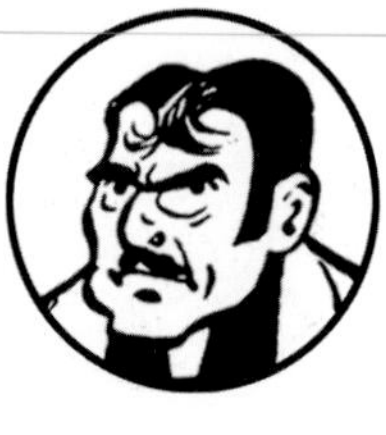

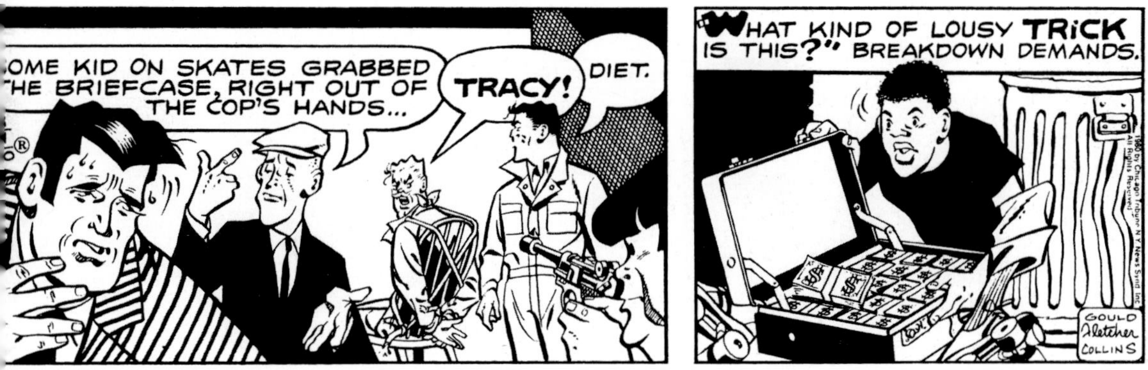

OME KID ON SKATES GRABBED THE BRIEFCASE, RIGHT OUT OF THE COP'S HANDS...
TRACY!
DIET.
"WHAT KIND OF LOUSY TRICK IS THIS?" BREAKDOWN DEMANDS.
GOULD Fletcher COLLINS

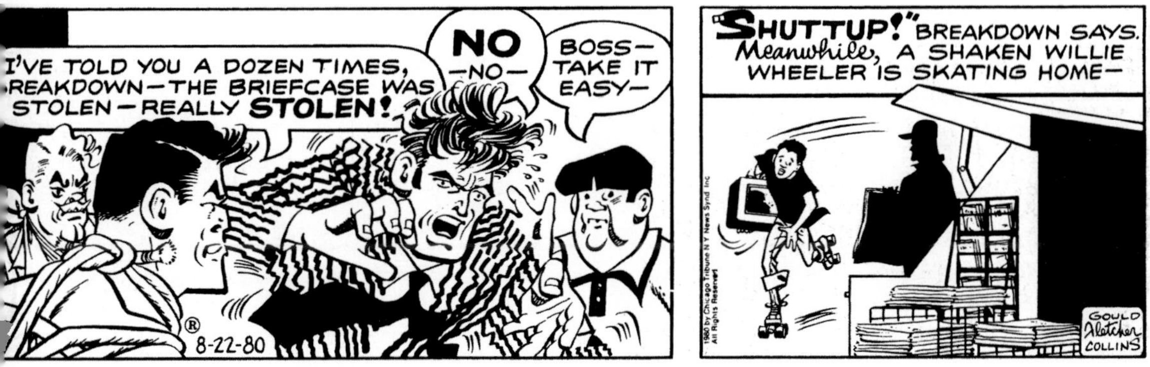

I'VE TOLD YOU A DOZEN TIMES, REAKDOWN—THE BRIEFCASE WAS STOLEN—REALLY STOLEN!
NO —NO—
BOSS— TAKE IT EASY—
8-22-80
"SHUTTUP!" BREAKDOWN SAYS. Meanwhile, A SHAKEN WILLIE WHEELER IS SKATING HOME—
1980 by Chicago Tribune N.Y. News Synd Inc All Rights Reserved
GOULD Fletcher COLLINS

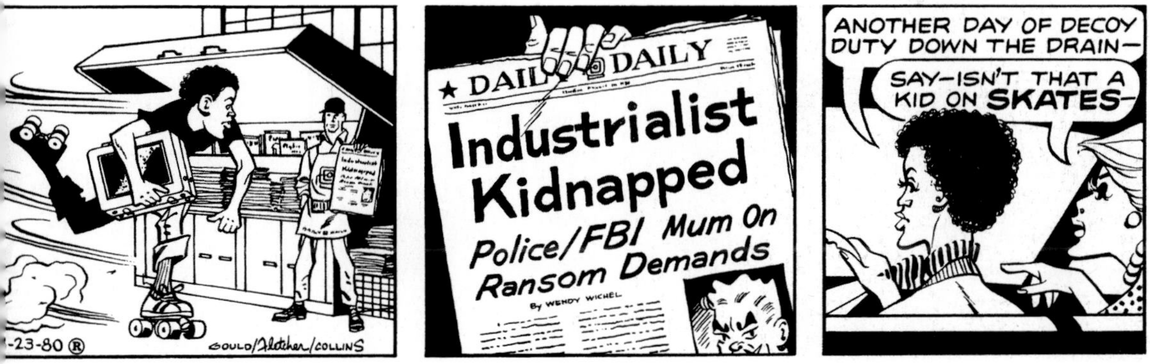

-23-80
GOULD/Fletcher/COLLINS
DAILY DAILY
Industrialist Kidnapped
Police/FBI Mum On Ransom Demands
BY WENDY WICHEL
ANOTHER DAY OF DECOY DUTY DOWN THE DRAIN—
SAY—ISN'T THAT A KID ON SKATES—

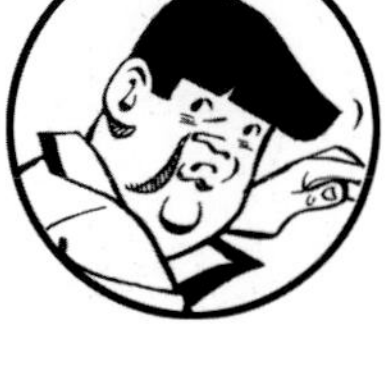

BREAKDOWN, YOU'RE GOING TO HAVE TO FACE IT—THE MONEY WAS STOLEN!
STOLEN! IMPOSSIBLE... CAN'T COPE WITH THAT...
BOSS, EASY—
SHUTTUP! CALL SMITH ENTERPRISES AND GIVE THEM ONE HOUR—
GOULD/Fletcher/COLLINS
"—TO RETRIEVE THAT MONEY—OR BOTH DIET SMITH AND TRACY DIE—
DID YOU SEE THAT KID ON SKATES?

"HE HAD A BRIEFCASE," LIZZ SAYS. "WHAT'S A KID DOING WITH A BRIEFCASE?"
YOU'LL HAVE TO GET OUT AND GO AFTER HIM ON FOOT—TRAFFIC'S ALL JAMMED UP.
CAB
BUT WITHIN MINUTES, WILLIE—AND $1,000,000—ARE HOME—
ALL THIS MONEY— I COULD TAKE MOM TO ARIZONA, FOR HER HEALTH— I COULD DO ANYTHING—
8-24-80

SO MUCH MONEY —OUR PROBLEMS WOULD BE OVER— WE COULD MOVE TO ARIZONA...
8-25-80 GOULD Fletcher COLLINS
BUT THAT NEWSPAPER HEADLINE...
Industrialist Kidnapped
Ransom Demand
"IS THAT WHAT THIS MONEY IS?"
THE RANSOM WAS STOLEN BY A KID ON SKATES
CRAZY BUT TRUE, DIET.

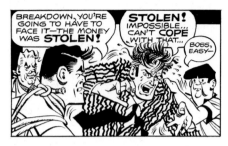

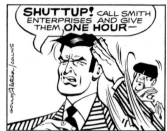

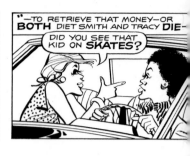

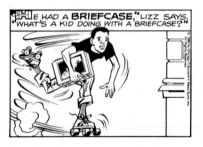

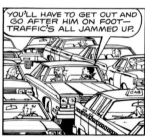

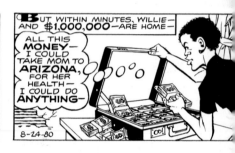

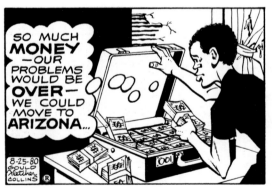

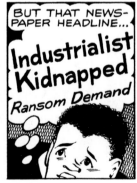

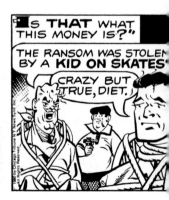

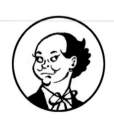

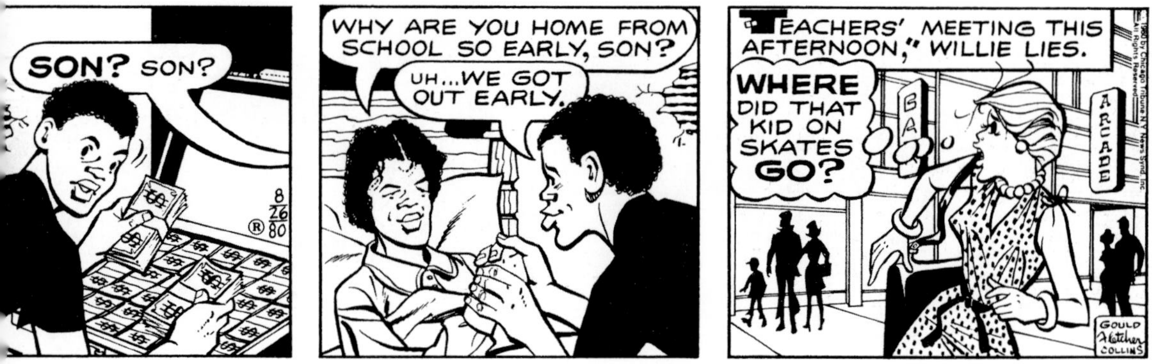
SON? SON?
8/26/80 ®
WHY ARE YOU HOME FROM SCHOOL SO EARLY, SON?
UH...WE GOT OUT EARLY.
"TEACHERS' MEETING THIS AFTERNOON," WILLIE LIES.
WHERE DID THAT KID ON SKATES GO?
ARCADE
© 1980 by Chicago Tribune-N.Y. News Synd. Inc. All Rights Reserved
GOULD Fletcher COLLINS

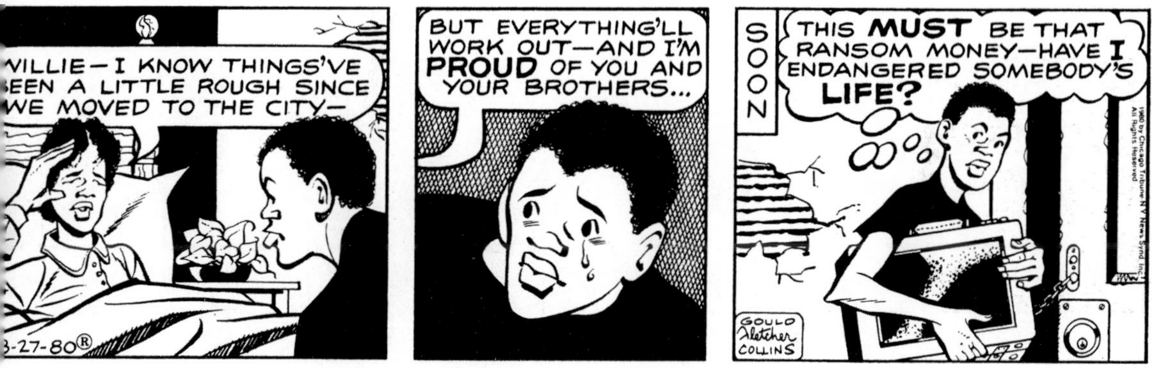
WILLIE—I KNOW THINGS'VE BEEN A LITTLE ROUGH SINCE WE MOVED TO THE CITY—
-27-80®
BUT EVERYTHING'LL WORK OUT—AND I'M PROUD OF YOU AND YOUR BROTHERS...
SOON
THIS MUST BE THAT RANSOM MONEY—HAVE I ENDANGERED SOMEBODY'S LIFE?
© 1980 by Chicago Tribune-N.Y. News Synd. Inc. All Rights Reserved
GOULD Fletcher COLLINS

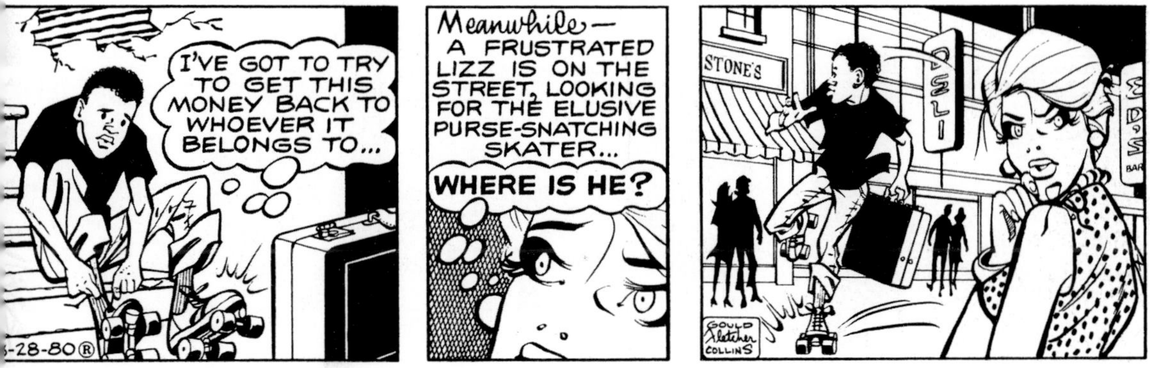
I'VE GOT TO TRY TO GET THIS MONEY BACK TO WHOEVER IT BELONGS TO...
-28-80®
Meanwhile—
A FRUSTRATED LIZZ IS ON THE STREET, LOOKING FOR THE ELUSIVE PURSE-SNATCHING SKATER...
WHERE IS HE?
STONE'S
DELI
BAR
GOULD Fletcher COLLINS

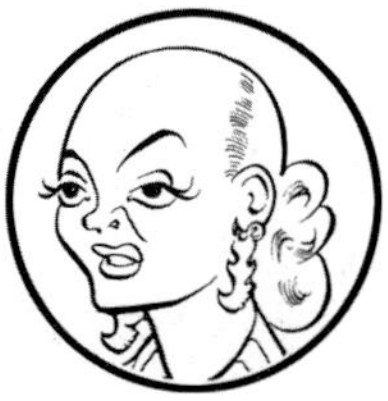

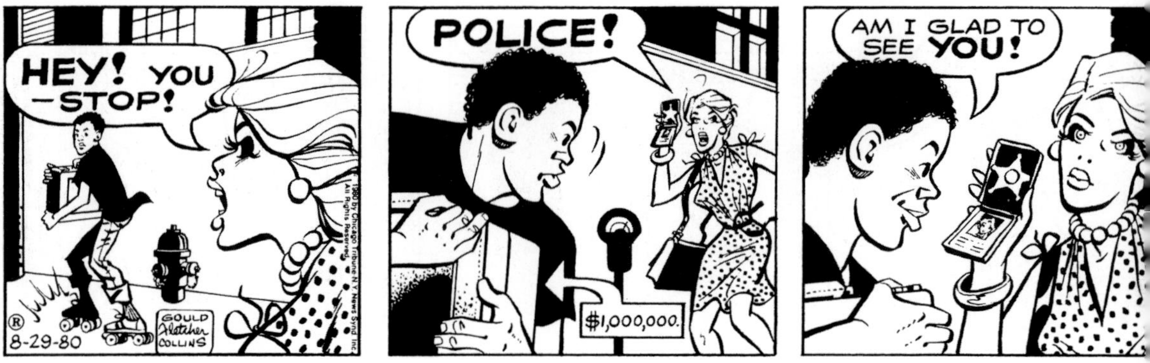
HEY! YOU —STOP!
8-29-80
GOULD Fletcher COLLINS
POLICE!
$1,000,000.
AM I GLAD TO SEE YOU!

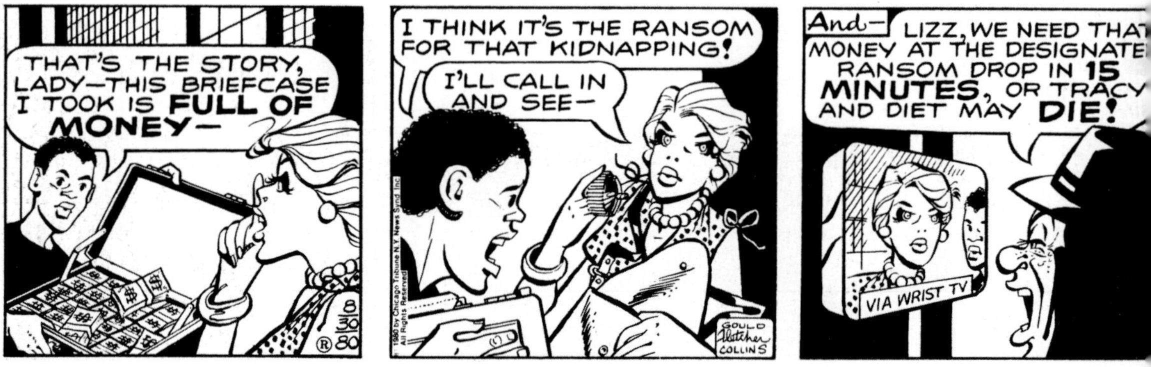
THAT'S THE STORY, LADY—THIS BRIEFCASE I TOOK IS FULL OF MONEY—
8 30 80
I THINK IT'S THE RANSOM FOR THAT KIDNAPPING!
I'LL CALL IN AND SEE—
GOULD Fletcher COLLINS
And—
LIZZ, WE NEED THAT MONEY AT THE DESIGNATE RANSOM DROP IN 15 MINUTES, OR TRACY AND DIET MAY DIE!
VIA WRIST TV

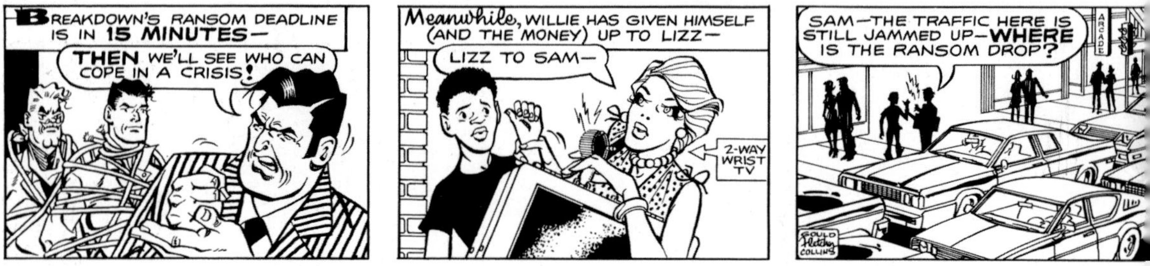
BREAKDOWN'S RANSOM DEADLINE IS IN 15 MINUTES—
THEN WE'LL SEE WHO CAN COPE IN A CRISIS!
Meanwhile, WILLIE HAS GIVEN HIMSELF (AND THE MONEY) UP TO LIZZ—
LIZZ TO SAM—
2-WAY WRIST TV
SAM—THE TRAFFIC HERE IS STILL JAMMED UP—WHERE IS THE RANSOM DROP?
ARCADE
GOULD Fletcher COLLINS

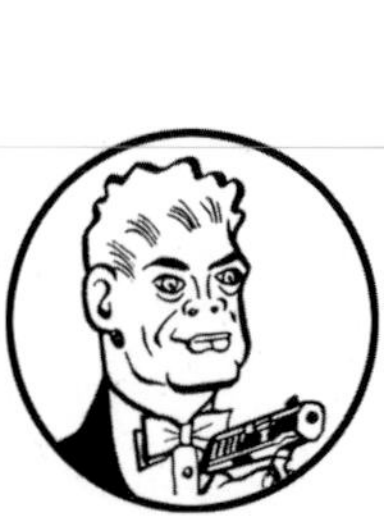

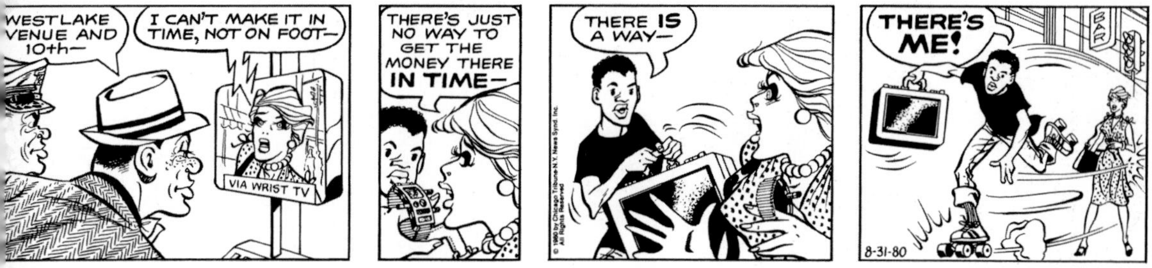
WESTLAKE
VENUE AND
10th—
I CAN'T MAKE IT IN
TIME, NOT ON FOOT—
VIA WRIST TV
THERE'S JUST
NO WAY TO
GET THE
MONEY THERE
IN TIME—
THERE IS
A WAY—
THERE'S
ME!
BAR
8-31-80

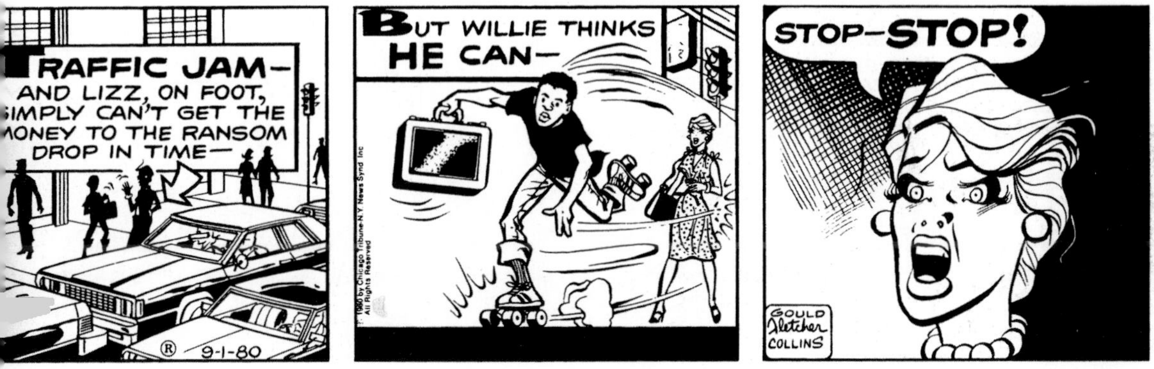
TRAFFIC JAM—
AND LIZZ, ON FOOT,
SIMPLY CAN'T GET THE
MONEY TO THE RANSOM
DROP IN TIME—
9-1-80
BUT WILLIE THINKS
HE CAN—
© 1980 by Chicago Tribune-N.Y. News Synd Inc
All Rights Reserved
STOP—STOP!
GOULD
Fletcher
COLLINS

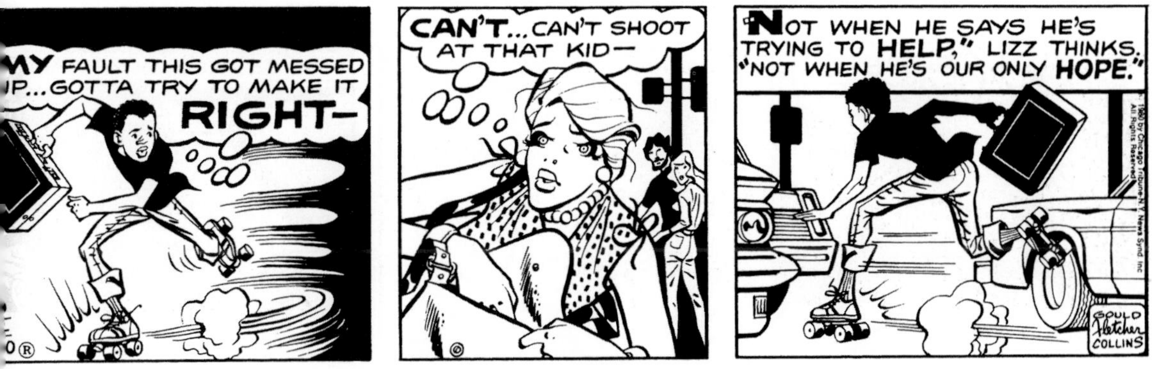
MY FAULT THIS GOT MESSED
UP... GOTTA TRY TO MAKE IT
RIGHT—
CAN'T... CAN'T SHOOT
AT THAT KID—
"NOT WHEN HE SAYS HE'S
TRYING TO HELP," LIZZ THINKS.
"NOT WHEN HE'S OUR ONLY HOPE."
© 1980 by Chicago Tribune-N.Y. News Synd Inc
All Rights Reserved
GOULD
Fletcher
COLLINS

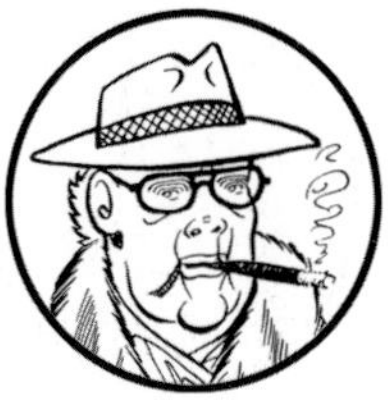

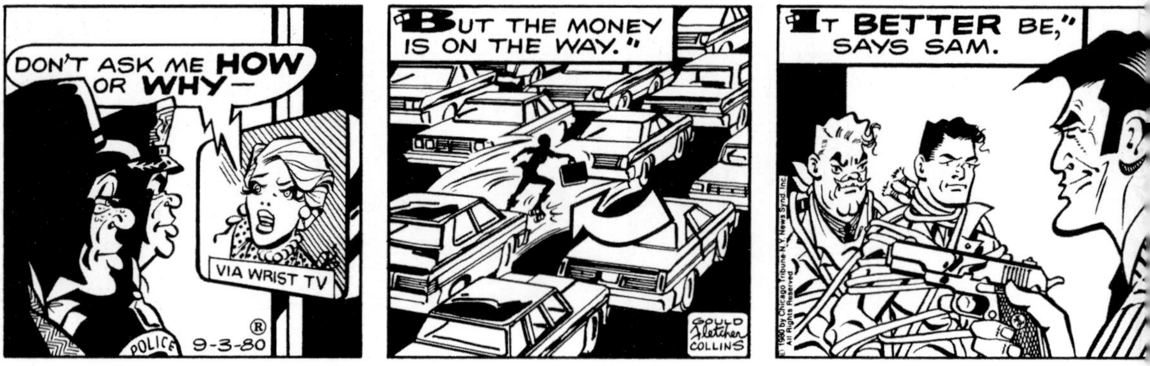
DON'T ASK ME HOW OR WHY—
VIA WRIST TV
POLICE
9-3-80
"BUT THE MONEY IS ON THE WAY."
GOULD Fletcher COLLINS
"IT BETTER BE," SAYS SAM.
© 1980 Chicago Tribune-N.Y. News Synd. Inc. All Rights Reserved

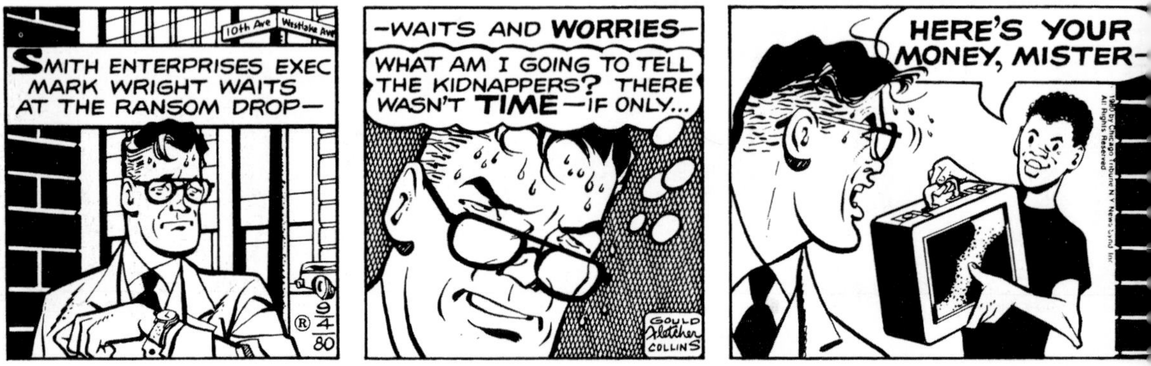
10th Ave
Westlake Ave
SMITH ENTERPRISES EXEC MARK WRIGHT WAITS AT THE RANSOM DROP—
9/4/80
—WAITS AND WORRIES—
WHAT AM I GOING TO TELL THE KIDNAPPERS? THERE WASN'T TIME—IF ONLY...
GOULD Fletcher COLLINS
HERE'S YOUR MONEY, MISTER—
© 1980 by Chicago Tribune-N.Y. News Synd. Inc. All Rights Reserved

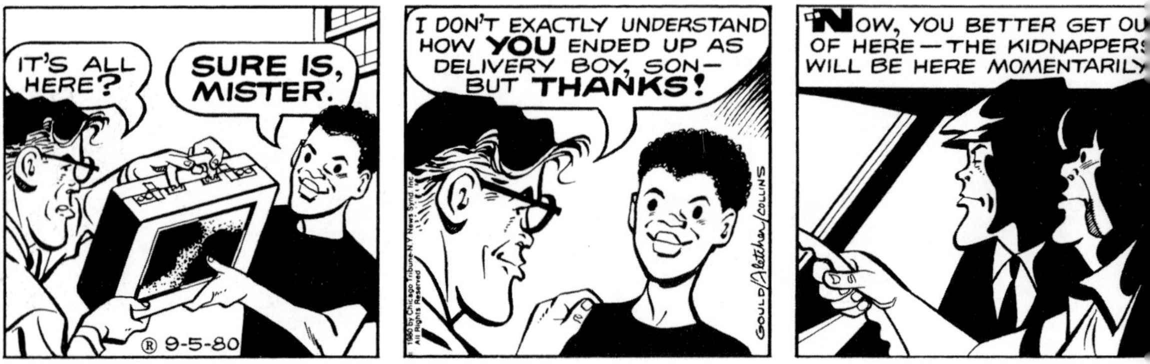
IT'S ALL HERE?
SURE IS, MISTER.
9-5-80
I DON'T EXACTLY UNDERSTAND HOW YOU ENDED UP AS DELIVERY BOY, SON— BUT THANKS!
© 1980 by Chicago Tribune-N.Y. News Synd. Inc. All Rights Reserved
GOULD/Fletcher/COLLINS
"NOW, YOU BETTER GET OU OF HERE—THE KIDNAPPERS WILL BE HERE MOMENTARILY

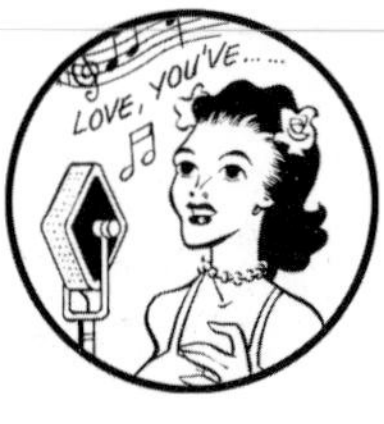
LOVE, YOU'VE.....

WE DON'T WANT YOU—
JUST THE DOUGH—
9-6-'80
THAT WAS EASY ENOUGH.
EASY ENOUGH.
$1,000,000.
GOULD/Fletcher/COLLINS

T'S THE CRAZIEST THING—A KID ON
SKATES DELIVERED THE BRIEF-
CASE OF RANSOM MONEY TO ME!
YES, AND THE KIDNAPPERS PICKED IT UP
SOON AFTER—WE GOT IT ON VIDEO TAPE,
FROM OUR POSITION ACROSS THE WAY.
And—
I DON'T KNOW HOW IT COULD'VE
GONE ANY SMOOTHER—
THE BOSS'LL
BE PLEASED—

BREAKDOWN WOULDN'T BE PLEASED,
ND NEITHER WOULD GAUNT AND PAUNCH,
F THEY KNEW ABOUT THEIR PASSENGER—
GOULD/Fletcher/COLLINS
© 1980 by Chicago Tribune-N.Y. News Synd. Inc.
All Rights Reserved
IT'S A GOOD THING
TRAFFIC'S SLOW—THIS
IS SCARY UNDER
ANY CONDITIONS!
While—
THE MONEY'LL BE
HERE SOON—THEN
THE REAL FUN
BEGINS!
9/7/80

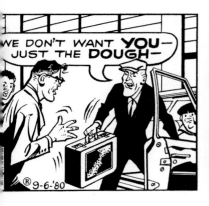

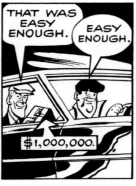

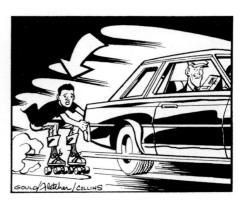

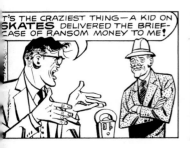

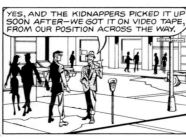

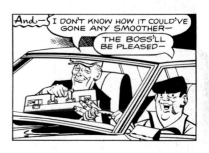

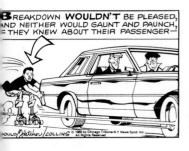

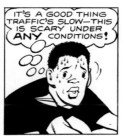

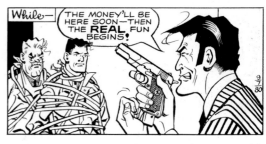

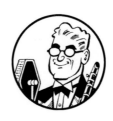

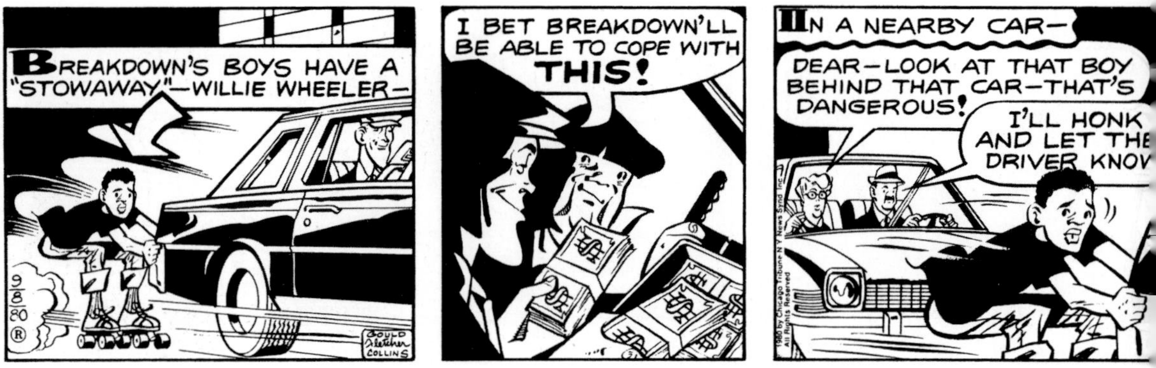
BREAKDOWN'S BOYS HAVE A "STOWAWAY"—WILLIE WHEELER—
9/8/80
I BET BREAKDOWN'LL BE ABLE TO COPE WITH THIS!
IN A NEARBY CAR—
DEAR—LOOK AT THAT BOY BEHIND THAT CAR—THAT'S DANGEROUS!
I'LL HONK AND LET THE DRIVER KNO

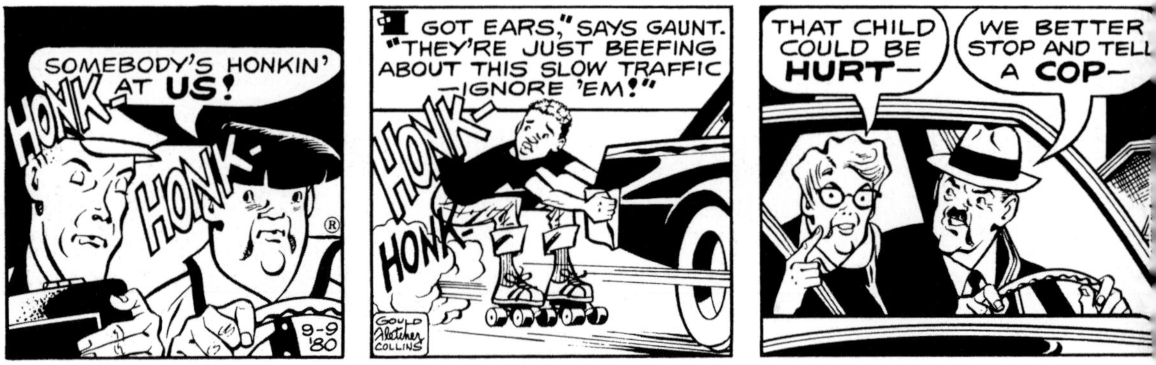
SOMEBODY'S HONKIN' AT US!
HONK-
HONK-
9-9 '80
"I GOT EARS," SAYS GAUNT. "THEY'RE JUST BEEFING ABOUT THIS SLOW TRAFFIC —IGNORE 'EM!"
HONK-
HONK-
THAT CHILD COULD BE HURT—
WE BETTER STOP AND TELL A COP—

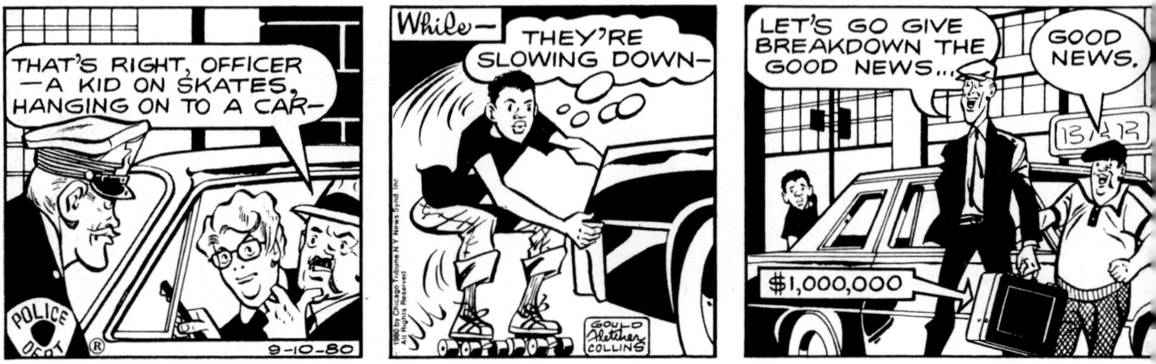
THAT'S RIGHT, OFFICER —A KID ON SKATES, HANGING ON TO A CAR—
POLICE DEPT
9-10-80
While—
THEY'RE SLOWING DOWN—
LET'S GO GIVE BREAKDOWN THE GOOD NEWS...
GOOD NEWS.
13 A 12
$1,000,000

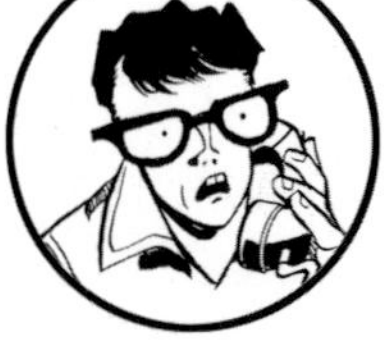

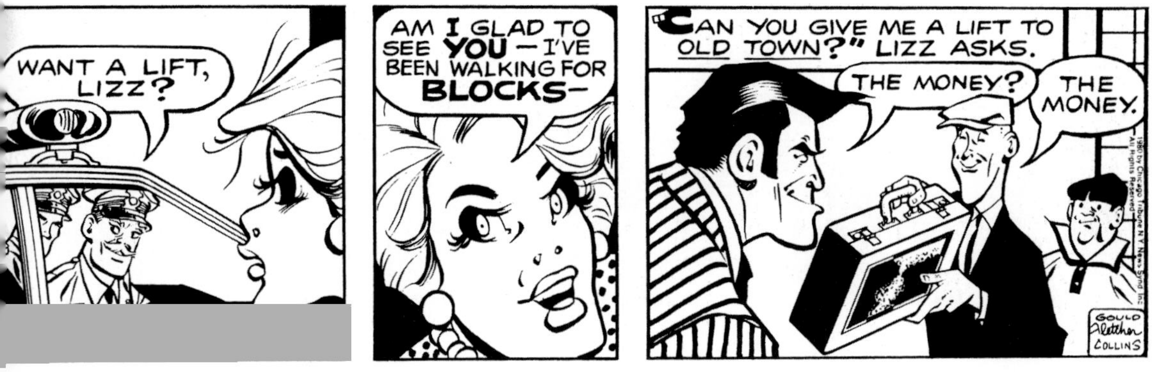
WANT A LIFT, LIZZ?
AM I GLAD TO SEE YOU — I'VE BEEN WALKING FOR BLOCKS—
"CAN YOU GIVE ME A LIFT TO OLD TOWN?" LIZZ ASKS.
THE MONEY?
THE MONEY.
GOULD Fletcher COLLINS

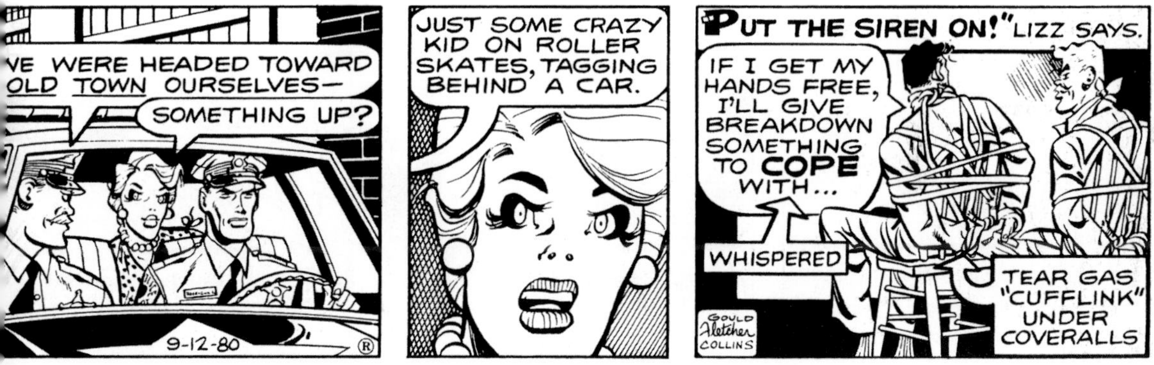
WE WERE HEADED TOWARD OLD TOWN OURSELVES—
SOMETHING UP?
9-12-80
JUST SOME CRAZY KID ON ROLLER SKATES, TAGGING BEHIND A CAR.
"PUT THE SIREN ON!" LIZZ SAYS.
IF I GET MY HANDS FREE, I'LL GIVE BREAKDOWN SOMETHING TO COPE WITH...
WHISPERED
TEAR GAS "CUFFLINK" UNDER COVERALLS
GOULD Fletcher COLLINS

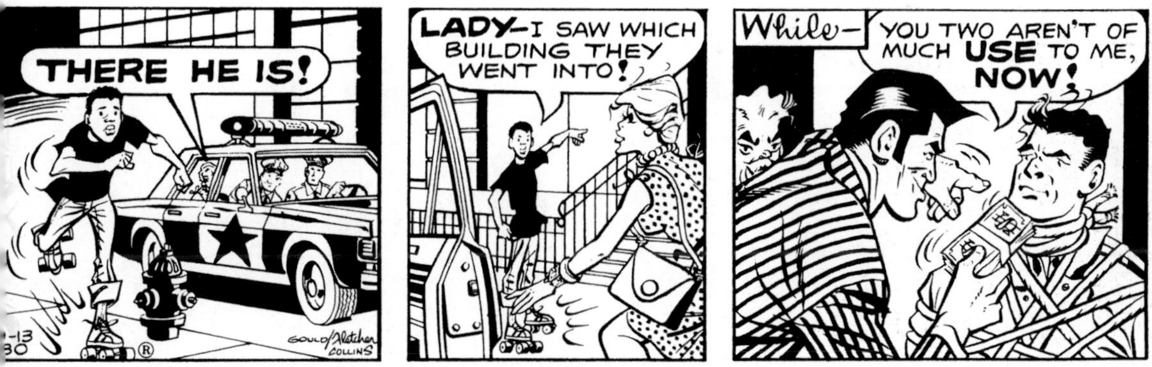
THERE HE IS!
GOULD/Fletcher COLLINS
LADY—I SAW WHICH BUILDING THEY WENT INTO!
While—
YOU TWO AREN'T OF MUCH USE TO ME, NOW!

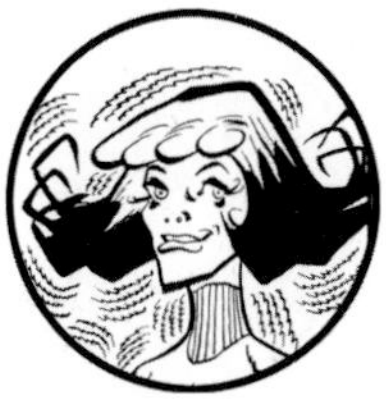

LIZZ TO SAM—OUR ROLLER SKATER TRAILED THE KIDNAPPERS TO A BUILDING IN UNDER TOWN— 1800 WEST BURNETT AVENUE.

2-WAY WRIST TV

ARE MORE COPS ON THE WAY, LADY?

THEY SURE ARE —THANKS TO YOU, SON...

THAT'S ONE LAW-BREAKER TURNING CRIMESTOPPER.

LIZZ—WE HAVE TO GET OFF THE STREET—

"HAVE TO KEEP A LOW PROFILE," SAYS GROOVY, "IN CASE THE KIDNAPPERS ARE KEEPING WATCH."

$1,000,000!

DON'T WORRY, BOYS—I'M NOT GOING TO KILL EITHER ONE OF YOU—

9 14 80

I'D RATHER HAVE YOU BOTH ALIVE AND HUMILIATED— —UNTIE 'EM...

I WANT YOU HUMILIATED!

TAKE IT EASY, BOSS.

9-15-80 ®

1980 by Chicago Tribune-N.Y. News Synd. Inc. All Rights Reserved

SHUTTUP!

HELLO, LIZZ—WHICH BUILDING IS IT?

RIGHT ACROSS FROM US, INSPECTOR TRAILER.

GOULD Fletcher COLLINS

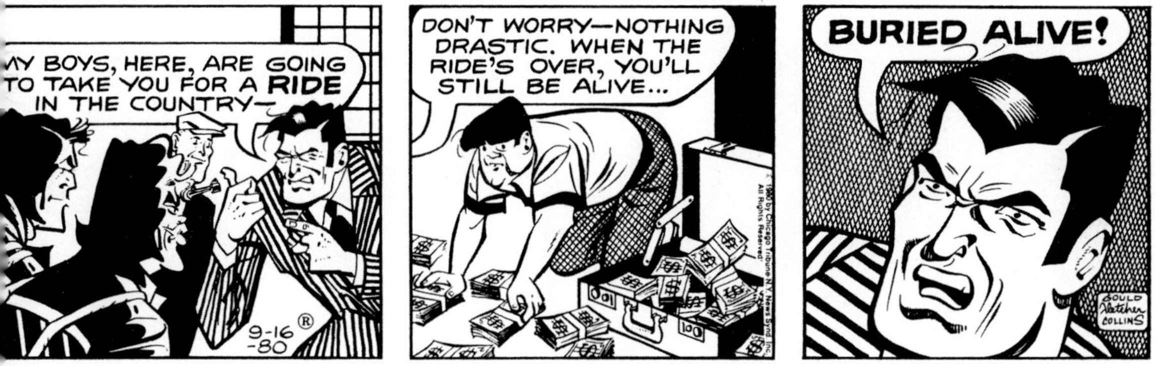
MY BOYS, HERE, ARE GOING TO TAKE YOU FOR A **RIDE** IN THE COUNTRY—
9-16 -80 ®
DON'T WORRY—NOTHING DRASTIC. WHEN THE RIDE'S OVER, YOU'LL STILL BE ALIVE...
© 1980 by Chicago Tribune-N.Y. News Synd. Inc. All Rights Reserved
BURIED ALIVE!
GOULD Fletcher COLLINS

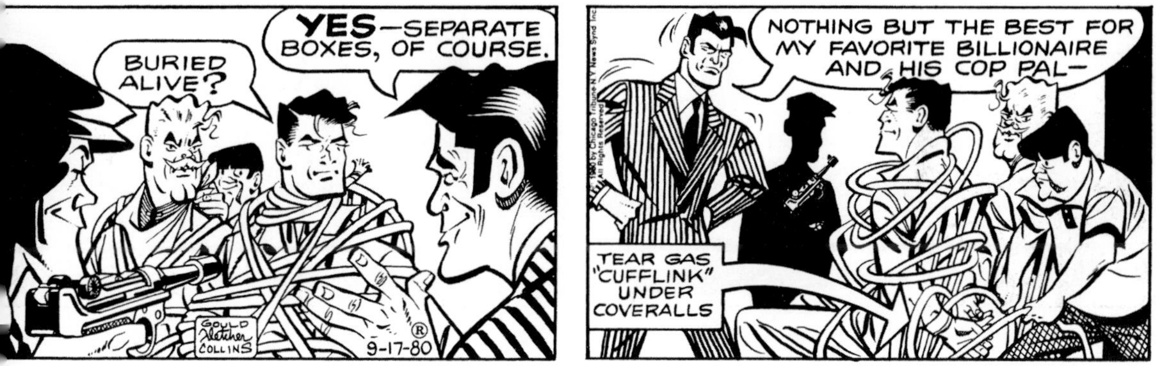
BURIED ALIVE?
YES—SEPARATE BOXES, OF COURSE.
GOULD Fletcher COLLINS
9-17-80 ®
© 1980 by Chicago Tribune-N.Y. News Synd. Inc. All Rights Reserved
NOTHING BUT THE BEST FOR MY FAVORITE BILLIONAIRE AND HIS COP PAL—
TEAR GAS "CUFFLINK" UNDER COVERALLS

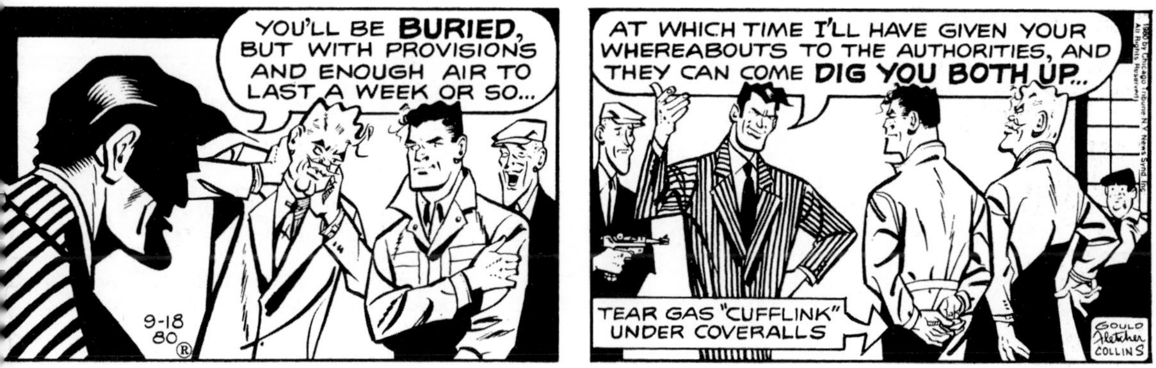
YOU'LL BE **BURIED**, BUT WITH PROVISIONS AND ENOUGH AIR TO LAST A WEEK OR SO...
9-18 80 ®
AT WHICH TIME I'LL HAVE GIVEN YOUR WHEREABOUTS TO THE AUTHORITIES, AND THEY CAN COME **DIG YOU BOTH UP**...
© 1980 by Chicago Tribune-N.Y. News Synd. Inc. All Rights Reserved
TEAR GAS "CUFFLINK" UNDER COVERALLS
GOULD Fletcher COLLINS

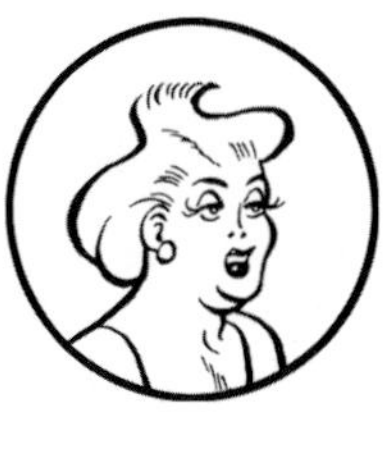

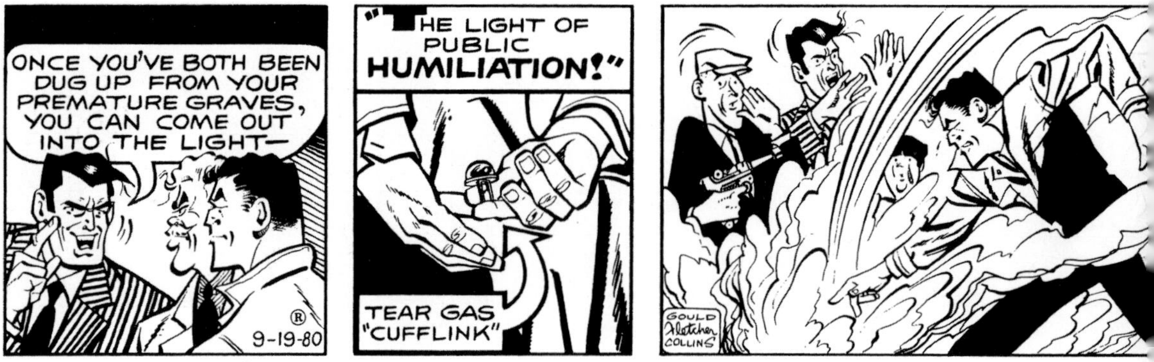
ONCE YOU'VE BOTH BEEN DUG UP FROM YOUR PREMATURE GRAVES, YOU CAN COME OUT INTO THE LIGHT—
9-19-80
"THE LIGHT OF PUBLIC HUMILIATION!"
TEAR GAS "CUFFLINK"
GOULD
Fletcher
COLLINS

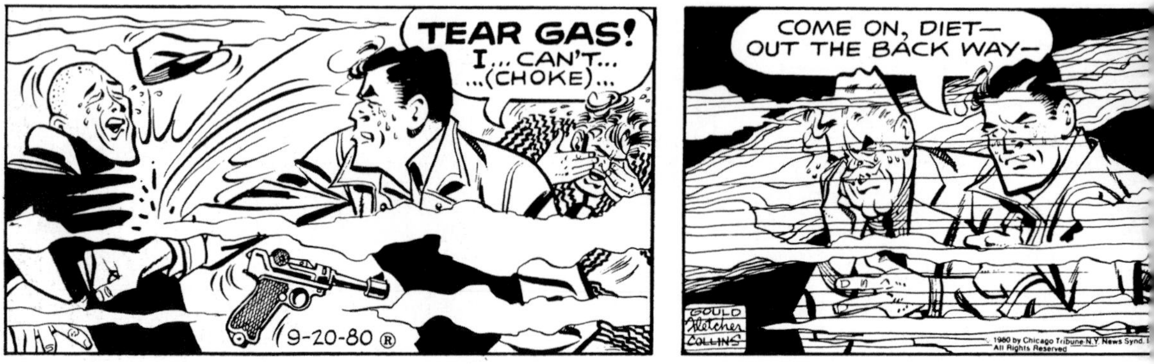
TEAR GAS! I... CAN'T... ...(CHOKE)...
9-20-80
COME ON, DIET— OUT THE BACK WAY—
GOULD
Fletcher
COLLINS
1980 by Chicago Tribune-N.Y. News Synd. I
All Rights Reserved

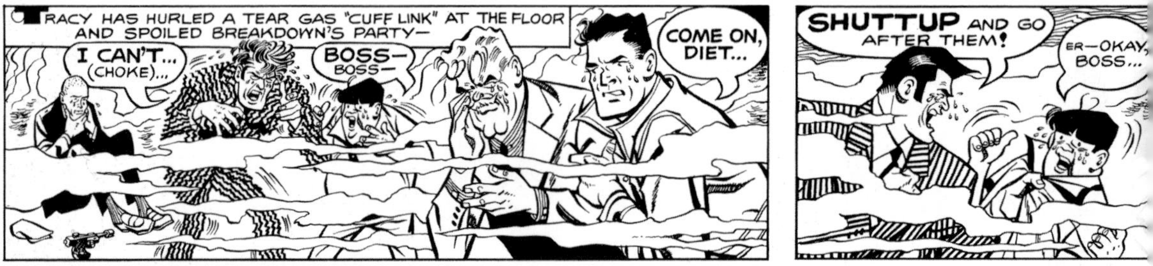
TRACY HAS HURLED A TEAR GAS "CUFF LINK" AT THE FLOOR AND SPOILED BREAKDOWN'S PARTY—
I CAN'T... (CHOKE)...
BOSS— BOSS—
COME ON, DIET...
SHUTTUP AND GO AFTER THEM!
ER—OKAY, BOSS...

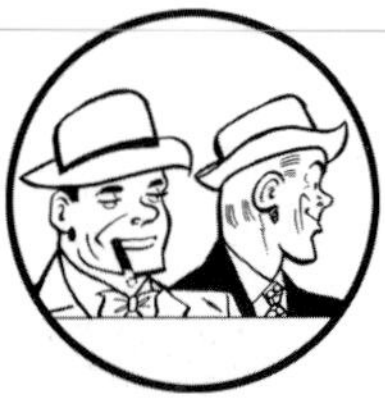

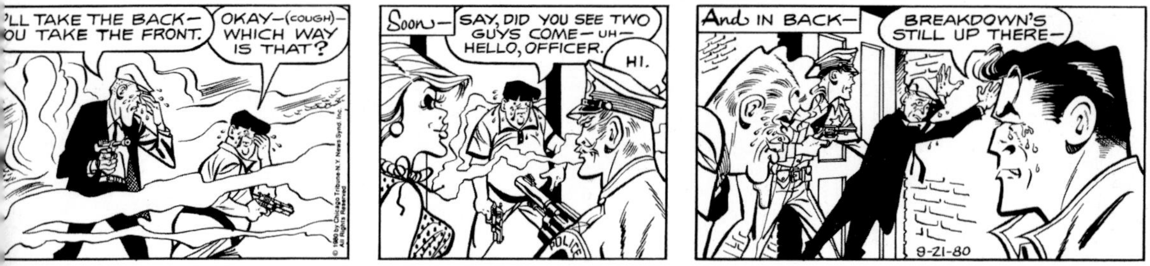

'LL TAKE THE BACK—
OU TAKE THE FRONT.
OKAY—(COUGH)—WHICH WAY IS THAT?
© 1980 by Chicago Tribune-N.Y. News Synd. Inc. All Rights Reserved
Soon—
SAY, DID YOU SEE TWO GUYS COME—UH—HELLO, OFFICER.
HI.
And IN BACK—
BREAKDOWN'S STILL UP THERE—
9-21-80

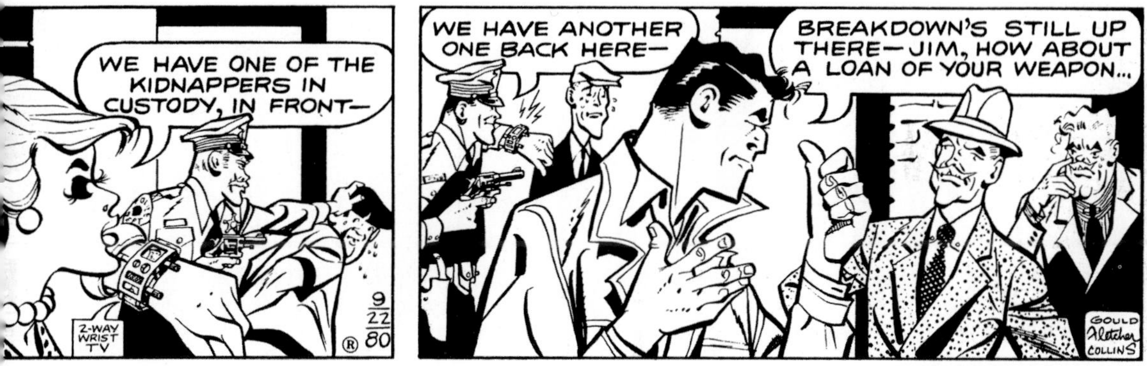

WE HAVE ONE OF THE KIDNAPPERS IN CUSTODY, IN FRONT—
2-WAY WRIST TV
9 22 80
®
WE HAVE ANOTHER ONE BACK HERE—
BREAKDOWN'S STILL UP THERE—JIM, HOW ABOUT A LOAN OF YOUR WEAPON...
GOULD Fletcher COLLINS

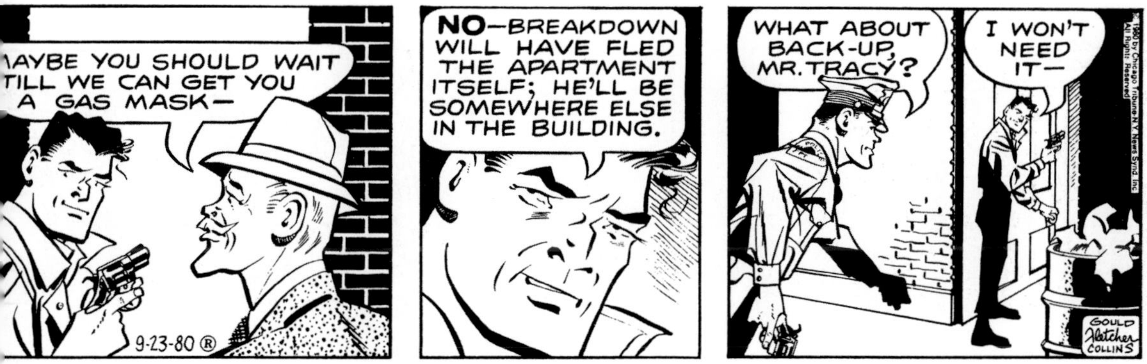

AYBE YOU SHOULD WAIT TILL WE CAN GET YOU A GAS MASK—
9-23-80 ®
NO—BREAKDOWN WILL HAVE FLED THE APARTMENT ITSELF; HE'LL BE SOMEWHERE ELSE IN THE BUILDING.
WHAT ABOUT BACK-UP, MR. TRACY?
I WON'T NEED IT—
© 1980 by Chicago Tribune-N.Y. News Synd. Inc. All Rights Reserved
GOULD Fletcher COLLINS

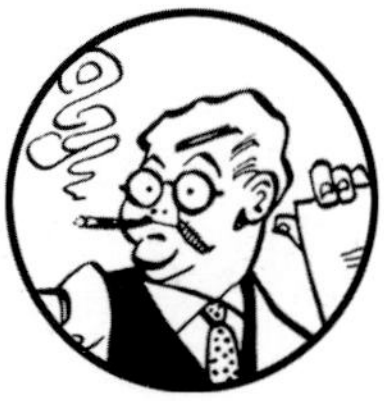

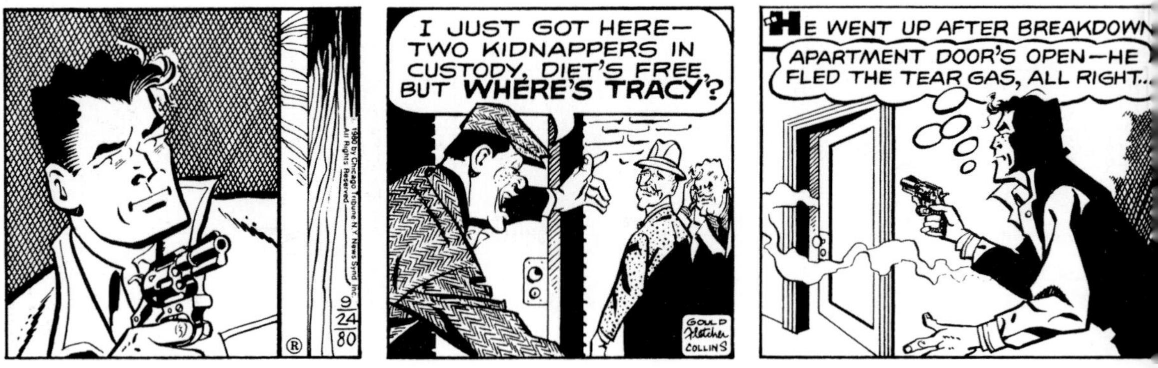
1980 by Chicago Tribune N.Y. News Synd Inc. All Rights Reserved
9/24/80
I JUST GOT HERE— TWO KIDNAPPERS IN CUSTODY, DIET'S FREE, BUT WHERE'S TRACY?
GOULD Fletcher COLLINS
HE WENT UP AFTER BREAKDOWN
APARTMENT DOOR'S OPEN—HE FLED THE TEAR GAS, ALL RIGHT...

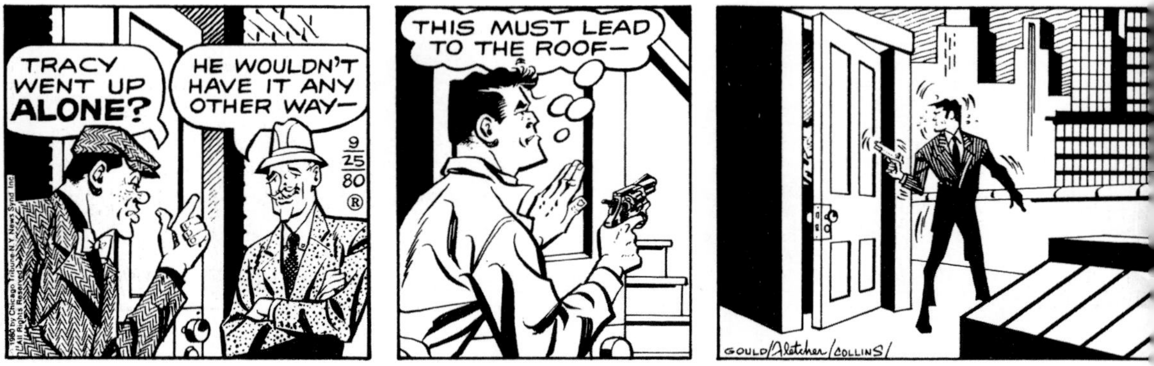
TRACY WENT UP ALONE?
HE WOULDN'T HAVE IT ANY OTHER WAY—
9/25/80
1980 by Chicago Tribune N.Y. News Synd Inc. All Rights Reserved
THIS MUST LEAD TO THE ROOF—
GOULD/Fletcher/COLLINS/

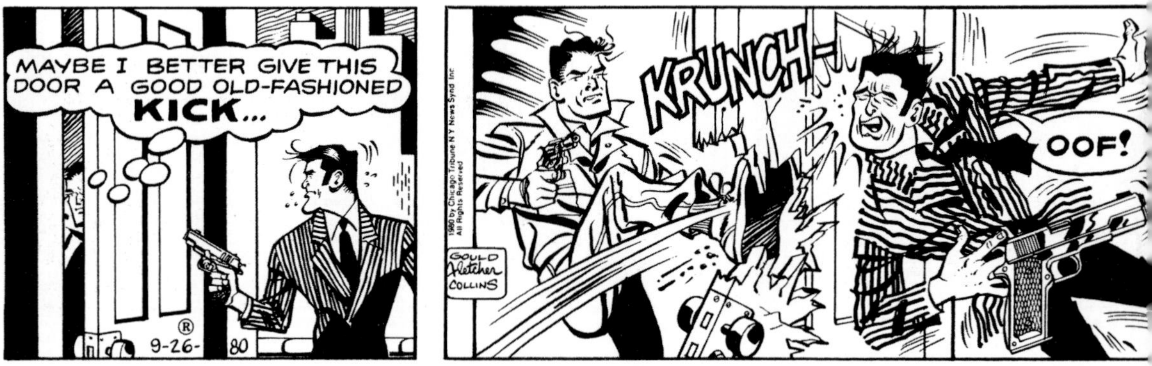
MAYBE I BETTER GIVE THIS DOOR A GOOD OLD-FASHIONED KICK...
9-26-80
1980 by Chicago Tribune N.Y. News Synd Inc. All Rights Reserved
GOULD Fletcher COLLINS
KRUNCH-
OOF!

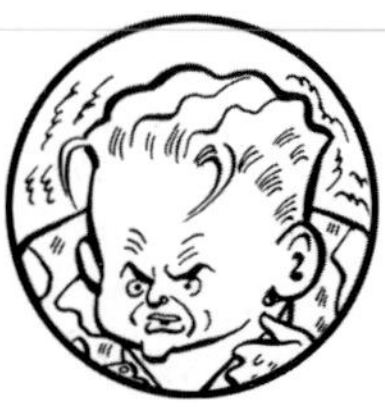

HELLO, BREAKDOWN—
9-27-80
© 1980 by Chicago Tribune-N.Y. News Synd. Inc. All Rights Reserved
GOULD Fletcher COLLINS
THINKING OF GOING FOR THAT GUN, ARE YOU? I CAN COPE WITH THAT...

RACY AND BREAKDOWN HAVE COME
ACE-TO-FACE, ON THE APARTMENT
BUILDING ROOF...
GOULD Fletcher COLLINS
I DIDN'T THINK YOU WANTED THAT GUN, BREAKDOWN—
© 1980 by Chicago Tribune-N.Y. News Synd. Inc. All Rights Reserved

CAN'T COPE—
AN'T COPE...
YOU CAN COPE WITH THE STAIRS, BREAK-DOWN—COME ON...
Soon—
THAT'S A MASTER KIDNAPPER?
HE JUST CAN'T COPE WITH COPS...
TRACY, THERE'S SOMEBODY YOU OUGHT TO MEET...
9 28 80

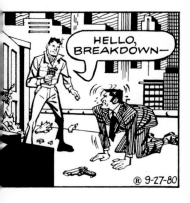

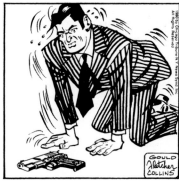

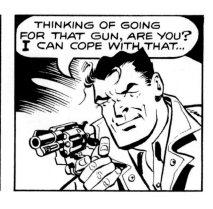

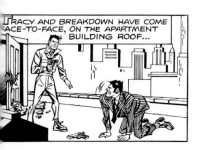

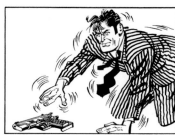

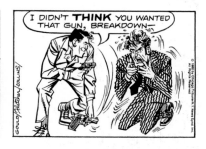

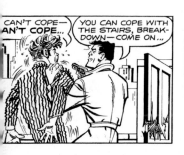

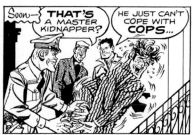

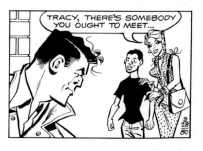

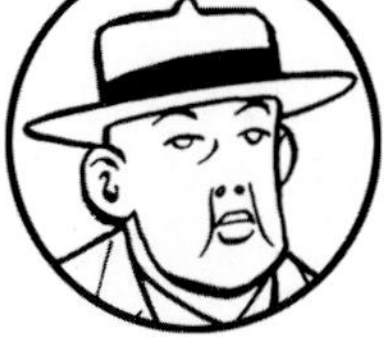

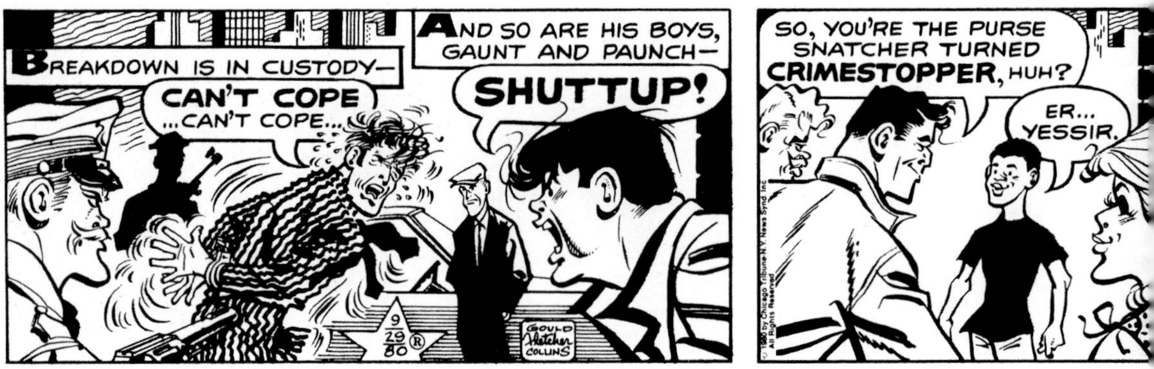
BREAKDOWN IS IN CUSTODY—
CAN'T COPE ...CAN'T COPE...
AND SO ARE HIS BOYS, GAUNT AND PAUNCH—
SHUTTUP!
9 29 80 ®
GOULD Fletcher COLLINS
SO, YOU'RE THE PURSE SNATCHER TURNED CRIMESTOPPER, HUH?
ER... YESSIR.
© 1980 by Chicago Tribune-N.Y. News Synd. Inc. All Rights Reserved

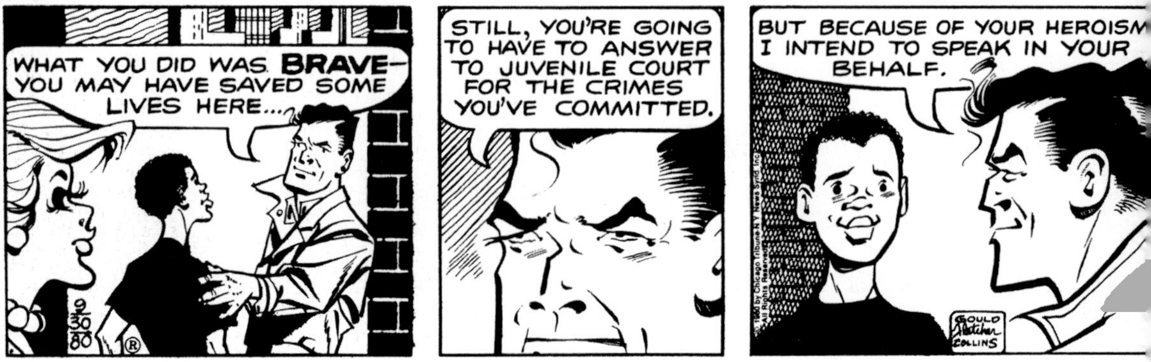
WHAT YOU DID WAS BRAVE— YOU MAY HAVE SAVED SOME LIVES HERE...
9 30 80 ®
STILL, YOU'RE GOING TO HAVE TO ANSWER TO JUVENILE COURT FOR THE CRIMES YOU'VE COMMITTED.
BUT BECAUSE OF YOUR HEROISM I INTEND TO SPEAK IN YOUR BEHALF.
© 1980 by Chicago Tribune-N.Y. News Synd. Inc. All Rights Reserved
GOULD Fletcher COLLINS

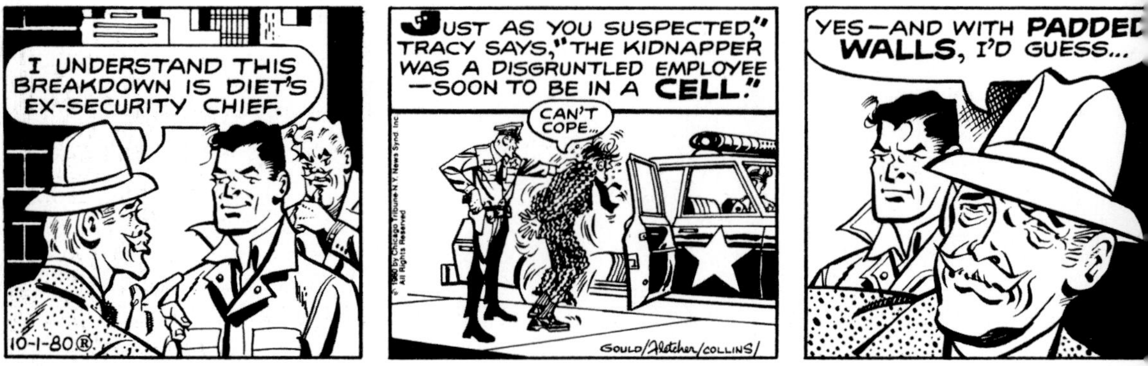
I UNDERSTAND THIS BREAKDOWN IS DIET'S EX-SECURITY CHIEF.
10-1-80 ®
"JUST AS YOU SUSPECTED," TRACY SAYS, "THE KIDNAPPER WAS A DISGRUNTLED EMPLOYEE —SOON TO BE IN A CELL."
CAN'T COPE...
© 1980 by Chicago Tribune-N.Y. News Synd. Inc. All Rights Reserved
GOULD/Fletcher/COLLINS/
YES—AND WITH PADDED WALLS, I'D GUESS...

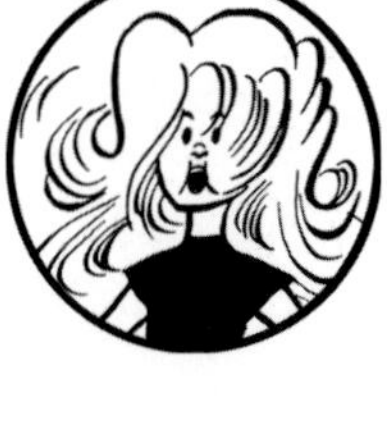

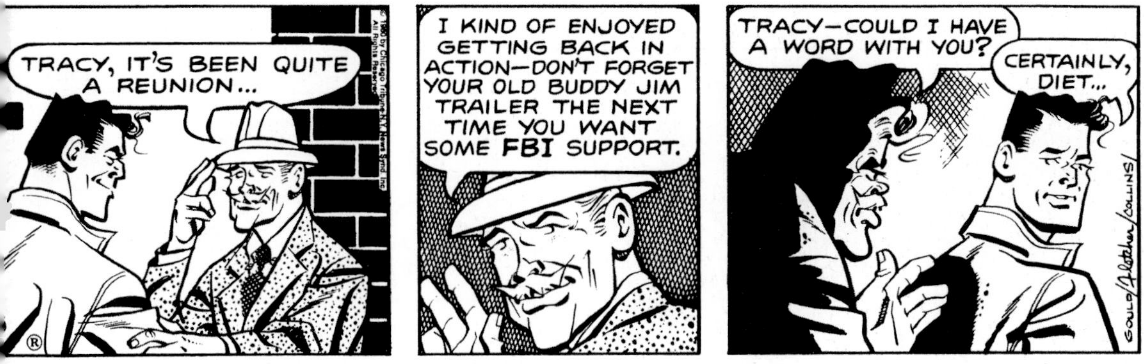
TRACY, IT'S BEEN QUITE A REUNION...
© 1980 by Chicago Tribune-N.Y. News Synd. Inc. All Rights Reserved
I KIND OF ENJOYED GETTING BACK IN ACTION—DON'T FORGET YOUR OLD BUDDY JIM TRAILER THE NEXT TIME YOU WANT SOME FBI SUPPORT.
TRACY—COULD I HAVE A WORD WITH YOU?
CERTAINLY, DIET...
GOULD / Fletcher / COLLINS

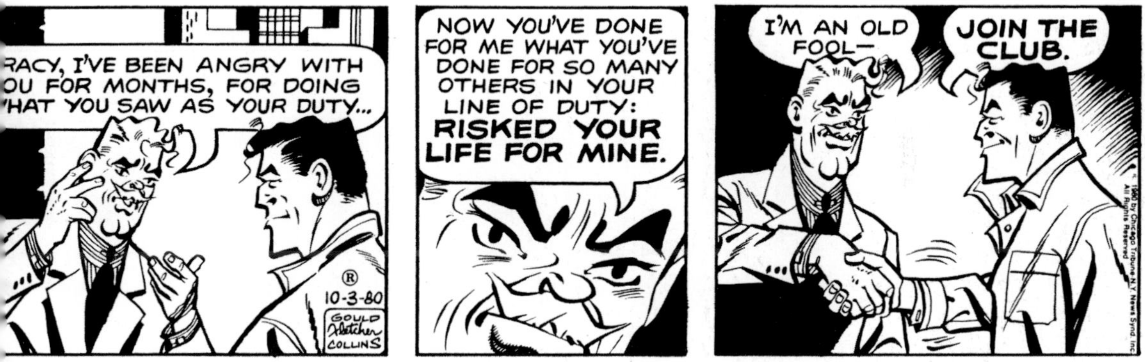
RACY, I'VE BEEN ANGRY WITH OU FOR MONTHS, FOR DOING HAT YOU SAW AS YOUR DUTY...
10-3-80
GOULD Fletcher COLLINS
NOW YOU'VE DONE FOR ME WHAT YOU'VE DONE FOR SO MANY OTHERS IN YOUR LINE OF DUTY: RISKED YOUR LIFE FOR MINE.
I'M AN OLD FOOL—
JOIN THE CLUB.
© 1980 by Chicago Tribune-N.Y. News Synd. Inc. All Rights Reserved

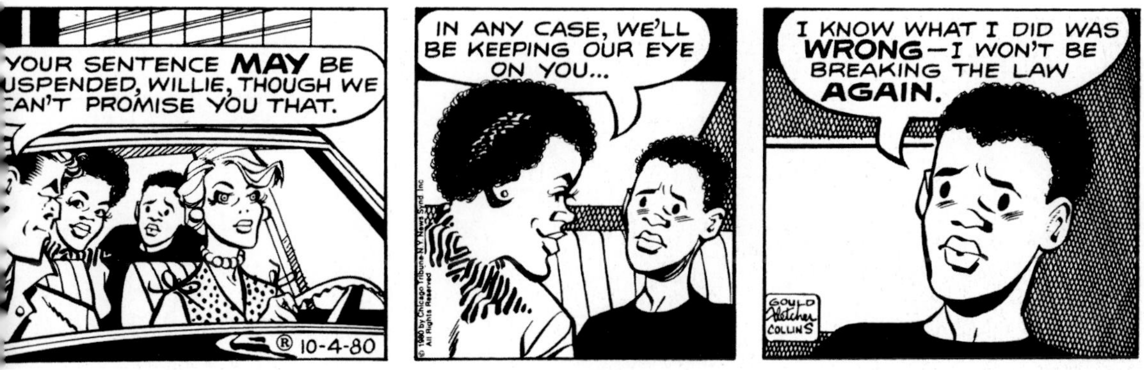
YOUR SENTENCE MAY BE USPENDED, WILLIE, THOUGH WE CAN'T PROMISE YOU THAT.
10-4-80
IN ANY CASE, WE'LL BE KEEPING OUR EYE ON YOU...
© 1980 by Chicago Tribune-N.Y. News Synd. Inc. All Rights Reserved
I KNOW WHAT I DID WAS WRONG—I WON'T BE BREAKING THE LAW AGAIN.
GOULD Fletcher COLLINS

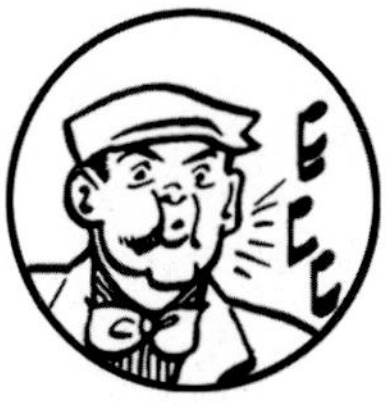

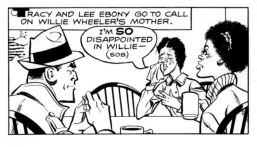

TRACY AND LEE EBONY GO TO CALL ON WILLIE WHEELER'S MOTHER.
I'M SO DISAPPOINTED IN WILLIE— (SOB)
MRS. WHEELER, YOU HAVE A RIGHT TO BE UPSET WITH WILLIE — HIS PURSE SNATCHING CAN'T BE JUSTIFIED...
BUT HE DID COME THROUGH IN THE CLUT
—RETURNED THE RANSOM MONEY, AN
FOLLOWED THE KIDNAPPERS, REPORTIN
THEIR LOCATION TO THE POLICE.

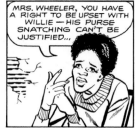

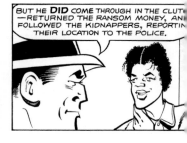

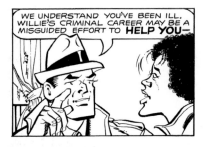

WE UNDERSTAND YOU'VE BEEN ILL. WILLIE'S CRIMINAL CAREER MAY BE A MISGUIDED EFFORT TO HELP YOU—
WHY HAVEN'T YOU SOUGHT HELP AT THE FREE CLINIC?" "I'M AFRAID OF A LENGTHY HOSPITAL STAY," SHE SAYS.
GOULD/Fletcher/COLLINS
I'M WORRIED I COULD LOSE MY BOY
THIS NEEDS BURNING.
CALL TORCHER?
© 1980 by Chicago Tribune-N.Y. News Synd. Inc All Rights Reserved

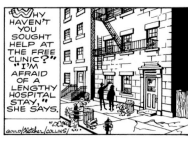

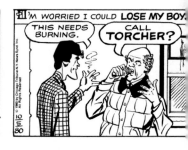

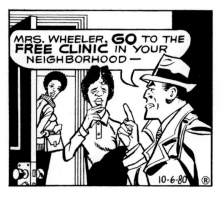

MRS. WHEELER, GO TO THE FREE CLINIC IN YOUR NEIGHBORHOOD—
10-6-80
YOU NEEDN'T WORRY ABOUT LOSING YOUR BOYS BECAUSE OF ANY HOSPITALIZATION YOU MIGHT NEED—
WAS THAT THE MAN WHO ARRESTED WILLIE, MOMMY?
YES—AND HE'S THE BES
FRIEND YOUR BROTHER
EVER HAD.
© 1980 by Chicago Tribune-N.Y. News Synd. Inc All Rights Reserved

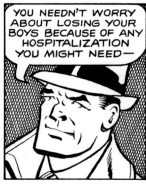

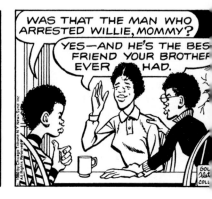

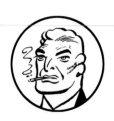

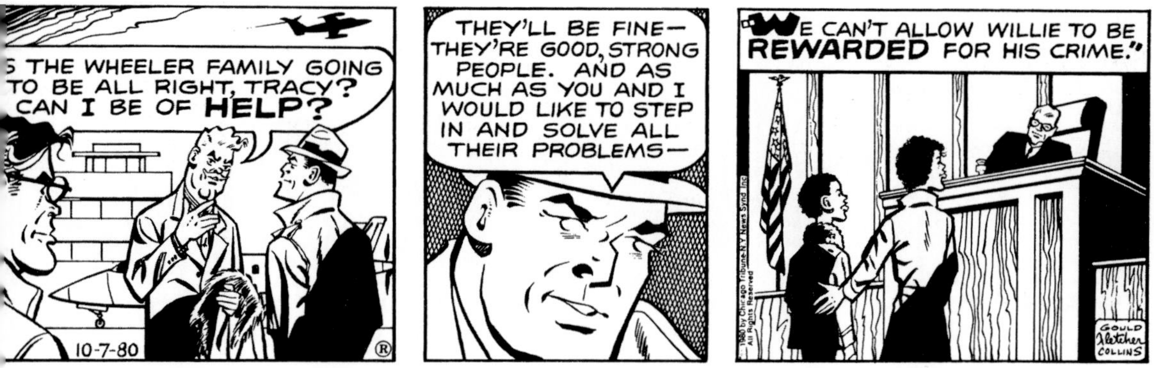
S THE WHEELER FAMILY GOING TO BE ALL RIGHT, TRACY? CAN I BE OF **HELP?**
10-7-80
THEY'LL BE FINE— THEY'RE GOOD, STRONG PEOPLE. AND AS MUCH AS YOU AND I WOULD LIKE TO STEP IN AND SOLVE ALL THEIR PROBLEMS—
"WE CAN'T ALLOW WILLIE TO BE **REWARDED** FOR HIS CRIME."
© 1980 by Chicago Tribune-N.Y. News Synd Inc All Rights Reserved
GOULD Fletcher COLLINS

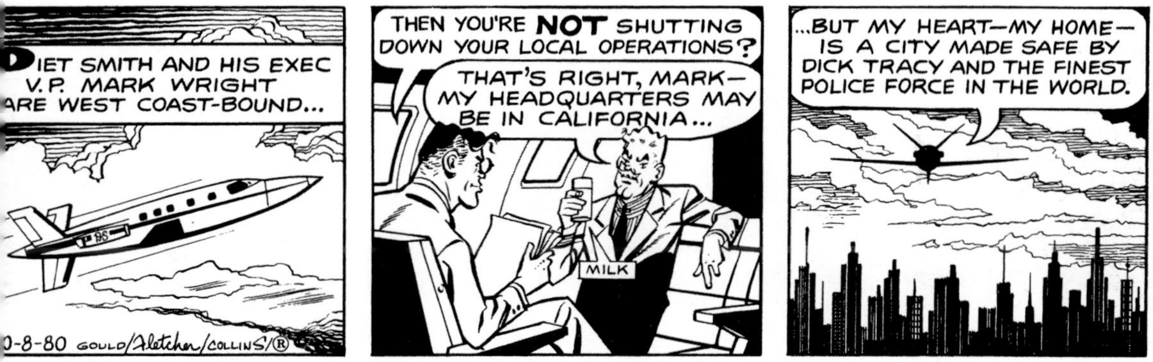
DIET SMITH AND HIS EXEC V.P. MARK WRIGHT ARE WEST COAST-BOUND...
0-8-80 GOULD/Fletcher/COLLINS/®
THEN YOU'RE **NOT** SHUTTING DOWN YOUR LOCAL OPERATIONS?
THAT'S RIGHT, MARK— MY HEADQUARTERS MAY BE IN CALIFORNIA...
MILK
...BUT MY HEART—MY HOME— IS A CITY MADE SAFE BY DICK TRACY AND THE FINEST POLICE FORCE IN THE WORLD.

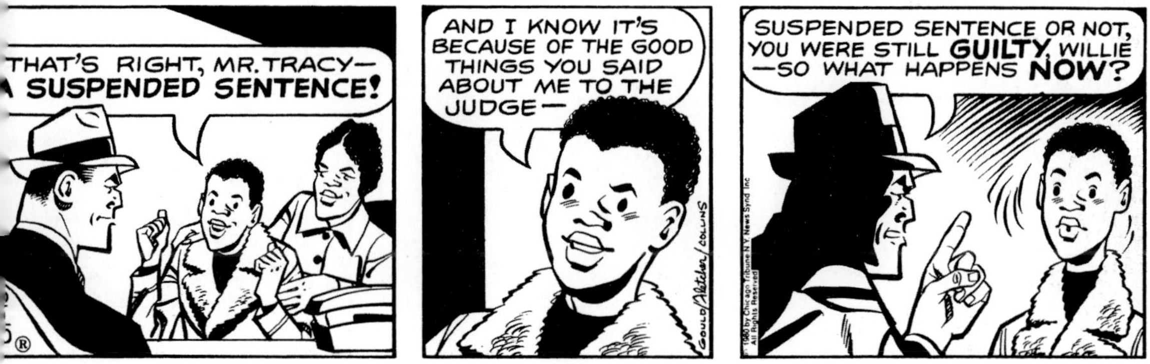
THAT'S RIGHT, MR. TRACY— A **SUSPENDED SENTENCE!**
AND I KNOW IT'S BECAUSE OF THE GOOD THINGS YOU SAID ABOUT ME TO THE JUDGE—
GOULD/Fletcher/COLLINS
SUSPENDED SENTENCE OR NOT, YOU WERE STILL **GUILTY**, WILLIE —SO WHAT HAPPENS **NOW?**
© 1980 by Chicago Tribune-N.Y. News Synd Inc All Rights Reserved

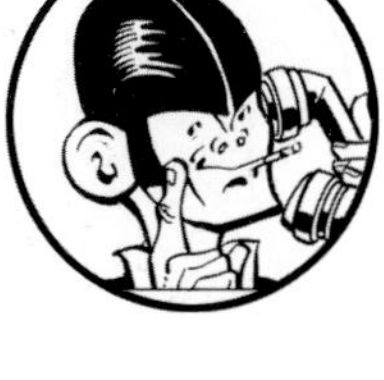

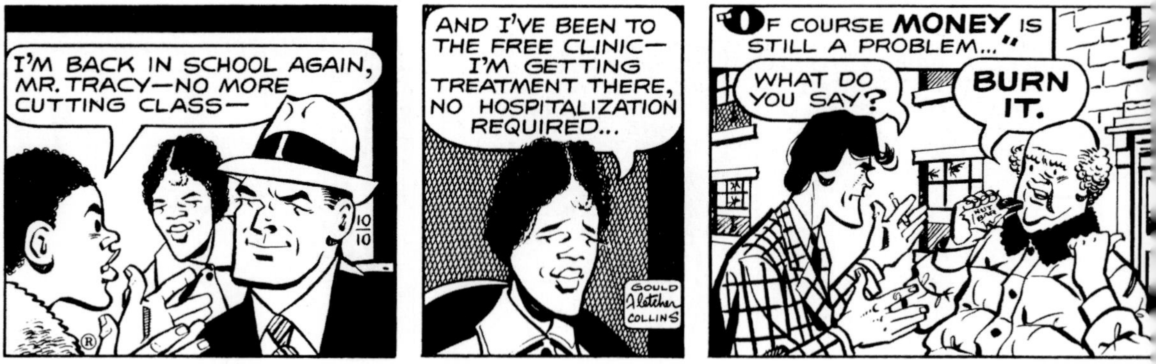
I'M BACK IN SCHOOL AGAIN, MR. TRACY—NO MORE CUTTING CLASS—
10/10
AND I'VE BEEN TO THE FREE CLINIC—I'M GETTING TREATMENT THERE, NO HOSPITALIZATION REQUIRED...
GOULD Fletcher COLLINS
"OF COURSE MONEY IS STILL A PROBLEM..."
WHAT DO YOU SAY?
BURN IT.

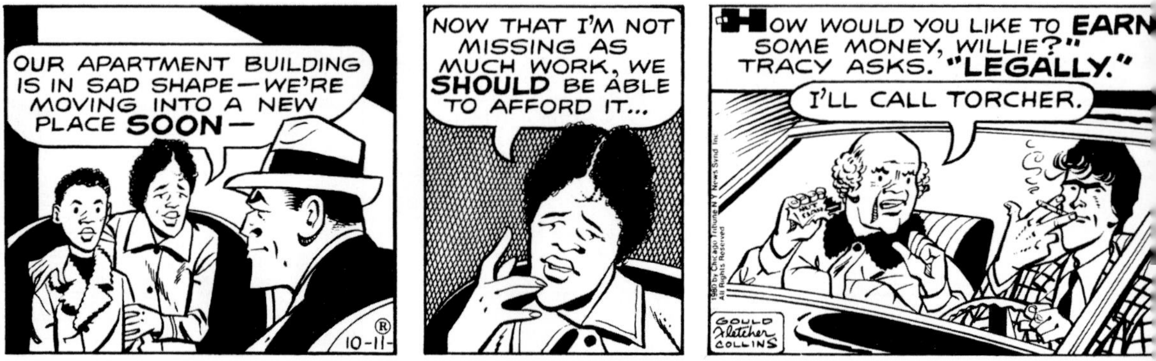
OUR APARTMENT BUILDING IS IN SAD SHAPE—WE'RE MOVING INTO A NEW PLACE SOON—
10-11-
NOW THAT I'M NOT MISSING AS MUCH WORK, WE SHOULD BE ABLE TO AFFORD IT...
"HOW WOULD YOU LIKE TO EARN SOME MONEY, WILLIE?" TRACY ASKS. "LEGALLY."
I'LL CALL TORCHER.
© 1980 by Chicago Tribune-N.Y. News Synd. Inc. All Rights Reserved
GOULD Fletcher COLLINS

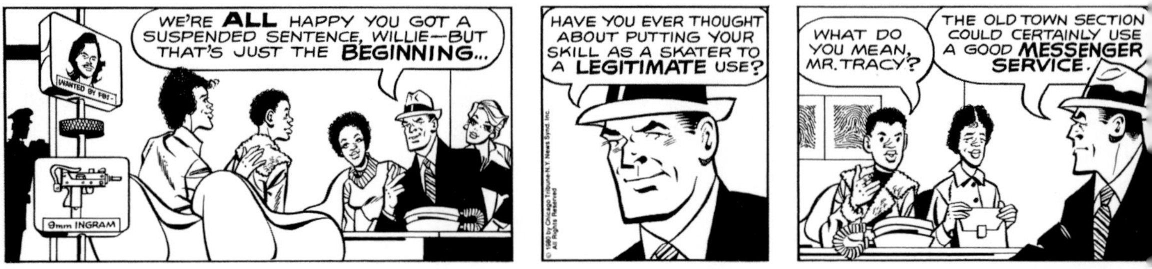
WANTED BY FBI
9mm INGRAM
WE'RE ALL HAPPY YOU GOT A SUSPENDED SENTENCE, WILLIE—BUT THAT'S JUST THE BEGINNING...
HAVE YOU EVER THOUGHT ABOUT PUTTING YOUR SKILL AS A SKATER TO A LEGITIMATE USE?
© 1980 by Chicago Tribune-N.Y. News Synd. Inc. All Rights Reserved
WHAT DO YOU MEAN, MR. TRACY?
THE OLD TOWN SECTION COULD CERTAINLY USE A GOOD MESSENGER SERVICE.

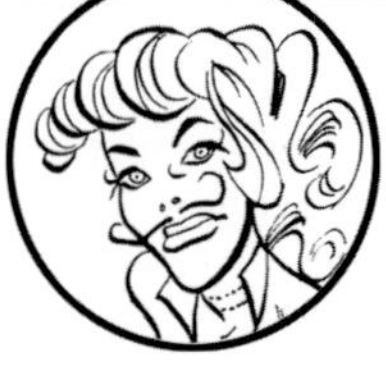

DICK TRACY

THE COLLINS CASEFILES, VOLUME 3

CHAPTER 3
DICK TRACY MEETS TORCHER

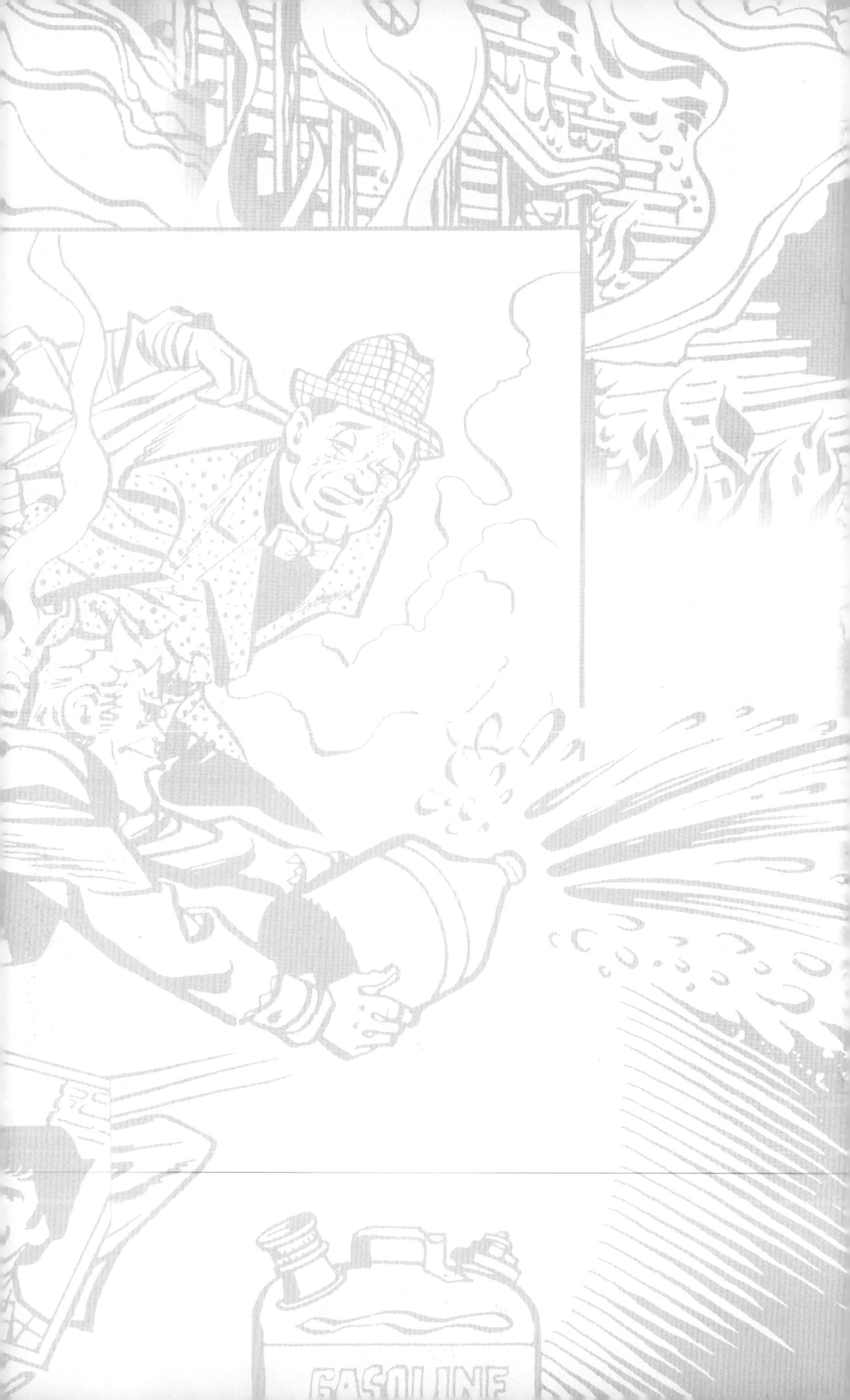
GASOLINE

"ERHAPS WITH SPECIAL ARRANGEMENTS WITH YOUR SCHOOL, YOU COULD RUN YOUR SERVICE IN THE AFTERNOONS, FROM 2 TO 6—

"DO YOU REALLY THINK SO?" WILLIE SAYS. "MOM, WE COULD USE EXTRA MONEY, NOW THAT WE'LL BE MOVING INTO A NEW PLACE!"

THE WHEELERS' CURRENT APARTMENT

GOULD/Fletcher/COLLINS

"THAT'S TRUE, SON," HIS MOTHER SAYS.

THIS IS TORCHER.

10/12/80

WHAT DO YOU THINK ABOUT MY SUGGESTION, WILLIE?

10-13-80

A MESSENGER SERVICE IN THE OLD TOWN AREA—

IT'D PUT YOUR SKATING SKILLS TO A GOOD USE...

© 1980 by Chicago Tribune-N.Y. News Synd. Inc. All Rights Reserved

"DO YOU REALLY THINK IT COULD WORK?" WILLIE ASKS.

USUAL MEETING PLACE? FINE.

GOULD/Fletcher/Collins

WE COULD CERTAINLY USE THE EXTRA MONEY YOU MIGHT BRING IN—

10-14-80

"OUR BUILDING HAS BEEN CONDEMNED," SAYS MRS. WHEELER. "WE'RE MOVING INTO A NICER, MORE EXPENSIVE PLACE IN A FEW WEEKS."

© 1980 by Chicago Tribune-N.Y. News Synd. Inc. All Rights Reserved

While—

THIS IS THE FIRETRAP IN QUESTION, TORCHER.

NO PROBLEM.

GOULD/Fletcher/COLLINS

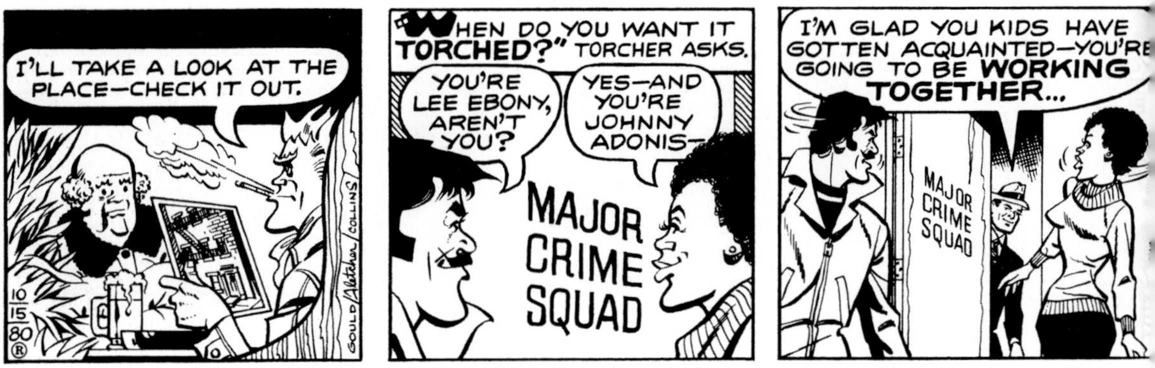
I'LL TAKE A LOOK AT THE PLACE—CHECK IT OUT.
GOULD / Fletcher / COLLINS
10/15/80 ®
"WHEN DO YOU WANT IT TORCHED?" TORCHER ASKS.
YOU'RE LEE EBONY, AREN'T YOU?
YES—AND YOU'RE JOHNNY ADONIS—
MAJOR CRIME SQUAD
I'M GLAD YOU KIDS HAVE GOTTEN ACQUAINTED—YOU'RE GOING TO BE WORKING TOGETHER...
MAJOR CRIME SQUAD

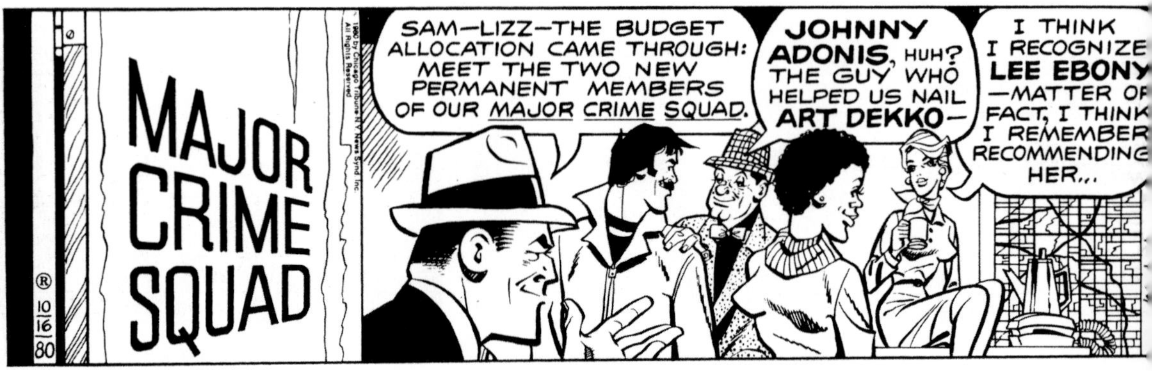
MAJOR CRIME SQUAD
® 10/16/80
© 1980 by Chicago Tribune-N.Y. News Synd. Inc. All Rights Reserved
SAM—LIZZ—THE BUDGET ALLOCATION CAME THROUGH: MEET THE TWO NEW PERMANENT MEMBERS OF OUR MAJOR CRIME SQUAD.
JOHNNY ADONIS, HUH? THE GUY WHO HELPED US NAIL ART DEKKO—
I THINK I RECOGNIZE LEE EBONY —MATTER OF FACT, I THINK I REMEMBER RECOMMENDING HER...

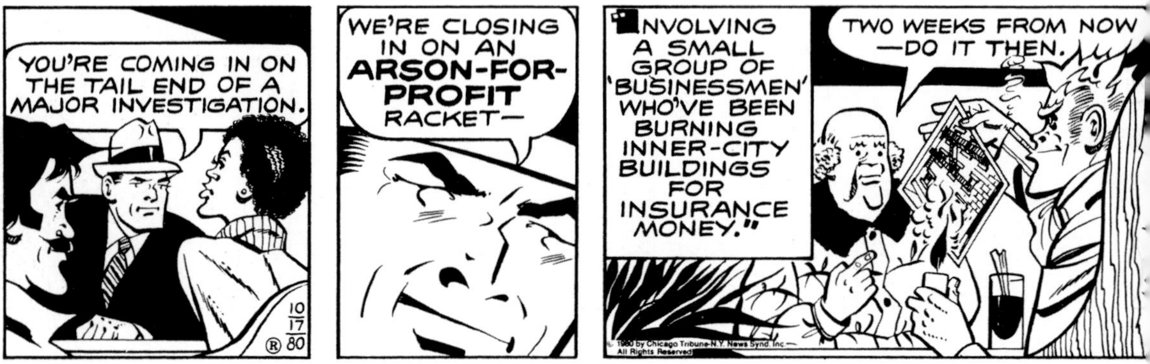
YOU'RE COMING IN ON THE TAIL END OF A MAJOR INVESTIGATION.
10/17/80 ®
WE'RE CLOSING IN ON AN ARSON-FOR-PROFIT RACKET—
"INVOLVING A SMALL GROUP OF 'BUSINESSMEN' WHO'VE BEEN BURNING INNER-CITY BUILDINGS FOR INSURANCE MONEY."
TWO WEEKS FROM NOW —DO IT THEN.
© 1980 by Chicago Tribune-N.Y. News Synd. Inc. All Rights Reserved

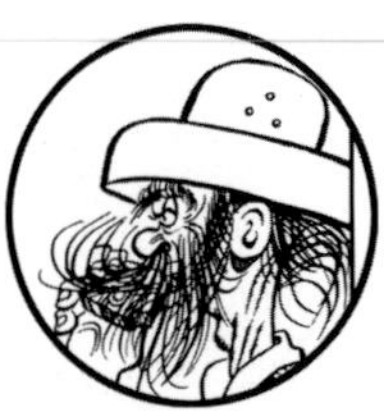

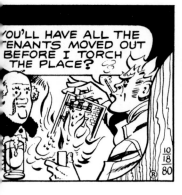

OU'LL HAVE ALL THE
ENANTS MOVED OUT
BEFORE I TORCH
THE PLACE?
10/18/80
YES—UNDER PRETENSE OF
REPAIRING THE PLACE.
SINCE **WHEN** ARE YOU
CONCERNED ABOUT
HUMAN LIFE, TORCHER?
THE ONLY HUMAN LIFE
I'M CONCERNED ABOUT'S
MY **OWN**—BUT HOMICIDE
MAKES COPS **MAD**—
© 1980 by Chicago Tribune-N.Y. News Synd Inc
All Rights Reserved
GOULD/Fletcher/COLLINS/

JOHNNY
DONIS AND
EE EBONY
—NOW
ERMANENT
MEMBERS
F TRACY'S
MAJOR
CRIME
SQUAD—
RE FILLED
N ON THE
LATEST
CASE—
ARSON—AMERICA'S FASTEST-
GROWING CRIME...
THE ARSON-FOR-PROFIT RING WE'RE
AFTER IS RESPONSIBLE FOR THE
BURNING OF **30** INNER-CITY BUILDINGS
—SLUMS, TRANSIENT HOTELS AND SO ON.

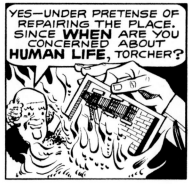

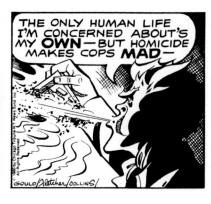

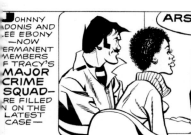

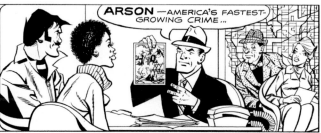

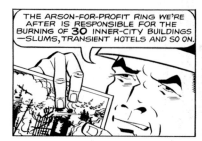

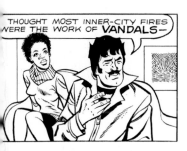

THOUGHT MOST INNER-CITY FIRES
WERE THE WORK OF **VANDALS**—
"THAT'S
WHAT THE
ARSON-
FOR-
PROFIT
BOYS
WANT
YOU TO
THINK," TRACY
SAYS.
POLICE
FILE
PHOTO
GOULD/Fletcher/COLLINS/
While—
I NEED TWO WEEKS
TO CLEAR OUT THE
TENANTS, TORCHER—
MEANTIME, I'LL
CHECK THE BUILDING
OUT—ACCIDENTAL
FIRES TAKE
PLANNING...
10/19/80

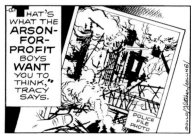

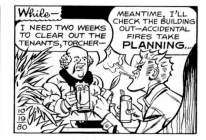

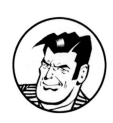

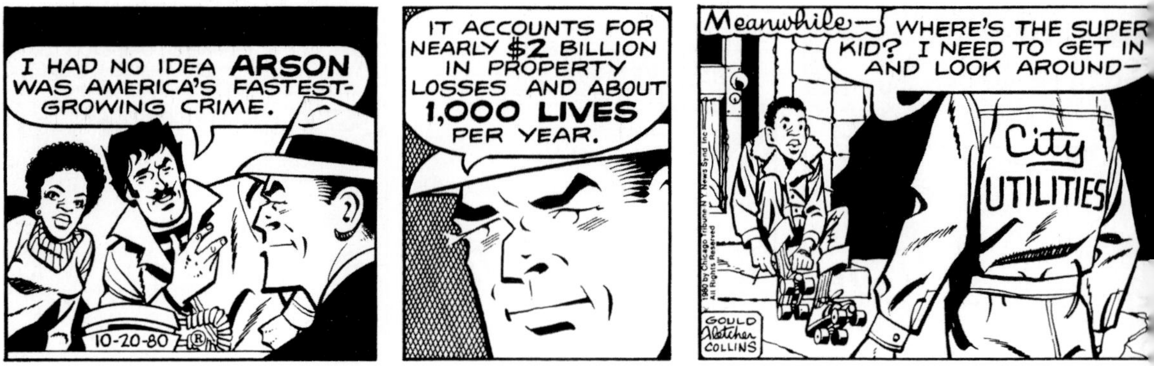
I HAD NO IDEA ARSON WAS AMERICA'S FASTEST-GROWING CRIME.
10-20-80 ®
IT ACCOUNTS FOR NEARLY $2 BILLION IN PROPERTY LOSSES AND ABOUT 1,000 LIVES PER YEAR.
Meanwhile—
WHERE'S THE SUPER KID? I NEED TO GET IN AND LOOK AROUND—
City UTILITIES
©1980 by Chicago Tribune-N.Y. News Synd. Inc. All Rights Reserved
GOULD Fletcher COLLINS

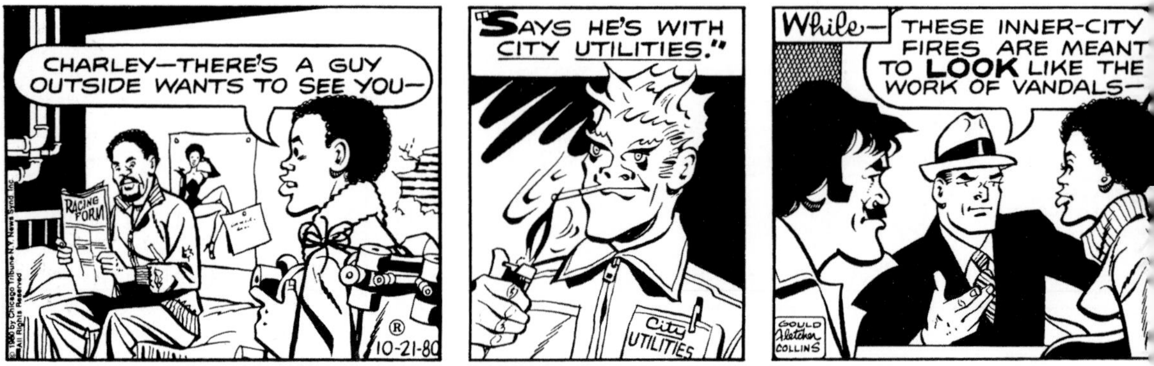
CHARLEY—THERE'S A GUY OUTSIDE WANTS TO SEE YOU—
RACING FORM
©1980 by Chicago Tribune-N.Y. News Synd. Inc. All Rights Reserved
® 10-21-80
"SAYS HE'S WITH CITY UTILITIES."
City UTILITIES
While—
THESE INNER-CITY FIRES ARE MEANT TO LOOK LIKE THE WORK OF VANDALS—
GOULD Fletcher COLLINS

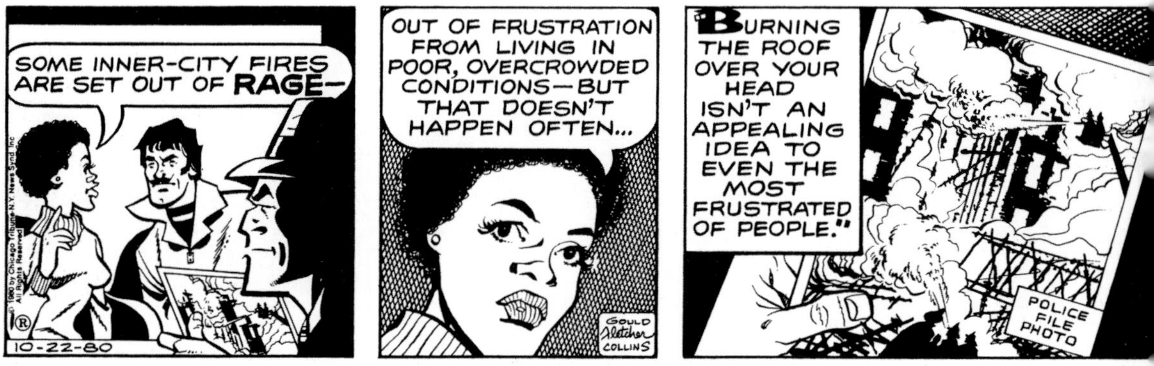
SOME INNER-CITY FIRES ARE SET OUT OF RAGE—
©1980 by Chicago Tribune-N.Y. News Synd. Inc. All Rights Reserved
® 10-22-80
OUT OF FRUSTRATION FROM LIVING IN POOR, OVERCROWDED CONDITIONS—BUT THAT DOESN'T HAPPEN OFTEN...
GOULD Fletcher COLLINS
"BURNING THE ROOF OVER YOUR HEAD ISN'T AN APPEALING IDEA TO EVEN THE MOST FRUSTRATED OF PEOPLE."
POLICE FILE PHOTO

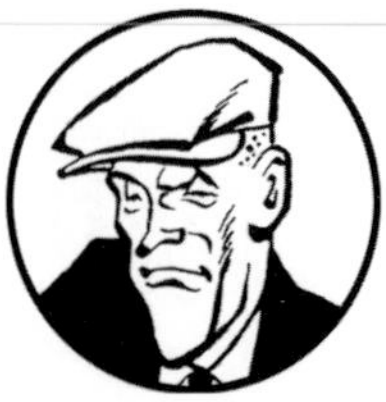

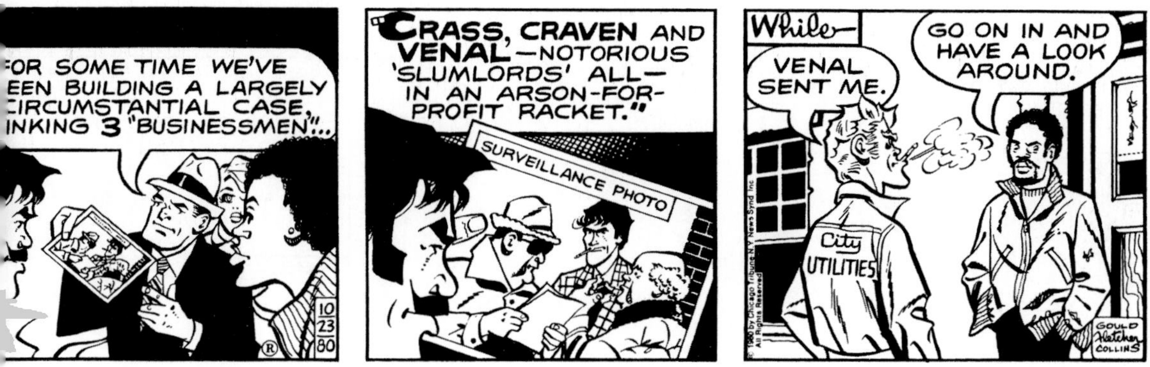
FOR SOME TIME WE'VE
EEN BUILDING A LARGELY
CIRCUMSTANTIAL CASE,
INKING 3 "BUSINESSMEN"...
10/23/80
"CRASS, CRAVEN AND VENAL—NOTORIOUS 'SLUMLORDS' ALL—IN AN ARSON-FOR-PROFIT RACKET."
SURVEILLANCE PHOTO
While—
VENAL SENT ME.
GO ON IN AND HAVE A LOOK AROUND.
CITY UTILITIES
© 1980 by Chicago Tribune N.Y. News Synd Inc All Rights Reserved
GOULD Fletcher COLLINS

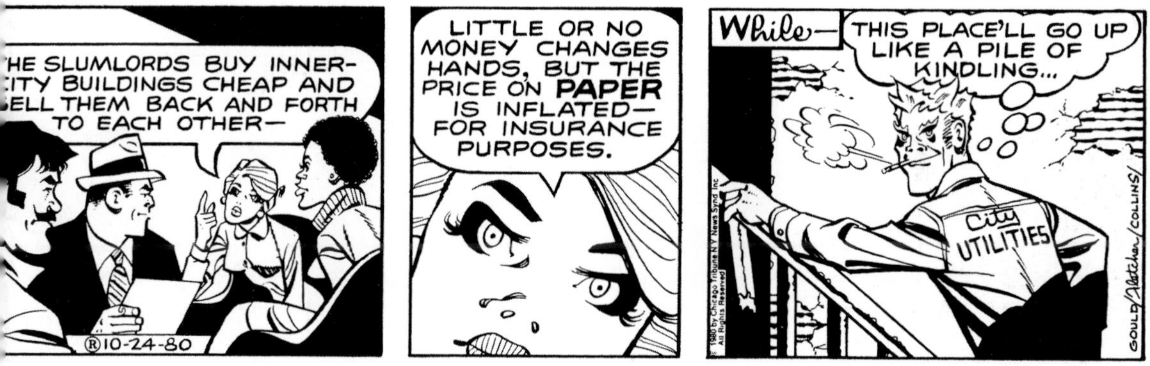
HE SLUMLORDS BUY INNER-
ITY BUILDINGS CHEAP AND
ELL THEM BACK AND FORTH
TO EACH OTHER—
®10-24-80
LITTLE OR NO MONEY CHANGES HANDS, BUT THE PRICE ON PAPER IS INFLATED—FOR INSURANCE PURPOSES.
While—
THIS PLACE'LL GO UP LIKE A PILE OF KINDLING...
CITY UTILITIES
© 1980 by Chicago Tribune N.Y. News Synd Inc All Rights Reserved
GOULD/Fletcher/COLLINS/

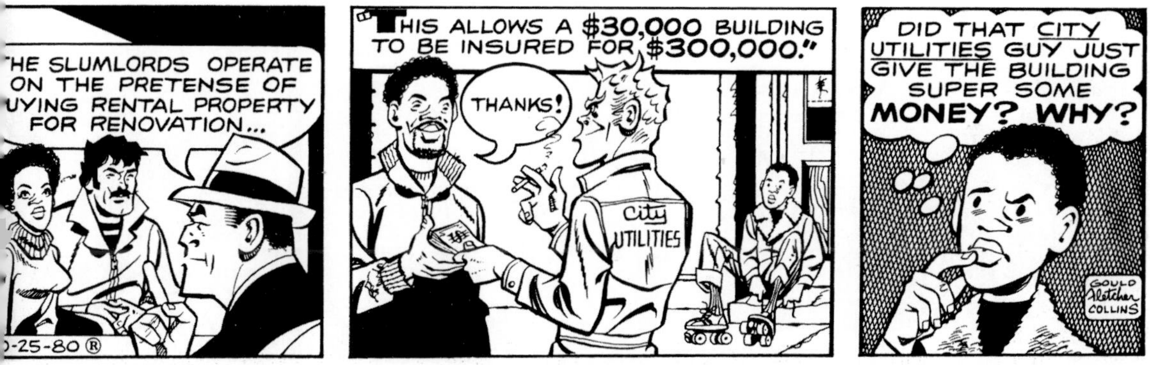
HE SLUMLORDS OPERATE
ON THE PRETENSE OF
UYING RENTAL PROPERTY
FOR RENOVATION...
-25-80 ®
"THIS ALLOWS A $30,000 BUILDING TO BE INSURED FOR $300,000."
THANKS!
CITY UTILITIES
DID THAT CITY UTILITIES GUY JUST GIVE THE BUILDING SUPER SOME MONEY? WHY?
GOULD Fletcher COLLINS

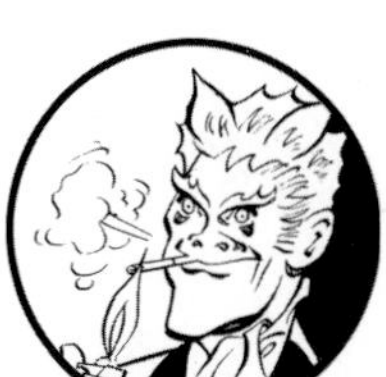

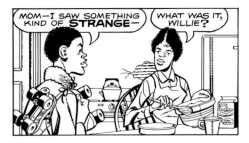

MOM—I SAW SOMETHING KIND OF STRANGE—
WHAT WAS IT, WILLIE?
A GUY FROM CITY UTILITIES HAD ME GET CHARLEY, THE BUILDING SUPER, FOR HIM...
© 1980 by Chicago Tribune-N.Y. News Synd. Inc. All Rights Reserved
"THEN THE GUY WENT INTO THE BUILDING AND LOOKED AROUND—BUT NEVER WENT IN THE BASEMENT WHERE THE METERS ARE."
City UTILITIES

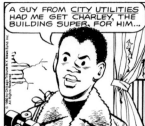

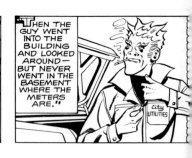

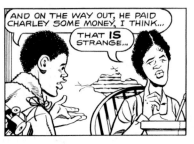

AND ON THE WAY OUT, HE PAID CHARLEY SOME MONEY, I THINK...
THAT IS STRANGE...
"BUT I DON'T THINK IT'S ANY OF OUR BUSINESS, SON."
YEAH— THIS IS TORCHER— A CINCH TO TORCH THAT FIRETRAP...
GOULD/Fletcher/COLLINS/
And—
THE ONLY POSITIVE THING ABOUT THIS ARSON-FOR-PROF RING IS NO LIVES HAVE BEEN LOST—YET.
10-26-80

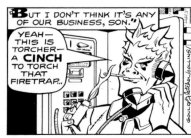

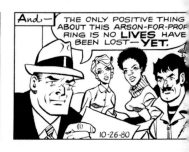

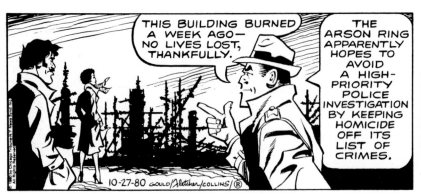

THIS BUILDING BURNED A WEEK AGO— NO LIVES LOST, THANKFULLY.
THE ARSON RING APPARENTLY HOPES TO AVOID A HIGH-PRIORITY POLICE INVESTIGATION BY KEEPING HOMICIDE OFF ITS LIST OF CRIMES.
© 1980 by Chicago Tribune-N.Y. News Synd. Inc. All Rights Reserved
10-27-80 GOULD/Fletcher/COLLINS/®
While—
JUST LET ME KNOW WHEN YOU WANT IT LIT—

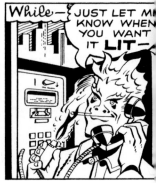

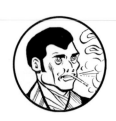

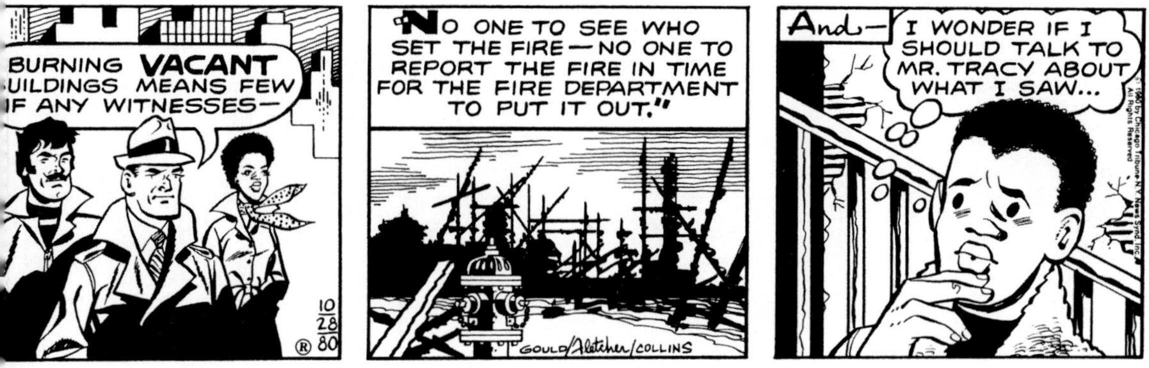
BURNING VACANT
UILDINGS MEANS FEW
IF ANY WITNESSES—
10 28 80
"NO ONE TO SEE WHO SET THE FIRE—NO ONE TO REPORT THE FIRE IN TIME FOR THE FIRE DEPARTMENT TO PUT IT OUT."
GOULD/Fletcher/COLLINS
And—
I WONDER IF I SHOULD TALK TO MR. TRACY ABOUT WHAT I SAW...
© 1980 by Chicago Tribune-N.Y. News Synd. Inc. All Rights Reserved

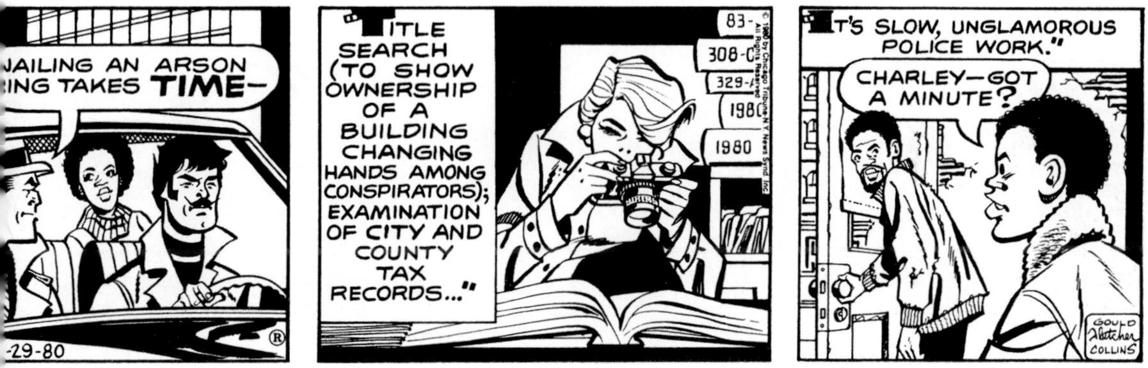
IAILING AN ARSON
ING TAKES TIME—
-29-80
"TITLE SEARCH (TO SHOW OWNERSHIP OF A BUILDING CHANGING HANDS AMONG CONSPIRATORS); EXAMINATION OF CITY AND COUNTY TAX RECORDS..."
83-
308-C
329-
1980
1980
© 1980 by Chicago Tribune-N.Y. News Synd. Inc. All Rights Reserved
"IT'S SLOW, UNGLAMOROUS POLICE WORK."
CHARLEY—GOT A MINUTE?
GOULD Fletcher COLLINS

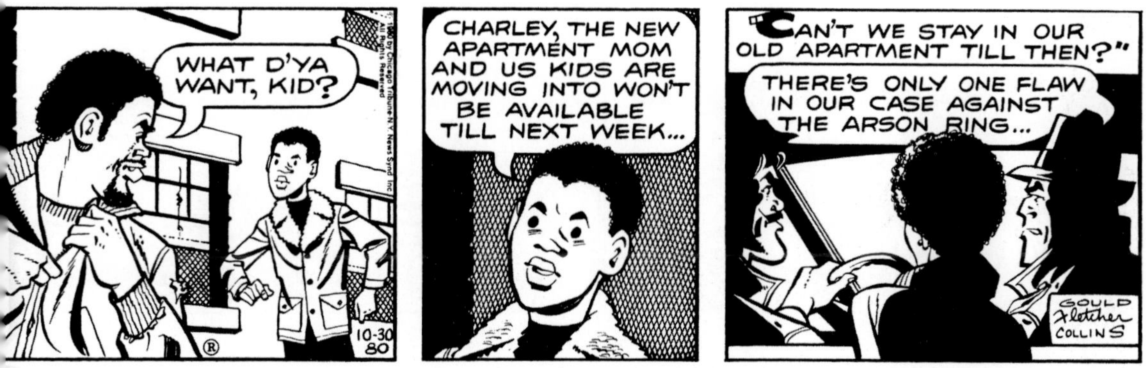
WHAT D'YA WANT, KID?
© 1980 by Chicago Tribune-N.Y. News Synd. Inc. All Rights Reserved
10-30 80
CHARLEY, THE NEW APARTMENT MOM AND US KIDS ARE MOVING INTO WON'T BE AVAILABLE TILL NEXT WEEK...
"CAN'T WE STAY IN OUR OLD APARTMENT TILL THEN?"
THERE'S ONLY ONE FLAW IN OUR CASE AGAINST THE ARSON RING...
GOULD Fletcher COLLINS

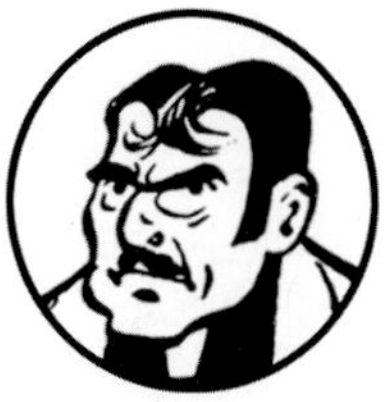

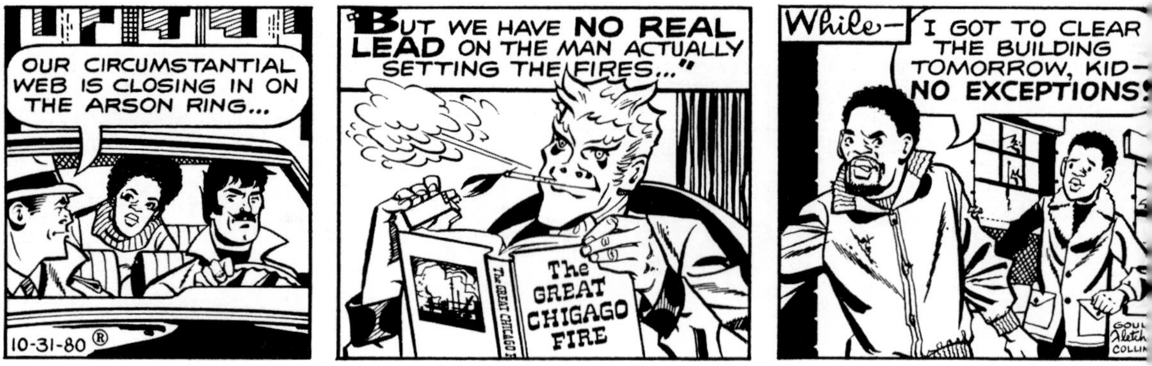
OUR CIRCUMSTANTIAL WEB IS CLOSING IN ON THE ARSON RING...
10-31-80 ®
"BUT WE HAVE NO REAL LEAD ON THE MAN ACTUALLY SETTING THE FIRES..."
The GREAT CHICAGO FIRE
While—
I GOT TO CLEAR THE BUILDING TOMORROW, KID—NO EXCEPTIONS!

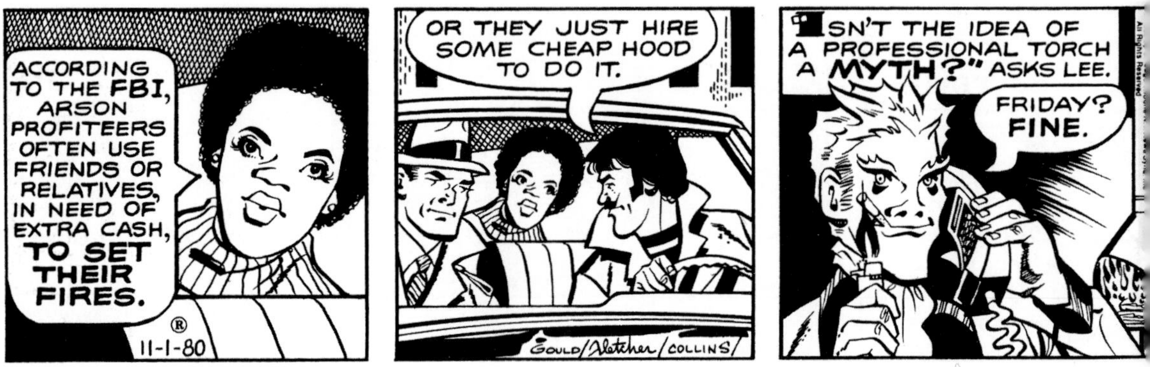
ACCORDING TO THE FBI, ARSON PROFITEERS OFTEN USE FRIENDS OR RELATIVES, IN NEED OF EXTRA CASH, TO SET THEIR FIRES.
® 11-1-80
OR THEY JUST HIRE SOME CHEAP HOOD TO DO IT.
GOULD/FLETCHER/COLLINS/
"ISN'T THE IDEA OF A PROFESSIONAL TORCH A MYTH?" ASKS LEE.
FRIDAY? FINE.
All Rights Reserved

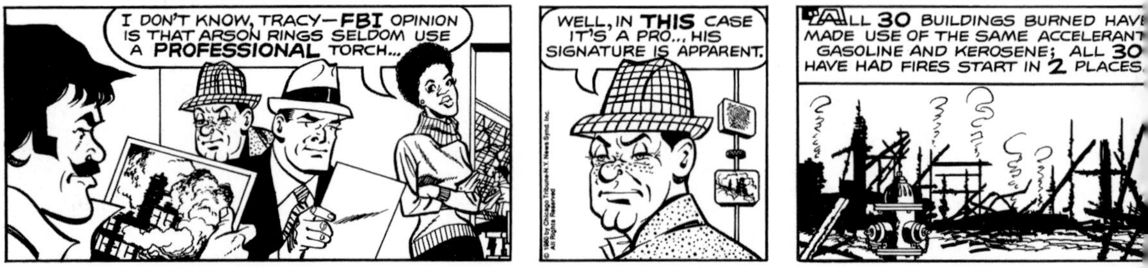
I DON'T KNOW, TRACY—FBI OPINION IS THAT ARSON RINGS SELDOM USE A PROFESSIONAL TORCH...
WELL, IN THIS CASE IT'S A PRO... HIS SIGNATURE IS APPARENT.
© 1980 by Chicago Tribune-N.Y. News Synd. Inc. All Rights Reserved
"ALL 30 BUILDINGS BURNED HAVE MADE USE OF THE SAME ACCELERANT GASOLINE AND KEROSENE; ALL 30 HAVE HAD FIRES START IN 2 PLACES.

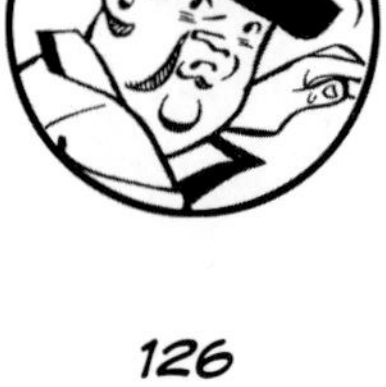

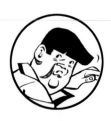

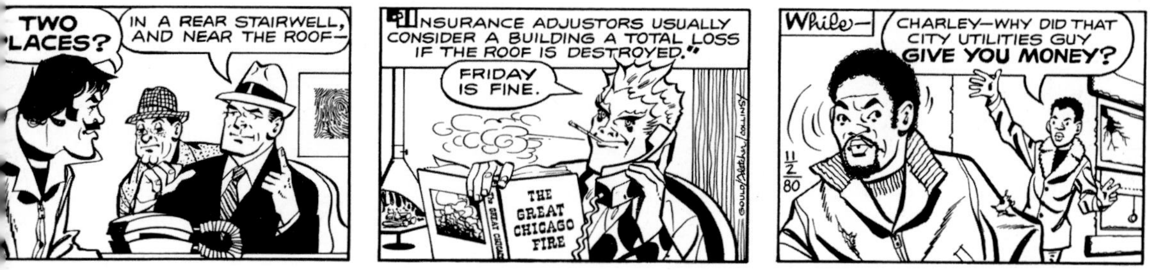
TWO
'LACES?
IN A REAR STAIRWELL, AND NEAR THE ROOF—
"INSURANCE ADJUSTORS USUALLY CONSIDER A BUILDING A TOTAL LOSS IF THE ROOF IS DESTROYED."
FRIDAY IS FINE.
THE GREAT CHICAGO FIRE
GOULD/Fletcher/COLLINS
While—
CHARLEY—WHY DID THAT CITY UTILITIES GUY GIVE YOU MONEY?
11/2/80

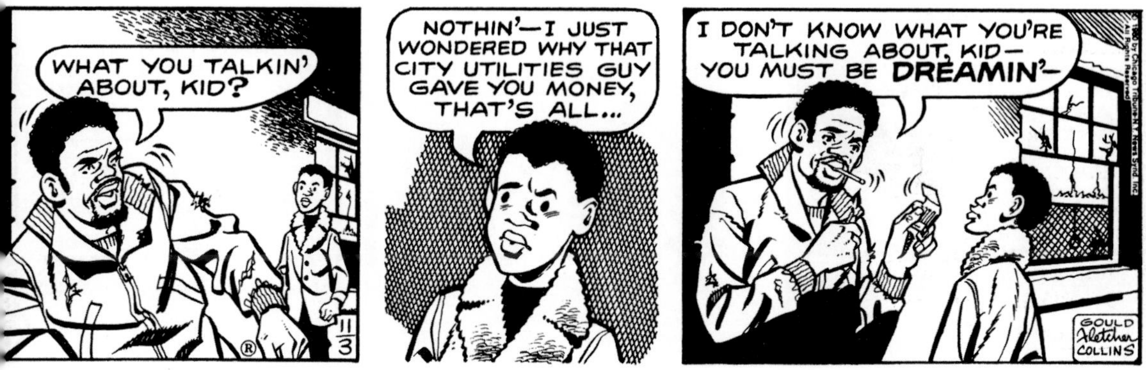
WHAT YOU TALKIN' ABOUT, KID?
11/3
NOTHIN'—I JUST WONDERED WHY THAT CITY UTILITIES GUY GAVE YOU MONEY, THAT'S ALL...
I DON'T KNOW WHAT YOU'RE TALKING ABOUT, KID— YOU MUST BE DREAMIN'—
© 1980 by Chicago Tribune-N.Y. News Synd. Inc. All Rights Reserved
GOULD Fletcher COLLINS

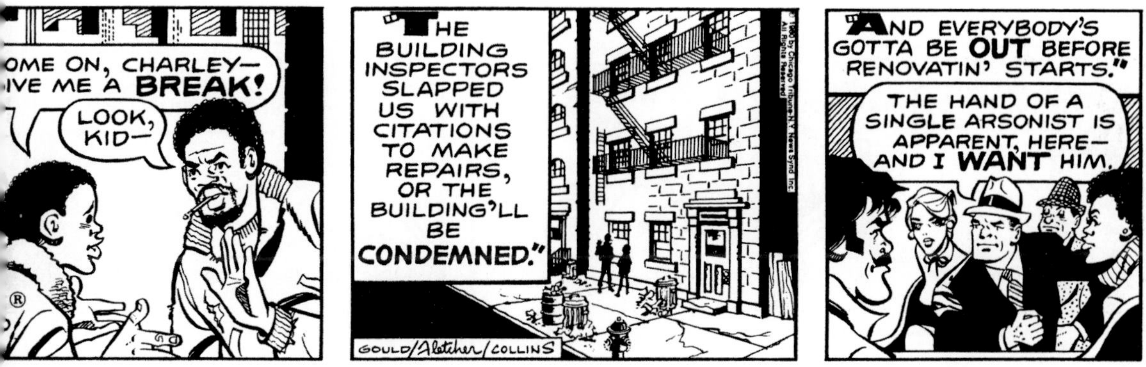
OME ON, CHARLEY— IVE ME A BREAK!
LOOK, KID—
"THE BUILDING INSPECTORS SLAPPED US WITH CITATIONS TO MAKE REPAIRS, OR THE BUILDING'LL BE CONDEMNED."
© 1980 by Chicago Tribune-N.Y. News Synd. Inc. All Rights Reserved
GOULD/Fletcher/COLLINS
"AND EVERYBODY'S GOTTA BE OUT BEFORE RENOVATIN' STARTS."
THE HAND OF A SINGLE ARSONIST IS APPARENT, HERE— AND I WANT HIM.

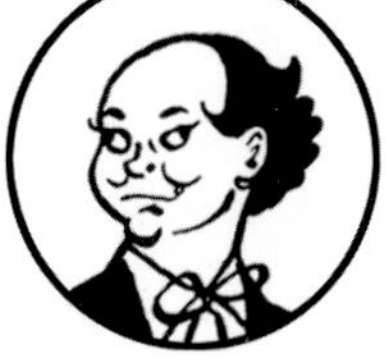

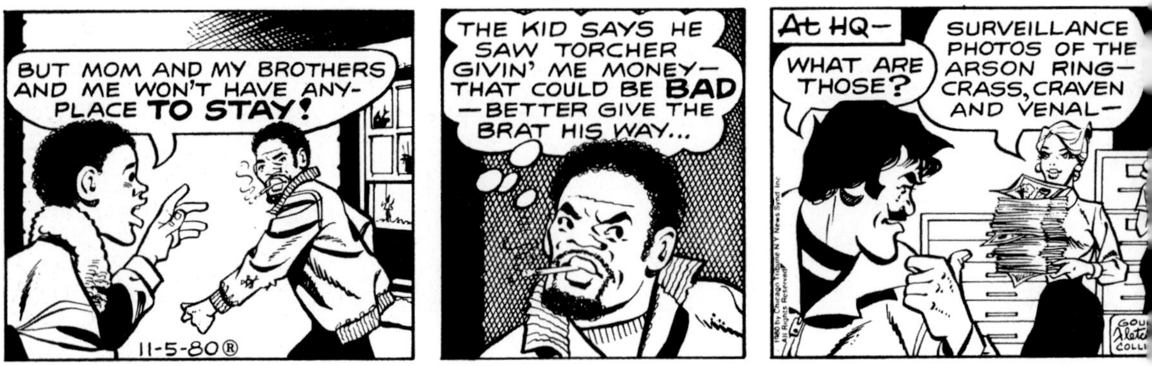

BUT MOM AND MY BROTHERS AND ME WON'T HAVE ANY-PLACE **TO STAY!**
11-5-80 ®
THE KID SAYS HE SAW TORCHER GIVIN' ME MONEY— THAT COULD BE **BAD** —BETTER GIVE THE BRAT HIS WAY...
At HQ—
WHAT ARE THOSE?
SURVEILLANCE PHOTOS OF THE ARSON RING— CRASS, CRAVEN AND VENAL—
© 1980 by Chicago Tribune-N.Y. News Synd Inc All Rights Reserved
GOUL Fletch COLLI

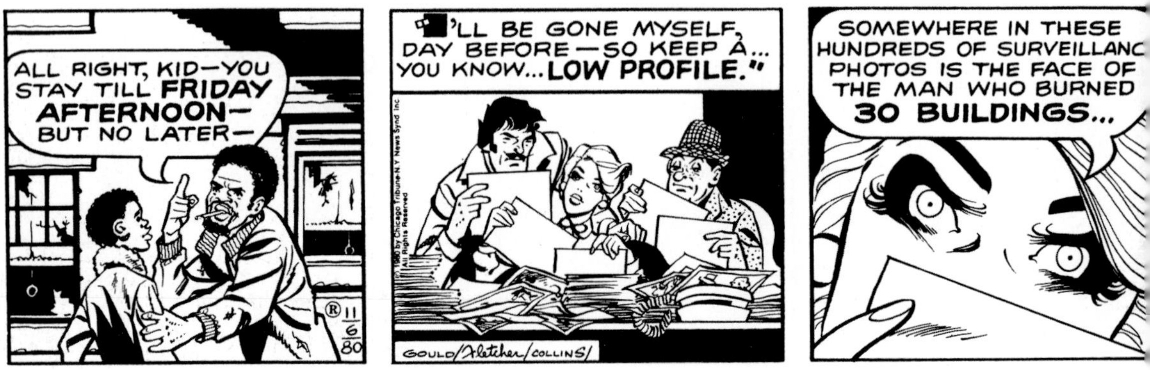

ALL RIGHT, KID—YOU STAY TILL **FRIDAY AFTERNOON**— BUT NO LATER—
® 11/6/80
"I'LL BE GONE MYSELF, DAY BEFORE—SO KEEP A... YOU KNOW... **LOW PROFILE.**"
© 1980 by Chicago Tribune-N.Y. News Synd Inc All Rights Reserved
GOULD/Fletcher/COLLINS/
SOMEWHERE IN THESE HUNDREDS OF SURVEILLANC PHOTOS IS THE FACE OF THE MAN WHO BURNED **30 BUILDINGS...**

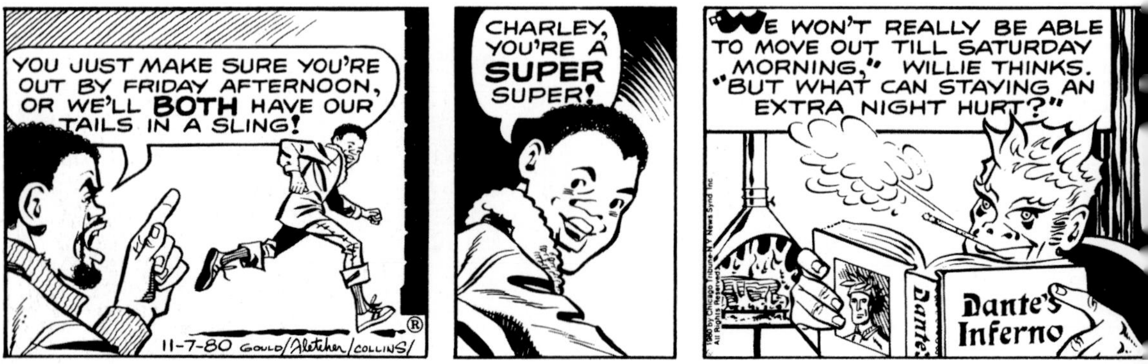

YOU JUST MAKE SURE YOU'RE OUT BY FRIDAY AFTERNOON, OR WE'LL **BOTH** HAVE OUR TAILS IN A SLING!
®
11-7-80 GOULD/Fletcher/COLLINS/
CHARLEY, YOU'RE A **SUPER** SUPER!
"WE WON'T REALLY BE ABLE TO MOVE OUT TILL SATURDAY MORNING," WILLIE THINKS. "BUT WHAT CAN STAYING AN EXTRA NIGHT HURT?"
© 1980 by Chicago Tribune-N.Y. News Synd Inc All Rights Reserved
Dante's Inferno
Dante's

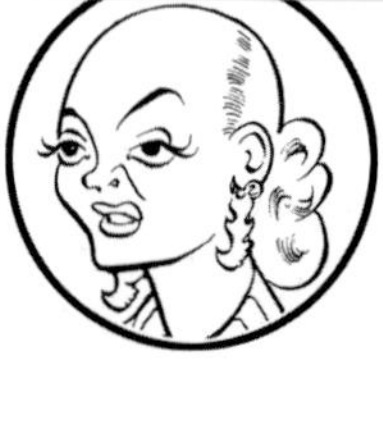

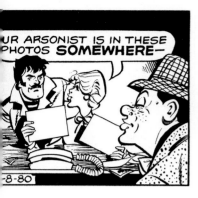

UR ARSONIST IS IN THESE PHOTOS **SOMEWHERE**—
-8-80
CRASS, CRAVEN AND VENAL ARE "BUSINESSMEN" WHO COME INTO CONTACT WITH DOZENS OF PEOPLE EACH DAY.
"HAVE YOU CHECKED 'EM ALL OUT?" "MUCH AS POSSIBLE," SAM SAYS, "WITHOUT BLOWING THE LID OFF OUR INVESTIGATION."
SURVEILLANCE PHOTO
1980 Chicago Tribune-N.Y. News Synd. Inc. All Rights Reserved
GOULD Fletcher COLLINS

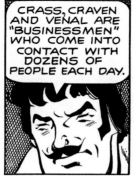

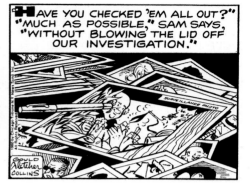

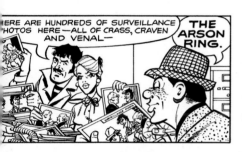

ERE ARE HUNDREDS OF SURVEILLANCE PHOTOS HERE—ALL OF CRASS, CRAVEN AND VENAL—
THE ARSON RING.
SURVEILLANCE PHOTO
ONLY A FEW OF THE DOZENS OF PEOPLE THESE "BUSINESSMEN" DEAL WITH **DON'T** HAVE CRIMINAL RECORDS.
USUALLY IT'S FOR BUSINESS FRAUD OF SOME KIND, BUT SOMETIMES IT'S FOR BURGLARY, ARMED ROBBERY, YOU NAME IT.

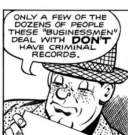

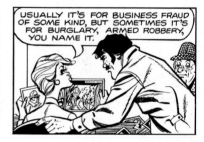

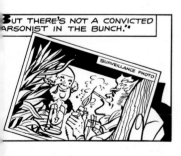

BUT THERE'S NOT A CONVICTED ARSONIST IN THE BUNCH."
SURVEILLANCE PHOTO
While—
MOM'S GOING TO BE REAL HAPPY WHEN YOU TELL HER THE SUPER SAID WE COULD STAY A FEW EXTRA DAYS—
"BUT CHARLEY SAID WE HAD TO LEAVE FRIDAY," SAYS KEENAN. "CAN WE GET AWAY WITH STAYING TILL SATURDAY?" "WHAT'S THE HARM?" ASKS WILLIE.
GOULD/Fletcher/COLLINS
11-9-80

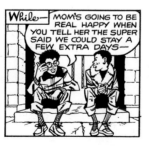

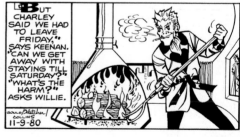

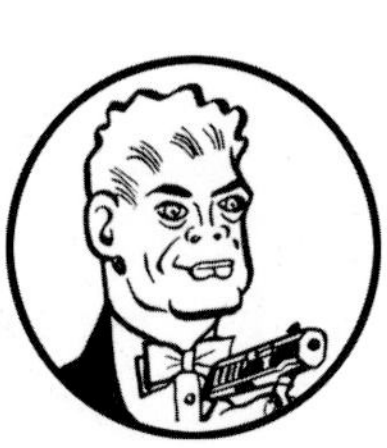

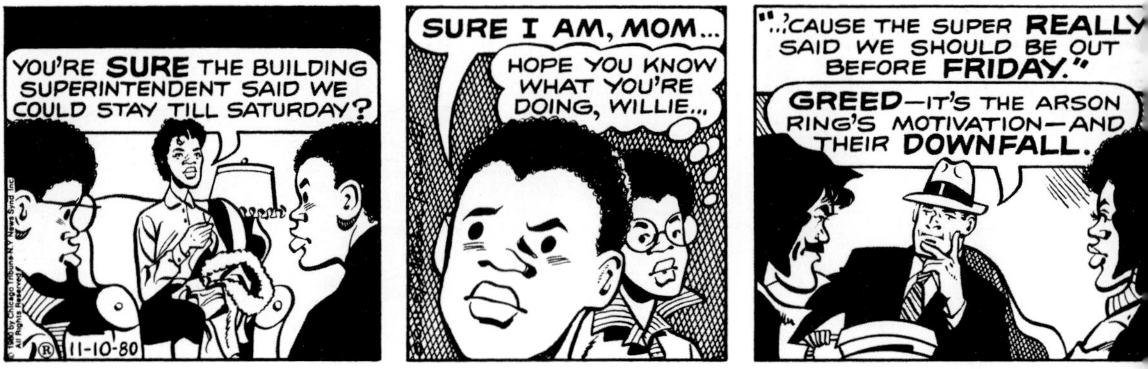
YOU'RE SURE THE BUILDING SUPERINTENDENT SAID WE COULD STAY TILL SATURDAY?
© 1980 by Chicago Tribune-N.Y. News Synd. Inc. All Rights Reserved
11-10-80
SURE I AM, MOM...
HOPE YOU KNOW WHAT YOU'RE DOING, WILLIE...
"...'CAUSE THE SUPER REALLY SAID WE SHOULD BE OUT BEFORE FRIDAY."
GREED—IT'S THE ARSON RING'S MOTIVATION—AND THEIR DOWNFALL.

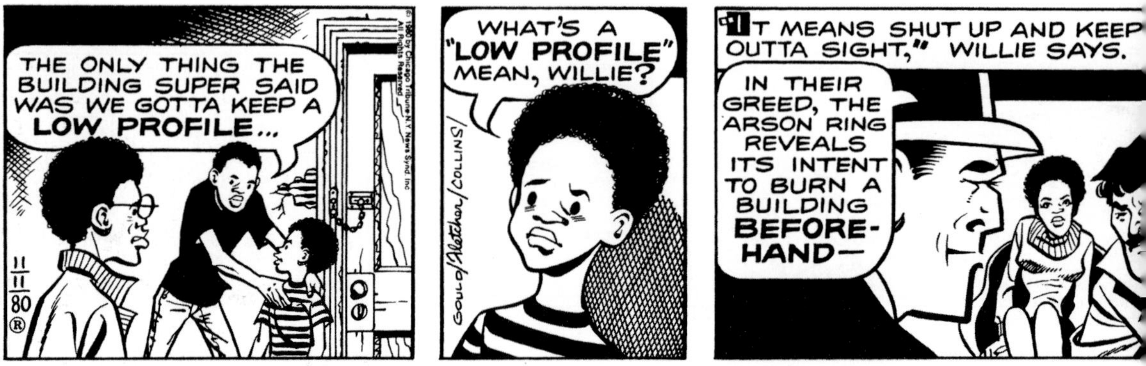
THE ONLY THING THE BUILDING SUPER SAID WAS WE GOTTA KEEP A LOW PROFILE...
11 11 80
© 1980 by Chicago Tribune-N.Y. News Synd. Inc. All Rights Reserved
WHAT'S A "LOW PROFILE" MEAN, WILLIE?
GOULD/Fletcher/COLLINS
"IT MEANS SHUT UP AND KEEP OUTTA SIGHT," WILLIE SAYS.
IN THEIR GREED, THE ARSON RING REVEALS ITS INTENT TO BURN A BUILDING BEFORE-HAND—

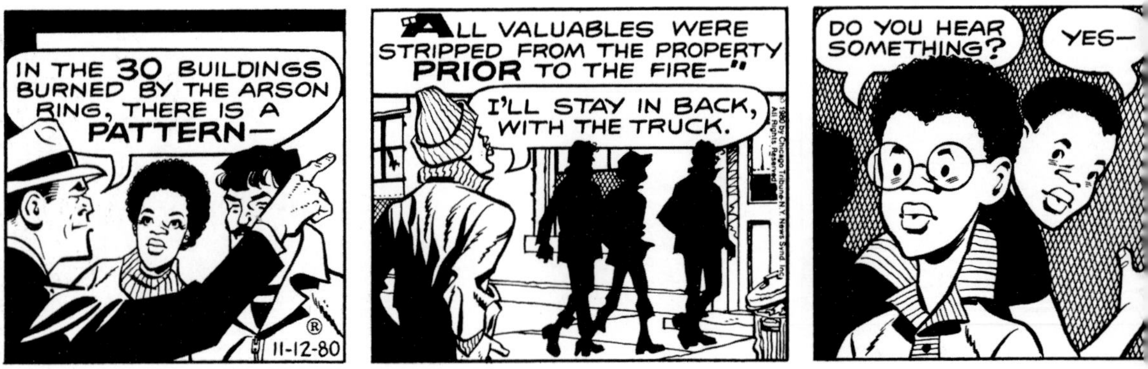
IN THE 30 BUILDINGS BURNED BY THE ARSON RING, THERE IS A PATTERN—
11-12-80
"ALL VALUABLES WERE STRIPPED FROM THE PROPERTY PRIOR TO THE FIRE—"
I'LL STAY IN BACK, WITH THE TRUCK.
© 1980 by Chicago Tribune-N.Y. News Synd. Inc. All Rights Reserved
DO YOU HEAR SOMETHING?
YES—

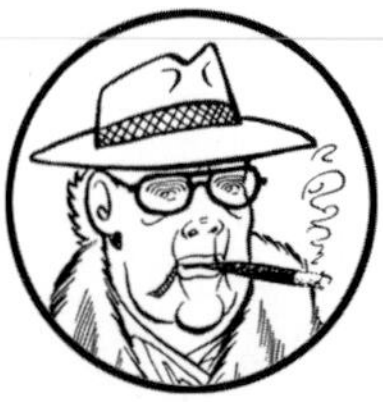

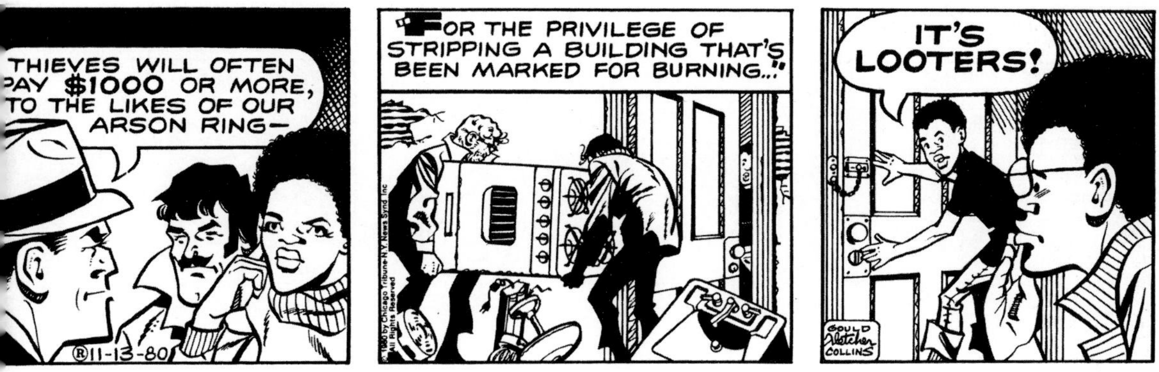
THIEVES WILL OFTEN PAY $1000 OR MORE, TO THE LIKES OF OUR ARSON RING—
"FOR THE PRIVILEGE OF STRIPPING A BUILDING THAT'S BEEN MARKED FOR BURNING..."
IT'S LOOTERS!

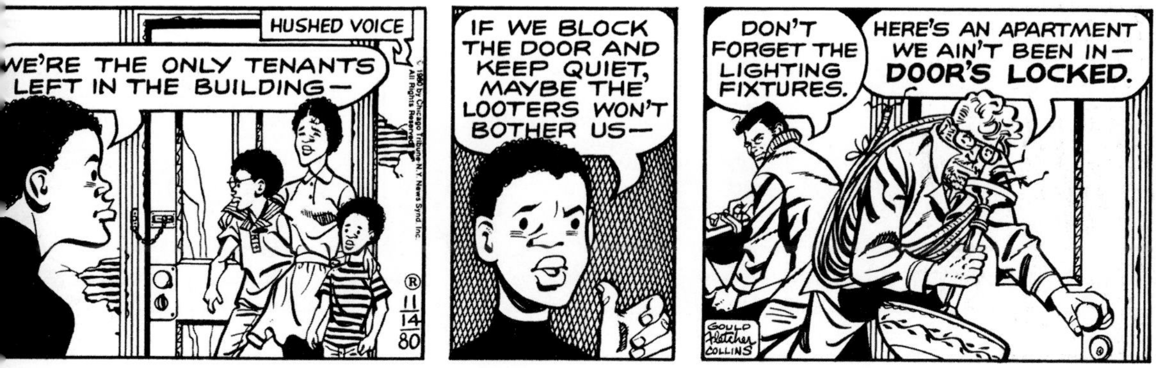
HUSHED VOICE
WE'RE THE ONLY TENANTS LEFT IN THE BUILDING—
IF WE BLOCK THE DOOR AND KEEP QUIET, MAYBE THE LOOTERS WON'T BOTHER US—
DON'T FORGET THE LIGHTING FIXTURES.
HERE'S AN APARTMENT WE AIN'T BEEN IN— DOOR'S LOCKED.

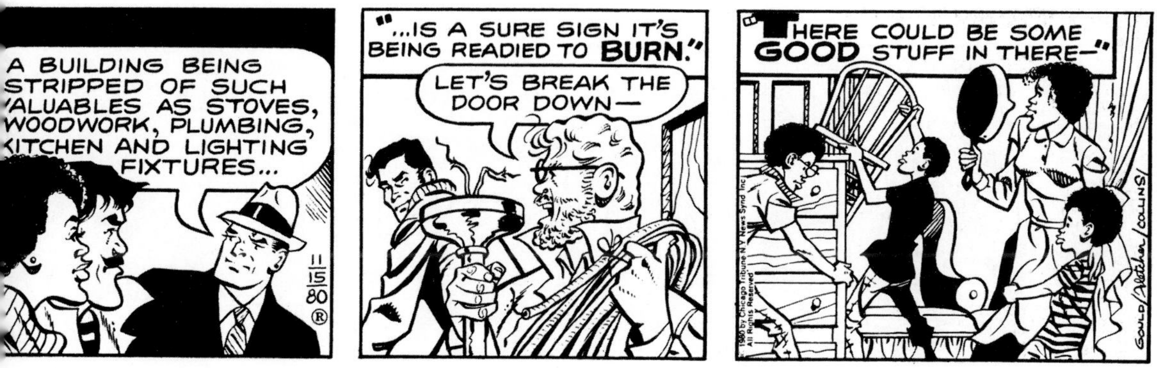
A BUILDING BEING STRIPPED OF SUCH VALUABLES AS STOVES, WOODWORK, PLUMBING, KITCHEN AND LIGHTING FIXTURES...
"...IS A SURE SIGN IT'S BEING READIED TO BURN."
LET'S BREAK THE DOOR DOWN—
"THERE COULD BE SOME GOOD STUFF IN THERE—"

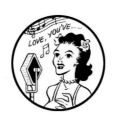

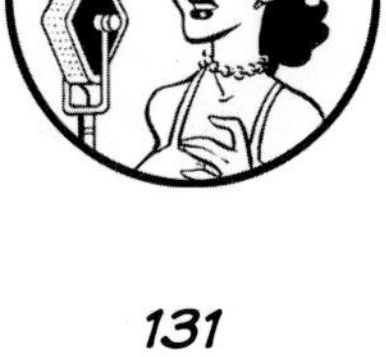
LOVE, YOU'VE.....

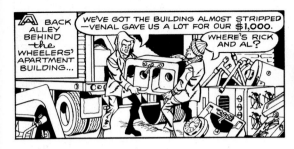

A BACK ALLEY BEHIND the WHEELERS' APARTMENT BUILDING...
WE'VE GOT THE BUILDING ALMOST STRIPPED —VENAL GAVE US A LOT FOR OUR $1,000.
WHERE'S RICK AND AL?
I THINK THEY FOUND A LOCKED ROOM THEY'RE BUSTIN' INTO.
GOULD/Fletcher/COLLINS
BAM-BAM-

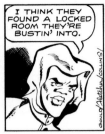

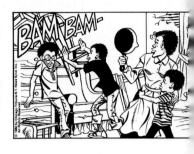

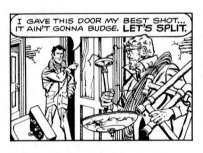

I GAVE THIS DOOR MY BEST SHOT... IT AIN'T GONNA BUDGE. LET'S SPLIT.
"YEAH—OKAY. WE GOT WHAT WE CAME FOR."
HUSHED VOICE
I THINK THEY'RE GOING... I THINK WE'RE SAFE—
SAFE, WILLIE? THAT WOULDN'T BE TRACY'S OPINION...
A VACATED BUILDING BEING STRIPPED OF ITS VALUABLES MEANS ONE THING: IT'S GOING TO BURN.

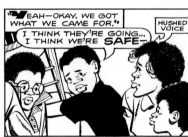

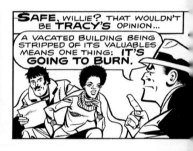

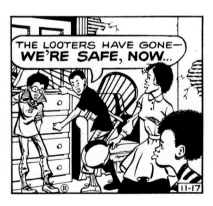

THE LOOTERS HAVE GONE— WE'RE SAFE, NOW...
11-17
In the ALLEY BEHIND the BUILDING—
THAT'S EVERYTHING.
EXCEPT FOR THAT ONE APARTMENT WE COULDN'T GET INTO—
IF SOMEBODY'S IN THERE THEY'RE GONNA GET A HECKUVA HOT FOOT 'FORE THE NIGHT'S OUT.
GOULD Fletcher COLLINS

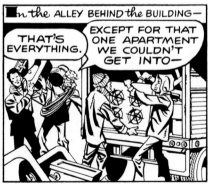

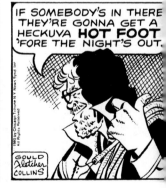

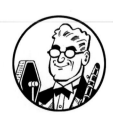

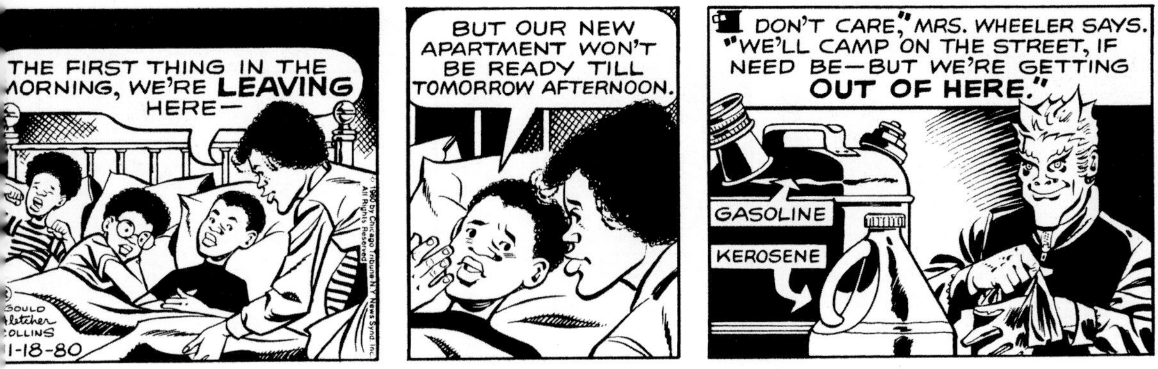

THE FIRST THING IN THE MORNING, WE'RE LEAVING HERE—
©1980 by Chicago Tribune-N.Y. News Synd. Inc. All Rights Reserved
GOULD Fletcher COLLINS
11-18-80
BUT OUR NEW APARTMENT WON'T BE READY TILL TOMORROW AFTERNOON.
"I DON'T CARE," MRS. WHEELER SAYS. "WE'LL CAMP ON THE STREET, IF NEED BE—BUT WE'RE GETTING OUT OF HERE."
GASOLINE
KEROSENE

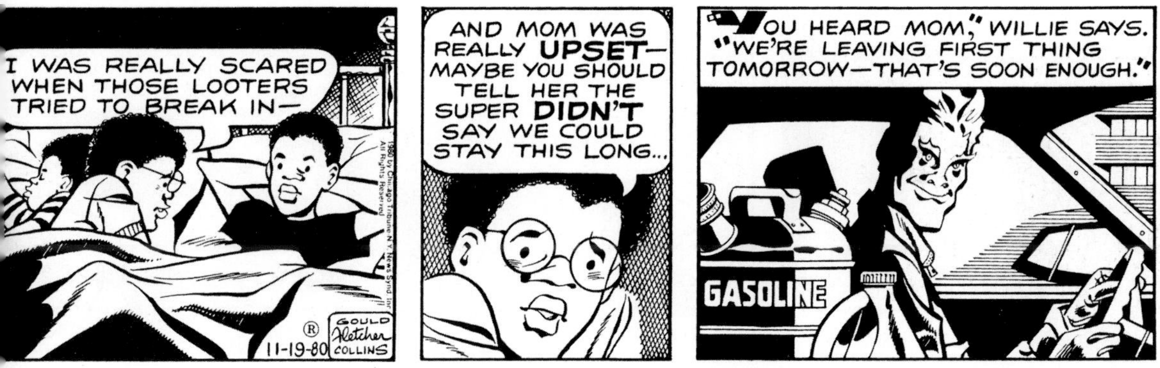

I WAS REALLY SCARED WHEN THOSE LOOTERS TRIED TO BREAK IN—
©1980 by Chicago Tribune-N.Y. News Synd. Inc. All Rights Reserved
11-19-80
GOULD Fletcher COLLINS
AND MOM WAS REALLY UPSET— MAYBE YOU SHOULD TELL HER THE SUPER DIDN'T SAY WE COULD STAY THIS LONG...
"YOU HEARD MOM," WILLIE SAYS. "WE'RE LEAVING FIRST THING TOMORROW—THAT'S SOON ENOUGH."
GASOLINE

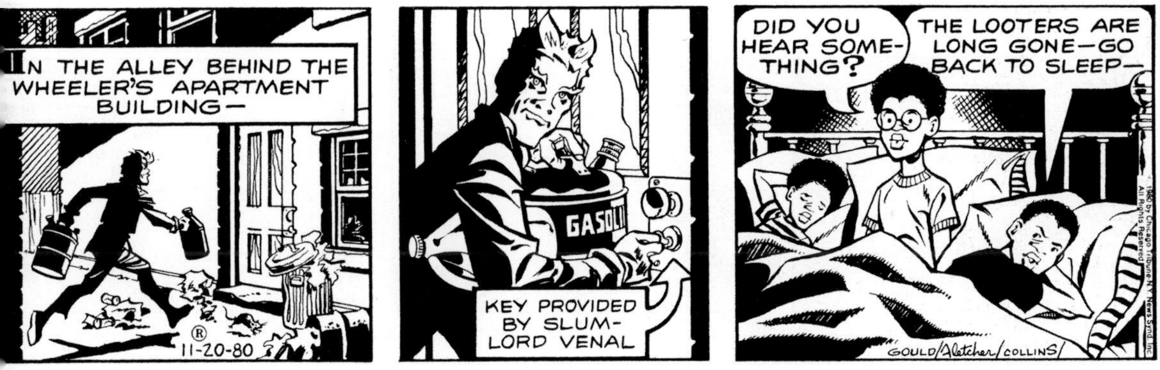

IN THE ALLEY BEHIND THE WHEELER'S APARTMENT BUILDING—
11-20-80
GASOLI
KEY PROVIDED BY SLUM-LORD VENAL
DID YOU HEAR SOME-THING?
THE LOOTERS ARE LONG GONE—GO BACK TO SLEEP—
©1980 by Chicago Tribune-N.Y. News Synd. Inc. All Rights Reserved
GOULD/Fletcher/COLLINS/

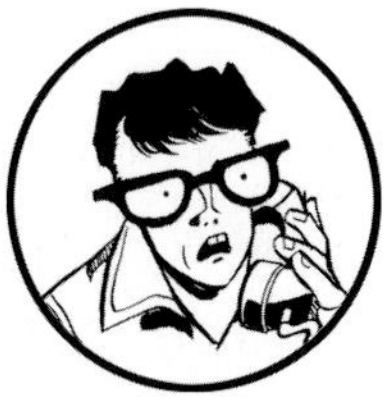

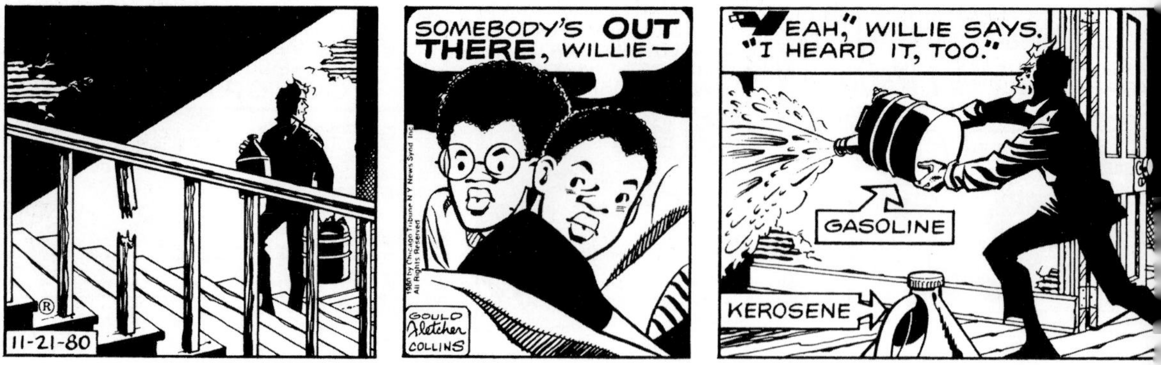
11-21-80
SOMEBODY'S OUT THERE, WILLIE—
©1980 by Chicago Tribune N.Y. News Synd. Inc. All Rights Reserved
GOULD Fletcher COLLINS
"YEAH," WILLIE SAYS. "I HEARD IT, TOO."
GASOLINE
KEROSENE

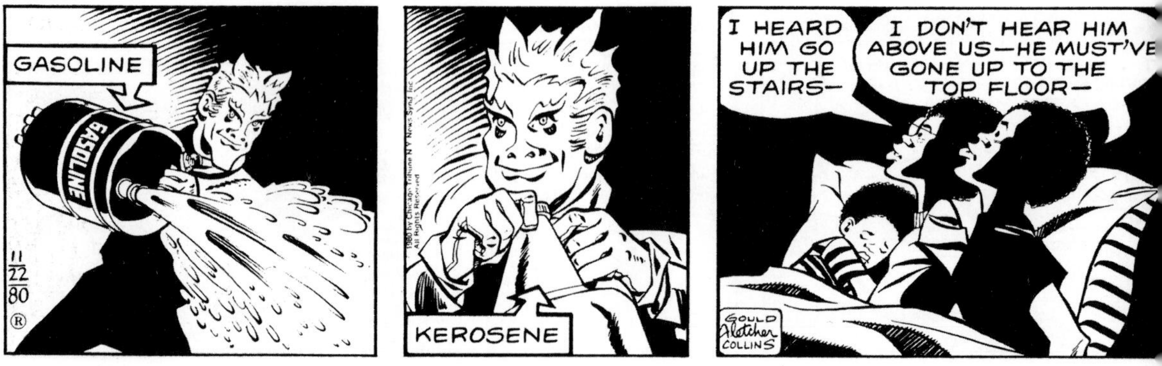
GASOLINE
GASOLINE
11/22/80
©1980 by Chicago Tribune N.Y. News Synd. Inc. All Rights Reserved
KEROSENE
I HEARD HIM GO UP THE STAIRS—
I DON'T HEAR HIM ABOVE US—HE MUST'VE GONE UP TO THE TOP FLOOR—
GOULD Fletcher COLLINS

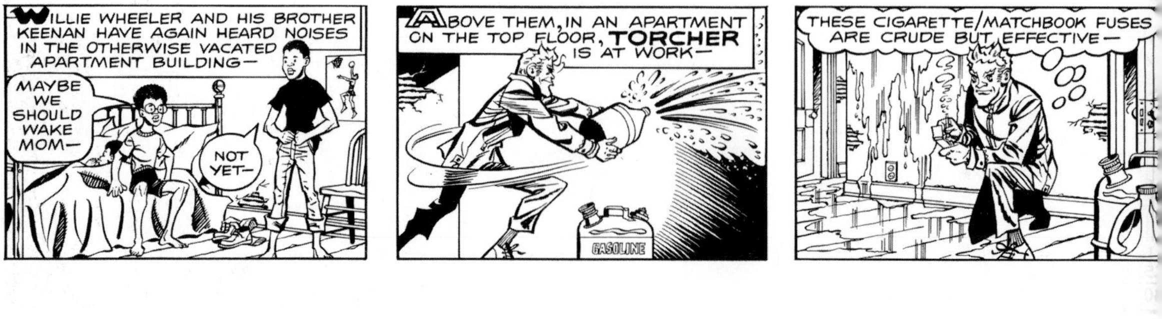
WILLIE WHEELER AND HIS BROTHER KEENAN HAVE AGAIN HEARD NOISES IN THE OTHERWISE VACATED APARTMENT BUILDING—
MAYBE WE SHOULD WAKE MOM—
NOT YET—
ABOVE THEM, IN AN APARTMENT ON THE TOP FLOOR, TORCHER IS AT WORK—
GASOLINE
THESE CIGARETTE/MATCHBOOK FUSES ARE CRUDE BUT EFFECTIVE—

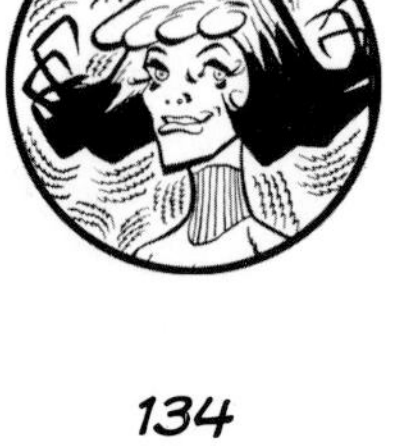

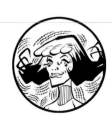

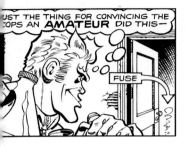

UST THE THING FOR CONVINCING THE
COPS AN AMATEUR DID THIS—
FUSE
NOW FOR THE REAR STAIRWELL, AND I SHOULD BE HOME IN TIME FOR THE LATE SHOW—"TOWERING INFERNO."
GASOLINE
GOULD/Fletcher/COLLINS/
© 1980 by Chicago Tribune-N.Y. News Synd. Inc. All Rights Reserved
IT'S THAT CITY UTILITIES GUY— THE ONE I SAW PAYING OFF CHARLEY, THE BUILDING SUPER!
11-23-80

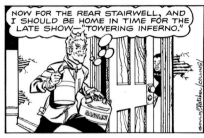

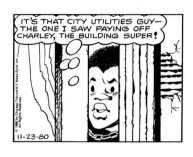

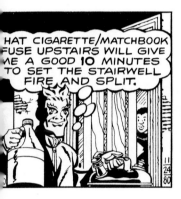

HAT CIGARETTE/MATCHBOOK FUSE UPSTAIRS WILL GIVE ME A GOOD 10 MINUTES TO SET THE STAIRWELL FIRE AND SPLIT.
11 24 80
THAT'S THE GUY I SAW GIVING MONEY TO CHARLEY, THE BUILDING SUPER...
HUSHED VOICE
GOULD Fletcher COLLINS
1980 by Chicago Tribune-N.Y. News Synd. Inc. All Rights Reserved
"THE UTILITIES GUY?" KEENAN ASKS. "YES!" WILLIE SAYS.
GASOLINE

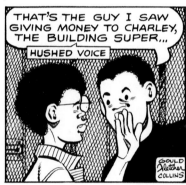

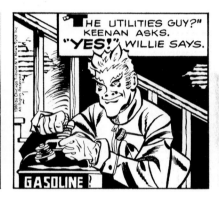

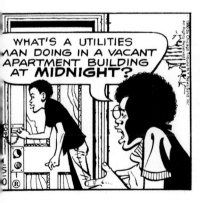

WHAT'S A UTILITIES MAN DOING IN A VACANT APARTMENT BUILDING AT MIDNIGHT?
1980 by Chicago Tribune-N.Y. News Synd. Inc. All Rights Reserved
I HAVE A BETTER QUESTION—
"WHAT WAS HE DOING WITH A CAN OF GASOLINE?"
GASOLINE
GOULD/Fletcher/COLLINS/

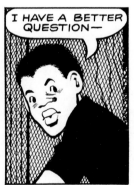

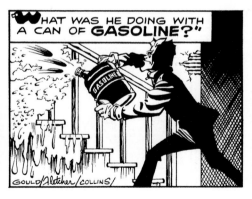

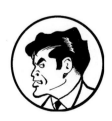

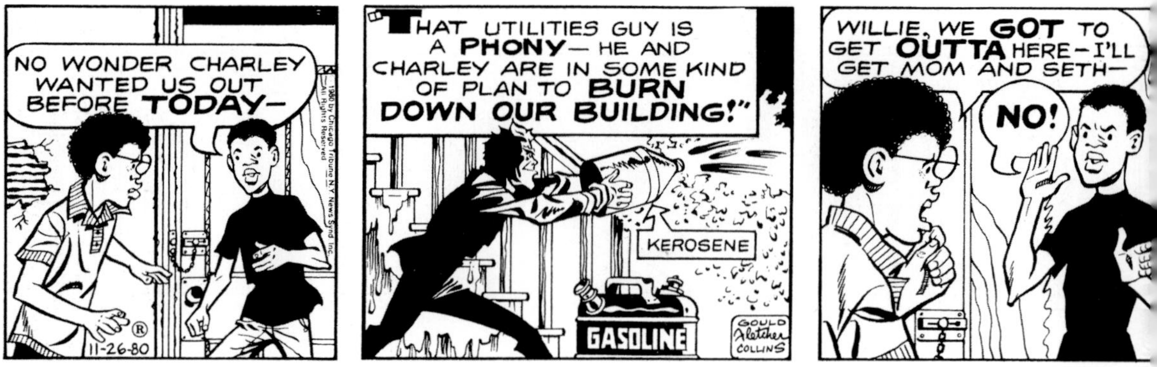
NO WONDER CHARLEY WANTED US OUT BEFORE TODAY—
© 1980 by Chicago Tribune-N.Y. News Synd. Inc. All Rights Reserved
11-26-80
"THAT UTILITIES GUY IS A PHONY— HE AND CHARLEY ARE IN SOME KIND OF PLAN TO BURN DOWN OUR BUILDING!"
KEROSENE
GASOLINE
GOULD Fletcher COLLINS
WILLIE, WE GOT TO GET OUTTA HERE—I'LL GET MOM AND SETH—
NO!

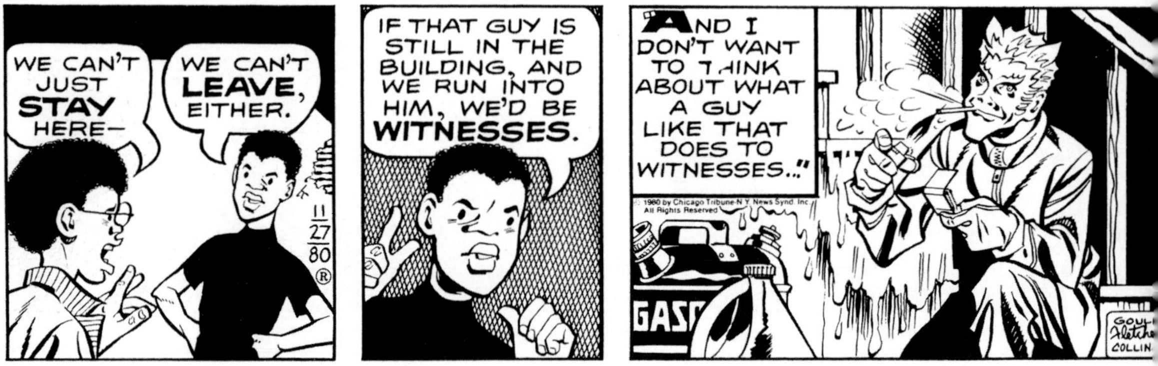
WE CAN'T JUST STAY HERE—
WE CAN'T LEAVE, EITHER.
11/27/80
IF THAT GUY IS STILL IN THE BUILDING, AND WE RUN INTO HIM, WE'D BE WITNESSES.
"AND I DON'T WANT TO THINK ABOUT WHAT A GUY LIKE THAT DOES TO WITNESSES.."
© 1980 by Chicago Tribune-N.Y. News Synd. Inc. All Rights Reserved

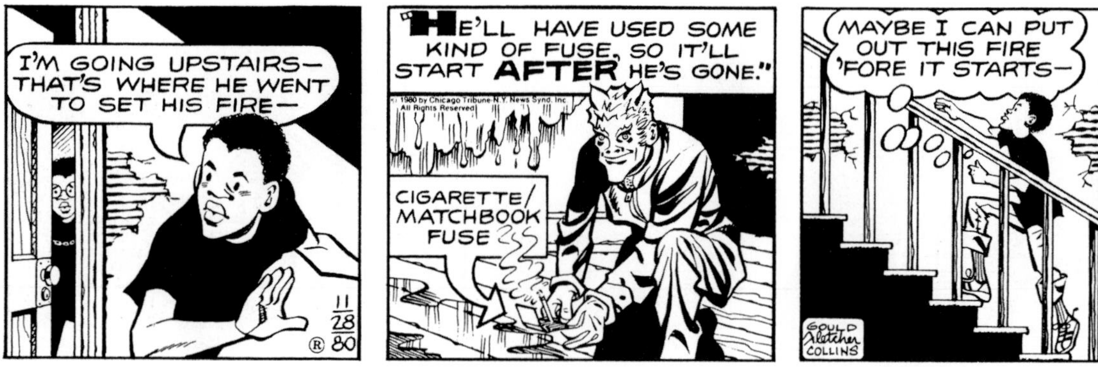
I'M GOING UPSTAIRS— THAT'S WHERE HE WENT TO SET HIS FIRE—
11/28/80
"HE'LL HAVE USED SOME KIND OF FUSE, SO IT'LL START AFTER HE'S GONE."
© 1980 by Chicago Tribune-N.Y. News Synd. Inc. All Rights Reserved
CIGARETTE/ MATCHBOOK FUSE
MAYBE I CAN PUT OUT THIS FIRE 'FORE IT STARTS—
GOULD Fletcher COLLINS

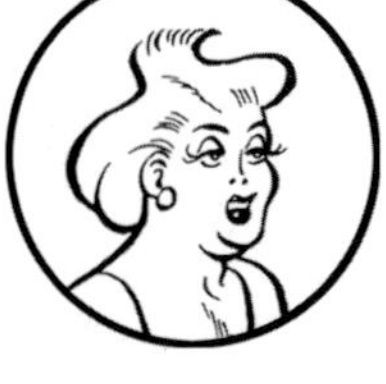

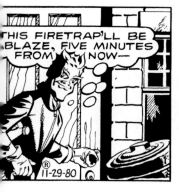

THIS FIRETRAP'LL BE
BLAZE, FIVE MINUTES
FROM NOW—
11-29-80
WILL IT? UPSTAIRS, IN THE APARTMENT BUILDING, WILLIE HAS FOUND ONE OF TORCHER'S CIGARETTE/ MATCHBOOK FUSES...
© 1980 by Chicago Tribune N.Y. News Synd. Inc. All Rights Reserved
BUT THERE IS STILL ANOTHER FUSE IN THE REAR STAIRWELL.
GOULD/FLETCHER/COLLINS

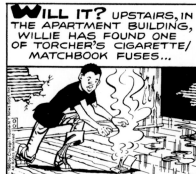

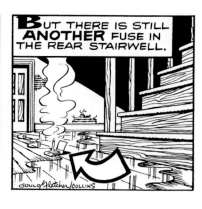

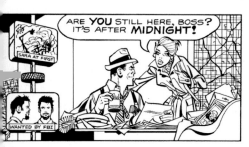

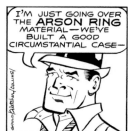

SARA AT FIRST
WANTED BY FBI
ARE YOU STILL HERE, BOSS? IT'S AFTER MIDNIGHT!
I'M JUST GOING OVER THE ARSON RING MATERIAL—WE'VE BUILT A GOOD CIRCUMSTANTIAL CASE—
GOULD/FLETCHER/COLLINS
"BUT I'D RATHER GO TO THE D.A. WHEN WE'VE GOT SOME HARD EVIDENCE TO BACK IT UP."
THAT WENT PERFECT—

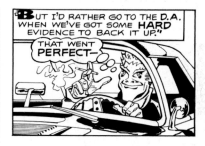

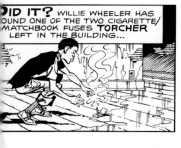

DID IT? WILLIE WHEELER HAS FOUND ONE OF THE TWO CIGARETTE/ MATCHBOOK FUSES TORCHER LEFT IN THE BUILDING...
WE WERE RIGHT ABOUT THAT GUY—THERE'S A ROOM UPSTAIRS WITH GAS SPLASHED EVERYPLACE—
© 1980 by Chicago Tribune N.Y. News Synd. Inc. All Rights Reserved
"THEN WE BETTER GET OUTTA HERE—" "NO," WILLIE SAYS. "WE'RE BETTER OFF STAYING— IT'S SAFE NOW."
SECOND FUSE IN REAR STAIRWELL
11-30-80

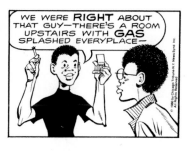

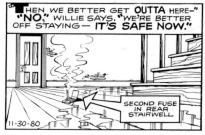

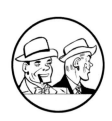

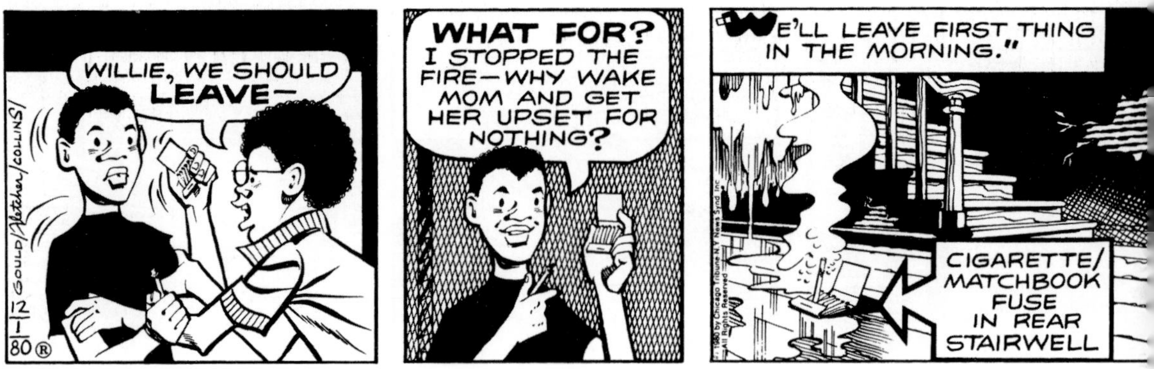
WILLIE, WE SHOULD LEAVE—
WHAT FOR? I STOPPED THE FIRE—WHY WAKE MOM AND GET HER UPSET FOR NOTHING?
"WE'LL LEAVE FIRST THING IN THE MORNING."
CIGARETTE/ MATCHBOOK FUSE IN REAR STAIRWELL
12/1/80 ®
GOULD/Fletcher/COLLINS/

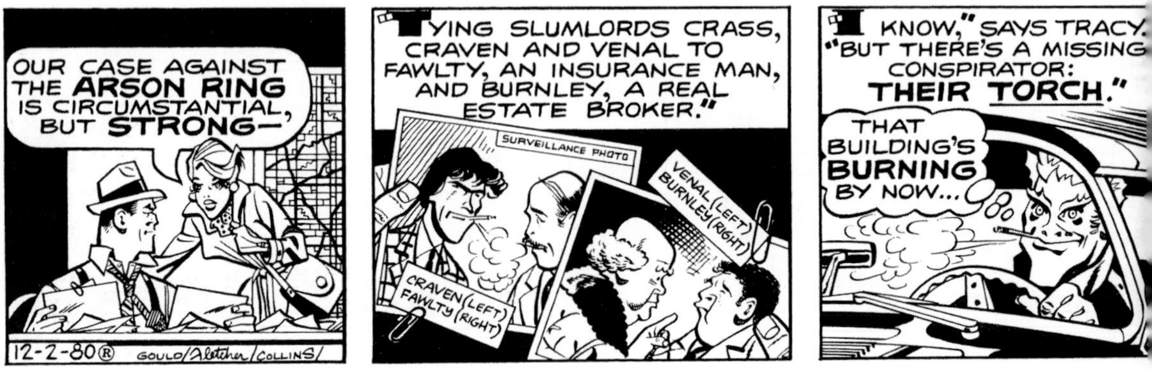
OUR CASE AGAINST THE ARSON RING IS CIRCUMSTANTIAL, BUT STRONG—
12-2-80 ®
GOULD/Fletcher/COLLINS/
"TYING SLUMLORDS CRASS, CRAVEN AND VENAL TO FAWLTY, AN INSURANCE MAN, AND BURNLEY, A REAL ESTATE BROKER."
SURVEILLANCE PHOTO
VENAL (LEFT) BURNLEY (RIGHT)
CRAVEN (LEFT) FAWLTY (RIGHT)
"I KNOW," SAYS TRACY. "BUT THERE'S A MISSING CONSPIRATOR: THEIR TORCH."
THAT BUILDING'S BURNING BY NOW...

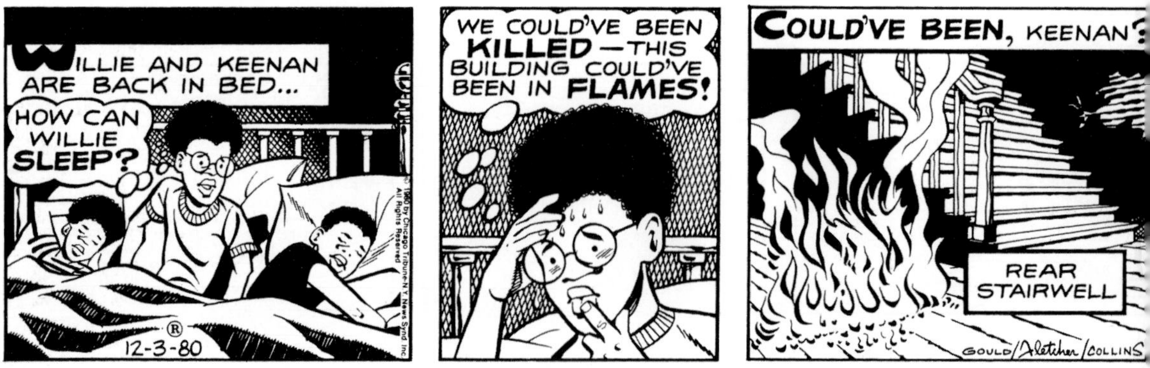
WILLIE AND KEENAN ARE BACK IN BED...
HOW CAN WILLIE SLEEP?
®
12-3-80
WE COULD'VE BEEN KILLED—THIS BUILDING COULD'VE BEEN IN FLAMES!
COULD'VE BEEN, KEENAN?
REAR STAIRWELL
GOULD/Fletcher/COLLINS

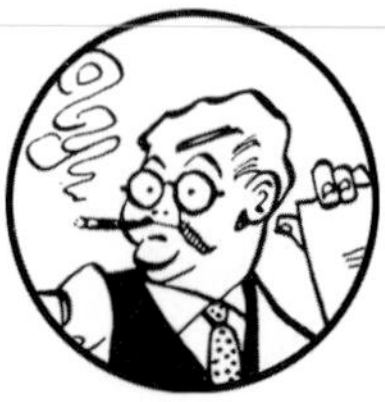

VILLIE—
VILLIE!
WHAT?
-4-80
I SMELL SMOKE!
"SO DO I!" WILLIE SAYS.
© 1980 by Chicago Tribune N.Y. News Synd. Inc. All Rights Reserved
GOULD/Fletcher/COLLINS/

AFTER A LONG DAY
T HQ, TRACY FINALLY HEADS HOME—
I WONDER HOW THE WHEELERS ARE DOING...
-5-80
NOT WELL, TRACY—
THIS DOOR IS HOT— THE FIRE'S RIGHT ON OUR DOORSTEP!
"YOU GET SETH— I'LL GET MOM—"
WHEELER APARTMENT
© 1980 by Chicago Tribune-N.Y. News Synd. Inc. All Rights Reserved
GOULD/Fletcher/COLLINS/

OME ON, MOM— LET'S NOT PANIC, NOW...
®
© 1980 by Chicago Tribune-N.Y. News Synd. Inc. All Rights Reserved
GOULD/Fletcher/COLLINS/
IN A CRUISING BLACK-AND-WHITE—
THE SKY'S AGLOW—
THAT'S A FIRE!

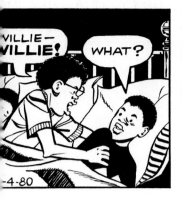

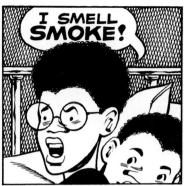

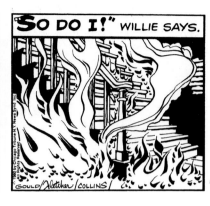

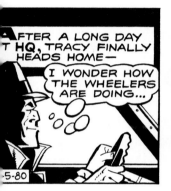

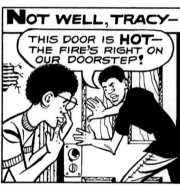

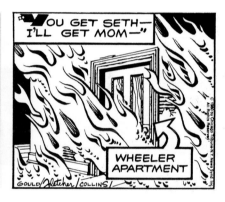

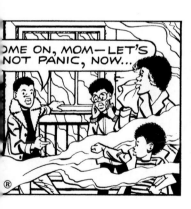

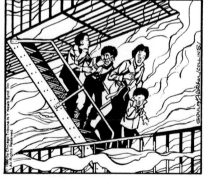

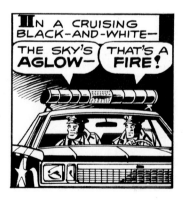

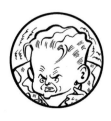

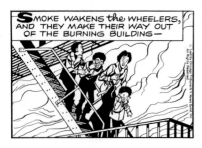

SMOKE WAKENS the WHEELERS, AND THEY MAKE THEIR WAY OUT OF THE BURNING BUILDING—
© 1980 by Chicago Tribune-N.Y. News Synd. Inc. All Rights Reserved
IS EVERYONE OUT OF THE BUILDING?
FAR AS WE KNOW—

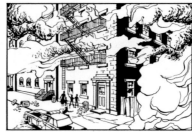

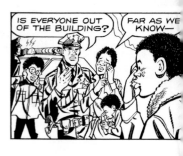

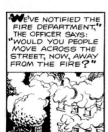

"WE'VE NOTIFIED THE FIRE DEPARTMENT," THE OFFICER SAYS: "WOULD YOU PEOPLE MOVE ACROSS THE STREET, NOW, AWAY FROM THE FIRE?"
I'VE REQUESTED BACK-UP—
2-WAY WRIST TV
"GOOD—NOW WE'VE GOT TO START EVACUATING RESIDENTS IN NEARBY BUILDINGS."
C.F.D.
CFD SNORKEL
GOULD/Fletcher/COLLINS/
I WONDER WHERE THOSE FIRE TRUCKS ARE HEADING...

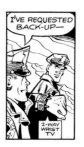

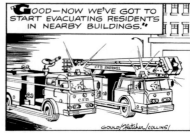

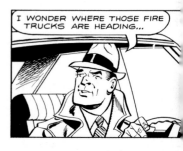

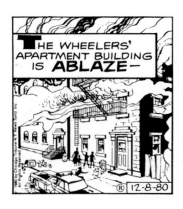

THE WHEELERS' APARTMENT BUILDING IS ABLAZE—
© 1980 by Chicago Tribune-N.Y. News Synd. Inc. All Rights Reserved
12-8-80
BUT THE FIRE TRUCKS ARE ON THEIR WAY—
CFD SNORKEL
C.F.D.
GOULD/Fletcher/COLLINS/
AND THE WHEELERS ARE SAFE!
OFFICER—DO YOU KNOW WHO DICK TRACY IS?

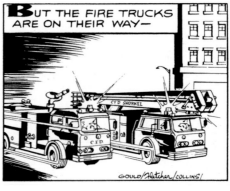

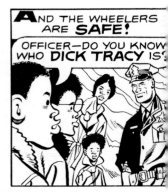

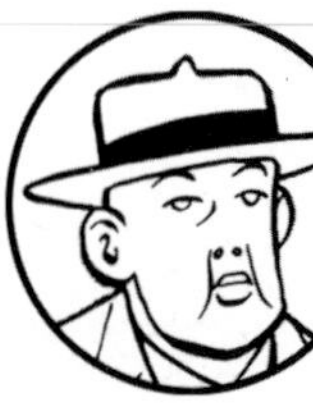

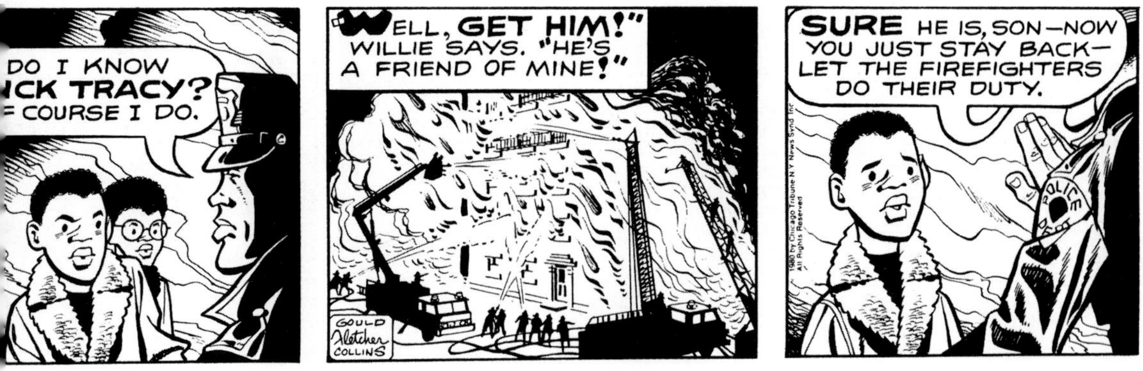
DO I KNOW
ICK TRACY?
F COURSE I DO.
WELL, GET HIM!" WILLIE SAYS. "HE'S A FRIEND OF MINE!"
GOULD
Fletcher
COLLINS
SURE HE IS, SON—NOW YOU JUST STAY BACK—LET THE FIREFIGHTERS DO THEIR DUTY.
POLICE
©1980 by Chicago Tribune-N.Y. News Synd Inc All Rights Reserved

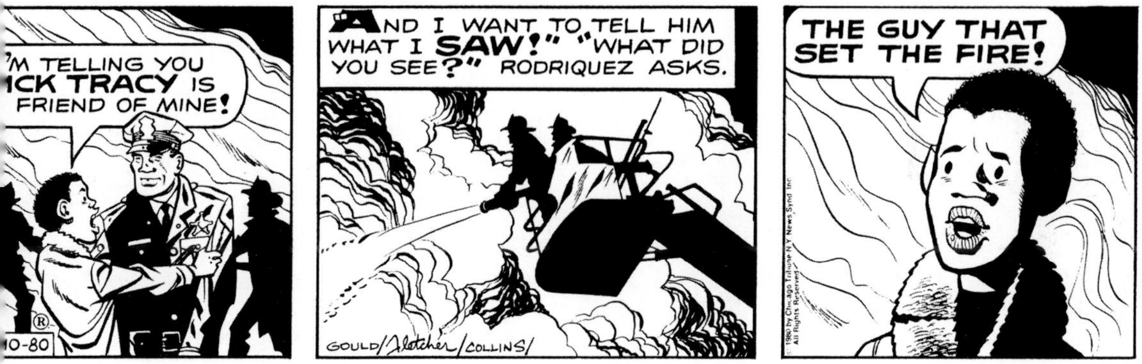
'M TELLING YOU
ICK TRACY IS
FRIEND OF MINE!
0-80
AND I WANT TO TELL HIM WHAT I SAW!" "WHAT DID YOU SEE?" RODRIQUEZ ASKS.
GOULD/Fletcher/COLLINS/
THE GUY THAT SET THE FIRE!
©1980 by Chicago Tribune-N.Y. News Synd Inc All Rights Reserved

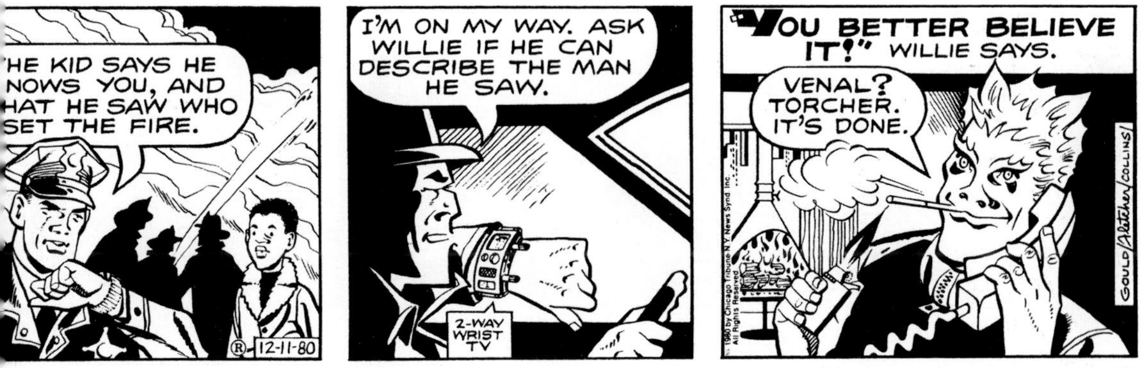
HE KID SAYS HE
NOWS YOU, AND
HAT HE SAW WHO
SET THE FIRE.
12-11-80
I'M ON MY WAY. ASK WILLIE IF HE CAN DESCRIBE THE MAN HE SAW.
2-WAY WRIST TV
YOU BETTER BELIEVE IT!" WILLIE SAYS.
VENAL? TORCHER. IT'S DONE.
GOULD/Fletcher/COLLINS/
©1980 by Chicago Tribune-N.Y. News Synd Inc All Rights Reserved

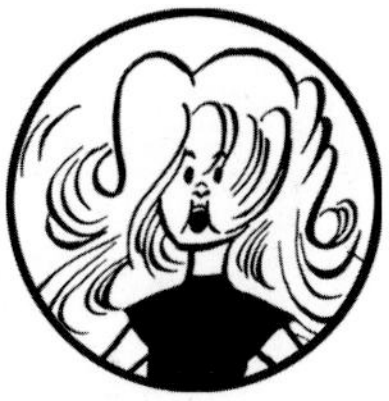

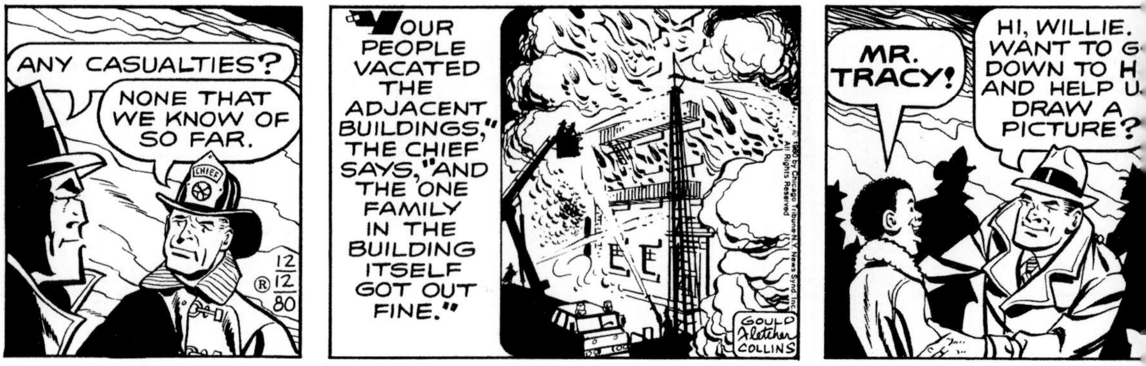
ANY CASUALTIES?
NONE THAT WE KNOW OF SO FAR.
12 12 80
"YOUR PEOPLE VACATED THE ADJACENT BUILDINGS," THE CHIEF SAYS, "AND THE ONE FAMILY IN THE BUILDING ITSELF GOT OUT FINE."
© 1980 by Chicago Tribune-N.Y. News Synd. Inc. All Rights Reserved
GOULD Fletcher COLLINS
MR. TRACY!
HI, WILLIE. WANT TO G DOWN TO H AND HELP U DRAW A PICTURE?

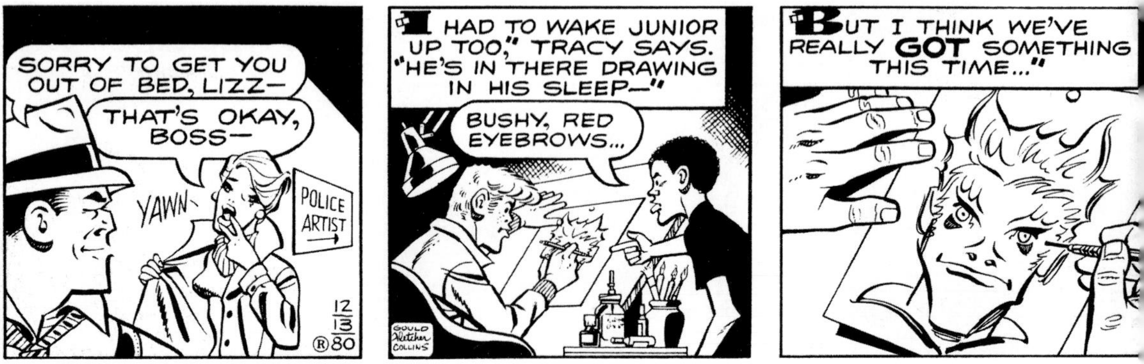
SORRY TO GET YOU OUT OF BED, LIZZ—
THAT'S OKAY, BOSS—
YAWN
POLICE ARTIST
12 13 80
"I HAD TO WAKE JUNIOR UP TOO," TRACY SAYS. "HE'S IN THERE DRAWING IN HIS SLEEP—"
BUSHY, RED EYEBROWS...
GOULD Fletcher COLLINS
"BUT I THINK WE'VE REALLY GOT SOMETHING THIS TIME..."

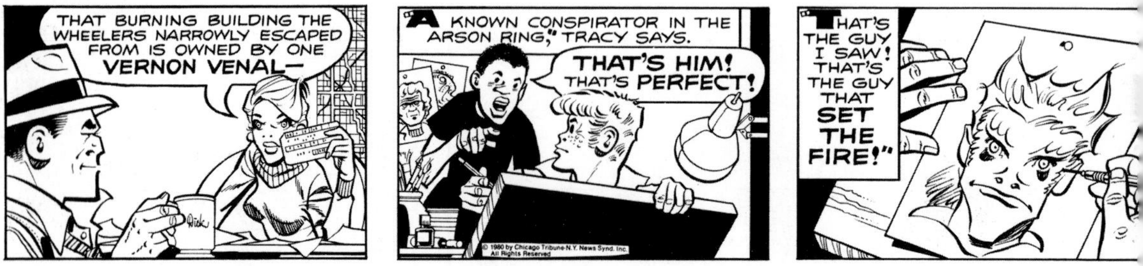
THAT BURNING BUILDING THE WHEELERS NARROWLY ESCAPED FROM IS OWNED BY ONE VERNON VENAL—
"A KNOWN CONSPIRATOR IN THE ARSON RING," TRACY SAYS.
THAT'S HIM! THAT'S PERFECT!
© 1980 by Chicago Tribune-N.Y. News Synd. Inc. All Rights Reserved
"THAT'S THE GUY I SAW! THAT'S THE GUY THAT SET THE FIRE!"

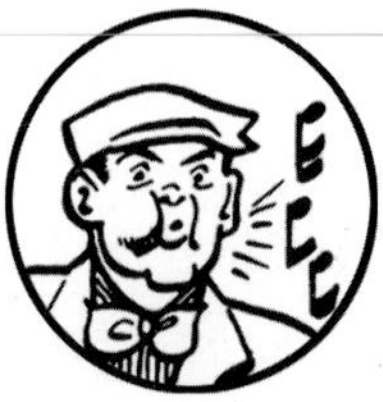

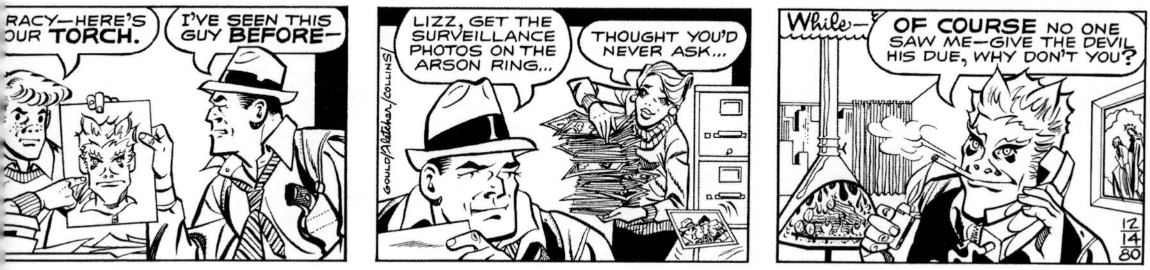
RACY—HERE'S
OUR TORCH.
I'VE SEEN THIS GUY BEFORE—
LIZZ, GET THE SURVEILLANCE PHOTOS ON THE ARSON RING...
THOUGHT YOU'D NEVER ASK...
GOULD/Fletcher/COLLINS/
While—
OF COURSE NO ONE SAW ME—GIVE THE DEVIL HIS DUE, WHY DON'T YOU?
12 14 80

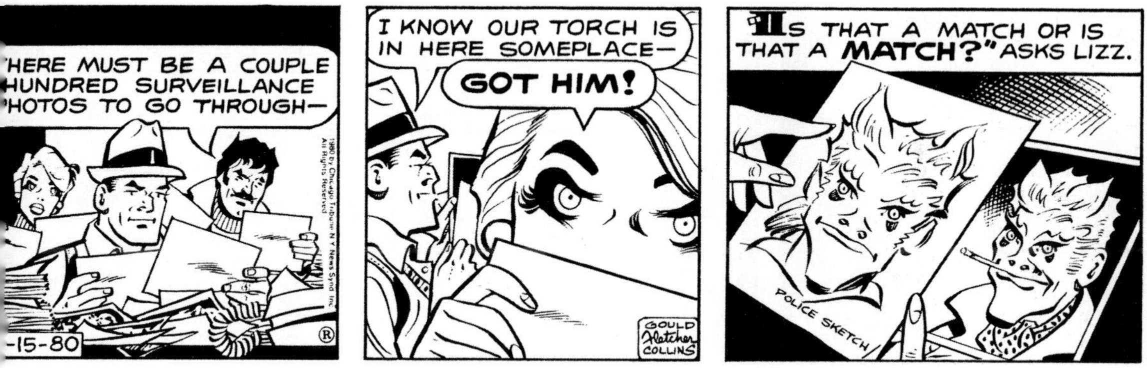
HERE MUST BE A COUPLE
HUNDRED SURVEILLANCE
PHOTOS TO GO THROUGH—
© 1980 by Chicago Tribune-N.Y. News Synd. Inc. All Rights Reserved
-15-80
I KNOW OUR TORCH IS IN HERE SOMEPLACE—
GOT HIM!
GOULD Fletcher COLLINS
"IS THAT A MATCH OR IS THAT A MATCH?" ASKS LIZZ.
POLICE SKETCH

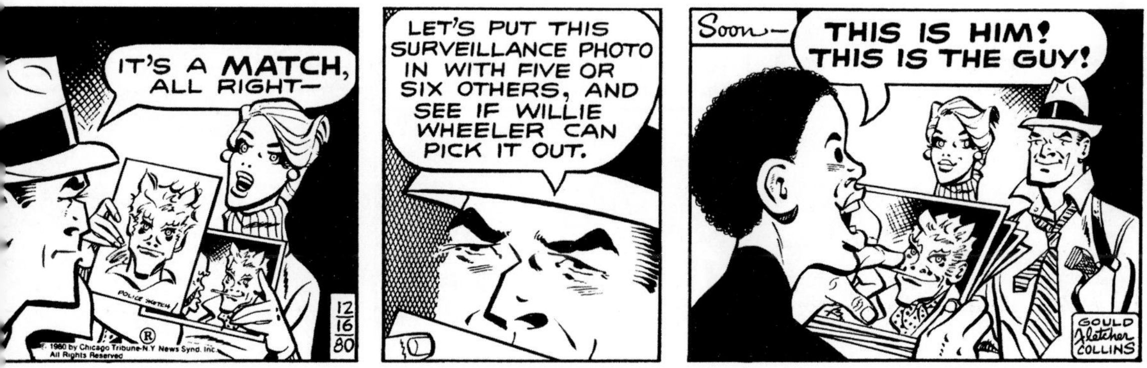
IT'S A MATCH, ALL RIGHT—
POLICE SKETCH
12 16 80
© 1980 by Chicago Tribune-N.Y. News Synd. Inc. All Rights Reserved
LET'S PUT THIS SURVEILLANCE PHOTO IN WITH FIVE OR SIX OTHERS, AND SEE IF WILLIE WHEELER CAN PICK IT OUT.
Soon—
THIS IS HIM! THIS IS THE GUY!
GOULD Fletcher COLLINS

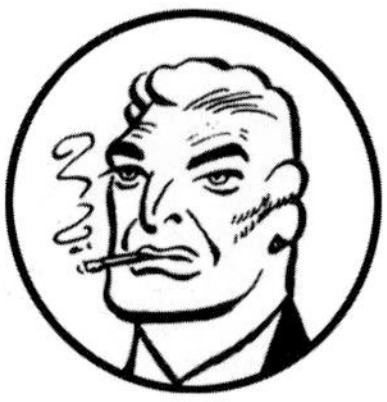

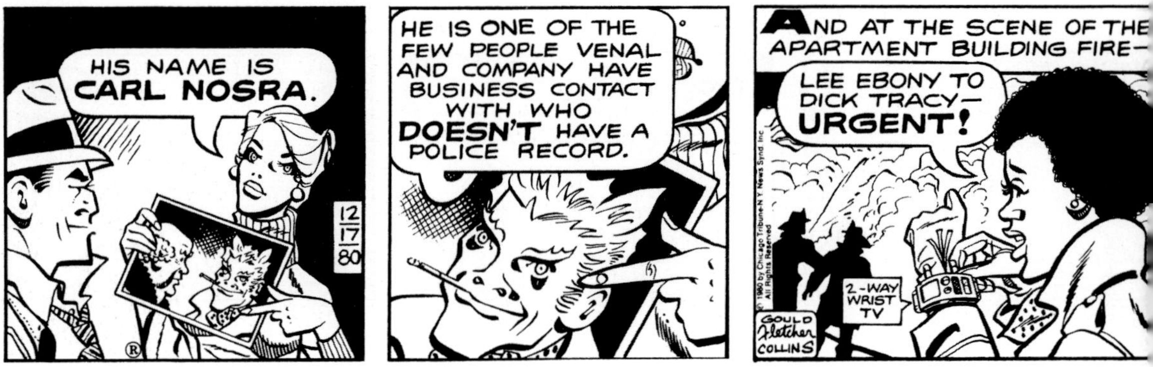
HIS NAME IS CARL NOSRA.
12/17/80
HE IS ONE OF THE FEW PEOPLE VENAL AND COMPANY HAVE BUSINESS CONTACT WITH WHO DOESN'T HAVE A POLICE RECORD.
AND AT THE SCENE OF THE APARTMENT BUILDING FIRE—
LEE EBONY TO DICK TRACY— URGENT!
2-WAY WRIST TV
© 1980 by Chicago Tribune-N.Y. News Synd. Inc. All Rights Reserved
GOULD Fletcher COLLINS

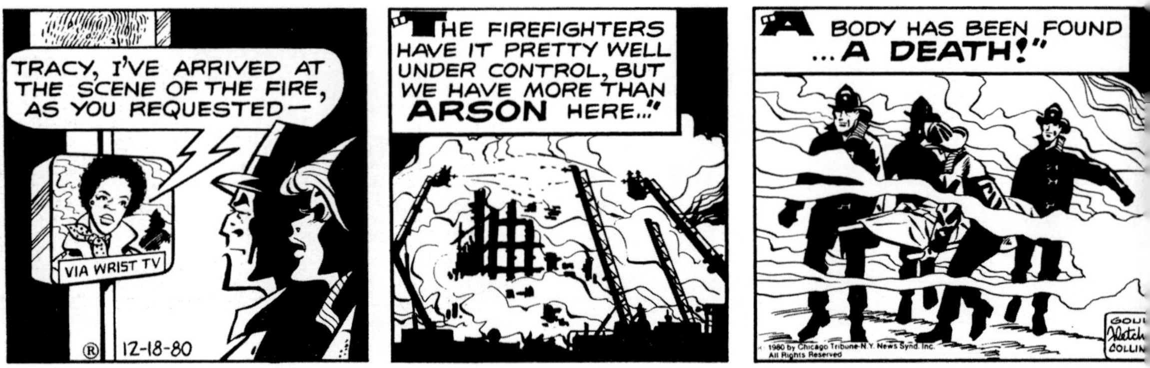
TRACY, I'VE ARRIVED AT THE SCENE OF THE FIRE, AS YOU REQUESTED—
VIA WRIST TV
12-18-80
"THE FIREFIGHTERS HAVE IT PRETTY WELL UNDER CONTROL, BUT WE HAVE MORE THAN ARSON HERE..."
"A BODY HAS BEEN FOUND ...A DEATH!"
© 1980 by Chicago Tribune-N.Y. News Synd. Inc. All Rights Reserved

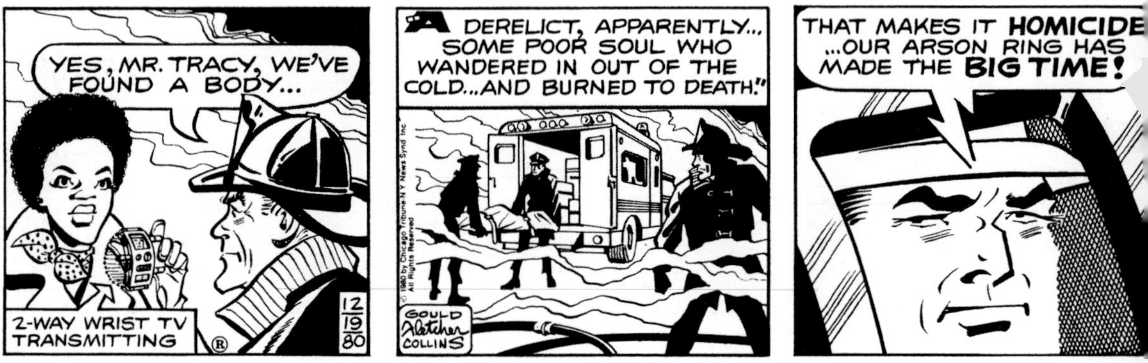
YES, MR. TRACY, WE'VE FOUND A BODY...
2-WAY WRIST TV TRANSMITTING
12/19/80
"A DERELICT, APPARENTLY... SOME POOR SOUL WHO WANDERED IN OUT OF THE COLD...AND BURNED TO DEATH."
© 1980 by Chicago Tribune-N.Y. News Synd. Inc. All Rights Reserved
GOULD Fletcher COLLINS
THAT MAKES IT HOMICIDE ...OUR ARSON RING HAS MADE THE BIG TIME!

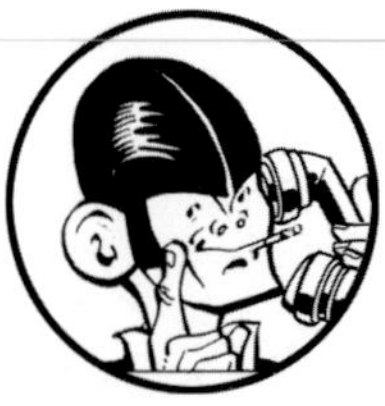

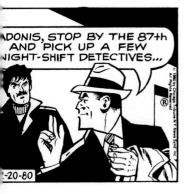

ADONIS, STOP BY THE 87th AND PICK UP A FEW IGHT-SHIFT DETECTIVES...
© 1980 by Chicago Tribune-N.Y. News Synd. Inc. All Rights Reserved
-20-80
"YOU'VE GOT SOME ARRESTS TO MAKE: VENAL, CRASS, CRAVEN, FAWLTY AND THE REST OF THE ARSON RING... THEY'RE MURDERERS NOW."
COME ON, LIZZ, SAM— I WANT TO CALL ON MR. NOSRA MYSELF—
GOULD Fletcher COLLINS

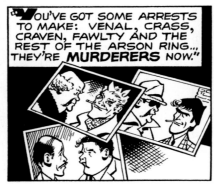

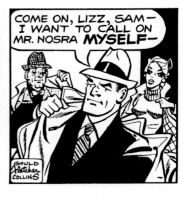

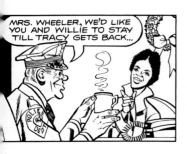

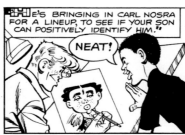

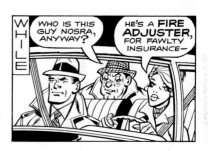

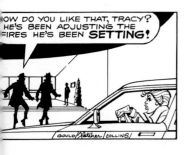

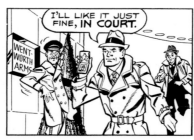

MRS. WHEELER, WE'D LIKE YOU AND WILLIE TO STAY TILL TRACY GETS BACK...
"HE'S BRINGING IN CARL NOSRA FOR A LINEUP, TO SEE IF YOUR SON CAN POSITIVELY IDENTIFY HIM."
NEAT!
WHILE
WHO IS THIS GUY NOSRA, ANYWAY?
HE'S A FIRE ADJUSTER, FOR FAWLTY INSURANCE—

OW DO YOU LIKE THAT, TRACY? HE'S BEEN ADJUSTING THE IRES HE'S BEEN SETTING!
GOULD Fletcher COLLINS
I'LL LIKE IT JUST FINE, IN COURT.
WENT-WORTH ARMS
Moments Later—
MR. NOSRA? POLICE. MAY WE HAVE A WORD WITH YOU?
CERTAINLY— COME IN, GENTLEMEN...
12/21/80
© 1980 by Chicago Tribune-N.Y. News Synd. Inc. All Rights Reserved

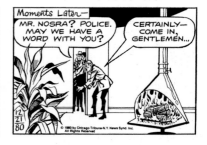

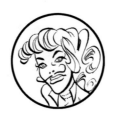

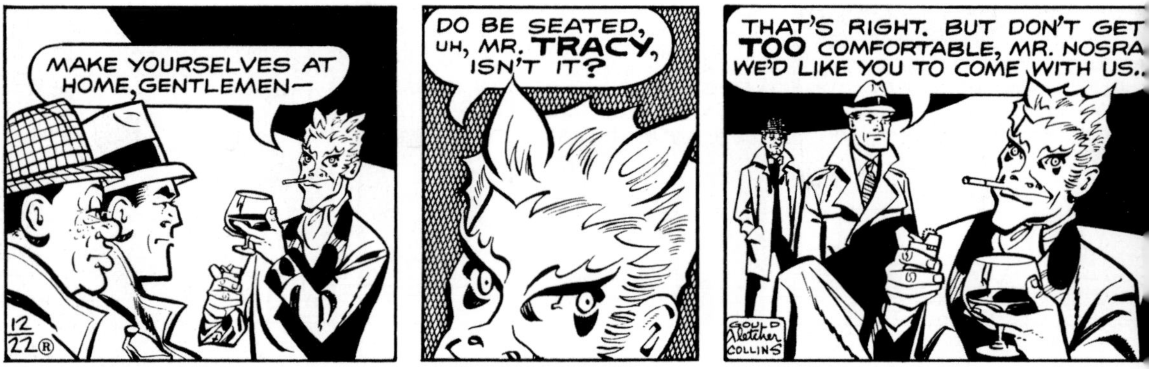
MAKE YOURSELVES AT HOME, GENTLEMEN—
12 22 ®
DO BE SEATED, UH, MR. TRACY, ISN'T IT?
THAT'S RIGHT. BUT DON'T GET TOO COMFORTABLE, MR. NOSRA
WE'D LIKE YOU TO COME WITH US..
GOULD Fletcher COLLINS

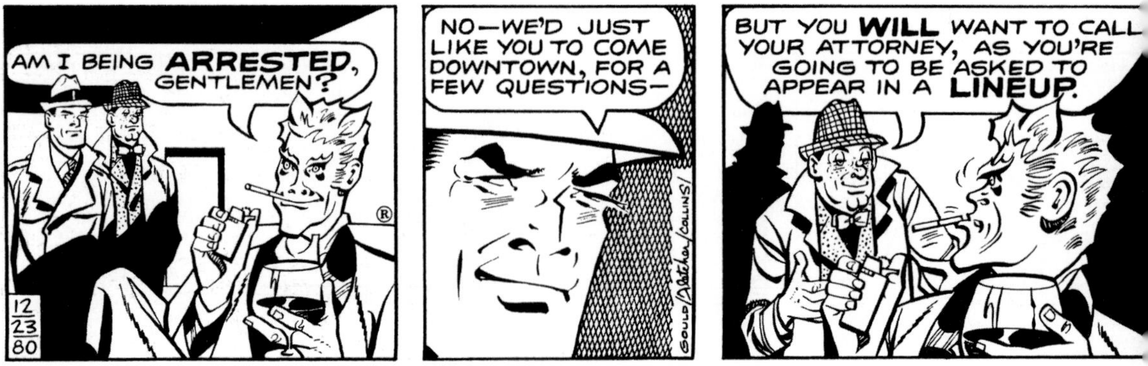
AM I BEING ARRESTED, GENTLEMEN?
12 23 80
®
NO—WE'D JUST LIKE YOU TO COME DOWNTOWN, FOR A FEW QUESTIONS—
GOULD/Fletcher/COLLINS/
BUT YOU WILL WANT TO CALL YOUR ATTORNEY, AS YOU'RE GOING TO BE ASKED TO APPEAR IN A LINEUP.

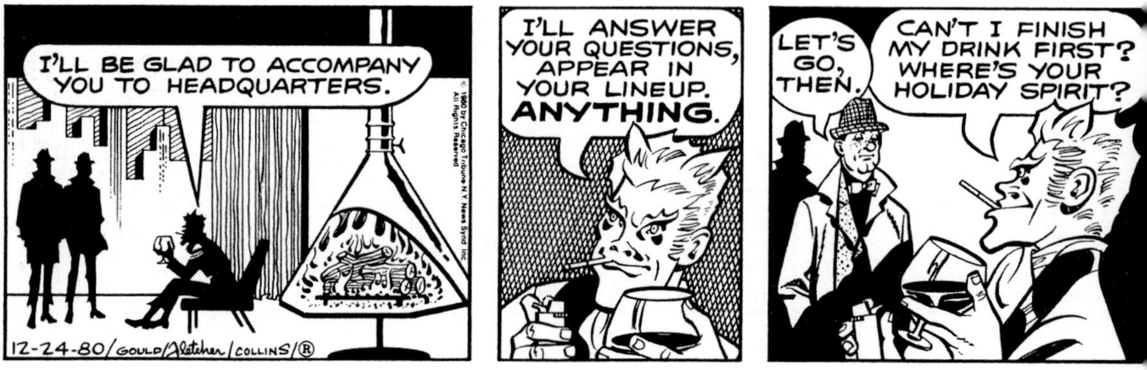
I'LL BE GLAD TO ACCOMPANY YOU TO HEADQUARTERS.
© 1980 by Chicago Tribune-N.Y. News Synd. Inc.
All Rights Reserved
12-24-80/GOULD/Fletcher/COLLINS/®
I'LL ANSWER YOUR QUESTIONS, APPEAR IN YOUR LINEUP. ANYTHING.
LET'S GO, THEN.
CAN'T I FINISH MY DRINK FIRST? WHERE'S YOUR HOLIDAY SPIRIT?

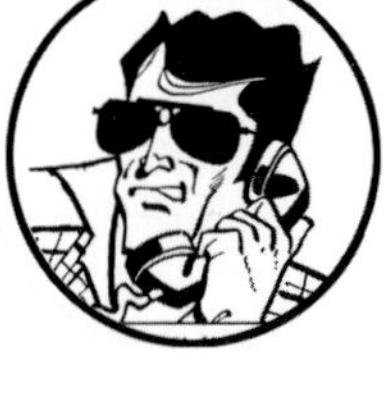

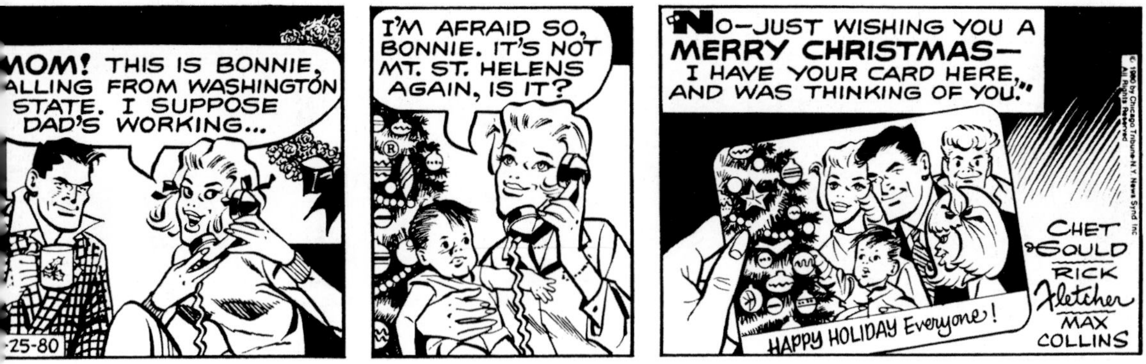
MOM! THIS IS BONNIE, ALLING FROM WASHINGTON STATE. I SUPPOSE DAD'S WORKING...
-25-80
I'M AFRAID SO, BONNIE. IT'S NOT MT. ST. HELENS AGAIN, IS IT?
"NO—JUST WISHING YOU A MERRY CHRISTMAS— I HAVE YOUR CARD HERE, AND WAS THINKING OF YOU."
HAPPY HOLIDAY Everyone!
© 1980 by Chicago Tribune-N.Y. News Synd. Inc. All Rights Reserved
CHET GOULD
RICK Fletcher
MAX COLLINS

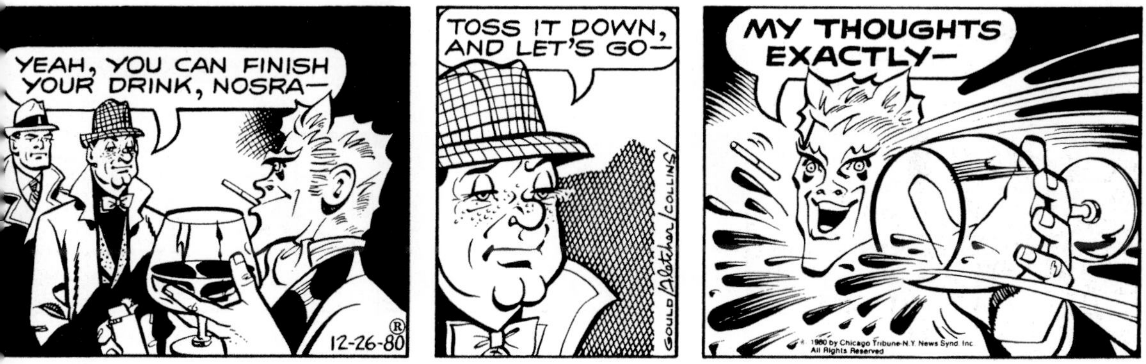
YEAH, YOU CAN FINISH YOUR DRINK, NOSRA—
12-26-80
TOSS IT DOWN, AND LET'S GO—
GOULD Fletcher COLLINS
MY THOUGHTS EXACTLY—
© 1980 by Chicago Tribune-N.Y. News Synd. Inc. All Rights Reserved

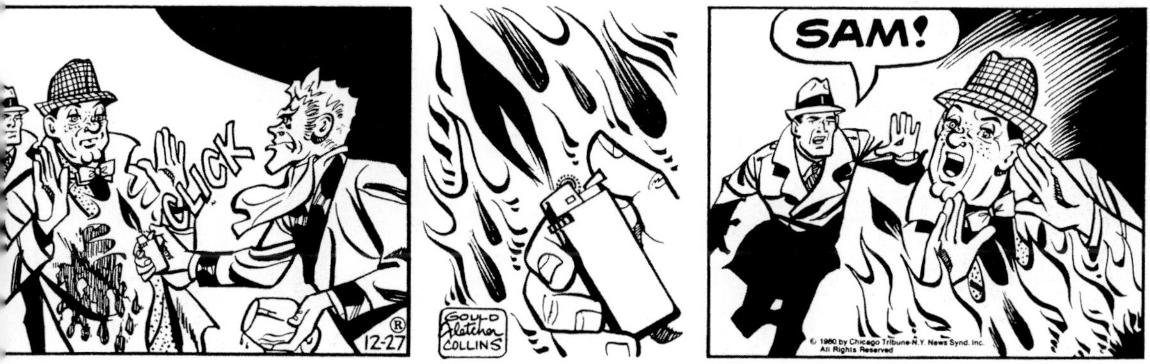
CLICK
12-27
GOULD Fletcher COLLINS
SAM!
© 1980 by Chicago Tribune-N.Y. News Synd. Inc. All Rights Reserved

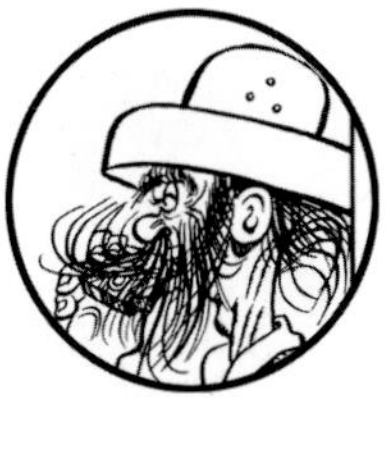

TORCHER SPLASHES SAM'S COAT WITH A DRINK AND—
YIIII!
BEATING OUT FLAMES

FIRE'S OUT. ARE YOU OKAY, SAM?
YEAH—MY PRIDE'S A LITTLE SINGED, THOUGH—
GOULD/Fletcher/COLLINS
"AND I THINK I NEED A NEW COAT," SAM SAYS. "WHERE'S NOSRA?" "LET'S FIND OUT," TRACY SAYS.
© 1980 by Chicago Tribune-N.Y. News Synd. Inc. All Rights Reserved
Moments Later—
CAN I HAVE A WORD WITH YOU, HARLEY?
CERTAINLY, MR. NOSRA—
WENT-WORTH ARMS

YOU SURE YOU'RE OKAY?
© 1980 by Chicago Tribune-N.Y. News Synd. Inc. All Rights Reserved
®
12 29 80
YEAH—BUT I GUESS MY COAT WASN'T FIREPROOF.
YOU UP TO GOING AFTER NOSRA?
GOULD Fletcher COLLINS
"TRY AND STOP ME!" SAM SAYS And AT THE FRONT ENTRANCE—
A WORD WITH ME, SIR?
YES, HARLEY—
WENT-WORTH ARMS

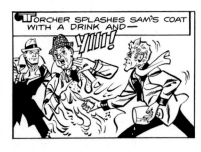

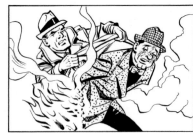

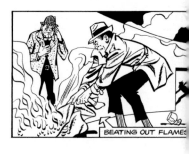

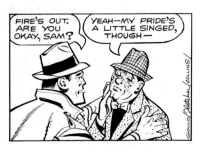

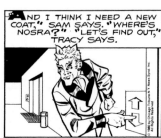

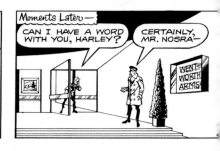

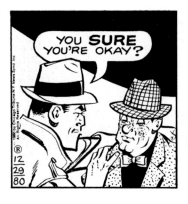

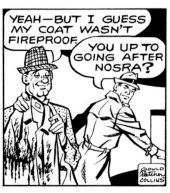

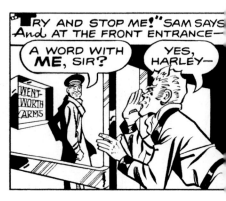

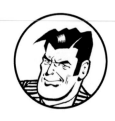

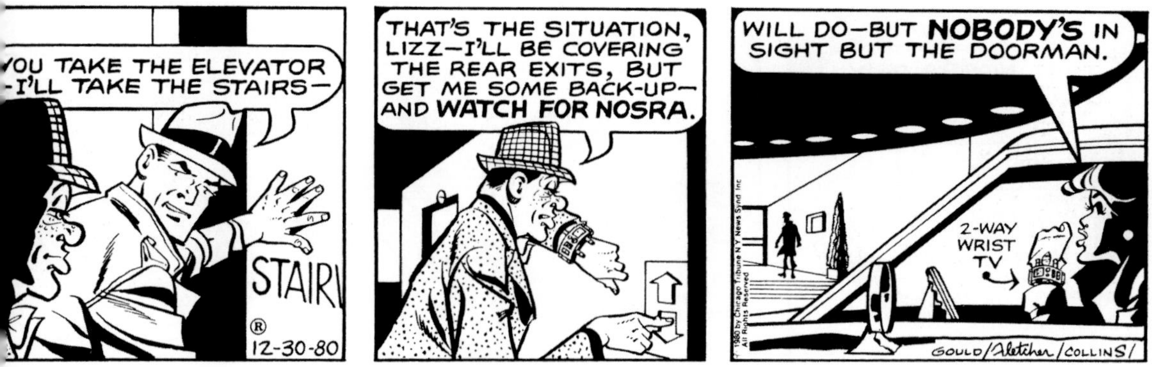
YOU TAKE THE ELEVATOR —I'LL TAKE THE STAIRS—
STAIR
12-30-80
THAT'S THE SITUATION, LIZZ—I'LL BE COVERING THE REAR EXITS, BUT GET ME SOME BACK-UP— AND **WATCH FOR NOSRA.**
WILL DO—BUT **NOBODY'S** IN SIGHT BUT THE DOORMAN.
2-WAY WRIST TV
© 1980 by Chicago Tribune-N.Y. News Synd. Inc. All Rights Reserved
GOULD/Fletcher/COLLINS/

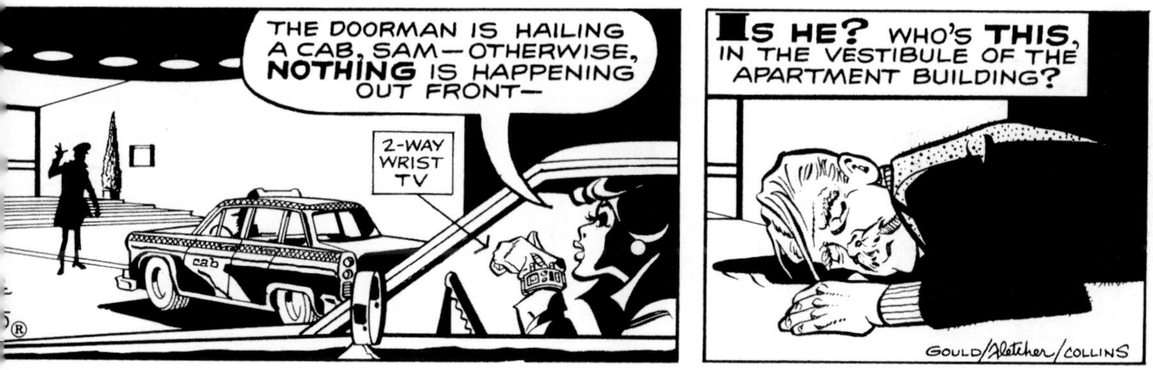
THE DOORMAN IS HAILING A CAB, SAM—OTHERWISE, **NOTHING** IS HAPPENING OUT FRONT—
2-WAY WRIST TV
cab
IS HE? WHO'S **THIS**, IN THE VESTIBULE OF THE APARTMENT BUILDING?
GOULD/Fletcher/COLLINS

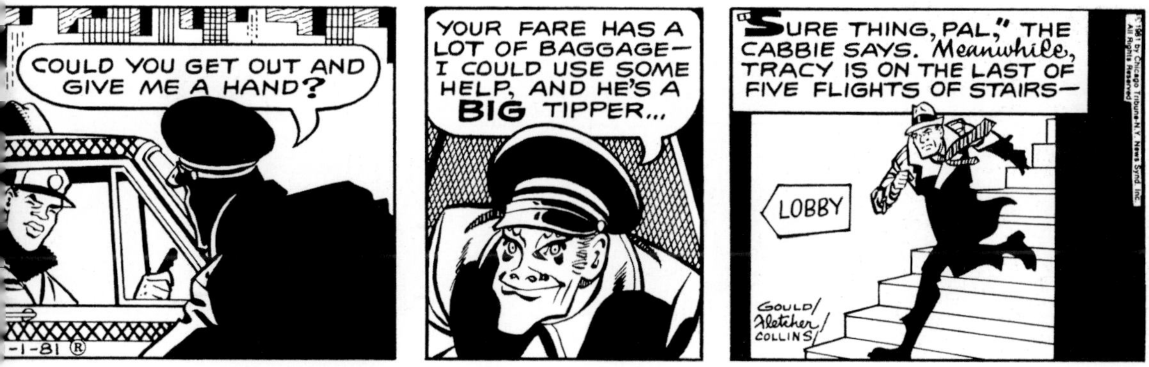
COULD YOU GET OUT AND GIVE ME A HAND?
-1-81
YOUR FARE HAS A LOT OF BAGGAGE— I COULD USE SOME HELP, AND HE'S A **BIG** TIPPER...
"SURE THING, PAL," THE CABBIE SAYS. *Meanwhile,* TRACY IS ON THE LAST OF FIVE FLIGHTS OF STAIRS—
LOBBY
© 1981 by Chicago Tribune-N.Y. News Synd. Inc. All Rights Reserved
GOULD/ Fletcher/ COLLINS/

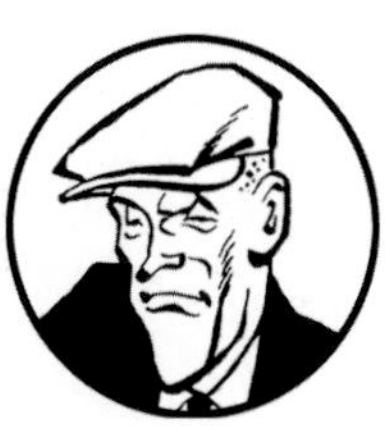

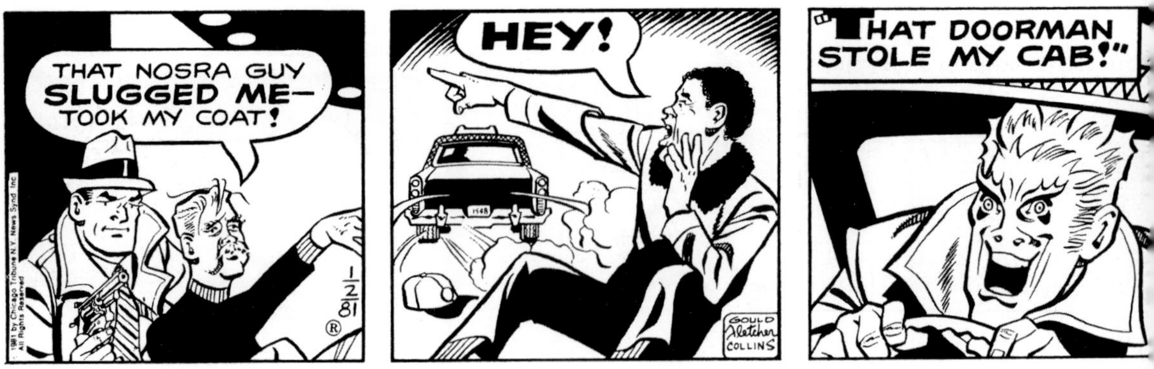
THAT NOSRA GUY SLUGGED ME— TOOK MY COAT!
1/2/81
HEY!
GOULD Fletcher COLLINS
"THAT DOORMAN STOLE MY CAB!"

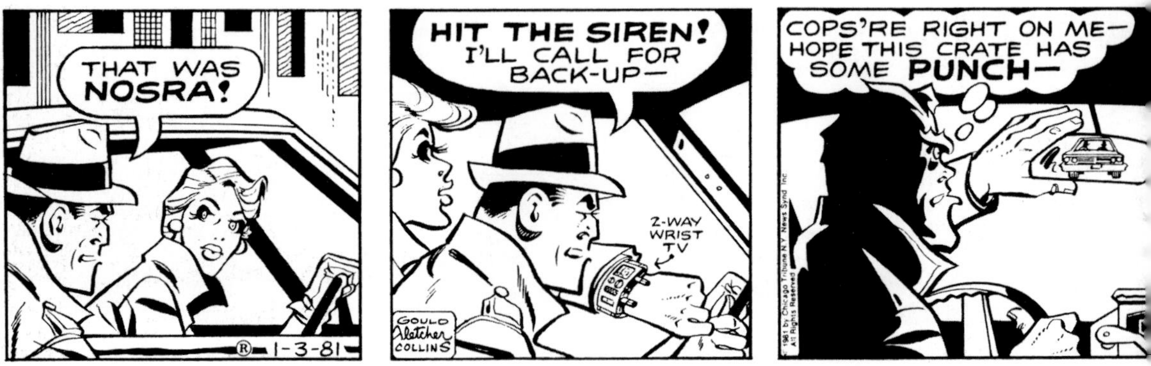
THAT WAS NOSRA!
1-3-81
HIT THE SIREN! I'LL CALL FOR BACK-UP—
2-WAY WRIST TV
GOULD Fletcher COLLINS
COPS'RE RIGHT ON ME— HOPE THIS CRATE HAS SOME PUNCH—

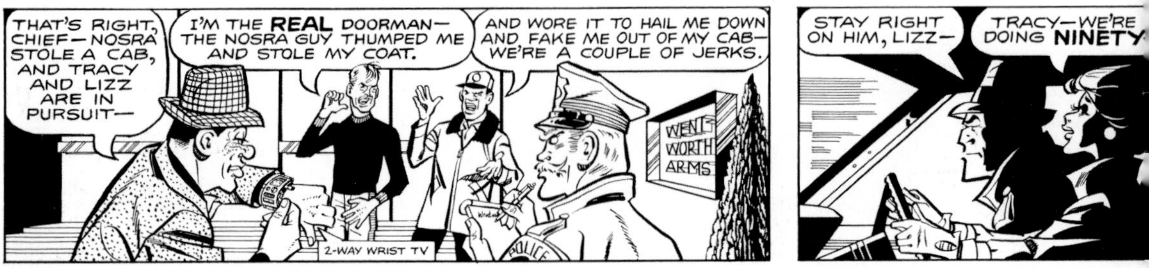
THAT'S RIGHT, CHIEF—NOSRA STOLE A CAB, AND TRACY AND LIZZ ARE IN PURSUIT—
I'M THE REAL DOORMAN— THE NOSRA GUY THUMPED ME AND STOLE MY COAT.
AND WORE IT TO HAIL ME DOWN AND FAKE ME OUT OF MY CAB— WE'RE A COUPLE OF JERKS.
WENTWORTH ARMS
2-WAY WRIST TV
STAY RIGHT ON HIM, LIZZ—
TRACY—WE'RE DOING NINETY

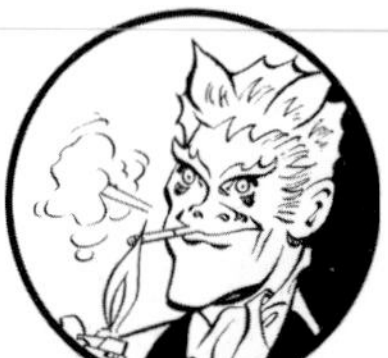

"I KNOW—STREETS ARE EMPTY, THIS TIME OF NIGHT, BUT STAY ALERT— AND STAY ON HIM!"
WHY DON'T THEY QUIT!
"GOTTA SHAKE 'EM," TORCHER THINKS.
© 1981 by Chicago Tribune-N.Y. News Synd. Inc. All Rights Reserved
GOULD/Fletcher/COLLINS/
HE'S TURNING INTO THAT ALLEY —NOT SLOWING DOWN—
DON'T FOLLOW HIM! THAT'S A DEAD END!
1-4-81

HIT YOUR BRAKES!
1/5/81
"NOSRA'S PULLING INTO A DEAD END —AT 100 MPH!"
Cab
SCREECH-
GOULD Fletcher COLLINS
1981 by Chicago Tribune-N.Y. News Synd. Inc. All Rights Reserved
BOOM-M-M

© 1981 by Chicago Tribune-N.Y. News Synd. Inc. All Rights Reserved
DON'T EVEN THINK OF IT, TRACY—
"THERE'S NO WAY YOU CAN SAVE HIM— HE'S DEAD BY NOW."
Cab

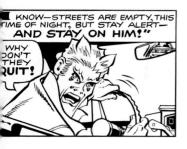

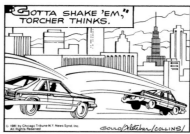

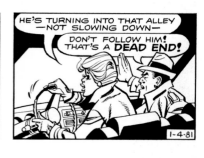

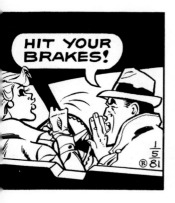

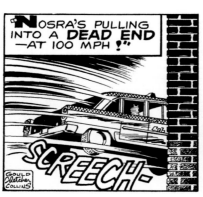

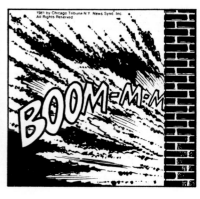

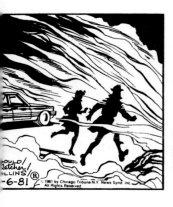

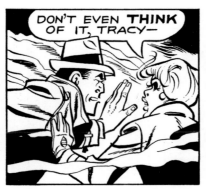

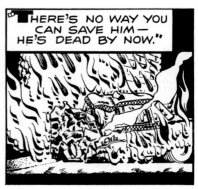

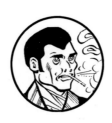

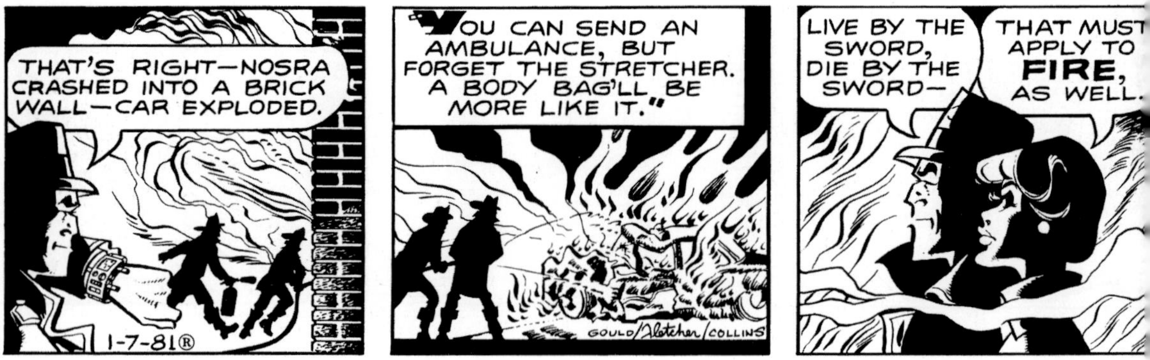
THAT'S RIGHT—NOSRA CRASHED INTO A BRICK WALL—CAR EXPLODED.
1-7-81®
"YOU CAN SEND AN AMBULANCE, BUT FORGET THE STRETCHER. A BODY BAG'LL BE MORE LIKE IT."
GOULD/Fletcher/COLLINS
LIVE BY THE SWORD, DIE BY THE SWORD—
THAT MUST APPLY TO **FIRE**, AS WELL.

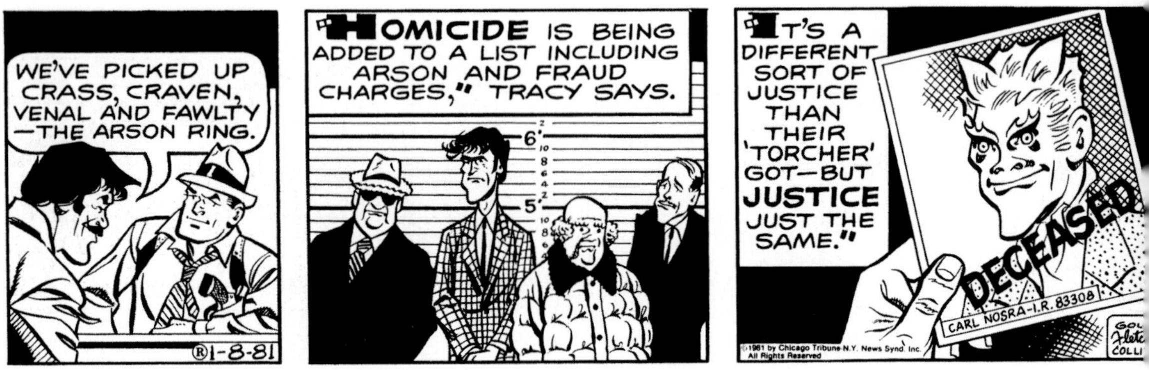
WE'VE PICKED UP CRASS, CRAVEN, VENAL AND FAWLTY —THE ARSON RING.
®1-8-81
"**HOMICIDE** IS BEING ADDED TO A LIST INCLUDING ARSON AND FRAUD CHARGES," TRACY SAYS.
"IT'S A DIFFERENT SORT OF JUSTICE THAN THEIR 'TORCHER' GOT—BUT **JUSTICE** JUST THE SAME."
DECEASED
CARL NOSRA—I.R. 83308
©1981 by Chicago Tribune-N.Y. News Synd. Inc. All Rights Reserved

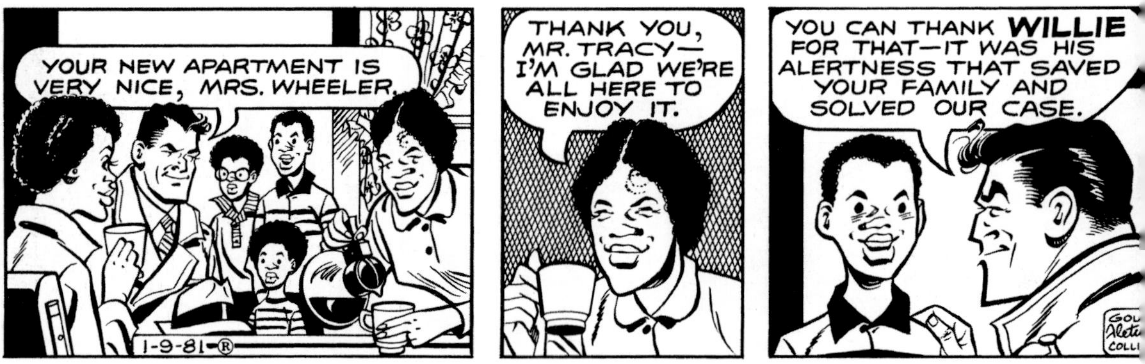
YOUR NEW APARTMENT IS VERY NICE, MRS. WHEELER.
1-9-81-®
THANK YOU, MR. TRACY— I'M GLAD WE'RE ALL HERE TO ENJOY IT.
YOU CAN THANK **WILLIE** FOR THAT—IT WAS HIS ALERTNESS THAT SAVED YOUR FAMILY AND SOLVED OUR CASE.

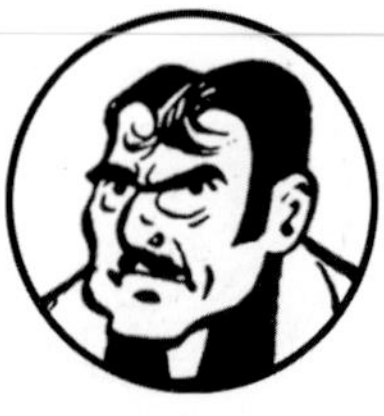

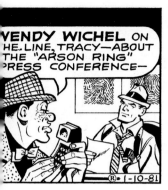

VENDY WICHEL ON HE LINE, TRACY—ABOUT THE "ARSON RING" PRESS CONFERENCE—
1-10-81
TELL HER IT'S IN AN HOUR, AND REMIND HER WHERE IT'S BEING HELD.
"THAT'S RIGHT, WENDY," SAM SAYS. "THAT IS AN INNER-CITY ADDRESS." While—
OPENING NIGHT DRAWS NEAR! WHERE IS B.U. TIFFIL?
GOULD Fletcher COLLINS
© 1981 by Chicago Tribune-N.Y. News Synd. Inc. All Rights Reserved

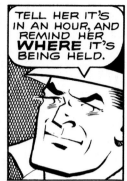

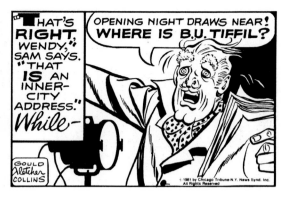

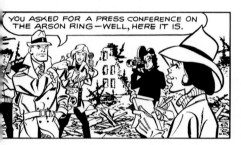

YOU ASKED FOR A PRESS CONFERENCE ON THE ARSON RING—WELL, HERE IT IS.
"AND HERE'S WHAT THE PROBLEM IS ABOUT: INNER-CITY BUILDINGS BURNED FOR PROFIT."
GOULD/Fletcher/COLLINS/
"MR. TRACY," WENDY WICHEL SAYS, "CARL NOSRA—THE 'TORCHER'—IS DEAD; THE ARSON RING IS JAILED."
AFTERMATH OF DEAD-END CRASH OF TORCHER'S CAR
1981 by Chicago Tribune-N.Y. News Synd. Inc. All Rights Reserved

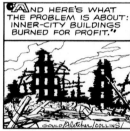

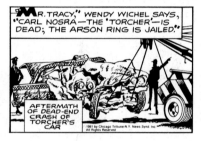

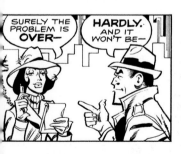

SURELY THE PROBLEM IS OVER—
HARDLY. AND IT WON'T BE—
NOT UNTIL EVERY STATE PASSES LAWS SO THAT A LANDLORD COLLECTS INSURANCE ON A FIRE-DAMAGED BUILDING ONLY IF HE REBUILDS IT.
"THEN THERE WOULD BE NO INCENTIVE FOR A SLUMLORD TO BURN HIS BUILDING." While—
1-11-81
B.U. TIFFIL! AT LAST! NOW, TO REHEARSE—

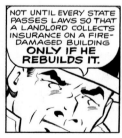

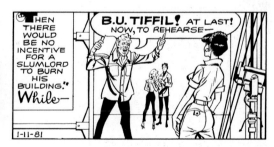

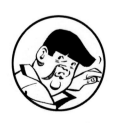

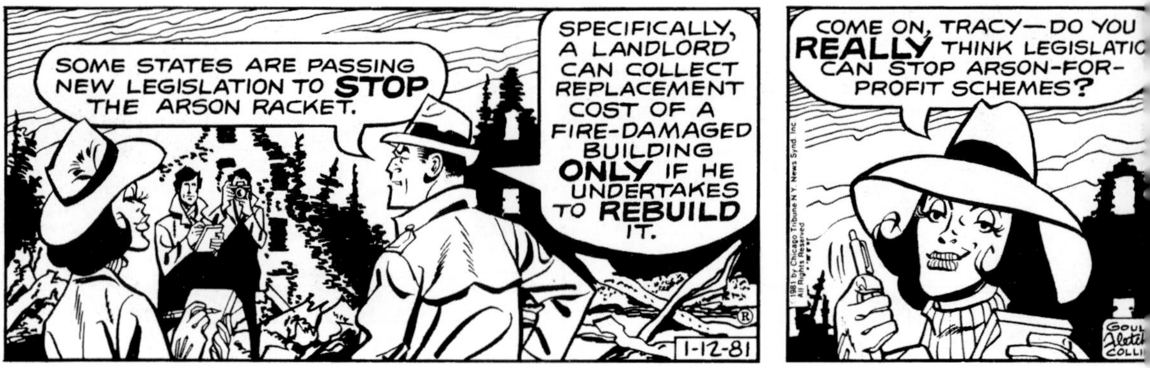
SOME STATES ARE PASSING NEW LEGISLATION TO STOP THE ARSON RACKET.
SPECIFICALLY, A LANDLORD CAN COLLECT REPLACEMENT COST OF A FIRE-DAMAGED BUILDING ONLY IF HE UNDERTAKES TO REBUILD IT.
1-12-81
COME ON, TRACY—DO YOU REALLY THINK LEGISLATIO CAN STOP ARSON-FOR-PROFIT SCHEMES?
1981 by Chicago Tribune-N.Y. News Synd. Inc. All Rights Reserved

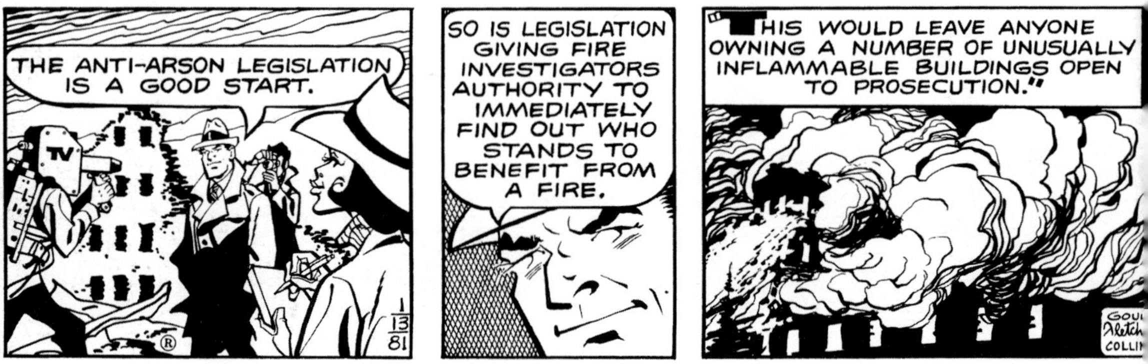
THE ANTI-ARSON LEGISLATION IS A GOOD START.
TV
1 13 81
SO IS LEGISLATION GIVING FIRE INVESTIGATORS AUTHORITY TO IMMEDIATELY FIND OUT WHO STANDS TO BENEFIT FROM A FIRE.
"THIS WOULD LEAVE ANYONE OWNING A NUMBER OF UNUSUALLY INFLAMMABLE BUILDINGS OPEN TO PROSECUTION."

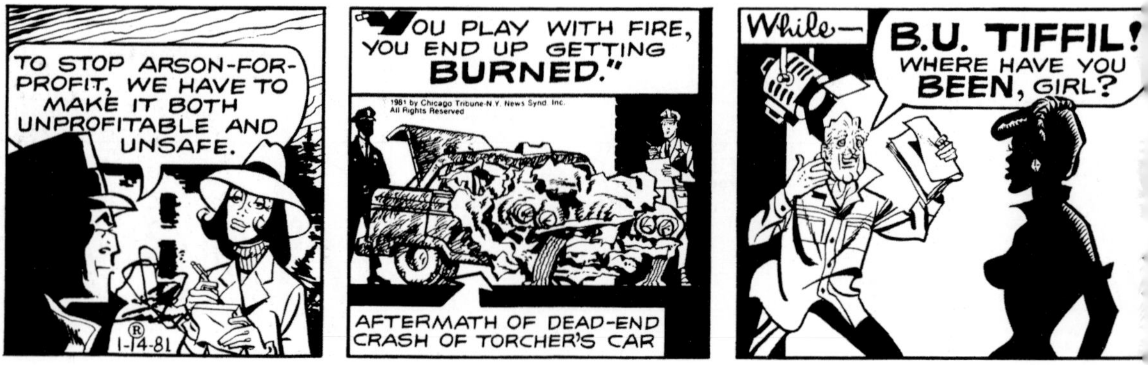
TO STOP ARSON-FOR-PROFIT, WE HAVE TO MAKE IT BOTH UNPROFITABLE AND UNSAFE.
1-14-81
"YOU PLAY WITH FIRE, YOU END UP GETTING BURNED."
1981 by Chicago Tribune-N.Y. News Synd. Inc. All Rights Reserved
AFTERMATH OF DEAD-END CRASH OF TORCHER'S CAR
While—
B.U. TIFFIL! WHERE HAVE YOU BEEN, GIRL?

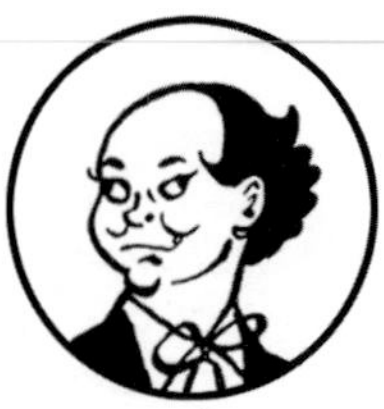

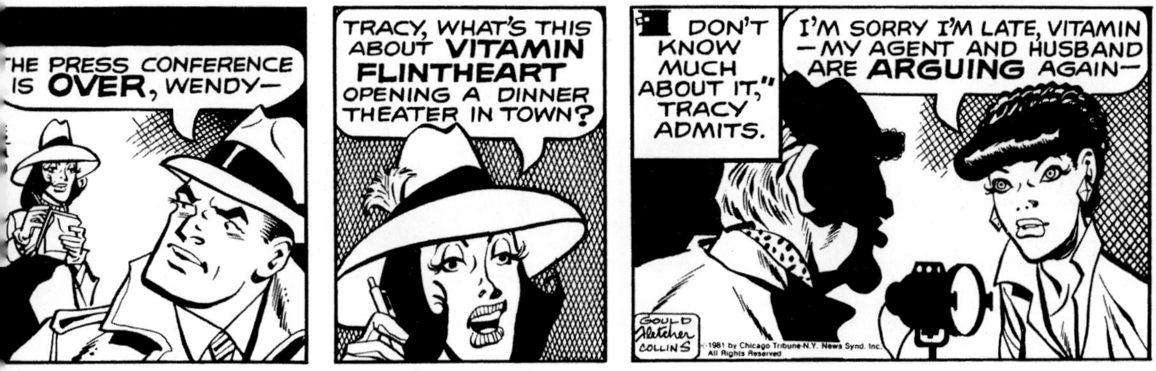
HE PRESS CONFERENCE IS OVER, WENDY—
TRACY, WHAT'S THIS ABOUT VITAMIN FLINTHEART OPENING A DINNER THEATER IN TOWN?
"I DON'T KNOW MUCH ABOUT IT," TRACY ADMITS.
I'M SORRY I'M LATE, VITAMIN—MY AGENT AND HUSBAND ARE ARGUING AGAIN—
GOULD Fletcher COLLINS
©1981 by Chicago Tribune-N.Y. News Synd. Inc. All Rights Reserved

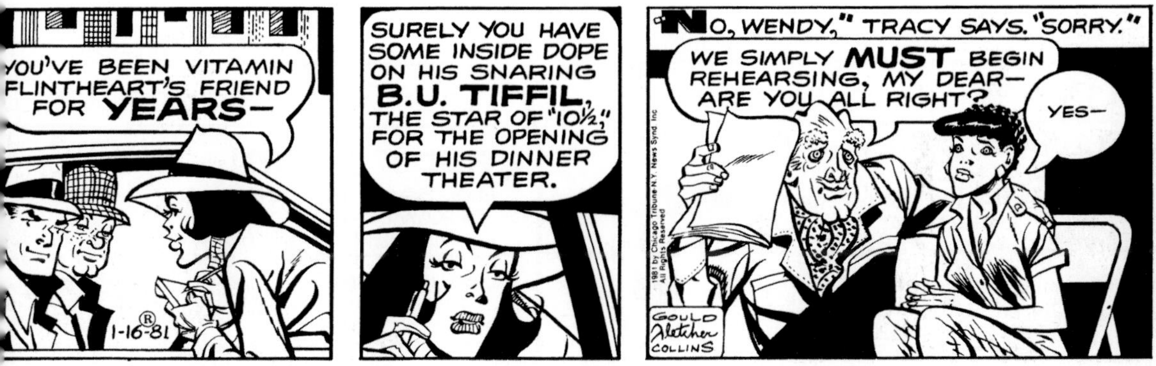
OU'VE BEEN VITAMIN FLINTHEART'S FRIEND FOR YEARS—
1-16-81 ®
SURELY YOU HAVE SOME INSIDE DOPE ON HIS SNARING B.U. TIFFIL, THE STAR OF "10½," FOR THE OPENING OF HIS DINNER THEATER.
"NO, WENDY," TRACY SAYS. "SORRY."
WE SIMPLY MUST BEGIN REHEARSING, MY DEAR—ARE YOU ALL RIGHT?
YES—
©1981 by Chicago Tribune-N.Y. News Synd. Inc All Rights Reserved
GOULD Fletcher COLLINS

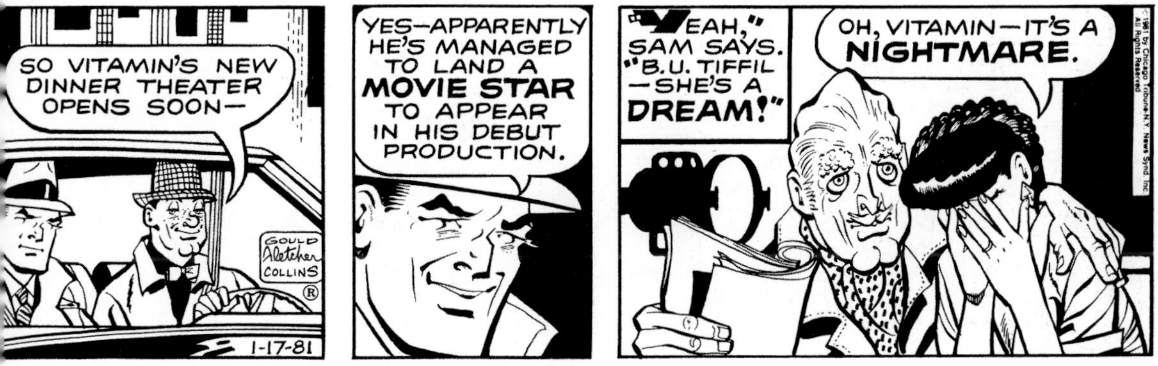
SO VITAMIN'S NEW DINNER THEATER OPENS SOON—
GOULD Fletcher COLLINS ®
1-17-81
YES—APPARENTLY HE'S MANAGED TO LAND A MOVIE STAR TO APPEAR IN HIS DEBUT PRODUCTION.
"YEAH," SAM SAYS. "B.U. TIFFIL—SHE'S A DREAM!"
OH, VITAMIN—IT'S A NIGHTMARE.
©1981 by Chicago Tribune-N.Y. News Synd. Inc. All Rights Reserved

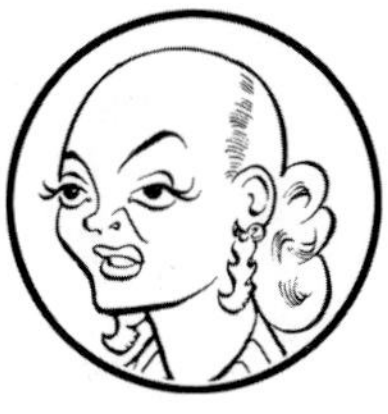

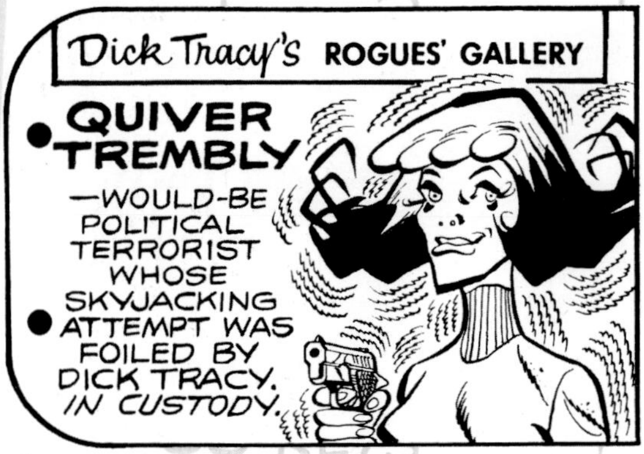
Dick Tracy's ROGUES' GALLERY
QUIVER TREMBLY
—WOULD-BE POLITICAL TERRORIST WHOSE SKYJACKING ATTEMPT WAS FOILED BY DICK TRACY. IN CUSTODY.

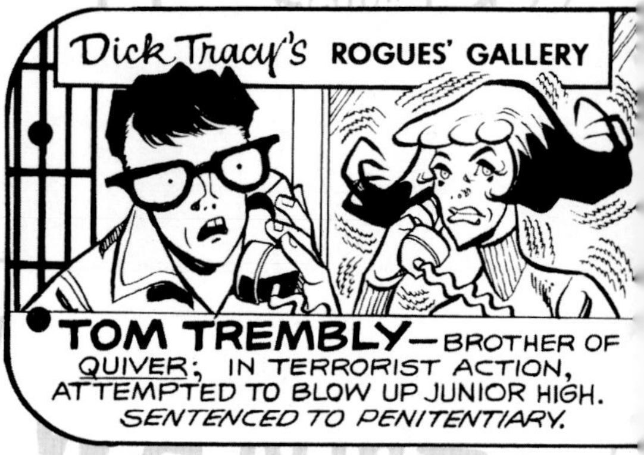
Dick Tracy's ROGUES' GALLERY
TOM TREMBLY—BROTHER OF QUIVER; IN TERRORIST ACTION, ATTEMPTED TO BLOW UP JUNIOR HIGH. SENTENCED TO PENITENTIARY.

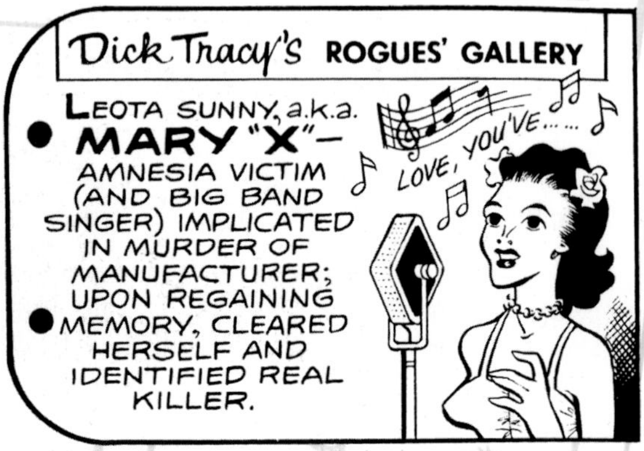
Dick Tracy's ROGUES' GALLERY
LEOTA SUNNY, a.k.a. MARY "X"—
AMNESIA VICTIM (AND BIG BAND SINGER) IMPLICATED IN MURDER OF MANUFACTURER; UPON REGAINING MEMORY, CLEARED HERSELF AND IDENTIFIED REAL KILLER.
LOVE, YOU'VE.....

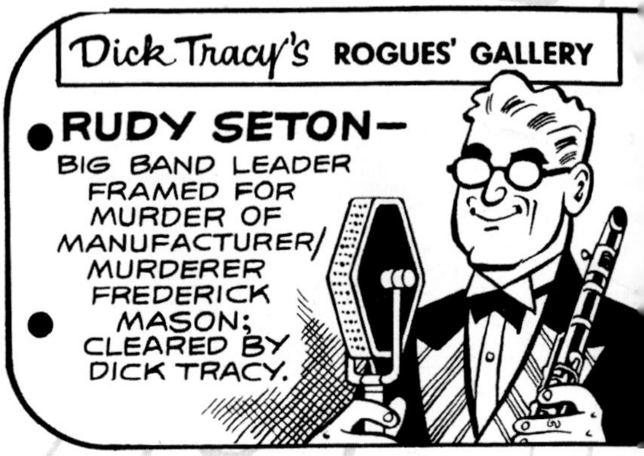
Dick Tracy's ROGUES' GALLERY
RUDY SETON—
BIG BAND LEADER FRAMED FOR MURDER OF MANUFACTURER/ MURDERER FREDERICK MASON; CLEARED BY DICK TRACY.

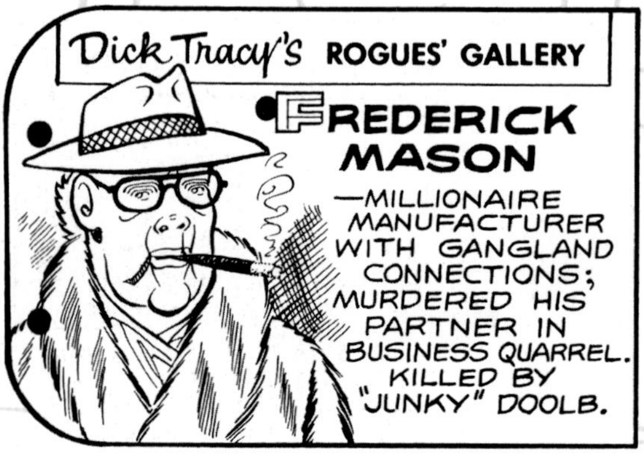
Dick Tracy's ROGUES' GALLERY
FREDERICK MASON
—MILLIONAIRE MANUFACTURER WITH GANGLAND CONNECTIONS; MURDERED HIS PARTNER IN BUSINESS QUARREL. KILLED BY "JUNKY" DOOLB.

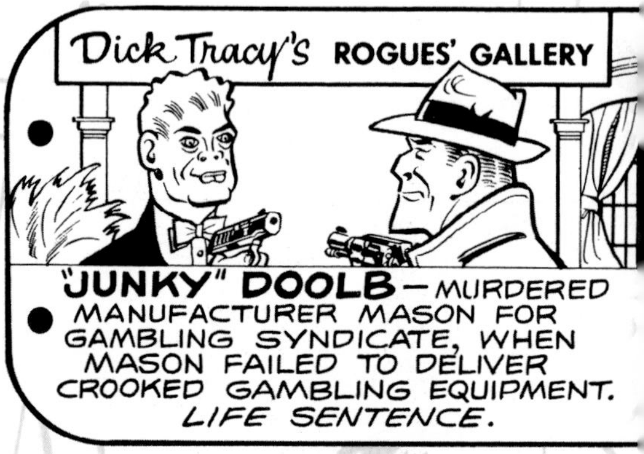
Dick Tracy's ROGUES' GALLERY
"JUNKY" DOOLB—MURDERED MANUFACTURER MASON FOR GAMBLING SYNDICATE, WHEN MASON FAILED TO DELIVER CROOKED GAMBLING EQUIPMENT. LIFE SENTENCE.

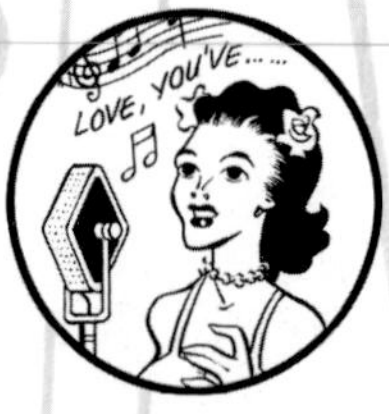
LOVE, YOU'VE.....

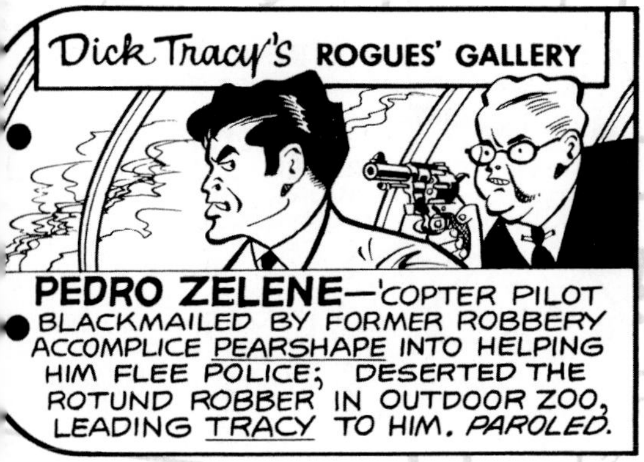
Dick Tracy's ROGUES' GALLERY
PEDRO ZELENE—'COPTER PILOT BLACKMAILED BY FORMER ROBBERY ACCOMPLICE PEARSHAPE INTO HELPING HIM FLEE POLICE; DESERTED THE ROTUND ROBBER IN OUTDOOR ZOO, LEADING TRACY TO HIM. PAROLED.

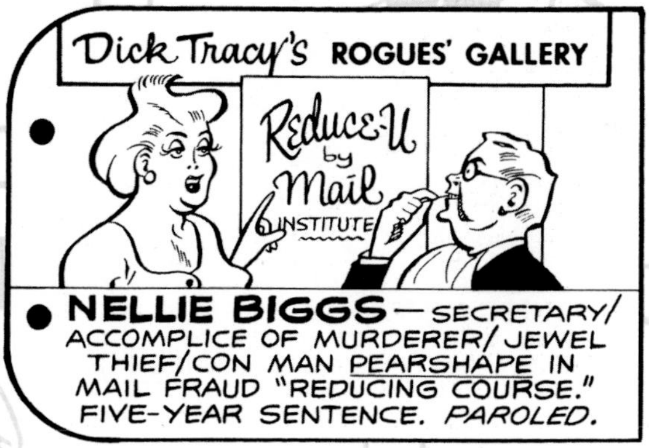
Dick Tracy's ROGUES' GALLERY
Reduce-U by Mail INSTITUTE
NELLIE BIGGS—SECRETARY/ ACCOMPLICE OF MURDERER/JEWEL THIEF/CON MAN PEARSHAPE IN MAIL FRAUD "REDUCING COURSE." FIVE-YEAR SENTENCE. PAROLED.

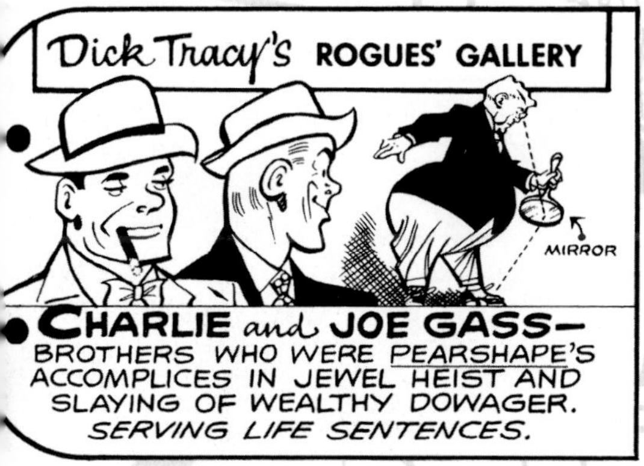
Dick Tracy's ROGUES' GALLERY
MIRROR
CHARLIE and JOE GASS—BROTHERS WHO WERE PEARSHAPE'S ACCOMPLICES IN JEWEL HEIST AND SLAYING OF WEALTHY DOWAGER. SERVING LIFE SENTENCES.

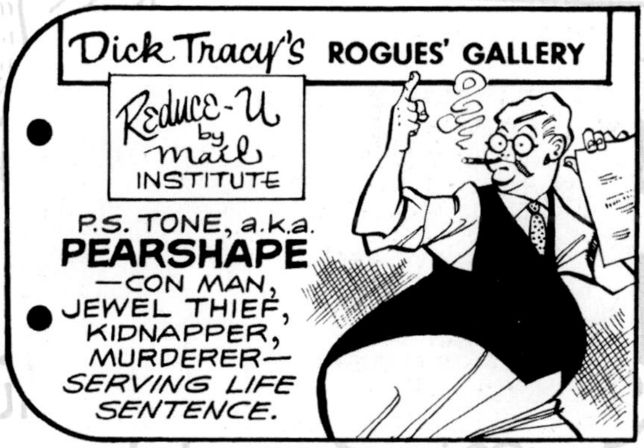
Dick Tracy's ROGUES' GALLERY
Reduce-U by Mail INSTITUTE
P.S. TONE, a.k.a. PEARSHAPE—CON MAN, JEWEL THIEF, KIDNAPPER, MURDERER—SERVING LIFE SENTENCE.

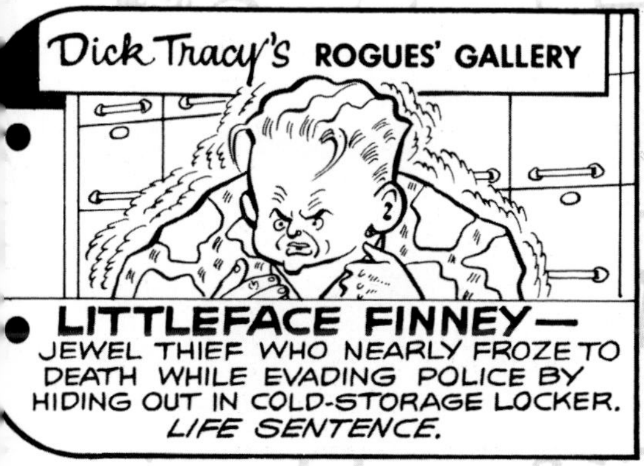
Dick Tracy's ROGUES' GALLERY
LITTLEFACE FINNEY—JEWEL THIEF WHO NEARLY FROZE TO DEATH WHILE EVADING POLICE BY HIDING OUT IN COLD-STORAGE LOCKER. LIFE SENTENCE.

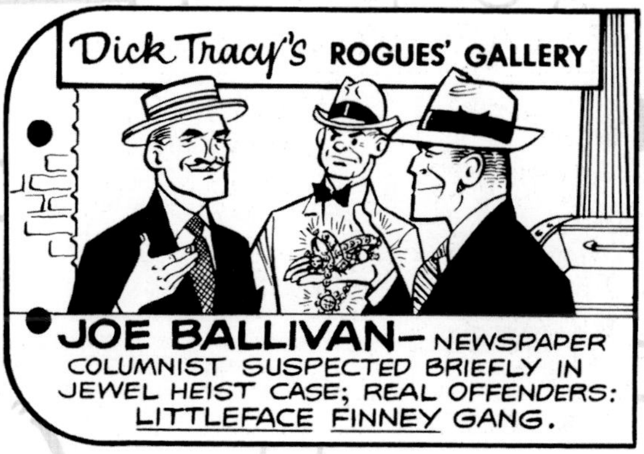
Dick Tracy's ROGUES' GALLERY
JOE BALLIVAN—NEWSPAPER COLUMNIST SUSPECTED BRIEFLY IN JEWEL HEIST CASE; REAL OFFENDERS: LITTLEFACE FINNEY GANG.

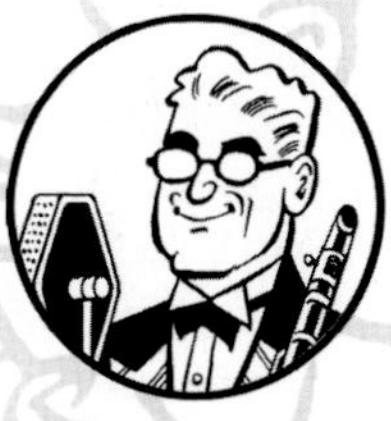

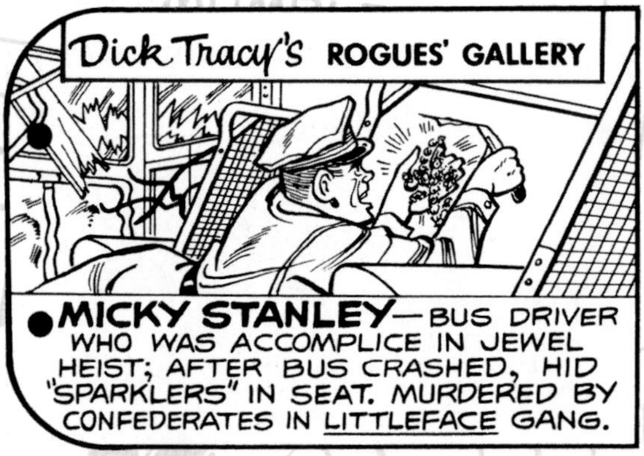
Dick Tracy's ROGUES' GALLERY
MICKY STANLEY—BUS DRIVER WHO WAS ACCOMPLICE IN JEWEL HEIST; AFTER BUS CRASHED, HID "SPARKLERS" IN SEAT. MURDERED BY CONFEDERATES IN LITTLEFACE GANG.

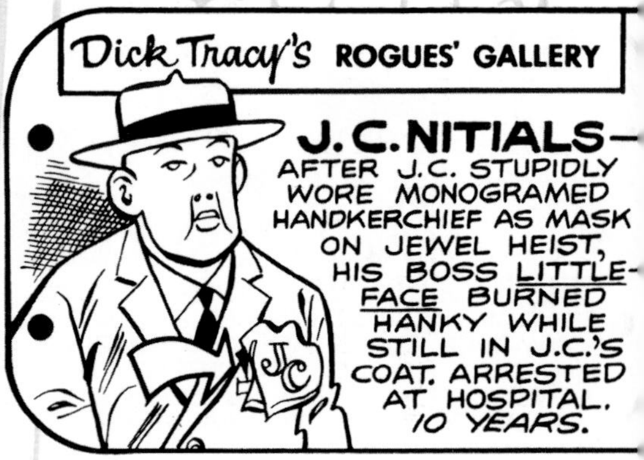
Dick Tracy's ROGUES' GALLERY
J.C. NITIALS—AFTER J.C. STUPIDLY WORE MONOGRAMED HANDKERCHIEF AS MASK ON JEWEL HEIST, HIS BOSS LITTLE-FACE BURNED HANKY WHILE STILL IN J.C.'S COAT. ARRESTED AT HOSPITAL. 10 YEARS.

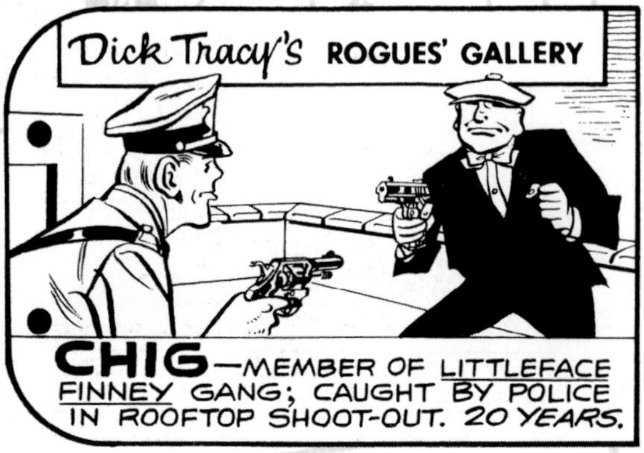
Dick Tracy's ROGUES' GALLERY
CHIG—MEMBER OF LITTLEFACE FINNEY GANG; CAUGHT BY POLICE IN ROOFTOP SHOOT-OUT. 20 YEARS.

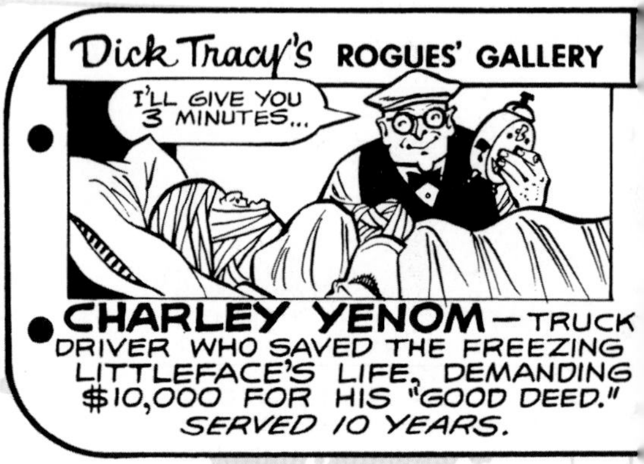
Dick Tracy's ROGUES' GALLERY
I'LL GIVE YOU 3 MINUTES...
CHARLEY YENOM—TRUCK DRIVER WHO SAVED THE FREEZING LITTLEFACE'S LIFE, DEMANDING $10,000 FOR HIS "GOOD DEED." SERVED 10 YEARS.

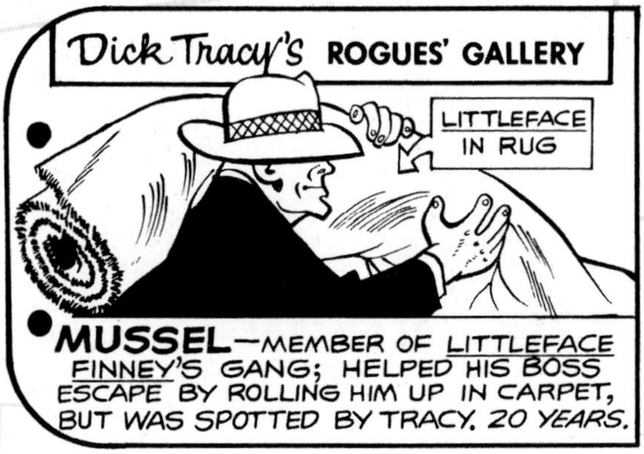
Dick Tracy's ROGUES' GALLERY
LITTLEFACE IN RUG
MUSSEL—MEMBER OF LITTLEFACE FINNEY'S GANG; HELPED HIS BOSS ESCAPE BY ROLLING HIM UP IN CARPET, BUT WAS SPOTTED BY TRACY. 20 YEARS.

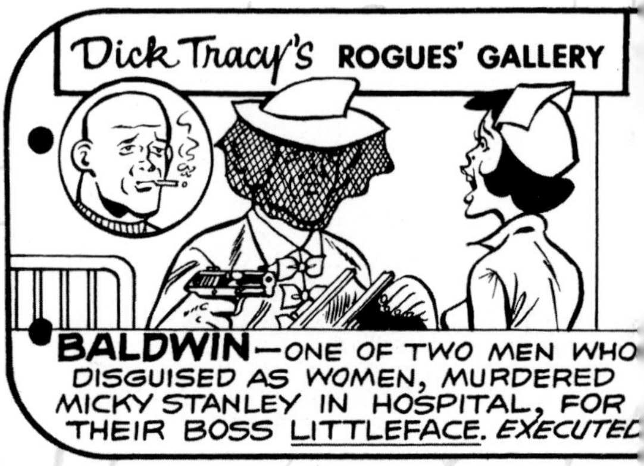
Dick Tracy's ROGUES' GALLERY
BALDWIN—ONE OF TWO MEN WHO DISGUISED AS WOMEN, MURDERED MICKY STANLEY IN HOSPITAL, FOR THEIR BOSS LITTLEFACE. EXECUTED

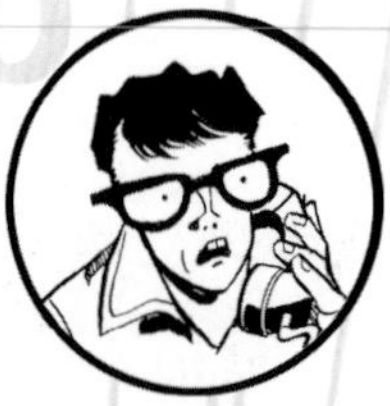

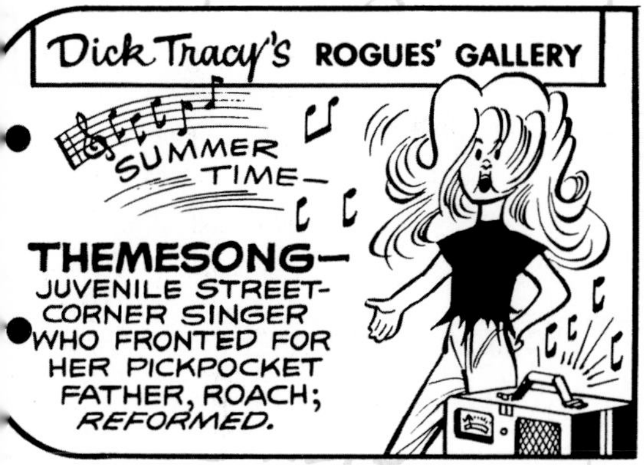
Dick Tracy's ROGUES' GALLERY
SUMMER TIME—
THEMESONG—
JUVENILE STREET-CORNER SINGER WHO FRONTED FOR HER PICKPOCKET FATHER, ROACH; REFORMED.

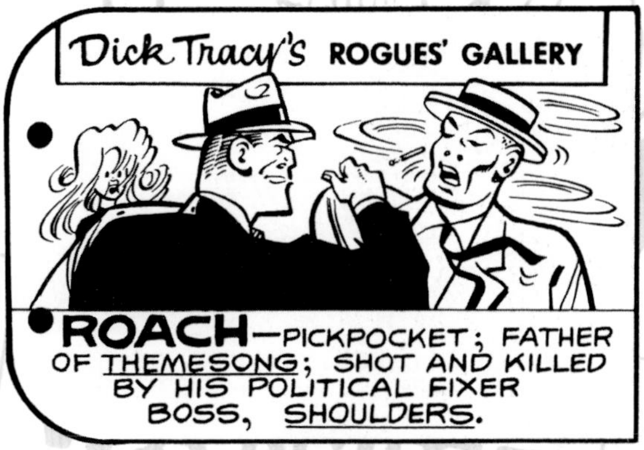
Dick Tracy's ROGUES' GALLERY
ROACH—PICKPOCKET; FATHER OF THEMESONG; SHOT AND KILLED BY HIS POLITICAL FIXER BOSS, SHOULDERS.

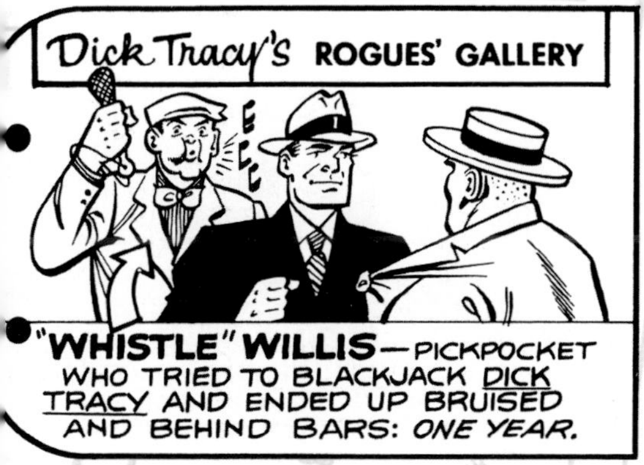
Dick Tracy's ROGUES' GALLERY
"WHISTLE" WILLIS—PICKPOCKET WHO TRIED TO BLACKJACK DICK TRACY AND ENDED UP BRUISED AND BEHIND BARS: ONE YEAR.

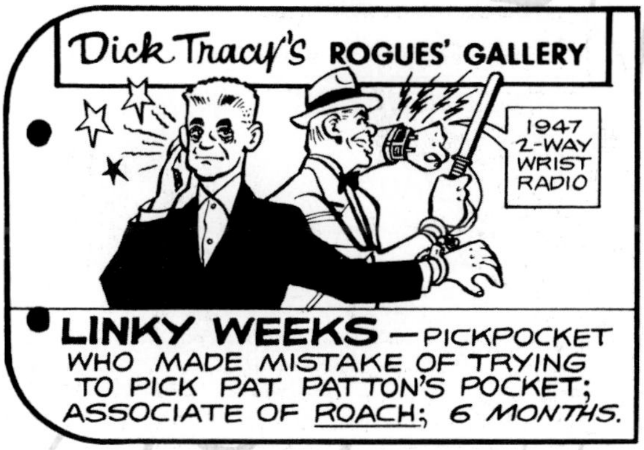
Dick Tracy's ROGUES' GALLERY
1947 2-WAY WRIST RADIO
LINKY WEEKS—PICKPOCKET WHO MADE MISTAKE OF TRYING TO PICK PAT PATTON'S POCKET; ASSOCIATE OF ROACH; 6 MONTHS.

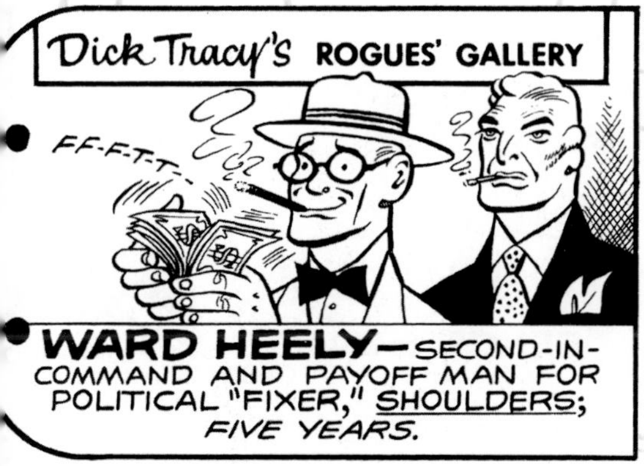
Dick Tracy's ROGUES' GALLERY
FF-F-T-T-
WARD HEELY—SECOND-IN-COMMAND AND PAYOFF MAN FOR POLITICAL "FIXER," SHOULDERS; FIVE YEARS.

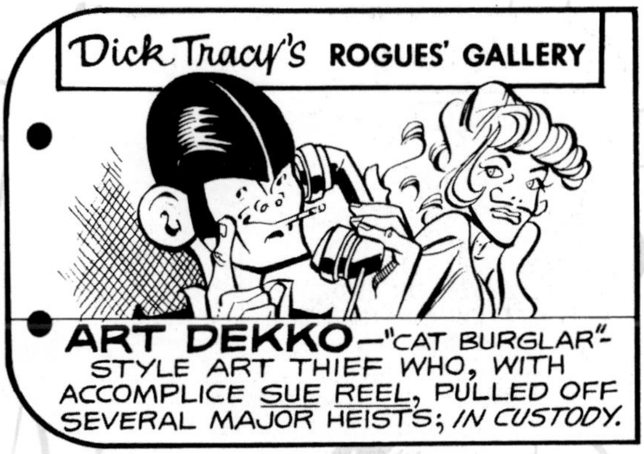
Dick Tracy's ROGUES' GALLERY
ART DEKKO—"CAT BURGLAR"-STYLE ART THIEF WHO, WITH ACCOMPLICE SUE REEL, PULLED OFF SEVERAL MAJOR HEISTS; IN CUSTODY.

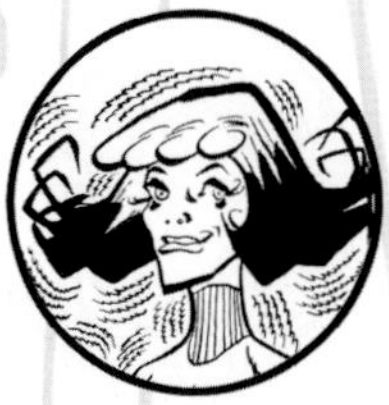

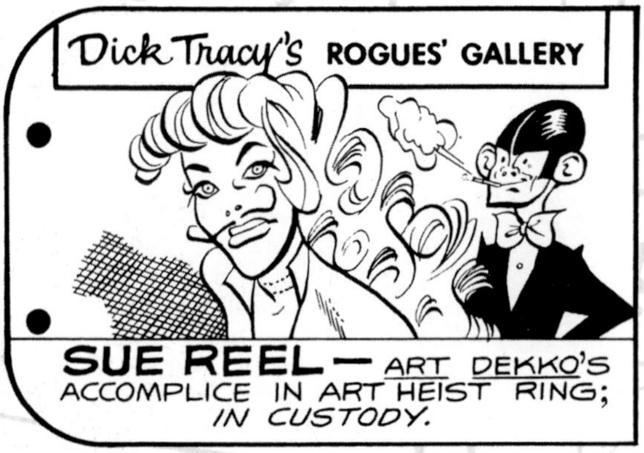
Dick Tracy's ROGUES' GALLERY
SUE REEL—ART DEKKO'S ACCOMPLICE IN ART HEIST RING; IN CUSTODY.

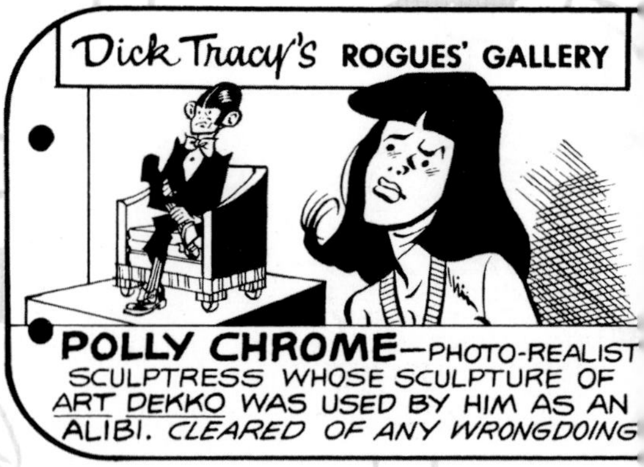
Dick Tracy's ROGUES' GALLERY
POLLY CHROME—PHOTO-REALIST SCULPTRESS WHOSE SCULPTURE OF ART DEKKO WAS USED BY HIM AS AN ALIBI. CLEARED OF ANY WRONGDOING

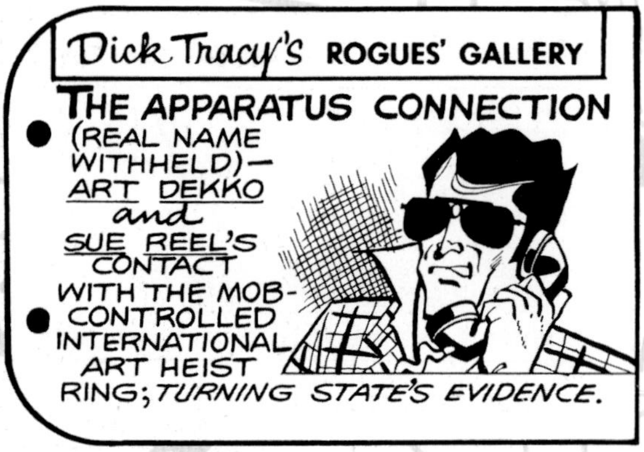
Dick Tracy's ROGUES' GALLERY
THE APPARATUS CONNECTION
(REAL NAME WITHHELD)— ART DEKKO and SUE REEL'S CONTACT WITH THE MOB-CONTROLLED INTERNATIONAL ART HEIST RING; TURNING STATE'S EVIDENCE.

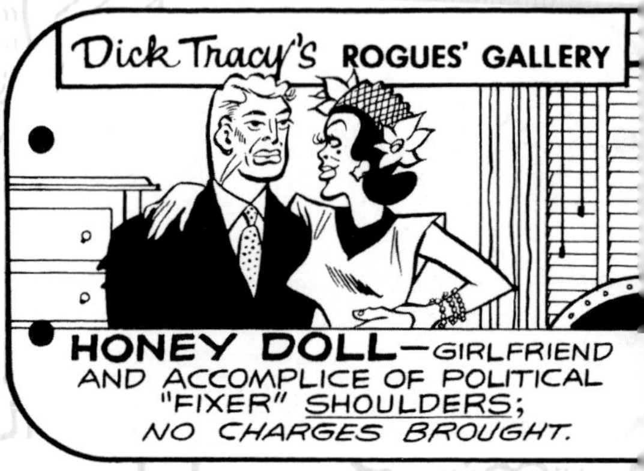
Dick Tracy's ROGUES' GALLERY
HONEY DOLL—GIRLFRIEND AND ACCOMPLICE OF POLITICAL "FIXER" SHOULDERS; NO CHARGES BROUGHT.

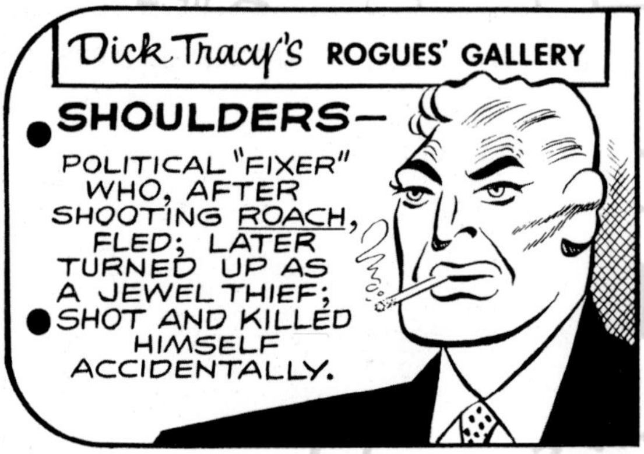
Dick Tracy's ROGUES' GALLERY
SHOULDERS—
POLITICAL "FIXER" WHO, AFTER SHOOTING ROACH, FLED; LATER TURNED UP AS A JEWEL THIEF; SHOT AND KILLED HIMSELF ACCIDENTALLY.

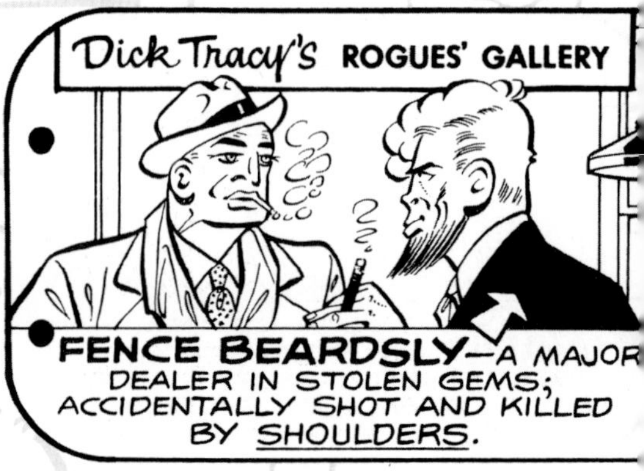
Dick Tracy's ROGUES' GALLERY
FENCE BEARDSLY—A MAJOR DEALER IN STOLEN GEMS; ACCIDENTALLY SHOT AND KILLED BY SHOULDERS.

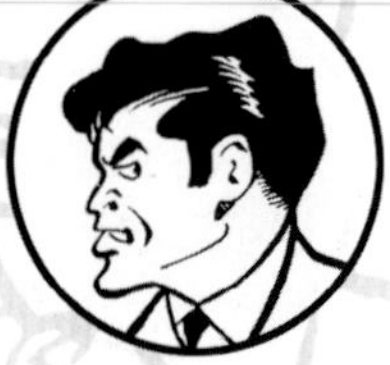

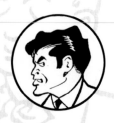

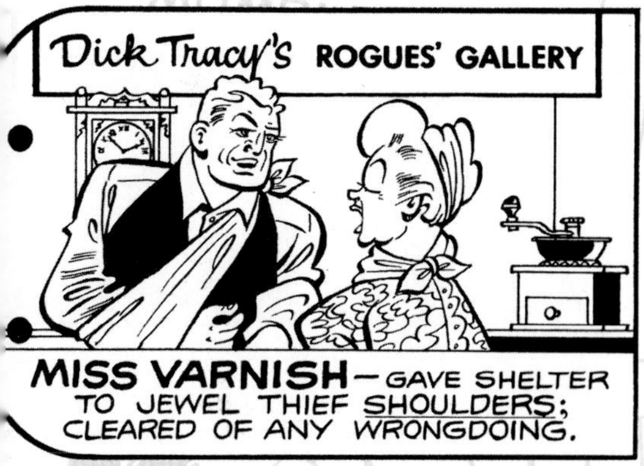
Dick Tracy's ROGUES' GALLERY
MISS VARNISH—GAVE SHELTER TO JEWEL THIEF SHOULDERS; CLEARED OF ANY WRONGDOING.

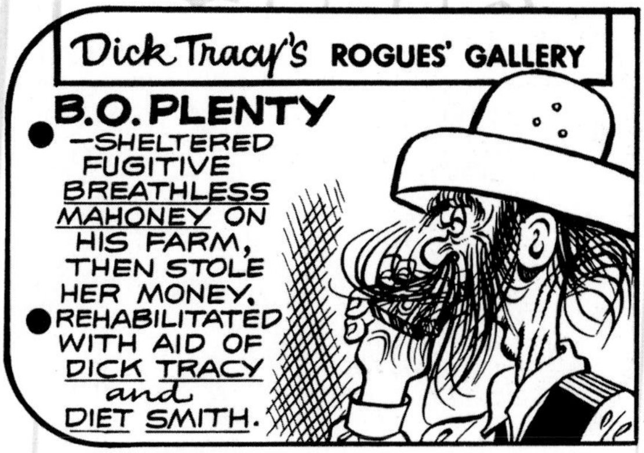
Dick Tracy's ROGUES' GALLERY
B.O. PLENTY —SHELTERED FUGITIVE BREATHLESS MAHONEY ON HIS FARM, THEN STOLE HER MONEY. REHABILITATED WITH AID OF DICK TRACY and DIET SMITH.

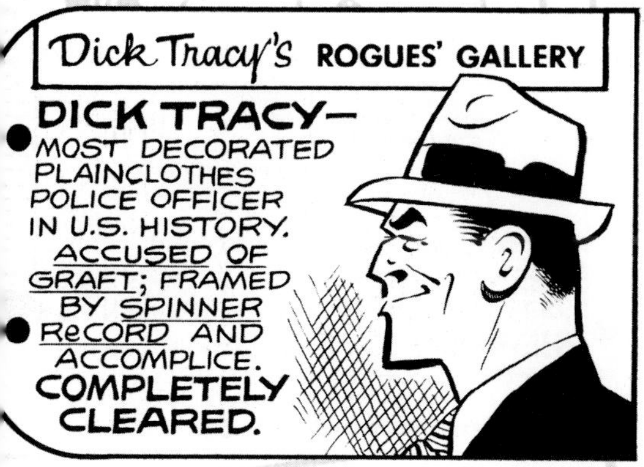
Dick Tracy's ROGUES' GALLERY
DICK TRACY— MOST DECORATED PLAINCLOTHES POLICE OFFICER IN U.S. HISTORY. ACCUSED OF GRAFT; FRAMED BY SPINNER RECORD AND ACCOMPLICE. COMPLETELY CLEARED.

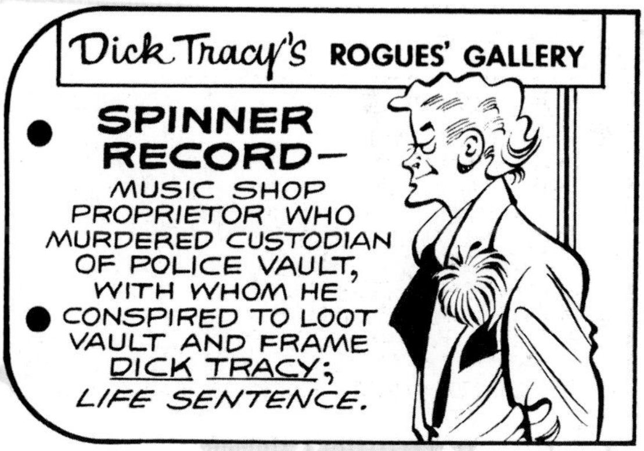
Dick Tracy's ROGUES' GALLERY
SPINNER RECORD— MUSIC SHOP PROPRIETOR WHO MURDERED CUSTODIAN OF POLICE VAULT, WITH WHOM HE CONSPIRED TO LOOT VAULT AND FRAME DICK TRACY; LIFE SENTENCE.

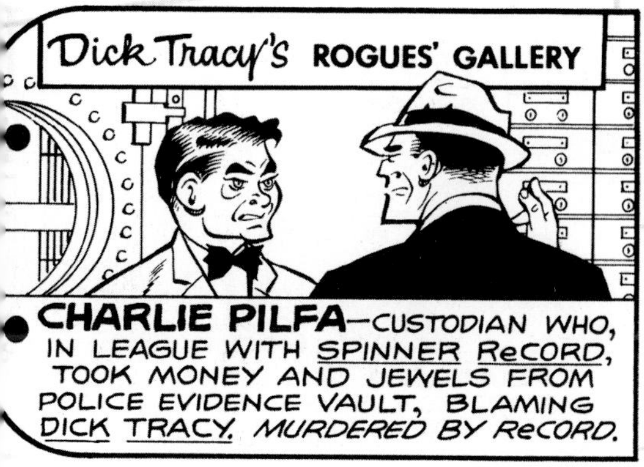
Dick Tracy's ROGUES' GALLERY
CHARLIE PILFA—CUSTODIAN WHO, IN LEAGUE WITH SPINNER RECORD, TOOK MONEY AND JEWELS FROM POLICE EVIDENCE VAULT, BLAMING DICK TRACY. MURDERED BY RECORD.

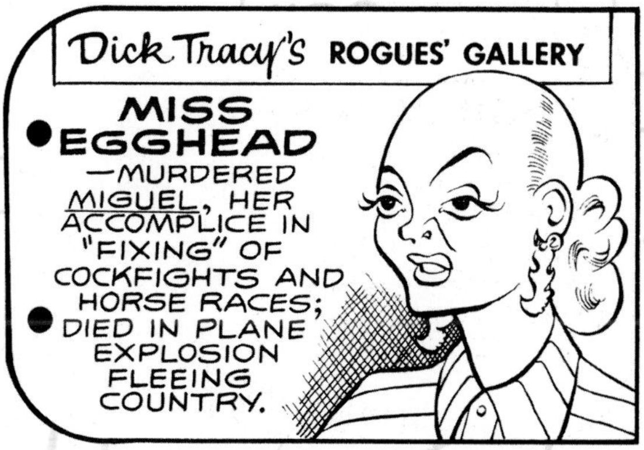
Dick Tracy's ROGUES' GALLERY
MISS EGGHEAD —MURDERED MIGUEL, HER ACCOMPLICE IN "FIXING" OF COCKFIGHTS AND HORSE RACES; DIED IN PLANE EXPLOSION FLEEING COUNTRY.

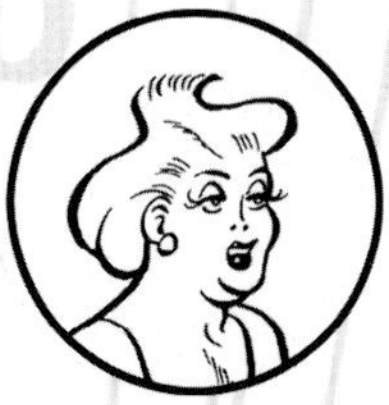

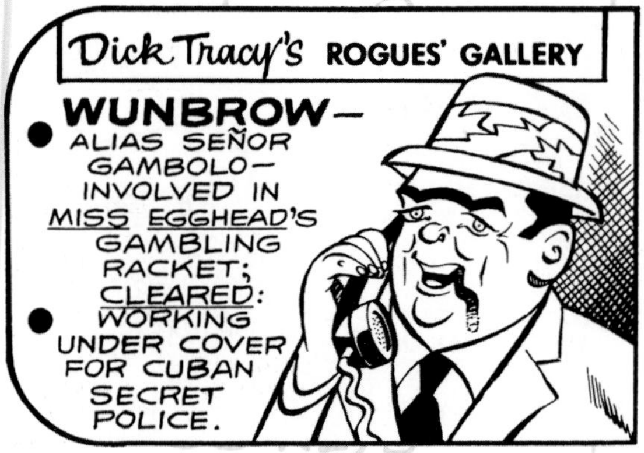
Dick Tracy's ROGUES' GALLERY
WUNBROW—ALIAS SEÑOR GAMBOLO—INVOLVED IN MISS EGGHEAD'S GAMBLING RACKET; CLEARED: WORKING UNDER COVER FOR CUBAN SECRET POLICE.

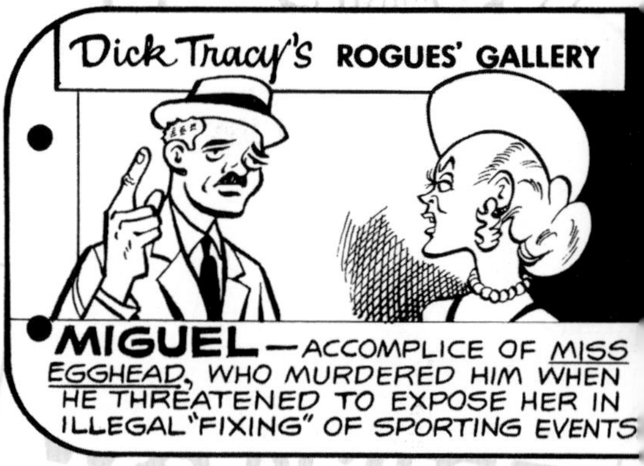
Dick Tracy's ROGUES' GALLERY
MIGUEL—ACCOMPLICE OF MISS EGGHEAD, WHO MURDERED HIM WHEN HE THREATENED TO EXPOSE HER IN ILLEGAL "FIXING" OF SPORTING EVENTS

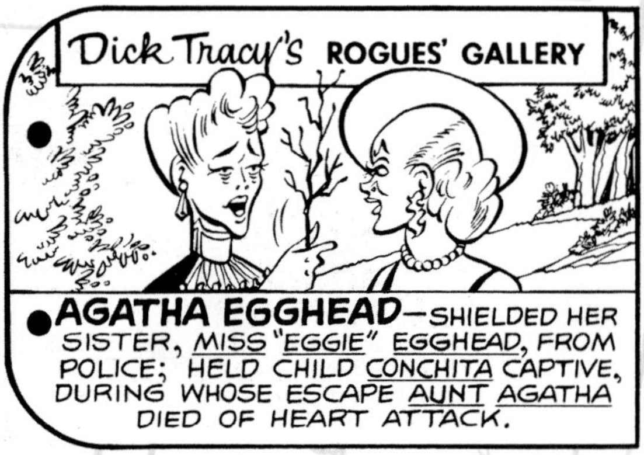
Dick Tracy's ROGUES' GALLERY
AGATHA EGGHEAD—SHIELDED HER SISTER, MISS "EGGIE" EGGHEAD, FROM POLICE; HELD CHILD CONCHITA CAPTIVE, DURING WHOSE ESCAPE AUNT AGATHA DIED OF HEART ATTACK.

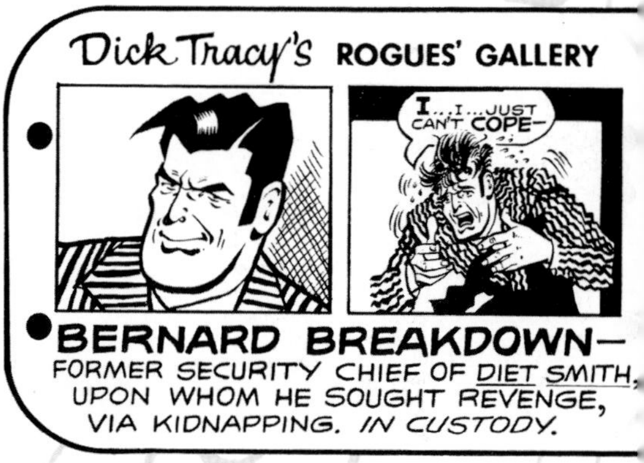
Dick Tracy's ROGUES' GALLERY
I...I...JUST CAN'T COPE—
BERNARD BREAKDOWN—FORMER SECURITY CHIEF OF DIET SMITH, UPON WHOM HE SOUGHT REVENGE, VIA KIDNAPPING. IN CUSTODY.

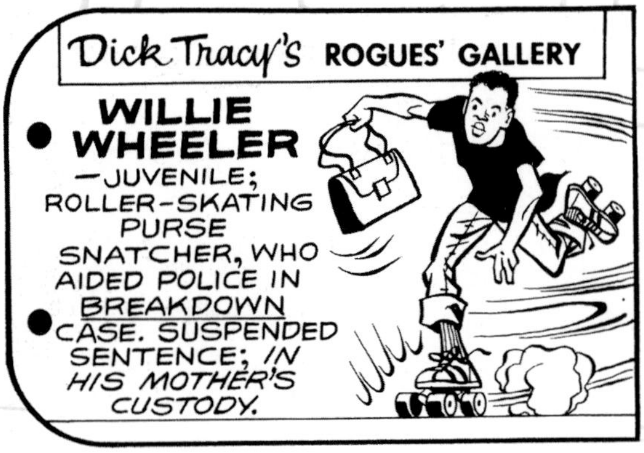
Dick Tracy's ROGUES' GALLERY
WILLIE WHEELER—JUVENILE; ROLLER-SKATING PURSE SNATCHER, WHO AIDED POLICE IN BREAKDOWN CASE. SUSPENDED SENTENCE; IN HIS MOTHER'S CUSTODY.

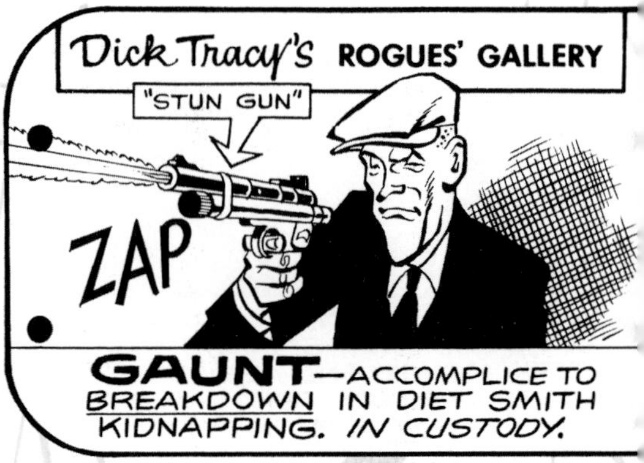
Dick Tracy's ROGUES' GALLERY
"STUN GUN"
ZAP
GAUNT—ACCOMPLICE TO BREAKDOWN IN DIET SMITH KIDNAPPING. IN CUSTODY.

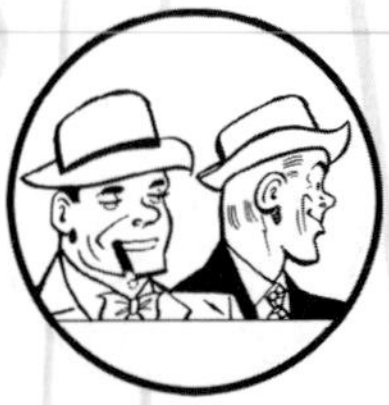

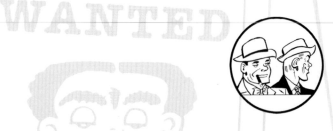

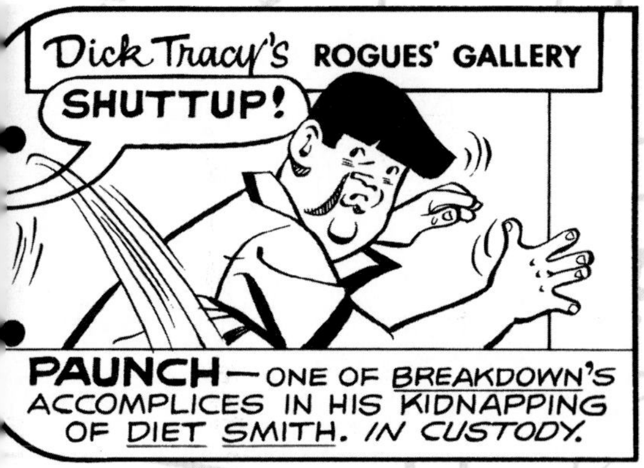
Dick Tracy's ROGUES' GALLERY
SHUTTUP!
PAUNCH—ONE OF BREAKDOWN'S ACCOMPLICES IN HIS KIDNAPPING OF DIET SMITH. IN CUSTODY.

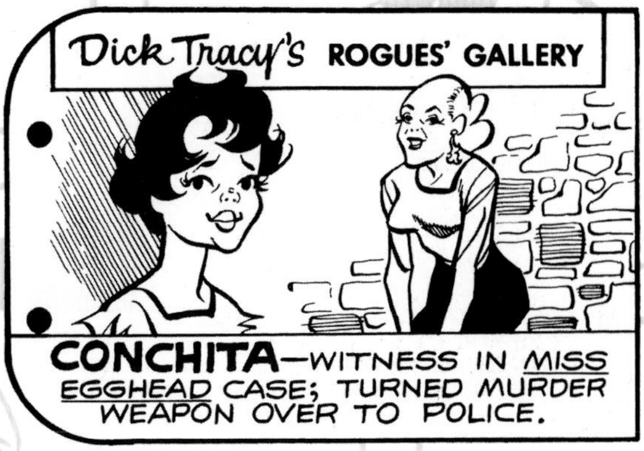
Dick Tracy's ROGUES' GALLERY
CONCHITA—WITNESS IN MISS EGGHEAD CASE; TURNED MURDER WEAPON OVER TO POLICE.

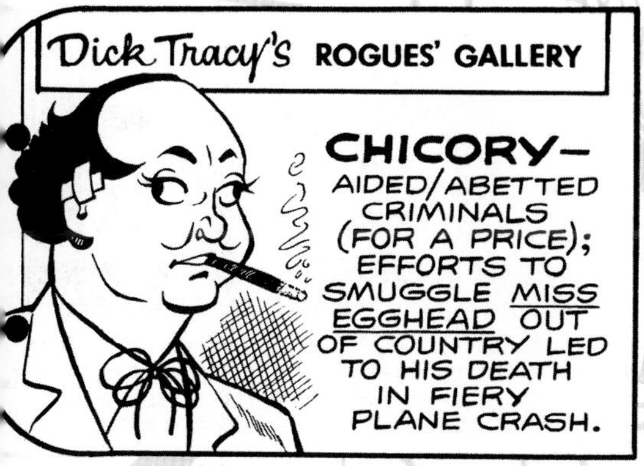
Dick Tracy's ROGUES' GALLERY
CHICORY—AIDED/ABETTED CRIMINALS (FOR A PRICE); EFFORTS TO SMUGGLE MISS EGGHEAD OUT OF COUNTRY LED TO HIS DEATH IN FIERY PLANE CRASH.

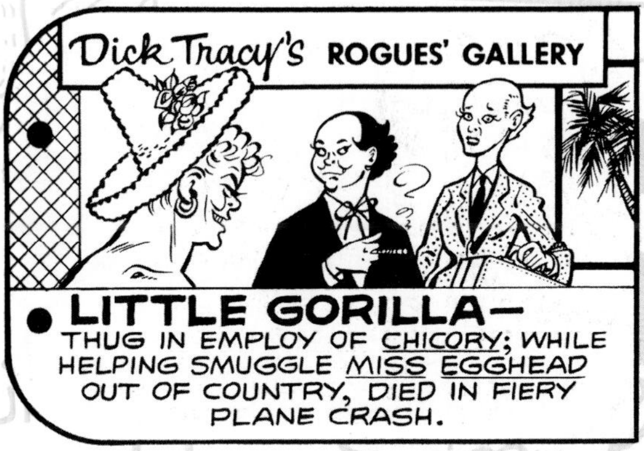
Dick Tracy's ROGUES' GALLERY
LITTLE GORILLA—THUG IN EMPLOY OF CHICORY; WHILE HELPING SMUGGLE MISS EGGHEAD OUT OF COUNTRY, DIED IN FIERY PLANE CRASH.

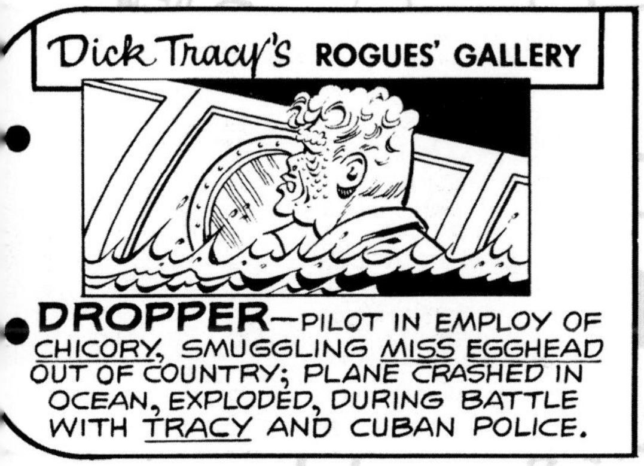
Dick Tracy's ROGUES' GALLERY
DROPPER—PILOT IN EMPLOY OF CHICORY, SMUGGLING MISS EGGHEAD OUT OF COUNTRY; PLANE CRASHED IN OCEAN, EXPLODED, DURING BATTLE WITH TRACY AND CUBAN POLICE.

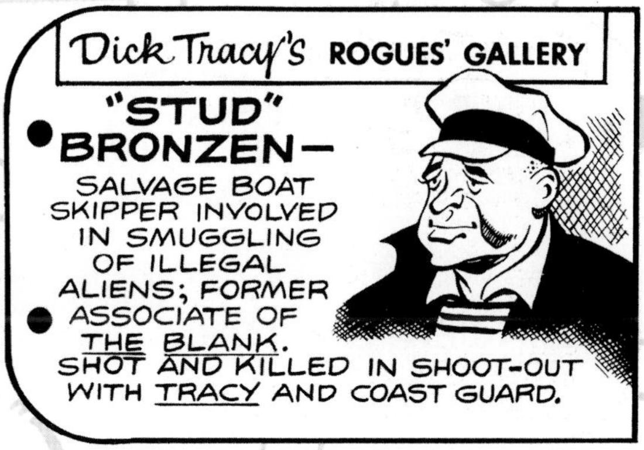
Dick Tracy's ROGUES' GALLERY
"STUD" BRONZEN—SALVAGE BOAT SKIPPER INVOLVED IN SMUGGLING OF ILLEGAL ALIENS; FORMER ASSOCIATE OF THE BLANK. SHOT AND KILLED IN SHOOT-OUT WITH TRACY AND COAST GUARD.

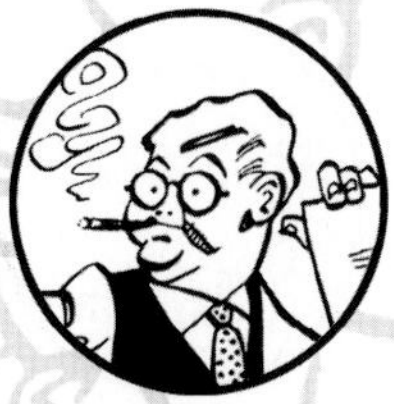

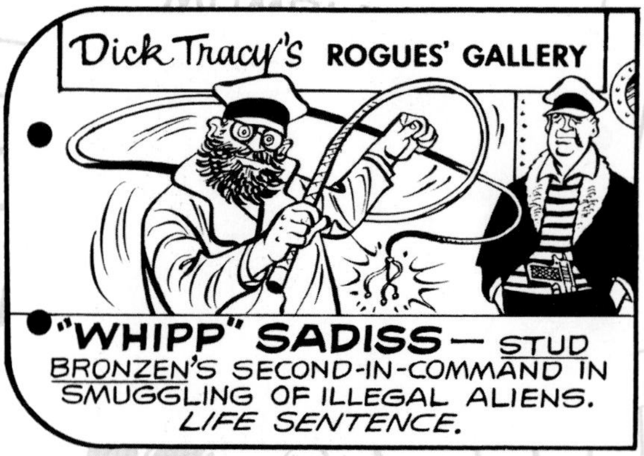
Dick Tracy's ROGUES' GALLERY
"WHIPP" SADISS — STUD BRONZEN'S SECOND-IN-COMMAND IN SMUGGLING OF ILLEGAL ALIENS. LIFE SENTENCE.

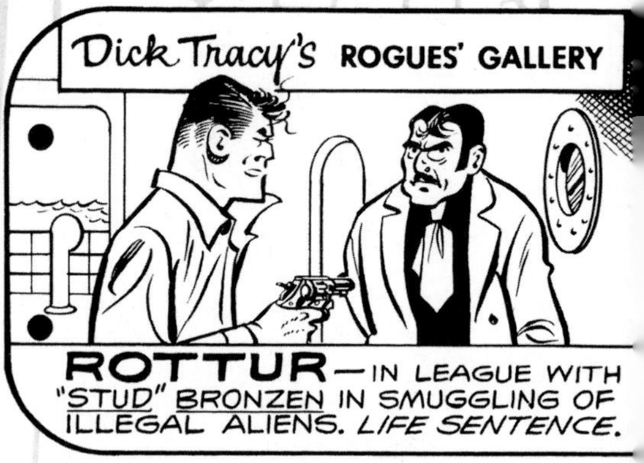
Dick Tracy's ROGUES' GALLERY
ROTTUR — IN LEAGUE WITH "STUD" BRONZEN IN SMUGGLING OF ILLEGAL ALIENS. LIFE SENTENCE.

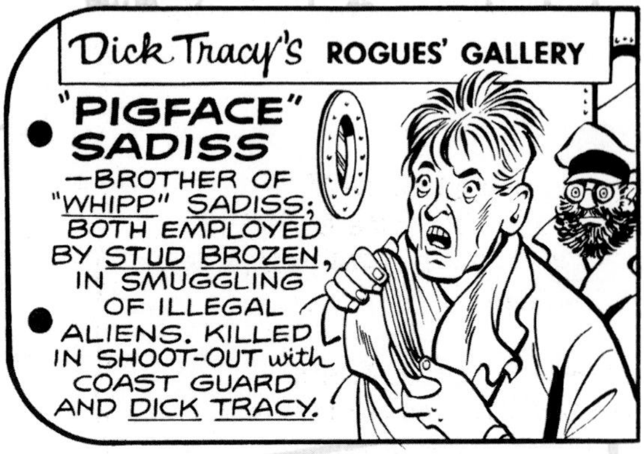
Dick Tracy's ROGUES' GALLERY
"PIGFACE" SADISS —BROTHER OF "WHIPP" SADISS; BOTH EMPLOYED BY STUD BROZEN, IN SMUGGLING OF ILLEGAL ALIENS. KILLED IN SHOOT-OUT with COAST GUARD AND DICK TRACY.

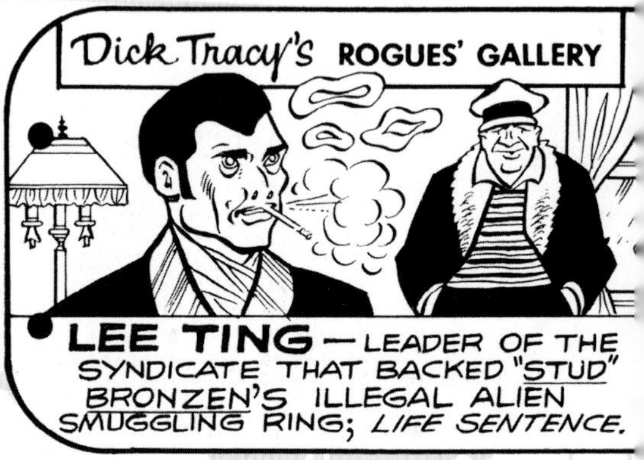
Dick Tracy's ROGUES' GALLERY
LEE TING — LEADER OF THE SYNDICATE THAT BACKED "STUD" BRONZEN'S ILLEGAL ALIEN SMUGGLING RING; LIFE SENTENCE.

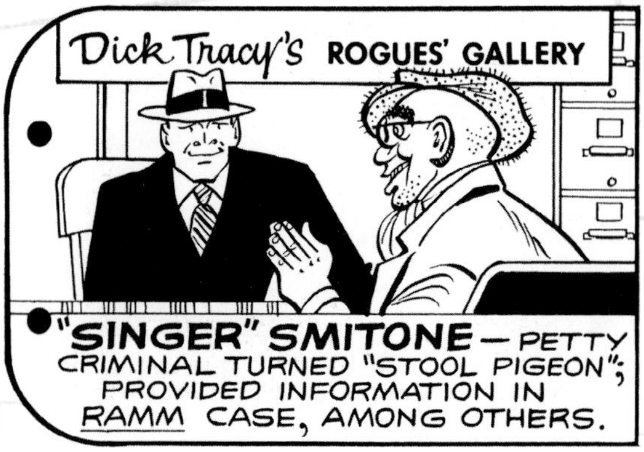
Dick Tracy's ROGUES' GALLERY
"SINGER" SMITONE — PETTY CRIMINAL TURNED "STOOL PIGEON"; PROVIDED INFORMATION IN RAMM CASE, AMONG OTHERS.

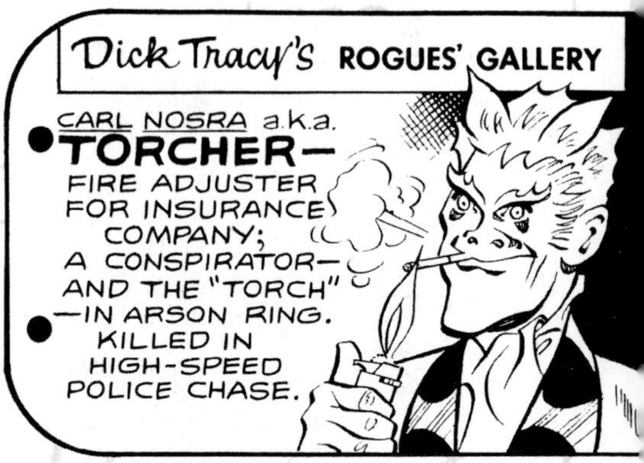
Dick Tracy's ROGUES' GALLERY
CARL NOSRA a.k.a. TORCHER — FIRE ADJUSTER FOR INSURANCE COMPANY; A CONSPIRATOR— AND THE "TORCH" —IN ARSON RING. KILLED IN HIGH-SPEED POLICE CHASE.

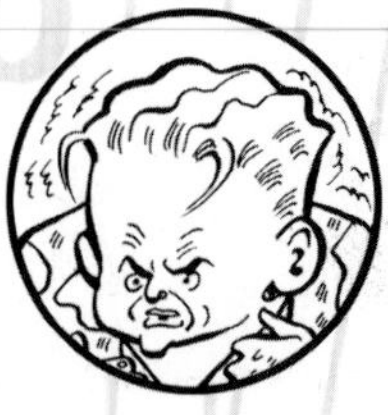

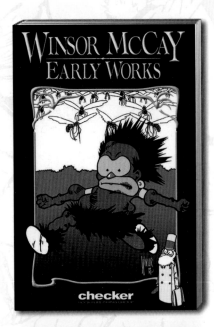
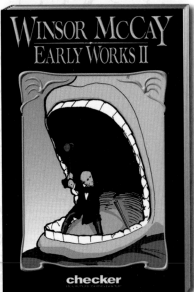

Alex Raymond's FLASH GORDON

Checker is proud to be involved in introducing a new generation of artists and writers to one of the most creative and talented men in cartooning history, while reminding those original fans of Flash Gordon of the past splendor of this landmark comic strip. Raymond is known for his wildly inventive stories and sprawling, extra-terrestrial landscapes that have inspired countless writers and artists, creating a visual imagery that persists in the science fiction genre to this day. Alex Raymond's vivid imagination finds new life in these archival-quality re-issues. These collections feature the Flash Gordon Sunday strips from 1934 to 1937.

Alex Raymond's Flash Gordon:
Volume 1 Collects January 7,
1934 to April 14, 1935
100 Full color pages, $14.95
Landscape hardcover format
ISBN 0-9741664-3-X

Alex Raymond's
Flash Gordon: Volume 2
Collects April 21, 1935 to
October 11, 1936
100 Full color pages, $19.95
Landscape hardcover format
ISBN 0-9741664-6-4

Alex Raymond's Flash Gordon:
Volume 3
Collects October 25, 1936 to
August 1, 1937
100 Full color pages, $19.95
Landscape hardcover format
ISBN 1-933160-25-X

checker
BOOK PUBLISHING GROUP
www.checkerbpg.com

COMIC CLASSICS

SPECIALIZING IN SMALL PRESS RUNS OF LARGE COMIC ADVENTURES

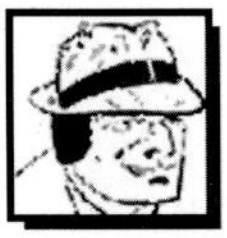 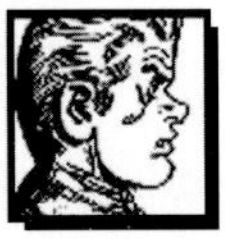 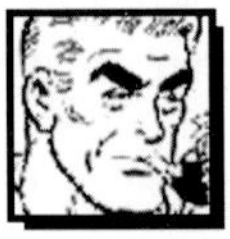 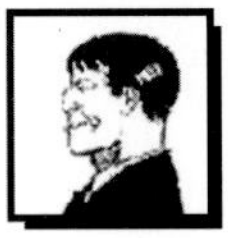 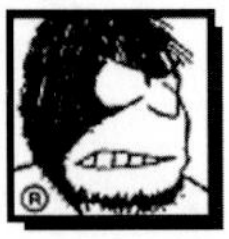

- DICK TRACY
- TERRY AND THE PIRATES
- KERRY DRAKE
- CAPTAIN EASY
- ALLEY OOP
- BUCK ROGERS
- MANDRAKE THE MAGICIAN
- GASOLINE ALLEY
- MOON MULLINS
- JOHNNY HAZARD

WHERE IS SPEC PRODUCTIONS HEADED?

THE NEW MILLENNIUM IS UPON US AND CLASSIC COMICS WILL BECOME EVEN MORE SO. LONGEVITY HAS SPREAD IT'S GNARLED HAND OVER MORE AND MORE COMIC STRIPS: ORPHAN ANNIE, DICK TRACY, GASOLINE ALLEY, PEANUTS, ALLEY OOP, KATZNJAMMER KIDS, BLONDIE, BRINGING UP FATHER, PRINCE VALLIANT, SNUFFY SMITH, NANCY AND TARZAN. (WE RECOGNIZE THAT NEARLY EVERY CONTINUING COMIC STRIP HAS HAD A NEW ARTIST OR ARTISTS AND STORY TELLER - SOME GOOD & SOME BAD) - BUT THE RECOGNITION OF THE NAME APPEALS TO A CHORD OF FAMILIARITY WE KNOW AND RELY ON.

MANY OF OUR FAVORITES NOW DWELL IN THE CARTOON RETIREMENT HOME - LEFT TO RESIDE WITHOUT THE SUPPORT OF THEIR OLD SYNDICATE - STILL BRIGHTLY COLORED BY THEIR SURVIVING SUNDAY PAGES - REVERED BY READERS AND COLLECTORS - READ WITH FOND MEMORY IF NOT UNFAIRLY PRICED - STILL DIFFICULT IN THE FINDING - AND WE DO LOVE THEM: KERRY DRAKE, ON STAGE, THE YELLOW KID, MUTT & JEFF, THE GUMPS, LIL' ABNER, JOE PALOOKA, SMILIN' JACK, CAPTAIN EASY, LIL' IODINE, THE LITTLE KING, BUSTER BROWN, FELIX THE CAT, MIN & BILL, TOONERVILLE TROLLEY, AND MANY MANY MORE.

SPEC LOVES THE COMICS, THE ARTISTS, AND THE MEMORIES THEY CONTINUE TO REFLECT IN OUR MINDS. THIS COMING CENTURY WE WILL CONTINUE REPRINTING DICK TRACY, TERRY AND THE PIRATES, KERRY DRAKE, JUNGLE JIM, MANDRAKE THE MAGICIAN, CAPTAIN EASY, ALLEY OOP, SECRET AGENT X-9, MOON MULLINS, BUCK ROGERS (DAILY AND SUNDAY EDITIONS) AND NEW/OLD FACES AND TITLES NOT SEEN IN MANY YEARS.

WE HOPE YOU WILL CONTINUE TO SUPPORT US - AND ENCOURAGE OUR EFFORTS TO BRING YOU ALL THE COMIC ADVENTURES WE CAN PRODUCE.

ANDY FEIGHERY - MANAGING EDITOR

SPEC Productions

COMIC ART RESTORATIONS

ANDREW FEIGHERY
SPEC PRODUCTIONS
P.O. BOX 32
MANITOU SPRINGS, CO 80829

FREE CATALOG ON REQUEST!

SPECPRODUCTIONS@MSN.COM